PROPERTY OF

_____
(Notary Public's legal signature)

IF FOUND, please immediately contact:

Notary's Printed Name: _____ Notary's Email: _____

Notary's Business Address: _____

Notary's Telephone: _____ _____ _____
                                 (cell)   (work)   (home)

COMMISSION & JOURNAL INFORMATION

My _____ notary public commission (# _____) runs from _____ to _____.
   (state of jurisdiction e.g. CA)   (commencement) (expiration)

Bond: _____ _____ _____ _____
        (issuing company)   (address)   (phone)   (bond number)

Errors & Omissions Insurance: _____ (policy # _____) runs from _____ to _____.
                               (issuing company)   (commencement) (expiration)

This journal _____ records official notarial acts from _____ to _____ and entry # _____ to ____
           (number)   (start date)   (end date)

DEATH/INCAPACITY and PRESERVATION INSTRUCTIONS

In the event of the death or incapacity of the above-named notary public, this journal must be mailed to: _____
_____
_____ within _____

Pursuant to state law, this notary journal shall be preserved for at least _____ years from its final entry or my commiss

NOTARY JOURNAL FOR CALIFORNIA: A Notary Public's Comprehensive Quick-Fill 250-Entry Log Book / Register of Official Notarial Acts & Records

TRADEMARK 2022 JENNA JACK

Guardian Notary Journals™ is a registered trademark of Jenna Jack

ANY UNAUTHORIZED DUPLICATION OR DISSEMINATION OF TRADEMARK, IN WHOLE OR IN PART, BY ANY MEANS WILL BE PROSECUTED TO THE FULLEST EXTENT OF THE LAW.

COPYRIGHT 2019 JENNA JACK

ALL RIGHTS RESERVED. NO PART OF THIS BOOK MAY BE REPRODUCED, DISTRIBUTED OR TRANSMITTED IN ANY FORM OR BY ANY MEANS, MECHANICAL OR ELECTRONIC (INCLUDING BUT NOT LIMITED TO VIA PHOTOCOPYING, RECORDING, INTERNET, INFORMATION STORAGE AND/OR RETRIEVAL SYSTEMS, OR OTHER METHODS), WITHOUT THE PRIOR EXPRESS WRITTEN PERMISSION OF THE AUTHOR OR PUBLISHER. ANY UNAUTHORIZED DUPLICATION OR DISSEMINATION, IN WHOLE OR IN PART, BY ANY MEANS WILL BE PROSECUTED TO THE FULLEST EXTENT OF THE LAW.

ISBN No. 978-1-69-694231-7: First paperback printing 2019

GUARDIAN NOTARY JOURNALS are authored and published solely by Jenna Jack

LEGAL DISCLAIMER: NEITHER THE AUTHOR NOR THE PUBLISHER ASSUMES ANY RESPONSIBILITY OR LIABILITY WHATSOEVER ON BEHALF OF THE CONSUMER OR READER OF THE MATERIAL IN THIS BOOK. THE INFORMATION PROVIDED IN THIS BOOK DOES NOT, AND IS NOT INTENDED TO, CONSTITUTE LEGAL ADVICE, IS INSTEAD PROVIDED ONLY FOR GENERAL INFORMATIONAL PURPOSES, AND SHOULD NOT BE USED TO REPLACE THE SPECIALIZED TRAINING AND PROFESSIONAL JUDGMENT OF A LICENSED/COMMISSIONED NOTARY PUBLIC OR COMPETENT ATTORNEY. NEITHER THE AUTHOR NOR THE PUBLISHER CAN BE HELD RESPONSIBLE OR LIABLE FOR THE USE OF THE INFORMATION PROVIDED VIA THIS BOOK.

Created by a Woman-Owned Business

★ ★ ★ Proudly Printed in the UNITED STATES OF AMERICA ★ ★ ★

NOTARY JOURNAL
for
CALIFORNIA

©2019 JENNA JACK

A NOTARY PUBLIC'S
COMPREHENSIVE QUICK-FILL 250-ENTRY LOG BOOK /
REGISTER OF OFFICIAL NOTARIAL ACTS & RECORDS

BY
JENNA JACK

!!!

iv

AUTHOR's NOTE

After years of searching for my ideal notary journal, I set out to create my own with 3 goals in mind.

GOAL 1 - create **the most** comprehensive yet efficient, spacious but compact and methodically organized journal on the market (2 entries per page with 100+ quick-fill checkboxes/items to circle all smartly grouped beside 4 intuitive tabs: Notary Service; Document; Signer; and Credible Witnesses).

GOAL 2 - create **truly** state-specific notary journals. My **NOTARY JOURNAL for CALIFORNIA** includes:
— both California mandates: "**Satisfactory Evidence**" checkbox and **1 notarial act per entry**
— only **California-authorized notarial acts** pre-printed (no other journal has them all) including:
 • *Proof of Execution of Subscribing Witness* • *Copy Certification of Power of Attorney*
— **ID-issuing agencies** (never write *California Department of Motor Vehicles* or *U.S. State Dept.* again)
— separate areas for **2 Credible Witnesses**
— notary's **personal knowledge** (or absence) **of Credible Witness** (but not Signer since prohibited)
— whether **oath or affirmation** was given (and which one)

GOAL 3 - incorporate one new game-changing attribute into my journal entry . . . our NOTARIAL PROTOCOLS. Beyond logging the standard data required by most sates (e.g. document type), one of a notary's key responsibilities is to **ensure the signer has capacity to and is voluntarily** participating in the notarization.[1] The National Notary Association (NNA) has directed notaries to carefully screen signers for capacity and voluntariness since 1998.[2] Here is why.

The meticulous and habitual nature of a notary's work makes each journal entry an official "business record" with inherent reliability in court (once admitted as evidence). So my thought was . . . why not bolster the reliability of our notarial protocols too, by recording *them* in our journal entries too. To my surprise, renowned notary public / author of *Professor Closen's Notary Best Practices* (2018) / law professor / attorney / National Notary Association lecturer Michael Closen set this **INDUSTRY STANDARD** in 2017 and has been instructing his notary students to log their Notarial Protocols in each journal entry ever since.[3]

As my logo reflects, **notaries protect the PUBLIC** from identity theft and fraud, but **NOTARIES deserve (and can now have) protection too** . . . by simply **checking off their pre-printed notarial protocols in a quick-fill GUARDIAN NOTARY JOURNAL** . . . log 'em all in **under 3 seconds**!

Order a Jenna Jack GUARDIAN NOTARY JOURNAL today . . . and give yourself extra peace of mind every day.

Jenna Jack

---

[1] David Thun, *10 Steps Notaries Can Take To Avoid Being Sued*, National Notary Association (Sep. 1, 2016), ¶ 4.

[2] National Notary Association (1998) NOTARY PUBLIC CODE OF PROFESSIONAL RESPONSIBILITY, Guiding Principle III-C-2.

[3] "[A] well-done, detailed notary journal entry could, and now should, reference the capacity/competence of the document signer to show … that the notary had exercised reasonable care in performing the notarization." Closen, M. & Phillips, M. (2017) *Issues Surrounding Mental Capacity for Document Signers* [Slideshow] National Notary Association, p.25.

ELEMENTS of JOURNAL ENTRY

Notaries protect the PUBLIC (their clients) and our LEGAL SYSTEM from identity theft and other fraud . . . but NOTARIES deserve protection too. Aside from continuing study, the most valuable tool we notaries have to protect ourselves from liability is the NOTARY JOURNAL we choose. Each journal entry is a 'business record' (with inherent reliability in court once admitted as evidence) that chronicles the facts of the particular notarized document or proceeding . . . but a good journal entry – *one that truly protects the notary* – also thoroughly evidences the notary's PROTOCOL. **Recording your compliance with California-mandated protocols (●)** - *that you already observe anyway* - **is easy in this quick-fill journal.**

I designed this notary journal exclusively for CALIFORNIA notaries [7 checkboxes for *California-specific* notarial acts; *affirmative statement* of satisfactory evidence; dedicated space for 2 credible witnesses]. Increasingly more states encourage their notaries to record more data than their state law requires ("any other information the notary considers appropriate" C.R.S. 12-55-111(3)(f)). This cutting-edge notary journal is EFFICIENT and ORDERLY *but also* COMPREHENSIVE. **Over 105 quick-fill**[1] **options** (checkboxes & pre-printed items to circle) throughout **data-dedicated spaces** equip you to quickly capture not only (1) mandatory **JOURNAL ELEMENTS** but also (2) California-mandated **PROTOCOLS** (3) California Secretary of State **GUIDELINES** and (4) industry **BEST PRACTICES** beside the **4 intuitive left-edge tabs** of the **spacious half-page entry:**

NOTARIZATION SERVICE	DOCUMENT/PROCEEDING	SIGNER	CREDIBLE WITNESS(ES)
● **date** of notarization	● doc/proceeding **type** [box]	● **satisfactory evidence** [box] via	● **printed names** of <u>both</u> credible witnesses
● **time** of notarization	● **doc subtype**: 30+ [circle]	● **credible witness** [box] *or*	● **personally known** to notary [box]
★ **address** of notarization	◖ doc/proceeding **date**	● **identification** [box] & **type** [circle]	★ **addresses** of <u>both</u> credible witnesses
☐ **signer's** address [box]	● doc/proceeding **title**	◖ signer's **printed name**	☐ address **non-disclosure** [box]
☐ notary's **office** [box]	☐ number of **pages** to doc	☐ signer's **representative capacity** [box]	credible witness **phone numbers** [circle]
● notarization **act type** [box]	★ **inspect/copy** request [box]	◖ signer's **address**	● credible witness **IDs types** [box]
● **notary service fee**	☐ entry **cross-reference #**	☐ address **non-disclosure** [box]	● **serial #s** of credible witness IDs
◖ related **clerical fees**		signer's **phone number** [circle]	● **agency** issuing credible witness IDs
☐ (travel, rush, copy) [boxes]		★ **voluntary** signer with **capacity** [boxes]	● **issue dates** of credible witness IDs *or*
◖ **mileage**		● **proper ID** from signer [box]	● **expiration dates** of credible witness IDs
◖ **notes**		● **serial #** of signer's ID	● **oaths** given to <u>both</u> credible witnesses [box]
★ **incomplete** service [box]		● **agency** issuing signer's ID	☐ **oath** indicators [circle]
★ **notary name**		● **issue date** of signer's ID *or*	☐ **affirmation** indicators [circle]
★ notary **commission #**		● **expiration date** of signer's ID	● **signatures** of <u>both</u> credible witnesses
● journal **entry #**		● any **oath** given to signer [box]	★ **miscellaneous** information [box]
● journal **page #**		☐ **oath** indicator [circle]	
		☐ **affirmation** indicator [circle]	
		● **signature** of signer	
		☐ signature **by mark** [box]	
		● **fingerprint** of signer	
		● **hand** indicator [circle]	
		● **finger** indicator [circle]	
		★ **miscellaneous** information [box]	

[1] **Quick-Fill options**
[box] indicates a checkbox to tick
[circle] indicates an item to circle

> ● journal element <u>required</u> by **California**
> ● notarial protocol <u>required</u> by **California**
> ◖ guideline <u>recommended</u> by **California**
> ★ best practices (NNA, AAoN, ASoN etc.)
> ☐ quick-fill convenience

vi

THIS CONTENT IS COPYRIGHTED © 2019 Jenna Jack

ATTRIBUTES of JOURNAL ENTRY
(entry is actual size relative to page)

pre-printed page numbers

sequential pre-printed journal entry numbers

4 distinct logical sections to capture all details of
1. notary <u>service</u>
2. underlying <u>document</u>
3. <u>signer</u> and
4. <u>credible witness</u> #1 & #2

note special circumstances (e.g. signer's physical condition; fee details like waiting time, travel start & stop time; check "Stop" and indicate reason for any unfulfilled notarization; describe "other" notarization acts)

large outside-edge fingerprint box with convenient horizontal imprint orientation and finger identification (right/left hand and thumb/index/middle/ring/pinky fingers)

over **105 quick-fill checkboxes** & items to circle to save time & enhance accuracy

track all **state-permitted fees** and record <u>advance</u> client consent via checkboxes

entry cross-reference inspection/copy checkbox

SERVICE | DATE 06-29-2019 | TIME 10:30 (am) pm | ADDRESS 789 Post St. SF-94111 | ☐ Office NOTES CareMore Convalescent | ☐ Stop MILES 8 | Notary $15 | ☒ Adv. Travel $24.64 | ☒ Rush $25 | ☐ Copy $0 | ☐ Other $0 TOTAL FEES $64.64 | **96**

DOCUMENT | TYPE ☒ Acknowledgment ☒ Jurat ☐ Copy Certification ☐ Oath/Affirmation ☐ Oath of Office ☐ Proof of Execution ☐ Protest ☐ Other
DOC TYPE ☐ Deed (Grant•Trust Transfer•Gift; Interspousal•Quitclaim•Warranty) ☐ DOT Mortgage Certification (Rev/Irrev•Am/Rest) ☐ Trust (Durable/Springing) ☐ POA General/Limited ☐ POAH AHCD Living Will ☒ Agreement Compliance•E&O Correction ☒ Affidavit (Borrower•Occupancy•Ownership•Refi•Survey; Debts & Liens•Name-Signature-ID•Marital•(Death)•Will•Safe Deposit Box) ☐ Other Vehicle Title | Fingerprint
DOC DATE J F M A M (J) J A S O N D 29, 2019 | DOC TITLE or TYPE Affidavit of Death of Trustee | # OF PAGES 1 ☒ Inspect/Copy Request Entry X-Ref # 106

SIGNER | ☒ SATISFACTORY EVIDENCE ☐ Driver's License / Passport / State ID / Military / Government / Tribal / Inmate / Other ID or ☒ Credible Witness(es)
SIGNER's NAME Jane M. Smith | ☐ For | ADDRESS 123 Main Street #4 | ☒ Non-Public ☒ Capacity # | ☒ Voluntary | ☐ Proper ID ISSUED | SIGNATURE ☒ (oath)/affirmation, if any) ☐ (by Mark)
PHONE C/H/W burn victim (fingerprint) | or ☒ MISC | San Francisco, CA 94104 | AGENCY ☐ CA DMV ☐ US State Dept EXPIRES | Jane M. Smith

CW #1 | #1 WITNESS's NAME Mary A. Jones | ☐ P/Known | ADDRESS 123 Main Street #6 | ☐ Non-Public ☒ Driver's License ☐ Passport ☐ Other ID # C1234321 ISSUED 2/14/17 | SIGNATURE ☒ (after oath/(affirmation))
PHONE (C)/H/W 415/555-1234 | or ☐ MISC | San Francisco, CA 94104 | AGENCY ☒ CA DMV ☐ US State Dept EXPIRES 2/14/22 | Mary A. Jones ❶

CW #2 | #2 WITNESS's NAME Roberta C. Adams | ☐ P/Known | ADDRESS 135 Main Street | ☐ Non-Public ☐ Driver's License ☒ Passport ☐ Other ID # 123456789 ISSUED 7/5/16 | SIGNATURE ☒ (after (oath)/affirmation)
PHONE C/H/(W) 415/555-1515 | or ☐ MISC | San Francisco, CA 94104 | AGENCY ☐ CA DMV ☒ US State Dept EXPIRES 7/5/26 | Roberta C. Adams ❷

Page **398**

---

dedicated space for printed name <u>and</u> address of signer and BOTH credible witnesses

credible witness personally known to notary checkboxes

signer's entity capacity checkbox (e.g. V.P. of ABC corporation)

3 miscellaneous catch-all checkboxes (for extra or unusual information)

note **public inspection prohibition** for battered signer/witness address

signer's capacity, voluntariness & proper ID checkboxes (e.g. current/recent and contains photo, description, serial # & signature)

easy locator symbols for signer (arrow) and witnesses (#1 & #2) with checkboxes for oath/affirmation and signature by mark in large outside-edge signature boxes

vii

Flowchart of U.S. Notary Laws by STATE - GUARDIAN NOTARY JOURNALS

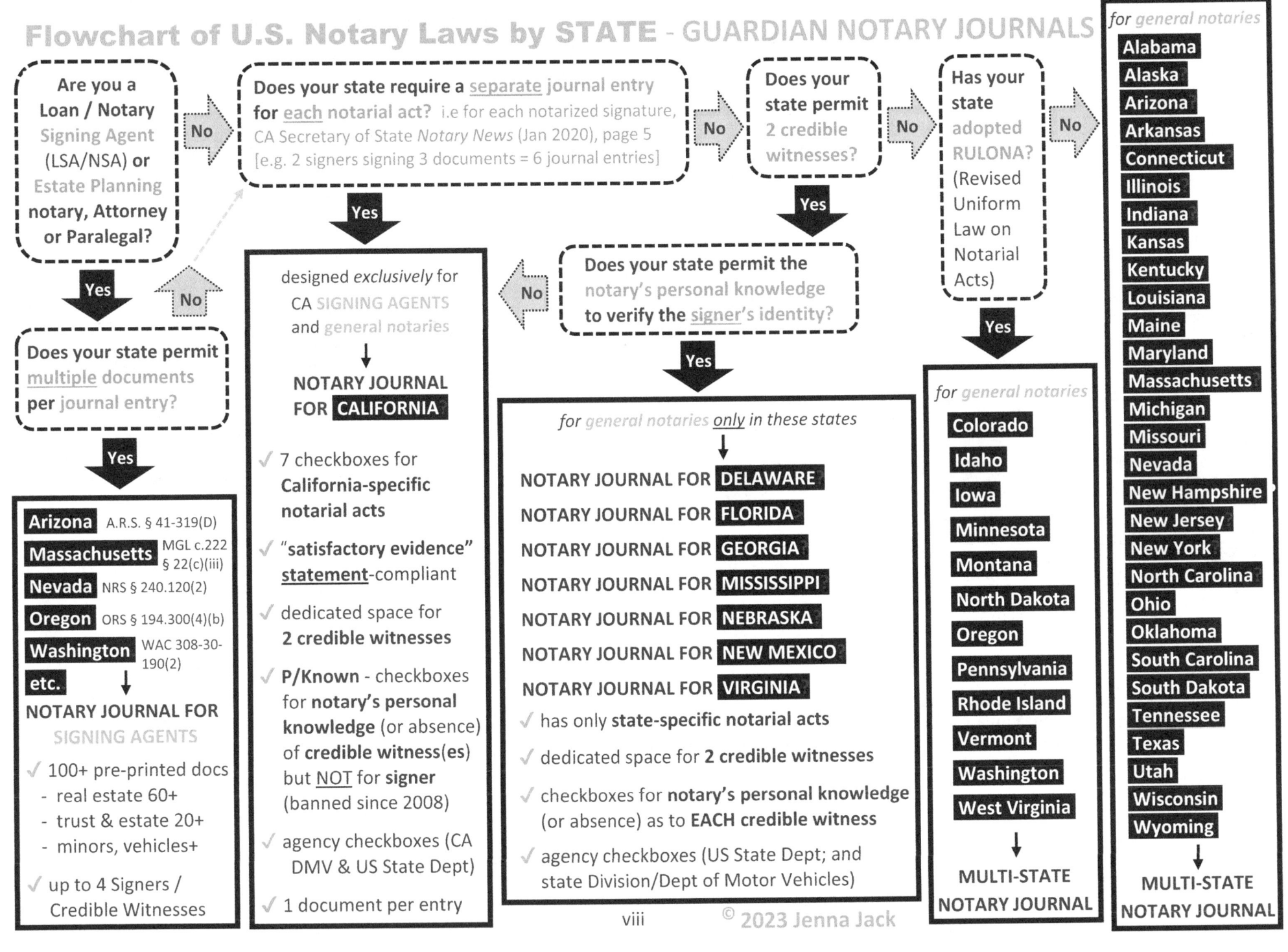

Are you a Loan / Notary Signing Agent (LSA/NSA) or Estate Planning notary, Attorney or Paralegal? → **No** →

Does your state require a separate journal entry for each notarial act? i.e for each notarized signature, CA Secretary of State *Notary News* (Jan 2020), page 5 [e.g. 2 signers signing 3 documents = 6 journal entries] → **No** →

Does your state permit 2 credible witnesses? → **No** →

Has your state adopted RULONA? (Revised Uniform Law on Notarial Acts) → **No** →

for general notaries

Alabama · Alaska · Arizona · Arkansas · Connecticut · Illinois · Indiana · Kansas · Kentucky · Louisiana · Maine · Maryland · Massachusetts · Michigan · Missouri · Nevada · New Hampshire · New Jersey · New York · North Carolina · Ohio · Oklahoma · South Carolina · South Dakota · Tennessee · Texas · Utah · Wisconsin · Wyoming

MULTI-STATE NOTARY JOURNAL

Yes ↓ (from "Are you a Loan / Notary Signing Agent...")

Does your state permit multiple documents per journal entry?

Yes ↓

Arizona A.R.S. § 41-319(D)
Massachusetts MGL c.222 § 22(c)(iii)
Nevada NRS § 240.120(2)
Oregon ORS § 194.300(4)(b)
Washington WAC 308-30-190(2)
etc.
↓
NOTARY JOURNAL FOR SIGNING AGENTS

✓ 100+ pre-printed docs
 - real estate 60+
 - trust & estate 20+
 - minors, vehicles+

✓ up to 4 Signers / Credible Witnesses

No ↑ (back to "Does your state require a separate journal entry for each notarial act?")

Yes ↓ (from "Does your state require a separate journal entry for each notarial act?")

designed *exclusively* for CA SIGNING AGENTS and *general notaries*
↓
NOTARY JOURNAL FOR CALIFORNIA

✓ 7 checkboxes for **California-specific notarial acts**

✓ **"satisfactory evidence" statement**-compliant

✓ dedicated space for **2 credible witnesses**

✓ **P/Known** - checkboxes for **notary's personal knowledge** (or absence) of **credible witness(es)** but **NOT** for **signer** (banned since 2008)

✓ agency checkboxes (CA DMV & US State Dept)

✓ 1 document per entry

Does your state permit the notary's personal knowledge to verify the signer's identity?

No → (to California)

Yes ↓

for general notaries only in these states
↓
NOTARY JOURNAL FOR **DELAWARE**
NOTARY JOURNAL FOR **FLORIDA**
NOTARY JOURNAL FOR **GEORGIA**
NOTARY JOURNAL FOR **MISSISSIPPI**
NOTARY JOURNAL FOR **NEBRASKA**
NOTARY JOURNAL FOR **NEW MEXICO**
NOTARY JOURNAL FOR **VIRGINIA**

✓ has only **state-specific notarial acts**

✓ dedicated space for **2 credible witnesses**

✓ checkboxes for **notary's personal knowledge** (or absence) as to **EACH credible witness**

✓ agency checkboxes (US State Dept; and state Division/Dept of Motor Vehicles)

Yes ↓ (from "Does your state permit 2 credible witnesses?")

for general notaries

Colorado · Idaho · Iowa · Minnesota · Montana · North Dakota · Oregon · Pennsylvania · Rhode Island · Vermont · Washington · West Virginia
↓
MULTI-STATE NOTARY JOURNAL

Yes ↓ (from "Has your state adopted RULONA?")

(leads to general notaries list)

viii © 2023 Jenna Jack

ILLUSTRATIONS
of
JOURNAL ENTRY USAGE OPTIONS

THIS CONTENT IS COPYRIGHTED

ENTRY ILLUSTRATION A © Jenna Jack

| SERVICE | DATE 06-29-2019 | TIME 9:05 (am) pm | ADDRESS 111 Broadway #1 SF 94111 | ☐ Signer's | ☐ Office | NOTES AAA Title Company | | ☐ Stop | MILES 16 | Notary $15 | ☒ Adv. Travel $9.28 | ☒ Rush $10 | ☐ Copy $0 | ☐ Other $0 | TOTAL FEES $34.28 | 98 |

DOCUMENT	TYPE ☒ Acknowledgment ☐ Jurat ☐ Copy Certification ☐ Oath/Affirmation ☐ Oath of Office ☐ Proof of Execution ☐ Protest ☐ Other

DOC TYPE ☒ Deed   ☐ DOT   ☐ Trust   ☐ POA   ☐ POAH   ☐ Agreement   ☐ Affidavit   ☐ Other
(Grant) Trust Transfer • Gift / Mortgage / Certification / General / Limited / AHCD / Compliance-E&O / Borrower • Occupancy • Ownership • Refi • Survey / Vehicle Title
Interspousal • Quitclaim • ToD • Warranty / Rev / Irrev • Am / Rest / Durable / Springing / Living Will / Correction / Debts & Liens • Name-Signature-ID • Marital • Death • Will / Safe Deposit Box

DOC DATE J F M A M (J) J A S O N D 28, 2019   **DOC TITLE or TYPE** Grant Deed   **# OF PAGES** 2   ☐ Inspect/Copy Request   Entry X-Ref #

Fingerprint — R T M R P / L

☒ **SATISFACTORY EVIDENCE** ☒ (Driver's License) / Passport / State ID / Military / Government / Tribal / Inmate / Other ID **or** ☐ Credible Witness(es)

| SIGNER | SIGNER's NAME John L. Smith | ☒ For | ADDRESS 123 Main Street #4 | ☐ Non-Public | ☒ Capacity | ☒ Voluntary | ☒ Proper ID | ISSUED 12/21/18 | SIGNATURE ☐ (oath / affirmation, if any) ☐ (by Mark) John L. Smith |
| | PHONE C / H / (W) 415/555-1111 | or ☐ MISC | San Francisco, CA 94104 | | # C1234567 AGENCY ☒ CA DMV ☐ US State Dept | | | EXPIRES 12/21/23 → | |

| CW #1 | #1 WITNESS's NAME | ☐ P/Known | ADDRESS | ☐ Non-Public | ☐ Driver's License ☐ Passport ☐ Other ID | ISSUED | SIGNATURE ☐ (after oath / affirmation) |
| | PHONE C / H / W | or ☐ MISC | | | # AGENCY ☐ CA DMV ☐ US State Dept | EXPIRES | ❶ |

| CW #2 | #2 WITNESS's NAME | ☐ P/Known | ADDRESS | ☐ Non-Public | ☐ Driver's License ☐ Passport ☐ Other ID | ISSUED | SIGNATURE ☐ (after oath / affirmation) |
| | PHONE C / H / W | or ☒ MISC V.P. / ABC Corporation - Real Estate Division | | | # AGENCY ☐ CA DMV ☐ US State Dept | EXPIRES | ❷ |

NOTE: The above illustration is an introduction on *how a notary public can efficiently use the format of this notary journal entry*. It is provided for general informational purposes only and is <u>not</u> to be used as an example of how to correctly perform notarization services for an acknowledgment, or any other notarial act, in any given U.S. state. This illustration does not, and is not intended to, constitute legal advice. <u>Each notary public is solely responsible for researching and keeping abreast of the notary laws currently applicable in the particular state in which she or he is commissioned.</u>

x

ENTRY ILLUSTRATION B © Jenna Jack

SERVICE											
DATE: 06-29-2019	TIME: 10:30 (am) pm	☒ ADDRESS ☐ Signer's ☒ Office	NOTES: acid burns (thumbs)	☐ Stop	MILES: 0	Notary $15	☐ Adv. Travel $0	☒ Rush $10	☐ Copy $0	☐ Other $0	TOTAL FEES $25.00 — 99

TYPE: ☒ Acknowledgment ☐ Jurat ☐ Copy Certification ☐ Oath/Affirmation ☐ Oath of Office ☐ Proof of Execution ☐ Protest ☐ Other

DOCUMENT

DOC TYPE: ☐ Deed (Grant • Trust Transfer • Gift • Interspousal • Quitclaim • ToD • Warranty) ☐ DOT (Mortgage) ☐ Trust (Certification • Rev/Irrev • Am/Rest) ☐ POA (General/Limited • Durable/Springing) ☐ POAH (AHCD • Living Will) ☐ Agreement (Compliance-E&O • Correction) ☐ Affidavit (Borrower • Occupancy • Ownership • Refi • Survey • Debts & Liens • Name-Signature-ID • Marital • Death • Will) ☒ Other (Vehicle Title • Safe Deposit Box)

DOC DATE: J F M A M (J) J A S O N D — 29, 2019
DOC TITLE or TYPE: Assignment of Property to Cho Revocable Trust
OF PAGES: 1
☒ Inspect / (Copy) Request
Entry X-Ref #: 132

Fingerprint (R T I M R P L)

☒ SATISFACTORY EVIDENCE ☐ Driver's License / Passport / State ID / Military / Government / Tribal / Inmate / Other ID **or** ☒ Credible Witness(es)

SIGNER

| SIGNER's NAME: Christina P. Cho | ☐ For | ADDRESS: 111 Oak Street | ☐ Non-Public ☒ Capacity # ☒ Voluntary ☐ Proper ID | ISSUED | SIGNATURE ☐ (oath / affirmation, if any) ☐ (by Mark) |
| PHONE (C) H / W: 415/555-5678 | or ☐ MISC | San Francisco, CA 94111 | AGENCY ☐ CA DMV ☐ US State Dept | EXPIRES | Christina P. Cho → |

CW #1

| #1 WITNESS's NAME: Amelia E. Gutierrez | ☒ P/Known | ADDRESS: 123 Penny Lane | ☐ Non-Public ☒ Driver's License ☐ Passport ☐ Other ID # C1231234 | ISSUED 4/12/19 | SIGNATURE ☒ (after oath /(affirmation)) |
| PHONE C (H) W: 415/555-5555 | or ☐ MISC | San Francisco, CA 94111 | AGENCY ☒ CA DMV ☐ US State Dept | EXPIRES 4/12/24 | Amelia E. Gutierrez ❶ |

CW #2

| #2 WITNESS's NAME: | ☐ P/Known | ADDRESS: | ☐ Non-Public ☐ Driver's License ☐ Passport ☐ Other ID # | ISSUED | SIGNATURE ☐ (after oath / affirmation) |
| PHONE C / H / W: /purse stolen (ID) | or ☒ MISC | | AGENCY ☐ CA DMV ☐ US State Dept | EXPIRES | ❷ |

NOTE: The above illustration is an introduction on *how a notary public can efficiently use the format of this notary journal entry.* It is provided for general informational purposes only and is <u>not</u> to be used as an example of how to correctly perform notarization services for a jurat, or any other notarial act, in any given U.S. state. This illustration does not, and is not intended to, constitute legal advice. <u>Each notary public is solely responsible for researching and keeping abreast of the notary laws currently applicable in the particular state in which she or he is commissioned.</u>

THIS CONTENT IS COPYRIGHTED

ENTRY ILLUSTRATION C © Jenna Jack

SERVICE

DATE	TIME	am	ADDRESS	☒ Signer's	☐ Office	NOTES		☐ Stop	MILES	Notary	☒ Adv. Travel	☒ Rush	☐ Copy	☐ Other	TOTAL FEES	100
06-29-2019	11:45 pm					burn victim (fingerprint)			8	$15	$24.64	$25	$0	$0	$64.64	

TYPE ☐ Acknowledgment ☒ Jurat ☐ Copy Certification ☐ Oath/Affirmation ☐ Oath of Office ☐ Proof of Execution ☐ Protest ☐ Other

DOCUMENT

DOC TYPE ☐ **Deed** ☐ **DOT** ☐ **Trust** ☐ **POA** ☐ **POAH** ☐ **Agreement** ☒ **Affidavit** ☐ **Other**
Grant • Trust Transfer • Gift | Mortgage | Certification | General / Limited | AHCD | Compliance-E&O | Borrower • Occupancy • Ownership • Refi • Survey | Vehicle Title
Interspousal • Quitclaim • ToD • Warranty | Rev / Irrev • Am / Rest | Durable / Springing | Living Will | Correction | Debts & Liens • Name-Signature-ID • Marital • Death • Will | Safe Deposit Box

DOC DATE J F M A M Ⓙ	DOC TITLE or TYPE	# OF PAGES	☒ Inspect/Copy Request
J A S O N D 29, 2019	Affidavit of Death of Trustee	1	Entry X-Ref # 106

Fingerprint (R T I M R P L)

☒ **SATISFACTORY EVIDENCE** ☐ Driver's License / Passport / State ID / Military / Government / Tribal / Inmate / Other ID **or** ☒ Credible Witness(es)

SIGNER

SIGNER's NAME	☐ For	ADDRESS	☒ Non-Public	☒ Capacity	☒ Voluntary	☐ Proper ID	ISSUED	SIGNATURE ☒ (oath / affirmation, if any)	☐ (by Mark)
Jane M. Smith		123 Main Street		#				Jane M. Smith	
PHONE C/Ⓗ/W 415/555-6789	or ☐ MISC	San Francisco, CA 94104		AGENCY ☐ CA DMV ☐ US State Dept			EXPIRES		

CW #1

#1 WITNESS's NAME	☐ P/Known	ADDRESS	☐ Non-Public	☒ Driver's License ☐ Passport ☐ Other ID	ISSUED	SIGNATURE ☒ (after oath / affirmation)
Mary A. Jones		123 Main Street #6		#C1234321	2/14/19	
PHONE Ⓒ/H/W 415/555-1234	or ☐ MISC	San Francisco, CA 94104		AGENCY ☒ CA DMV ☐ US State Dept	EXPIRES 2/14/24 ❶	Mary A. Jones

CW #2

#2 WITNESS's NAME	☐ P/Known	ADDRESS	☐ Non-Public	☐ Driver's License ☒ Passport ☐ Other ID	ISSUED	SIGNATURE ☒ (after oath / affirmation)
Roberta C. Adams		135 Main Street		#123456789	7/3/16	
PHONE C/H/Ⓦ 415/555-1515	or ☐ MISC	San Francisco, CA 94104		AGENCY ☐ CA DMV ☒ US State Dept	EXPIRES 7/3/26 ❷	Roberta C. Adams

NOTE: The above illustration is an introduction on *how a notary public can efficiently use the format of this notary journal entry*. It is provided for general informational purposes only and is <u>not</u> to be used as an example of how to correctly perform notarization services for a signature by mark, or any other notarial act, in any given U.S. state. This illustration does not, and is not intended to, constitute legal advice. <u>Each notary public is solely responsible for researching and keeping abreast of the notary laws currently applicable in the particular state in which she or he is commissioned.</u>

THIS CONTENT IS COPYRIGHTED

JOURNAL USAGE EXPLAINED via STATE-SPECIFIC* NOTARIAL LAW COMPARISONS © 2019 Jenna Jack

[NOTARIZATION] SERVICE TAB

1. **TIME** - - **California, Colorado, Hawaii, Idaho, Iowa, Massachusetts, Minnesota, Mississippi, Montana, North Dakota, Oregon, Pennsylvania, Rhode Island, Vermont, Washington** and **West Virginia** require recording of the time of notarization of each notarial act in the notary journal.

2. **SERVICE ADDRESS** - - **Massachusetts** and **Mississippi** require recording of the address where the notarization occurs. To avoid having to write addresses out longhand, just mark the "Signer's" checkbox for mobile notarizations performed at the client's address or mark the "Office" checkbox if done at the notary's business address.

3. **NOTES** - - Record any special circumstances in the "NOTES" box (e.g. the signer's physical condition, waiting time, extra fee details or as **Nevada** requires the notary's start and stop travel times). If any notarization goes unfulfilled, just mark the "Stop" checkbox and note the reason as **Massachusetts** requires.

4. **FEES** - - Many states including **Mississippi, Missouri, Montana, Nevada, Oregon, Pennsylvania** and **Washington** require the notary service fee to be separately itemized in the notary journal from any clerical or administrative costs (e.g. mileage reimbursement, travel time, rush charge, waiting time, cancellation and copy costs). Each notary should research her or his own state's particular laws which may require (1) advance disclosure of all clerical/administrative costs as separate, unregulated and optional from any notary service fee and (2) the client's advance agreement to pay them. Mark the various fee checkboxes to evidence your *advance disclosure* of any clerical/administrative costs (however **Pennsylvania** requires clerical fees on the client's receipt rather than in the notary journal). If no fee is charged for the notarial service, many states require recording of that fact such as **Arizona** (enter ø), **California** (enter $0) or **Pennsylvania** (enter N/C or $0).

5. **SERVICE TYPE** - - This is the ONLY journal with checkboxes for all 7 specific notarial acts that **California** notaries are authorized to perform (acknowledgment, jurat, proof of execution of subscribing witness etc.; CA prohibits signature witnessing). California admonishes act abbreviations and acronyms, so just mark the applicable checkbox.

* The information provided herein does not, and is not intended to, constitute legal advice and instead is provided only for general informational purposes. References to specific notary laws of the 50 U.S. states serve only as illustration and are not exhaustive. Because all such references are current only through July 2019, **EACH NOTARY IS SOLELY RESPONSIBLE FOR RESEARCHING AND KEEPING ABREAST OF THE NOTARY LAWS APPLICABLE IN THE PARTICULAR STATE IN WHICH SHE OR HE IS COMMISSIONED.**

THIS CONTENT IS COPYRIGHTED

JOURNAL USAGE EXPLAINED via STATE-SPECIFIC* NOTARIAL LAW COMPARISONS © 2019 Jenna Jack

DOCUMENT TAB

6 DOCUMENT DATE - - **Colorado, Hawaii, Montana** and **Texas** require recording of the date of the document being notarized. Because multiple dates are often recorded for any given notarization, this journal's unique date format (notary hand writes the numeric day and year but circles the 1st letter of the appropriate month) helps to call attention to this critical date to ensure the correct document date is legibly recorded.

7 DOCUMENT LENGTH - - It is good notarial practice to record the <u>number of pages</u> to any document being notarized (to discourage fraudulent document or page swapping) but be sure to count accurately. **Hawaii** requires recording the number of pages of the notarized document in the *notarial certificate*.

8 INSPECTION/COPY REQUEST - - **Mississippi** and the Revised Uniform Law On Notarial Acts ("RULONA" adopted by **Colorado, Idaho, Iowa, Minnesota, Montana, North Dakota, Oregon, Pennsylvania, Rhode Island, Vermont, Washington** and **West Virginia**) require any <u>request to inspect or copy a notary journal entry</u> to be recorded as a <u>separate distinct entry</u> in the notary's journal. Mark the checkbox, circle "Inspect" or "Copy" in both the original (if permissible) and current journal entries and write the original journal entry number as a cross-reference in the (current) inspection/copy request journal entry after "Entry X-Ref #.

9 FINGERPRINT - - Many states require recording of the signer's <u>right thumbprint</u> for notarization of certain documents (e.g. powers of attorney and most documents affecting real estate in **California**) so circle "R" for right hand and "T" for thumb. **California** and **Illinois** notaries must designate if an alternate finger is used so simply circle the corresponding letter to denote the thumb, index, middle, ring or pinky finger and "L" if the left hand is used. Do <u>not</u> fingerprint clients in states like **Texas** that prohibit doing so due to their strict regulations regarding collection and retention of biometric data.

SERVICE

DATE	TIME	am / pm	ADDRESS	☐ Signer's	☐ Office	NOTES	☐ Stop	MILES	Notary	☐ Adv. Travel	☐ Rush	☐ Copy	☐ Other	TOTAL FEES	**97**
- -20	:								$ $		$	$	$	$	

TYPE ☐ Acknowledgment ☐ Jurat ☐ Copy Certification ☐ Oath/Affirmation ☐ Oath of Office ☐ Proof of Execution ☐ Protest ☐ Other

DOCUMENT

DOC TYPE	☐ Deed	☐ DOT	☐ Trust	☐ POA	☐ POAH	☐ Agreement	☐ Affidavit	☐ Other
	Grant ▪ Trust Transfer ▪ Gift	Mortgage	Certification	General / Limited	AHCD	Compliance-E&O	Borrower ▪ Occupancy ▪ Ownership ▪ Refi ▪ Survey	Vehicle Title
	Interspousal ▪ Quitclaim ▪ ToD ▪ Warranty		Rev / Irrev ▪ Am / Rest	Durable / Springing	Living Will	Correction	Debts & Liens ▪ Name-Signature-ID ▪ Marital ▪ Death ▪ Will	Safe Deposit Box

DOC DATE J F M A M J / J A S O N D , | DOC TITLE or TYPE | # OF PAGES | ☐ Inspect/Copy Request / Entry X-Ref #

Fingerprint column (right side): R / T / I / M / R / P / L

☐ **SATISFACTORY EVIDENCE** ☐ Driver's License / Passport / State ID / Military / Government / Tribal / Inmate / Other ID *or* ☐ Credible Witness(es)

SIGNER

SIGNER's NAME	☐ For	ADDRESS	☐ Non-Public	☐ Capacity	☐ Voluntary	☐ Proper ID	ISSUED	SIGNATURE ☐ *(oath / affirmation, if any)* ☐ (by Mark)
				#				
PHONE C / H / W *or* ☐ MISC /			AGENCY	☐ CA DMV	☐ US State Dept	EXPIRES	➤

CW #1

#1 WITNESS's NAME	☐ P/Known	ADDRESS	☐ Non-Public	☐ Driver's License	☐ Passport	☐ Other ID	ISSUED	SIGNATURE ☐ *(after oath / affirmation)*
				#				
PHONE C / H / W *or* ☐ MISC /			AGENCY	☐ CA DMV	☐ US State Dept	EXPIRES	❶

CW #2

#2 WITNESS's NAME	☐ P/Known	ADDRESS	☐ Non-Public	☐ Driver's License	☐ Passport	☐ Other ID	ISSUED	SIGNATURE ☐ *(after oath / affirmation)*
				#				
PHONE C / H / W *or* ☐ MISC /			AGENCY	☐ CA DMV	☐ US State Dept	EXPIRES	❷

---

* See complete legal disclaimer regarding non-exhaustive illustrations and notary's absolute duty to research the laws of their own state on pages ii and xiii.

THIS CONTENT IS COPYRIGHTED

JOURNAL USAGE EXPLAINED via STATE-SPECIFIC* NOTARIAL LAW COMPARISONS © 2019 Jenna Jack

SIGNER TAB

⑩ SATISFACTORY EVIDENCE - - States like **Colorado, Massachusetts, Nevada, Oregon** and **Tennessee** require satisfactory evidence of signer's identity by proper identification, credible witness or personal knowledge. **California** now prohibits the notary's *personal knowledge* of signer BUT requires an *affirmative statement* of "satisfactory evidence" in the journal, so just mark that checkbox. Record full ID numbers (e.g. driver's license #) unless your state prohibits them or allows only terminal numbers.

⑪ SIGNER'S NAME - - **Arizona, Colorado, Hawaii, Maryland, Massachusetts, Mississippi, Missouri, Montana, Nevada, Oregon, Pennsylvania, Tennessee, Texas** and **Washington** require recording the signer's printed name. While **California** does not, it is good notarial practice to do so because signatures are often illegible. For those signing in a representative capacity (e.g. President or Vice-President of a corporation), mark the "For" checkbox and a "MISC" checkbox (in an empty Credible Witness tab) and record the signer's work title (capacity) and employer/entity name beside it, or alternatively in the NOTES area (in the Service tab.)

⑫ MISCELLANEOUS - - Mark the "MISC" checkbox and record any extra information required by your state (e.g. **Nevada** requires the notary's travel start and stop times).

⑬ SIGNER'S ADDRESS - - Although **Pennsylvania** requires only the city and state, **Arizona, Colorado**, the **District of Columbia, Hawaii, Maryland, Massachusetts, Mississippi, Missouri, Montana, Oregon, Texas** and **Washington** require recording the signer's full address. **California** requires neither but more data tends to better protect the notary. For states like **Massachusetts** that require noting in the journal that a battered signer's address is not subject to public inspection, mark the "Non-Public" checkbox.

⑭ ASSESSMENT OF SIGNER - - *Proper identification* and signer's *awareness of* and *willingness* regarding the notarization are crucial (and can easily impact a notary's potential liability). Mark these 3 checkboxes *only after* you are satisfied (1) signer has this capacity (2) their participation is voluntary and if used (3) proper ID was presented (current ID or issued within 5 years; has signer's photograph, description, signature & identifying number). Ensure descriptions & signatures match (on ID, document & your journal).

⑮ IDENTIFICATION DATES - - While **Oregon** requires recording only the date of issuance of signer or witness's identification, **Idaho, Iowa, Montana, North Dakota, Oregon, Pennsylvania, Rhode Island, Vermont, Washington** and **West Virginia** require recording both the *date of issuance* AND the *date of expiration*.

⑯ SIGNER'S SIGNATURE - - A large black arrow differentiates the signer's signature box that is conveniently located on the *right outside edge* of the journal for the client's comfort. Mark the checkbox to indicate a 'signature by mark' or as **Nevada** requires any oath or affirmation taken by the signer and circle which one was administered.

See complete legal disclaimer regarding non-exhaustive illustrations and notary's absolute duty to research the laws of their own state on pages ii and xiii.

THIS CONTENT IS COPYRIGHTED

JOURNAL USAGE EXPLAINED via STATE-SPECIFIC* NOTARIAL LAW COMPARISONS © 2019 Jenna Jack

CREDIBLE WITNESS TAB

17 CREDIBLE WITNESS NAME - - **California**, **Colorado**, **Hawaii** and **Massachusetts** require recording of the printed name of any witnesses to the notarization. Many states like **California** permit a single credible witness to serve as satisfactory evidence of the identity of a signer who does not possess (and it would be difficult/impossible to obtain) proper identification IF the witness personally knows the signer and is personally known by the notary. **Montana** and **Texas** permit a single credible witness not personally know by the notary IF proper identification is presented. Indicate the notary's personal knowledge (or lack thereof) of a credible witness via the "P/Known" checkbox.

18 CREDIBLE WITNESS ADDRESS - - **Colorado**, **Hawaii** and **Massachusetts** require recording of the address of any witnesses to the notarization. Mark the "Non-Public" checkbox for states like **Massachusetts** that require notation in the journal that a battered witness's address is not subject to public inspection for safety/privacy reasons.

19 CREDIBLE WITNESS #1 SIGNATURE - - A black-circled #1 differentiates the signature box for the 1st credible witness that is conveniently located on the journal's *right outside edge*. As **Nevada** requires, affirmatively evidence the oath/affirmation given to the 1st credible witness by marking the checkbox and circling which one was given.

20 CREDIBLE WITNESS #2 SIGNATURE - - **California**, **Delaware**, **Florida**, **Georgia**, **Mississippi**, **Nebraska**, **New Mexico** and **Virginia** permit two credible witnesses (who are not personally known by the notary) to serve as satisfactory evidence of the identity of the signer (who does not possess proper identification) IF both credible witnesses personally know the signer and present proper identification. A black-circled #2 differentiates the signature box for the 2nd credible witness that is conveniently located on the journal's *right outside edge* for their comfort. Mark the checkbox to affirmatively evidence the oath/affirmation given to the 2nd credible witness and circle which one was given. **Pennsylvania** requires recording of the credible witness data (name, address, ID) in the *same journal entry* as the underlying notarization being conducted on the signer's behalf. For states like **Oregon** that require recording of the credible witness data in a *separate journal entry* from the signer's underlying notarization, enter the two corresponding journal entry cross-reference numbers in the respective "Entry X-ref #" spaces of both journal entries (in the Inspect/Copy Request box).

SERVICE	DATE - -20	TIME : am pm	ADDRESS ☐ Signer's ☐ Office	NOTES	☐ Stop	MILES	Notary ☐ Adv. Travel ☐ Rush ☐ Copy ☐ Other TOTAL FEES $ $ $ $ $ $	97

TYPE ☐ Acknowledgment ☐ Jurat ☐ Copy Certification ☐ Oath/Affirmation ☐ Oath of Office ☐ Proof of Execution ☐ Protest ☐ Other

R T I M R P **Fingerprint**

DOC TYPE ☐ **Deed** ☐ **DOT** ☐ **Trust** ☐ **POA** ☐ **POAH** ☐ **Agreement** ☐ **Affidavit** ☐ **Other**
Grant • Trust Transfer • Gift   Mortgage   Certification   General / Limited   AHCD   Compliance-E&O   Borrower • Occupancy • Ownership • Refi • Survey   Vehicle Title
Interspousal • Quitclaim • ToD • Warranty   Rev / Irrev • Am / Rest   Durable / Springing   Living Will   Correction   Debts & Liens • Name-Signature-ID • Marital • Death • Will   Safe Deposit Box

DOC DATE J F M A M J J A S O N D , | DOC TITLE or TYPE | # OF PAGES | ☐ Inspect/Copy Request | Entry X-Ref #

☐ **SATISFACTORY EVIDENCE** ☐ Driver's License / Passport / State ID / Military / Government / Tribal / Inmate / Other ID *or* ☐ Credible Witness(es)   L

SIGNER	SIGNER's NAME	☐ For	ADDRESS	☐ Non-Public	☐ Capacity ☐ Voluntary ☐ Proper ID #	ISSUED	SIGNATURE ☐ (oath / affirmation, if any) ☐ (by Mark)
	PHONE C / H / W /	*or* ☐ MISC			AGENCY ☐ CA DMV ☐ US State Dept	EXPIRES	➡

CW #1	#1 WITNESS's NAME	☐ P/Known	ADDRESS	☐ Non-Public	☐ Driver's License ☐ Passport ☐ Other ID #	ISSUED	SIGNATURE ☐ (after oath / affirmation)
	PHONE C / H / W /	*or* ☐ MISC			AGENCY ☐ CA DMV ☐ US State Dept	EXPIRES	❶

CW #2	#2 WITNESS's NAME	☐ P/Known	ADDRESS	☐ Non-Public	☐ Driver's License ☐ Passport ☐ Other ID #	ISSUED	SIGNATURE ☐ (after oath / affirmation)
	PHONE C / H / W /	*or* ☐ MISC			AGENCY ☐ CA DMV ☐ US State Dept	EXPIRES	❷

* See complete legal disclaimer regarding non-exhaustive illustrations and notary's absolute duty to research the laws of their own state on pages ii and xiii.

THIS CONTENT IS COPYRIGHTED

JOURNAL USAGE EXPLAINED via STATE-SPECIFIC* NOTARIAL LAW COMPARISONS © 2019 Jenna Jack

JOURNAL FORMAT & MAINTENANCE

㉑ NOTARY's INFORMATION - - **Hawaii** requires the notary to legibly print her or his <u>name</u> and <u>commission number</u> respectively at the top left and top right of the page for any journal entry.

㉒ SEQUENTIAL JOURNAL ENTRY NUMBERS - - Many states like **Montana, Oregon** and **Pennsylvania** require a permanently bound notary journal with pre-printed sequential numbered journal entries.

㉓ SEQUENTIAL PAGE NUMBERS - - Many states like **Nevada, Oregon, Pennsylvania** and **Washington** require notary journal pages to be sequentially numbered.

㉔ JOURNAL SIZE - - This landscape-oriented notary journal accommodates the book size laws of 49 U.S. states (*excluding Hawaii*). Some journals claim to be 50-state compliant when they are not (i.e. they lack page and journal entry numbers OR exceed Hawaii's maximum size of 11 inches high & 16.5 inches wide *when open*). Ensure the notary journal you choose meets <u>all of YOUR STATE's requirements</u> (view my <u>Flowchart By State</u> on **page viii** to see which of my journals was designed for your state).

㉕ JOURNAL ABBREVIATIONS - - Some states like **Oregon** require the abbreviations used by the notary to be listed in a Legend or Glossary in the journal (see page xxi).

㉖ JOURNAL RETENTION - - Many states like **Arizona** (5 years), **Massachusetts** (7 years), **Montana** (10 years), **Nevada** (7 years), **Oregon** (10 years), **Washington** (10 years) and **states adopting RULONA** (10 years) require notary journals to be retained for specified periods after the final entry is complete or the notary's commission ends. This requirement is addressed in the notary's information page (see page i).

㉗ JOURNAL SURRENDER - - In the event of a notary's death, incapacity, or other circumstances where she or he is no longer commissioned, many states like **Arizona, California, Colorado, Hawaii, Mississippi, Montana** (optional for resignation/termination), **Oregon, Pennsylvania, Texas**, states adopting **RULONA** and the **District of Columbia** require surrender of the notary journal (some to the Secretary of State, County Clerk/Recorder, Office of the Attorney General, state archives or other specified agency/entity). This requirement is addressed in the notary's information page (see page i).

NOTARY NAME (printed): ㉑   COMMISSION #: ㉑   ㉒

SERVICE | DATE - -20 | TIME : am/pm | ADDRESS | ☐ Signer's ☐ Office | NOTES | ☐ Stop MILES | Notary $ | ☐ Adv. Travel $ | ☐ Rush $ | ☐ Copy $ | ☐ Other $ | TOTAL FEES $ | 97

TYPE ☐ Acknowledgment ☐ Jurat ☐ Copy Certification ☐ Oath/Affirmation ☐ Oath of Office ☐ Proof of Execution ☐ Protest ☐ Other | R **Fingerprint**

DOCUMENT
DOC TYPE ☐ Deed   ☐ DOT   ☐ Trust   ☐ POA   ☐ POAH   ☐ Agreement   ☐ Affidavit   ☐ Other
Grant • Trust Transfer • Gift | Mortgage | Certification | General / Limited | AHCD | Compliance-E&O | Borrower • Occupancy • Ownership • Refi • Survey | Vehicle Title
Interspousal • Quitclaim • ToD • Warranty | Rev / Irrev • Am / Rest | Durable / Springing | Living Will | Correction | Debts & Liens • Name-Signature-ID • Marital • Death • Will | Safe Deposit Box

T I M R P

DOC DATE   J F M A M J   DOC TITLE or TYPE   # OF PAGES   ☐ Inspect/Copy Request
           J A S O N D   ,   Entry X-Ref #

☐ **SATISFACTORY EVIDENCE**   ☐ Driver's License / Passport / State ID / Military / Government / Tribal / Inmate / Other ID   *or*   ☐ Credible Witness(es)   L

SIGNER
SIGNER's NAME | ☐ For | ADDRESS | ☐ Non-Public | ☐ Capacity # | ☐ Voluntary | ☐ Proper ID | ISSUED | SIGNATURE | ☐ (oath / affirmation, if any) | ☐ (by Mark)
PHONE C / H / W / | *or* ☐ MISC | | | AGENCY | ☐ CA DMV | ☐ US State Dept | EXPIRES | ➡ |

CW #1
#1 WITNESS's NAME | ☐ P/Known | ADDRESS | ☐ Non-Public | ☐ Driver's License # | ☐ Passport | ☐ Other ID | ISSUED | SIGNATURE | ☐ (after oath / affirmation)
PHONE C / H / W / | *or* ☐ MISC | | | AGENCY | ☐ CA DMV | ☐ US State Dept | EXPIRES | ❶

CW #2
#2 WITNESS's NAME | ☐ P/Known | ADDRESS | ☐ Non-Public | ☐ Driver's License # | ☐ Passport | ☐ Other ID | ISSUED | SIGNATURE | ☐ (after oath / affirmation)
PHONE C / H / W / | *or* ☐ MISC | | | AGENCY | ☐ CA DMV | ☐ US State Dept | EXPIRES | ❷   ㉓

---

* See complete legal disclaimer regarding non-exhaustive illustrations and notary's absolute duty to research the laws of their own state on pages ii and xiii.

FEE SCHEDULE

Consider storing a laminated copy of your fee schedule here (rush, after hours, waiting time, cancellation, travel, mileage & copy costs)

DUTY OF CONFIDENTIALITY

Regardless of the state in which you are commissioned, **safeguarding the confidentiality of the client data recorded in your notary journal is one of the most fundamental and paramount of a notary public's duties**. The American Association of Notaries directs notaries to "cover any previous journal entries" when meeting with clients. That means concealing ALL prior entries from the current client, credible witness(es) and anyone else present during EACH of your notarizations.

Fines, criminal charges, and suspension or even revocation of a notary's commission are among the disciplinary sanctions that many states impose for failure to follow applicable notarial laws. Because many states have enacted umbrella legislation (e.g. "failure to discharge fully and faithfully any of the duties or responsibilities required of a notary public" Cal. Gov. Code § 8214.1(d)), the violation of which is subject to discipline, preserving client data confidentiality is a serious matter.

Fortunately, **concealing all prior journal entries from your next client is now easy** … due to the innovative half-page entry format of this landscape-orientated notary journal (it opens upwards like a calendar). Regardless of which of the 4 entries you use (top entry on upper page, bottom entry on upper page, top entry on lower page, or bottom entry on lower page), my companion Data Shield effortlessly conceals all visible prior entries recorded in any of the Jenna Jack notary journals.

Email to learn more or to order your budget-friendly bi-fold DATA SHIELD for your GUARDIAN NOTARY JOURNAL.

NotaryRecords@gmail.com

Jenna Jack

OATH & AFFIRMATION SCRIPTS

Consider attaching a printed copy of the verbiage for oaths and affirmations that you administer to signers, credible witnesses and others

LEGEND of NOTARY's ABBREVIATIONS

Consider attaching a printed copy of abbreviations that you build over the course of your notary career for courts & peace officers

Pre-printed Abbreviations

Adv Travel - advance client notice of travel fee	Deed ToD - Transfer on Death Deed	POAH - Power of Attorney for Health Care
AHCD - Advance Health Care Directive	DOT - Deed of Trust	Trust Am - Amended Trust
CA DMV - California Department of Motor Vehicles	Fingerprint R / L - right hand or left hand	Trust Cert - Trust Certification
CW #1 - credible witness #1	Fingerprint T / I / M / R / P - thumb, index, middle, ring, pinky	Trust Irrev - irrevocable Trust
CW #2 - credible witness #2	P/Known - personally known to notary public	Trust Rest - Restated Trust
Copy Certification - Power of Attorney/journal entry	POA - Power of Attorney	Trust Rev - revocable Trust

TO MOST EFFECTIVELY USE THIS NOTARY JOURNAL

(e.g. why and how best to use the "For" "Non-Public" or "Stop" checkboxes)

see

"JOURNAL USAGE EXPLAINED via STATE-SPECIFIC NOTARIAL LAW COMPARISONS"

for explanations about items in the

SERVICE tab . . . . page xiii

DOCUMENT tab . . . . page xiv

SIGNER tab . . . . page xv

CREDIBLE WITNESS tab . . . . page xvi

JOURNAL FORMAT & MAINTENANCE . . . . page xvii

NOTARY NAME (printed): _____   COMMISSION #: _____

Entry 1

| SERVICE | DATE __ - __ -20 | TIME __ : __ ☐ am ☐ pm | ADDRESS | ☐ Signer's | ☐ Office | NOTES | ☐ Stop | MILES | Notary $__ $__ | ☐ Adv. Travel $__ | ☐ Rush $__ | ☐ Copy $__ | ☐ Other $__ | TOTAL FEES | **1** |

TYPE ☐ Acknowledgment ☐ Jurat ☐ Copy Certification ☐ Oath/Affirmation ☐ Oath of Office ☐ Proof of Execution ☐ Protest ☐ Other

R · T · I · M · R · P — **Fingerprint**

DOCUMENT

DOC TYPE ☐ Deed ☐ DOT ☐ Trust ☐ POA ☐ POAH ☐ Agreement ☐ Affidavit ☐ Other

Grant · Trust Transfer · Gift / Mortgage / Certification / General / Limited / AHCD / Compliance-E&O / Borrower · Occupancy · Ownership · Refi · Survey / Vehicle Title

Interspousal · Quitclaim · ToD · Warranty / Rev / Irrev · Am / Rest / Durable / Springing / Living Will / Correction / Debts & Liens · Name-Signature-ID · Marital · Death · Will / Safe Deposit Box

DOC DATE J F M A M J J A S O N D , ____   **DOC TITLE or TYPE** _____   **# OF PAGES** ____   ☐ Inspect/Copy Request   Entry X-Ref # ____

L

☐ **SATISFACTORY EVIDENCE** ☐ Driver's License / Passport / State ID / Military / Government / Tribal / Inmate / Other ID *or* ☐ Credible Witness(es)

SIGNER

| SIGNER's NAME | ☐ For | ADDRESS | ☐ Non-Public | ☐ Capacity | ☐ Voluntary | ☐ Proper ID | ISSUED | SIGNATURE ☐ (oath / affirmation, if any) ☐ (by Mark) |
| PHONE C / H / W ___/___ | *or* ☐ MISC | | | AGENCY | ☐ CA DMV | ☐ US State Dept | EXPIRES | # ➤ |

CW #1

| #1 WITNESS's NAME | ☐ P/Known | ADDRESS | ☐ Non-Public | ☐ Driver's License | ☐ Passport | ☐ Other ID | ISSUED | SIGNATURE ☐ (after oath / affirmation) |
| PHONE C / H / W ___/___ | *or* ☐ MISC | | | AGENCY | ☐ CA DMV | ☐ US State Dept | EXPIRES | # ❶ |

CW #2

| #2 WITNESS's NAME | ☐ P/Known | ADDRESS | ☐ Non-Public | ☐ Driver's License | ☐ Passport | ☐ Other ID | ISSUED | SIGNATURE ☐ (after oath / affirmation) |
| PHONE C / H / W ___/___ | *or* ☐ MISC | | | AGENCY | ☐ CA DMV | ☐ US State Dept | EXPIRES | # ❷ |

Entry 2

| SERVICE | DATE __ - __ -20 | TIME __ : __ ☐ am ☐ pm | ADDRESS | ☐ Signer's | ☐ Office | NOTES | ☐ Stop | MILES | Notary $__ $__ | ☐ Adv. Travel $__ | ☐ Rush $__ | ☐ Copy $__ | ☐ Other $__ | TOTAL FEES | **2** |

TYPE ☐ Acknowledgment ☐ Jurat ☐ Copy Certification ☐ Oath/Affirmation ☐ Oath of Office ☐ Proof of Execution ☐ Protest ☐ Other

R · T · I · M · R · P — **Fingerprint**

DOCUMENT

DOC TYPE ☐ Deed ☐ DOT ☐ Trust ☐ POA ☐ POAH ☐ Agreement ☐ Affidavit ☐ Other

Grant · Trust Transfer · Gift / Mortgage / Certification / General / Limited / AHCD / Compliance-E&O / Borrower · Occupancy · Ownership · Refi · Survey / Vehicle Title

Interspousal · Quitclaim · ToD · Warranty / Rev / Irrev · Am / Rest / Durable / Springing / Living Will / Correction / Debts & Liens · Name-Signature-ID · Marital · Death · Will / Safe Deposit Box

DOC DATE J F M A M J J A S O N D , ____   **DOC TITLE or TYPE** _____   **# OF PAGES** ____   ☐ Inspect/Copy Request   Entry X-Ref # ____

L

☐ **SATISFACTORY EVIDENCE** ☐ Driver's License / Passport / State ID / Military / Government / Tribal / Inmate / Other ID *or* ☐ Credible Witness(es)

SIGNER

| SIGNER's NAME | ☐ For | ADDRESS | ☐ Non-Public | ☐ Capacity | ☐ Voluntary | ☐ Proper ID | ISSUED | SIGNATURE ☐ (oath / affirmation, if any) ☐ (by Mark) |
| PHONE C / H / W ___/___ | *or* ☐ MISC | | | AGENCY | ☐ CA DMV | ☐ US State Dept | EXPIRES | # ➤ |

CW #1

| #1 WITNESS's NAME | ☐ P/Known | ADDRESS | ☐ Non-Public | ☐ Driver's License | ☐ Passport | ☐ Other ID | ISSUED | SIGNATURE ☐ (after oath / affirmation) |
| PHONE C / H / W ___/___ | *or* ☐ MISC | | | AGENCY | ☐ CA DMV | ☐ US State Dept | EXPIRES | # ❶ |

CW #2

| #2 WITNESS's NAME | ☐ P/Known | ADDRESS | ☐ Non-Public | ☐ Driver's License | ☐ Passport | ☐ Other ID | ISSUED | SIGNATURE ☐ (after oath / affirmation) |
| PHONE C / H / W ___/___ | *or* ☐ MISC | | | AGENCY | ☐ CA DMV | ☐ US State Dept | EXPIRES | # ❷ |

NOTARY NAME (printed): COMMISSION #:

Entry 3

SERVICE — DATE: - -20 | TIME: : am/pm | ADDRESS ☐ Signer's ☐ Office | NOTES | ☐ Stop | MILES | Notary $ | ☐ Adv. Travel $ | ☐ Rush $ | ☐ Copy $ | ☐ Other $ | TOTAL FEES $

TYPE: ☐ Acknowledgment ☐ Jurat ☐ Copy Certification ☐ Oath/Affirmation ☐ Oath of Office ☐ Proof of Execution ☐ Protest ☐ Other

Fingerprint R T I M R P L

DOCUMENT
DOC TYPE: ☐ Deed (Grant • Trust Transfer • Gift / Interspousal • Quitclaim • ToD • Warranty) ☐ DOT (Mortgage) ☐ Trust (Certification / Rev / Irrev • Am / Rest) ☐ POA (General / Limited / Durable / Springing) ☐ POAH (AHCD / Living Will) ☐ Agreement (Compliance-E&O / Correction) ☐ Affidavit (Borrower • Occupancy • Ownership • Refi • Survey / Debts & Liens • Name-Signature-ID • Marital • Death • Will) ☐ Other (Vehicle Title / Safe Deposit Box)

DOC DATE: J F M A M J J A S O N D , | DOC TITLE or TYPE | # OF PAGES | ☐ Inspect/Copy Request | Entry X-Ref #

☐ **SATISFACTORY EVIDENCE** ☐ Driver's License / Passport / State ID / Military / Government / Tribal / Inmate / Other ID **or** ☐ Credible Witness(es)

SIGNER
SIGNER's NAME | ☐ For | ADDRESS | ☐ Non-Public | ☐ Capacity # | ☐ Voluntary | ☐ Proper ID | ISSUED | SIGNATURE ☐ (oath / affirmation, if any) ☐ (by Mark)
PHONE C / H / W / | or ☐ MISC | | | AGENCY | ☐ CA DMV | ☐ US State Dept | EXPIRES | ➡

CW #1
#1 WITNESS's NAME | ☐ P/Known | ADDRESS | ☐ Non-Public | ☐ Driver's License # | ☐ Passport | ☐ Other ID | ISSUED | SIGNATURE ☐ (after oath / affirmation)
PHONE C / H / W / | or ☐ MISC | | | AGENCY | ☐ CA DMV | ☐ US State Dept | EXPIRES | ❶

CW #2
#2 WITNESS's NAME | ☐ P/Known | ADDRESS | ☐ Non-Public | ☐ Driver's License # | ☐ Passport | ☐ Other ID | ISSUED | SIGNATURE ☐ (after oath / affirmation)
PHONE C / H / W / | or ☐ MISC | | | AGENCY | ☐ CA DMV | ☐ US State Dept | EXPIRES | ❷

Entry 4

SERVICE — DATE: - -20 | TIME: : am/pm | ADDRESS ☐ Signer's ☐ Office | NOTES | ☐ Stop | MILES | Notary $ | ☐ Adv. Travel $ | ☐ Rush $ | ☐ Copy $ | ☐ Other $ | TOTAL FEES $

TYPE: ☐ Acknowledgment ☐ Jurat ☐ Copy Certification ☐ Oath/Affirmation ☐ Oath of Office ☐ Proof of Execution ☐ Protest ☐ Other

Fingerprint R T I M R P L

DOCUMENT
DOC TYPE: ☐ Deed (Grant • Trust Transfer • Gift / Interspousal • Quitclaim • ToD • Warranty) ☐ DOT (Mortgage) ☐ Trust (Certification / Rev / Irrev • Am / Rest) ☐ POA (General / Limited / Durable / Springing) ☐ POAH (AHCD / Living Will) ☐ Agreement (Compliance-E&O / Correction) ☐ Affidavit (Borrower • Occupancy • Ownership • Refi • Survey / Debts & Liens • Name-Signature-ID • Marital • Death • Will) ☐ Other (Vehicle Title / Safe Deposit Box)

DOC DATE: J F M A M J J A S O N D , | DOC TITLE or TYPE | # OF PAGES | ☐ Inspect/Copy Request | Entry X-Ref #

☐ **SATISFACTORY EVIDENCE** ☐ Driver's License / Passport / State ID / Military / Government / Tribal / Inmate / Other ID **or** ☐ Credible Witness(es)

SIGNER
SIGNER's NAME | ☐ For | ADDRESS | ☐ Non-Public | ☐ Capacity # | ☐ Voluntary | ☐ Proper ID | ISSUED | SIGNATURE ☐ (oath / affirmation, if any) ☐ (by Mark)
PHONE C / H / W / | or ☐ MISC | | | AGENCY | ☐ CA DMV | ☐ US State Dept | EXPIRES | ➡

CW #1
#1 WITNESS's NAME | ☐ P/Known | ADDRESS | ☐ Non-Public | ☐ Driver's License # | ☐ Passport | ☐ Other ID | ISSUED | SIGNATURE ☐ (after oath / affirmation)
PHONE C / H / W / | or ☐ MISC | | | AGENCY | ☐ CA DMV | ☐ US State Dept | EXPIRES | ❶

CW #2
#2 WITNESS's NAME | ☐ P/Known | ADDRESS | ☐ Non-Public | ☐ Driver's License # | ☐ Passport | ☐ Other ID | ISSUED | SIGNATURE ☐ (after oath / affirmation)
PHONE C / H / W / | or ☐ MISC | | | AGENCY | ☐ CA DMV | ☐ US State Dept | EXPIRES | ❷

NOTARY NAME (printed):   COMMISSION #:

Entry 5

SERVICE | DATE - -20 | TIME : am/pm | ADDRESS ☐ Signer's ☐ Office | NOTES | ☐ Stop | MILES | Notary ☐ Adv. Travel ☐ Rush ☐ Copy ☐ Other TOTAL FEES | $ $ $ $ $ $ | **5**

TYPE ☐ Acknowledgment ☐ Jurat ☐ Copy Certification ☐ Oath/Affirmation ☐ Oath of Office ☐ Proof of Execution ☐ Protest ☐ Other

R   **Fingerprint**
T
I
M
R
P
L

DOCUMENT
DOC TYPE ☐ Deed ☐ DOT ☐ Trust ☐ POA ☐ POAH ☐ Agreement ☐ Affidavit ☐ Other
Grant • Trust Transfer • Gift | Mortgage | Certification | General / Limited | AHCD | Compliance-E&O | Borrower • Occupancy • Ownership • Refi • Survey | Vehicle Title
Interspousal • Quitclaim • ToD • Warranty | Rev / Irrev • Am / Rest | Durable / Springing | Living Will | Correction | Debts & Liens • Name-Signature-ID • Marital • Death • Will | Safe Deposit Box

DOC DATE   J F M A M J   J A S O N D   ,   DOC TITLE or TYPE   # OF PAGES   ☐ Inspect/Copy Request   Entry X-Ref #

☐ **SATISFACTORY EVIDENCE** ☐ Driver's License / Passport / State ID / Military / Government / Tribal / Inmate / Other ID *or* ☐ Credible Witness(es)

SIGNER
SIGNER's NAME ☐ For | ADDRESS ☐ Non-Public | ☐ Capacity ☐ Voluntary ☐ Proper ID | ISSUED # | SIGNATURE ☐ (oath / affirmation, if any) ☐ (by Mark)
PHONE C / H / W   *or* ☐ MISC   / | AGENCY ☐ CA DMV ☐ US State Dept | EXPIRES | ➡

CW #1
#1 WITNESS's NAME ☐ P/Known | ADDRESS ☐ Non-Public | ☐ Driver's License ☐ Passport ☐ Other ID | ISSUED # | SIGNATURE ☐ (after oath / affirmation)
PHONE C / H / W   *or* ☐ MISC   / | AGENCY ☐ CA DMV ☐ US State Dept | EXPIRES | ❶

CW #2
#2 WITNESS's NAME ☐ P/Known | ADDRESS ☐ Non-Public | ☐ Driver's License ☐ Passport ☐ Other ID | ISSUED # | SIGNATURE ☐ (after oath / affirmation)
PHONE C / H / W   *or* ☐ MISC   / | AGENCY ☐ CA DMV ☐ US State Dept | EXPIRES | ❷

Entry 6

SERVICE | DATE - -20 | TIME : am/pm | ADDRESS ☐ Signer's ☐ Office | NOTES | ☐ Stop | MILES | Notary ☐ Adv. Travel ☐ Rush ☐ Copy ☐ Other TOTAL FEES | $ $ $ $ $ $ | **6**

TYPE ☐ Acknowledgment ☐ Jurat ☐ Copy Certification ☐ Oath/Affirmation ☐ Oath of Office ☐ Proof of Execution ☐ Protest ☐ Other

R   **Fingerprint**
T
I
M
R
P
L

DOCUMENT
DOC TYPE ☐ Deed ☐ DOT ☐ Trust ☐ POA ☐ POAH ☐ Agreement ☐ Affidavit ☐ Other
Grant • Trust Transfer • Gift | Mortgage | Certification | General / Limited | AHCD | Compliance-E&O | Borrower • Occupancy • Ownership • Refi • Survey | Vehicle Title
Interspousal • Quitclaim • ToD • Warranty | Rev / Irrev • Am / Rest | Durable / Springing | Living Will | Correction | Debts & Liens • Name-Signature-ID • Marital • Death • Will | Safe Deposit Box

DOC DATE   J F M A M J   J A S O N D   ,   DOC TITLE or TYPE   # OF PAGES   ☐ Inspect/Copy Request   Entry X-Ref #

☐ **SATISFACTORY EVIDENCE** ☐ Driver's License / Passport / State ID / Military / Government / Tribal / Inmate / Other ID *or* ☐ Credible Witness(es)

SIGNER
SIGNER's NAME ☐ For | ADDRESS ☐ Non-Public | ☐ Capacity ☐ Voluntary ☐ Proper ID | ISSUED # | SIGNATURE ☐ (oath / affirmation, if any) ☐ (by Mark)
PHONE C / H / W   *or* ☐ MISC   / | AGENCY ☐ CA DMV ☐ US State Dept | EXPIRES | ➡

CW #1
#1 WITNESS's NAME ☐ P/Known | ADDRESS ☐ Non-Public | ☐ Driver's License ☐ Passport ☐ Other ID | ISSUED # | SIGNATURE ☐ (after oath / affirmation)
PHONE C / H / W   *or* ☐ MISC   / | AGENCY ☐ CA DMV ☐ US State Dept | EXPIRES | ❶

CW #2
#2 WITNESS's NAME ☐ P/Known | ADDRESS ☐ Non-Public | ☐ Driver's License ☐ Passport ☐ Other ID | ISSUED # | SIGNATURE ☐ (after oath / affirmation)
PHONE C / H / W   *or* ☐ MISC   / | AGENCY ☐ CA DMV ☐ US State Dept | EXPIRES | ❷

NOTARY NAME (printed):   COMMISSION #:

Entry 7

SERVICE
- DATE: - -20
- TIME: : am/pm
- ADDRESS: ☐ Signer's ☐ Office
- NOTES
- ☐ Stop MILES Notary ☐ Adv. Travel ☐ Rush ☐ Copy ☐ Other TOTAL FEES
- $ $ $ $ $ $

TYPE: ☐ Acknowledgment ☐ Jurat ☐ Copy Certification ☐ Oath/Affirmation ☐ Oath of Office ☐ Proof of Execution ☐ Protest ☐ Other

Fingerprint — R T I M R P L

DOCUMENT
- DOC TYPE: ☐ Deed (Grant • Trust Transfer • Gift • Interspousal • Quitclaim • ToD • Warranty) ☐ DOT (Mortgage • Rev/Irrev • Am/Rest) ☐ Trust (Certification • Durable/Springing) ☐ POA (General/Limited) ☐ POAH (AHCD • Living Will) ☐ Agreement (Compliance-E&O • Correction) ☐ Affidavit (Borrower • Occupancy • Ownership • Refi • Survey • Debts & Liens • Name-Signature-ID • Marital • Death • Will) ☐ Other (Vehicle Title • Safe Deposit Box)
- DOC DATE: J F M A M J J A S O N D ,
- DOC TITLE or TYPE:
- # OF PAGES:
- ☐ Inspect/Copy Request
- Entry X-Ref #:

☐ **SATISFACTORY EVIDENCE** ☐ Driver's License / Passport / State ID / Military / Government / Tribal / Inmate / Other ID *or* ☐ Credible Witness(es)

SIGNER
- SIGNER's NAME | ☐ For | ADDRESS | ☐ Non-Public | ☐ Capacity | ☐ Voluntary | ☐ Proper ID | ISSUED # | SIGNATURE | ☐ (oath / affirmation, if any) | ☐ (by Mark)
- PHONE C/H/W / | or ☐ MISC | | | AGENCY | ☐ CA DMV | ☐ US State Dept | EXPIRES

CW #1
- #1 WITNESS's NAME | ☐ P/Known | ADDRESS | ☐ Non-Public | ☐ Driver's License | ☐ Passport | ☐ Other ID | ISSUED # | SIGNATURE | ☐ (after oath / affirmation)
- PHONE C/H/W / | or ☐ MISC | | | AGENCY | ☐ CA DMV | ☐ US State Dept | EXPIRES | ❶

CW #2
- #2 WITNESS's NAME | ☐ P/Known | ADDRESS | ☐ Non-Public | ☐ Driver's License | ☐ Passport | ☐ Other ID | ISSUED # | SIGNATURE | ☐ (after oath / affirmation)
- PHONE C/H/W / | or ☐ MISC | | | AGENCY | ☐ CA DMV | ☐ US State Dept | EXPIRES | ❷

Entry 8

SERVICE
- DATE: - -20
- TIME: : am/pm
- ADDRESS: ☐ Signer's ☐ Office
- NOTES
- ☐ Stop MILES Notary ☐ Adv. Travel ☐ Rush ☐ Copy ☐ Other TOTAL FEES
- $ $ $ $ $ $

TYPE: ☐ Acknowledgment ☐ Jurat ☐ Copy Certification ☐ Oath/Affirmation ☐ Oath of Office ☐ Proof of Execution ☐ Protest ☐ Other

Fingerprint — R T I M R P L

DOCUMENT
- DOC TYPE: ☐ Deed (Grant • Trust Transfer • Gift • Interspousal • Quitclaim • ToD • Warranty) ☐ DOT (Mortgage • Rev/Irrev • Am/Rest) ☐ Trust (Certification • Durable/Springing) ☐ POA (General/Limited) ☐ POAH (AHCD • Living Will) ☐ Agreement (Compliance-E&O • Correction) ☐ Affidavit (Borrower • Occupancy • Ownership • Refi • Survey • Debts & Liens • Name-Signature-ID • Marital • Death • Will) ☐ Other (Vehicle Title • Safe Deposit Box)
- DOC DATE: J F M A M J J A S O N D ,
- DOC TITLE or TYPE:
- # OF PAGES:
- ☐ Inspect/Copy Request
- Entry X-Ref #:

☐ **SATISFACTORY EVIDENCE** ☐ Driver's License / Passport / State ID / Military / Government / Tribal / Inmate / Other ID *or* ☐ Credible Witness(es)

SIGNER
- SIGNER's NAME | ☐ For | ADDRESS | ☐ Non-Public | ☐ Capacity | ☐ Voluntary | ☐ Proper ID | ISSUED # | SIGNATURE | ☐ (oath / affirmation, if any) | ☐ (by Mark)
- PHONE C/H/W / | or ☐ MISC | | | AGENCY | ☐ CA DMV | ☐ US State Dept | EXPIRES

CW #1
- #1 WITNESS's NAME | ☐ P/Known | ADDRESS | ☐ Non-Public | ☐ Driver's License | ☐ Passport | ☐ Other ID | ISSUED # | SIGNATURE | ☐ (after oath / affirmation)
- PHONE C/H/W / | or ☐ MISC | | | AGENCY | ☐ CA DMV | ☐ US State Dept | EXPIRES | ❶

CW #2
- #2 WITNESS's NAME | ☐ P/Known | ADDRESS | ☐ Non-Public | ☐ Driver's License | ☐ Passport | ☐ Other ID | ISSUED # | SIGNATURE | ☐ (after oath / affirmation)
- PHONE C/H/W / | or ☐ MISC | | | AGENCY | ☐ CA DMV | ☐ US State Dept | EXPIRES | ❷

NOTARY NAME (printed): _____ COMMISSION #: _____

Entry 9

SERVICE

DATE	TIME	am	ADDRESS	☐ Signer's	☐ Office	NOTES	☐ Stop	MILES	Notary	☐ Adv. Travel	☐ Rush	☐ Copy	☐ Other	TOTAL FEES	**9**
- -20	:	pm							$ $		$	$	$	$	

TYPE ☐ Acknowledgment ☐ Jurat ☐ Copy Certification ☐ Oath/Affirmation ☐ Oath of Office ☐ Proof of Execution ☐ Protest ☐ Other

Fingerprint — R T I M R P L

DOCUMENT

DOC TYPE ☐ Deed ☐ DOT ☐ Trust ☐ POA ☐ POAH ☐ Agreement ☐ Affidavit ☐ Other
Grant • Trust Transfer • Gift / Mortgage / Certification / General / Limited / AHCD / Compliance-E&O / Borrower • Occupancy • Ownership • Refi • Survey / Vehicle Title
Interspousal • Quitclaim • ToD • Warranty / Rev / Irrev • Am / Rest / Durable / Springing / Living Will / Correction / Debts & Liens • Name-Signature-ID • Marital • Death • Will / Safe Deposit Box

DOC DATE J F M A M J J A S O N D , DOC TITLE or TYPE _____ # OF PAGES ☐ Inspect/Copy Request Entry X-Ref #

☐ **SATISFACTORY EVIDENCE** ☐ Driver's License / Passport / State ID / Military / Government / Tribal / Inmate / Other ID *or* ☐ Credible Witness(es)

SIGNER

SIGNER's NAME	☐ For	ADDRESS	☐ Non-Public	☐ Capacity	☐ Voluntary	☐ Proper ID	ISSUED	SIGNATURE	☐ (oath / affirmation, if any)	☐ (by Mark)
PHONE C / H / W /	*or* ☐ MISC			#	AGENCY ☐ CA DMV ☐ US State Dept	EXPIRES		➡		

CW #1

#1 WITNESS's NAME	☐ P/Known	ADDRESS	☐ Non-Public	☐ Driver's License	☐ Passport	☐ Other ID	ISSUED	SIGNATURE	☐ (after oath / affirmation)
PHONE C / H / W /	*or* ☐ MISC			#	AGENCY ☐ CA DMV ☐ US State Dept	EXPIRES		❶	

CW #2

#2 WITNESS's NAME	☐ P/Known	ADDRESS	☐ Non-Public	☐ Driver's License	☐ Passport	☐ Other ID	ISSUED	SIGNATURE	☐ (after oath / affirmation)
PHONE C / H / W /	*or* ☐ MISC			#	AGENCY ☐ CA DMV ☐ US State Dept	EXPIRES		❷	

Entry 10

SERVICE

DATE	TIME	am	ADDRESS	☐ Signer's	☐ Office	NOTES	☐ Stop	MILES	Notary	☐ Adv. Travel	☐ Rush	☐ Copy	☐ Other	TOTAL FEES	**10**
- -20	:	pm							$ $		$	$	$	$	

TYPE ☐ Acknowledgment ☐ Jurat ☐ Copy Certification ☐ Oath/Affirmation ☐ Oath of Office ☐ Proof of Execution ☐ Protest ☐ Other

Fingerprint — R T I M R P L

DOCUMENT

DOC TYPE ☐ Deed ☐ DOT ☐ Trust ☐ POA ☐ POAH ☐ Agreement ☐ Affidavit ☐ Other
Grant • Trust Transfer • Gift / Mortgage / Certification / General / Limited / AHCD / Compliance-E&O / Borrower • Occupancy • Ownership • Refi • Survey / Vehicle Title
Interspousal • Quitclaim • ToD • Warranty / Rev / Irrev • Am / Rest / Durable / Springing / Living Will / Correction / Debts & Liens • Name-Signature-ID • Marital • Death • Will / Safe Deposit Box

DOC DATE J F M A M J J A S O N D , DOC TITLE or TYPE _____ # OF PAGES ☐ Inspect/Copy Request Entry X-Ref #

☐ **SATISFACTORY EVIDENCE** ☐ Driver's License / Passport / State ID / Military / Government / Tribal / Inmate / Other ID *or* ☐ Credible Witness(es)

SIGNER

SIGNER's NAME	☐ For	ADDRESS	☐ Non-Public	☐ Capacity	☐ Voluntary	☐ Proper ID	ISSUED	SIGNATURE	☐ (oath / affirmation, if any)	☐ (by Mark)
PHONE C / H / W /	*or* ☐ MISC			#	AGENCY ☐ CA DMV ☐ US State Dept	EXPIRES		➡		

CW #1

#1 WITNESS's NAME	☐ P/Known	ADDRESS	☐ Non-Public	☐ Driver's License	☐ Passport	☐ Other ID	ISSUED	SIGNATURE	☐ (after oath / affirmation)
PHONE C / H / W /	*or* ☐ MISC			#	AGENCY ☐ CA DMV ☐ US State Dept	EXPIRES		❶	

CW #2

#2 WITNESS's NAME	☐ P/Known	ADDRESS	☐ Non-Public	☐ Driver's License	☐ Passport	☐ Other ID	ISSUED	SIGNATURE	☐ (after oath / affirmation)
PHONE C / H / W /	*or* ☐ MISC			#	AGENCY ☐ CA DMV ☐ US State Dept	EXPIRES		❷	

NOTARY NAME (printed):   **COMMISSION #:**

Entry 11

SERVICE
- DATE: - -20
- TIME: : am/pm
- ADDRESS: ☐ Signer's ☐ Office
- NOTES: ☐ Stop
- MILES | Notary $ | ☐ Adv. Travel $ | ☐ Rush $ | ☐ Copy $ | ☐ Other $ | TOTAL FEES $

TYPE: ☐ Acknowledgment ☐ Jurat ☐ Copy Certification ☐ Oath/Affirmation ☐ Oath of Office ☐ Proof of Execution ☐ Protest ☐ Other

Fingerprint   R T I M R P L

DOCUMENT
- DOC TYPE: ☐ Deed ☐ DOT ☐ Trust ☐ POA ☐ POAH ☐ Agreement ☐ Affidavit ☐ Other
  - Grant • Trust Transfer • Gift | Mortgage | Certification | General / Limited | AHCD | Compliance-E&O | Borrower • Occupancy • Ownership • Refi • Survey | Vehicle Title
  - Interspousal • Quitclaim • ToD • Warranty | Rev / Irrev • Am / Rest | Durable / Springing | Living Will | Correction | Debts & Liens • Name-Signature-ID • Marital • Death • Will | Safe Deposit Box
- DOC DATE: J F M A M J / J A S O N D ,
- DOC TITLE or TYPE:
- # OF PAGES:
- ☐ Inspect/Copy Request
- Entry X-Ref #:

☐ **SATISFACTORY EVIDENCE** ☐ Driver's License / Passport / State ID / Military / Government / Tribal / Inmate / Other ID *or* ☐ Credible Witness(es)

SIGNER
- SIGNER's NAME | ☐ For | ADDRESS | ☐ Non-Public | ☐ Capacity # | ☐ Voluntary | ☐ Proper ID | ISSUED | SIGNATURE ☐ (oath / affirmation, if any) ☐ (by Mark)
- PHONE C / H / W / | *or* ☐ MISC | | | AGENCY | ☐ CA DMV | ☐ US State Dept | EXPIRES | ➡

CW #1
- #1 WITNESS's NAME | ☐ P/Known | ADDRESS | ☐ Non-Public | ☐ Driver's License ☐ Passport ☐ Other ID # | ISSUED | SIGNATURE ☐ (after oath / affirmation)
- PHONE C / H / W / | *or* ☐ MISC | | | AGENCY ☐ CA DMV ☐ US State Dept | EXPIRES | ❶

CW #2
- #2 WITNESS's NAME | ☐ P/Known | ADDRESS | ☐ Non-Public | ☐ Driver's License ☐ Passport ☐ Other ID # | ISSUED | SIGNATURE ☐ (after oath / affirmation)
- PHONE C / H / W / | *or* ☐ MISC | | | AGENCY ☐ CA DMV ☐ US State Dept | EXPIRES | ❷

Entry 12

SERVICE
- DATE: - -20
- TIME: : am/pm
- ADDRESS: ☐ Signer's ☐ Office
- NOTES: ☐ Stop
- MILES | Notary $ | ☐ Adv. Travel $ | ☐ Rush $ | ☐ Copy $ | ☐ Other $ | TOTAL FEES $

TYPE: ☐ Acknowledgment ☐ Jurat ☐ Copy Certification ☐ Oath/Affirmation ☐ Oath of Office ☐ Proof of Execution ☐ Protest ☐ Other

Fingerprint   R T I M R P L

DOCUMENT
- DOC TYPE: ☐ Deed ☐ DOT ☐ Trust ☐ POA ☐ POAH ☐ Agreement ☐ Affidavit ☐ Other
  - Grant • Trust Transfer • Gift | Mortgage | Certification | General / Limited | AHCD | Compliance-E&O | Borrower • Occupancy • Ownership • Refi • Survey | Vehicle Title
  - Interspousal • Quitclaim • ToD • Warranty | Rev / Irrev • Am / Rest | Durable / Springing | Living Will | Correction | Debts & Liens • Name-Signature-ID • Marital • Death • Will | Safe Deposit Box
- DOC DATE: J F M A M J / J A S O N D ,
- DOC TITLE or TYPE:
- # OF PAGES:
- ☐ Inspect/Copy Request
- Entry X-Ref #:

☐ **SATISFACTORY EVIDENCE** ☐ Driver's License / Passport / State ID / Military / Government / Tribal / Inmate / Other ID *or* ☐ Credible Witness(es)

SIGNER
- SIGNER's NAME | ☐ For | ADDRESS | ☐ Non-Public | ☐ Capacity # | ☐ Voluntary | ☐ Proper ID | ISSUED | SIGNATURE ☐ (oath / affirmation, if any) ☐ (by Mark)
- PHONE C / H / W / | *or* ☐ MISC | | | AGENCY ☐ CA DMV ☐ US State Dept | EXPIRES | ➡

CW #1
- #1 WITNESS's NAME | ☐ P/Known | ADDRESS | ☐ Non-Public | ☐ Driver's License ☐ Passport ☐ Other ID # | ISSUED | SIGNATURE ☐ (after oath / affirmation)
- PHONE C / H / W / | *or* ☐ MISC | | | AGENCY ☐ CA DMV ☐ US State Dept | EXPIRES | ❶

CW #2
- #2 WITNESS's NAME | ☐ P/Known | ADDRESS | ☐ Non-Public | ☐ Driver's License ☐ Passport ☐ Other ID # | ISSUED | SIGNATURE ☐ (after oath / affirmation)
- PHONE C / H / W / | *or* ☐ MISC | | | AGENCY ☐ CA DMV ☐ US State Dept | EXPIRES | ❷

NOTARY NAME (printed):   COMMISSION #:

Entry 13

SERVICE

DATE	TIME	am	ADDRESS	☐ Signer's	☐ Office	NOTES	☐ Stop	MILES	Notary	☐ Adv. Travel	☐ Rush	☐ Copy	☐ Other	TOTAL FEES
- -20	:	pm						$	$		$	$	$	$

TYPE ☐ Acknowledgment ☐ Jurat ☐ Copy Certification ☐ Oath/Affirmation ☐ Oath of Office ☐ Proof of Execution ☐ Protest ☐ Other

R   **Fingerprint**

DOCUMENT

DOC TYPE ☐ Deed ☐ DOT ☐ Trust ☐ POA ☐ POAH ☐ Agreement ☐ Affidavit ☐ Other
Grant • Trust Transfer • Gift | Mortgage | Certification | General / Limited | AHCD | Compliance-E&O | Borrower • Occupancy • Ownership • Refi • Survey | Vehicle Title
Interspousal • Quitclaim • ToD • Warranty | Rev / Irrev • Am / Rest | Durable / Springing | Living Will | Correction | Debts & Liens • Name-Signature-ID • Marital • Death • Will | Safe Deposit Box

T
I
M
R
P

DOC DATE J F M A M J / J A S O N D , | DOC TITLE or TYPE | # OF PAGES | ☐ Inspect/Copy Request | Entry X-Ref #

☐ **SATISFACTORY EVIDENCE** ☐ Driver's License / Passport / State ID / Military / Government / Tribal / Inmate / Other ID **or** ☐ Credible Witness(es)   **L**

SIGNER

SIGNER's NAME | ☐ For | ADDRESS | ☐ Non-Public | ☐ Capacity | ☐ Voluntary | ☐ Proper ID | ISSUED | SIGNATURE | ☐ (oath / affirmation, if any) | ☐ (by Mark)

PHONE C / H / W | **or** ☐ MISC | AGENCY | ☐ CA DMV | ☐ US State Dept | EXPIRES | ➡

CW #1

#1 WITNESS's NAME | ☐ P/Known | ADDRESS | ☐ Non-Public | ☐ Driver's License | ☐ Passport | ☐ Other ID | ISSUED | SIGNATURE | ☐ (after oath / affirmation)
#
PHONE C / H / W | **or** ☐ MISC | AGENCY | ☐ CA DMV | ☐ US State Dept | EXPIRES | ❶

CW #2

#2 WITNESS's NAME | ☐ P/Known | ADDRESS | ☐ Non-Public | ☐ Driver's License | ☐ Passport | ☐ Other ID | ISSUED | SIGNATURE | ☐ (after oath / affirmation)
#
PHONE C / H / W | **or** ☐ MISC | AGENCY | ☐ CA DMV | ☐ US State Dept | EXPIRES | ❷

Entry 14

SERVICE

DATE	TIME	am	ADDRESS	☐ Signer's	☐ Office	NOTES	☐ Stop	MILES	Notary	☐ Adv. Travel	☐ Rush	☐ Copy	☐ Other	TOTAL FEES
- -20	:	pm						$	$		$	$	$	$

TYPE ☐ Acknowledgment ☐ Jurat ☐ Copy Certification ☐ Oath/Affirmation ☐ Oath of Office ☐ Proof of Execution ☐ Protest ☐ Other

R   **Fingerprint**

DOCUMENT

DOC TYPE ☐ Deed ☐ DOT ☐ Trust ☐ POA ☐ POAH ☐ Agreement ☐ Affidavit ☐ Other
Grant • Trust Transfer • Gift | Mortgage | Certification | General / Limited | AHCD | Compliance-E&O | Borrower • Occupancy • Ownership • Refi • Survey | Vehicle Title
Interspousal • Quitclaim • ToD • Warranty | Rev / Irrev • Am / Rest | Durable / Springing | Living Will | Correction | Debts & Liens • Name-Signature-ID • Marital • Death • Will | Safe Deposit Box

T
I
M
R
P

DOC DATE J F M A M J / J A S O N D , | DOC TITLE or TYPE | # OF PAGES | ☐ Inspect/Copy Request | Entry X-Ref #

☐ **SATISFACTORY EVIDENCE** ☐ Driver's License / Passport / State ID / Military / Government / Tribal / Inmate / Other ID **or** ☐ Credible Witness(es)   **L**

SIGNER

SIGNER's NAME | ☐ For | ADDRESS | ☐ Non-Public | ☐ Capacity | ☐ Voluntary | ☐ Proper ID | ISSUED | SIGNATURE | ☐ (oath / affirmation, if any) | ☐ (by Mark)
#
PHONE C / H / W | **or** ☐ MISC | AGENCY | ☐ CA DMV | ☐ US State Dept | EXPIRES | ➡

CW #1

#1 WITNESS's NAME | ☐ P/Known | ADDRESS | ☐ Non-Public | ☐ Driver's License | ☐ Passport | ☐ Other ID | ISSUED | SIGNATURE | ☐ (after oath / affirmation)
#
PHONE C / H / W | **or** ☐ MISC | AGENCY | ☐ CA DMV | ☐ US State Dept | EXPIRES | ❶

CW #2

#2 WITNESS's NAME | ☐ P/Known | ADDRESS | ☐ Non-Public | ☐ Driver's License | ☐ Passport | ☐ Other ID | ISSUED | SIGNATURE | ☐ (after oath / affirmation)
#
PHONE C / H / W | **or** ☐ MISC | AGENCY | ☐ CA DMV | ☐ US State Dept | EXPIRES | ❷

NOTARY NAME (printed):   COMMISSION #:

Entry 15

SERVICE — DATE - -20 | TIME : am/pm | ADDRESS ☐ Signer's ☐ Office | NOTES | ☐ Stop MILES | Notary $ | ☐ Adv. Travel $ | ☐ Rush $ | ☐ Copy $ | ☐ Other $ | TOTAL FEES $

TYPE: ☐ Acknowledgment ☐ Jurat ☐ Copy Certification ☐ Oath/Affirmation ☐ Oath of Office ☐ Proof of Execution ☐ Protest ☐ Other

DOCUMENT
- DOC TYPE: ☐ Deed (Grant • Trust Transfer • Gift • Interspousal • Quitclaim • ToD • Warranty) ☐ DOT (Mortgage • Certification • Rev / Irrev • Am / Rest) ☐ Trust ☐ POA (General / Limited • Durable / Springing) ☐ POAH (AHCD • Living Will) ☐ Agreement (Compliance-E&O • Correction) ☐ Affidavit (Borrower • Occupancy • Ownership • Refi • Survey • Debts & Liens • Name-Signature-ID • Marital • Death • Will) ☐ Other (Vehicle Title • Safe Deposit Box)
- DOC DATE: J F M A M J J A S O N D ,   DOC TITLE or TYPE   # OF PAGES   ☐ Inspect/Copy Request   Entry X-Ref #

☐ **SATISFACTORY EVIDENCE** ☐ Driver's License / Passport / State ID / Military / Government / Tribal / Inmate / Other ID *or* ☐ Credible Witness(es)

SIGNER: SIGNER's NAME | ☐ For | ADDRESS | ☐ Non-Public | ☐ Capacity # | ☐ Voluntary | ☐ Proper ID | ISSUED | SIGNATURE ☐ (oath / affirmation, if any) ☐ (by Mark)
PHONE C / H / W / | *or* ☐ MISC | | | AGENCY | ☐ CA DMV | ☐ US State Dept | EXPIRES

CW #1: #1 WITNESS's NAME | ☐ P/Known | ADDRESS | ☐ Non-Public | ☐ Driver's License ☐ Passport ☐ Other ID # | ISSUED | SIGNATURE ☐ (after oath / affirmation)
PHONE C / H / W / | *or* ☐ MISC | | | AGENCY ☐ CA DMV ☐ US State Dept | EXPIRES | ❶

CW #2: #2 WITNESS's NAME | ☐ P/Known | ADDRESS | ☐ Non-Public | ☐ Driver's License ☐ Passport ☐ Other ID # | ISSUED | SIGNATURE ☐ (after oath / affirmation)
PHONE C / H / W / | *or* ☐ MISC | | | AGENCY ☐ CA DMV ☐ US State Dept | EXPIRES | ❷

Fingerprint (R T I M R P L)

Entry 16

SERVICE — DATE - -20 | TIME : am/pm | ADDRESS ☐ Signer's ☐ Office | NOTES | ☐ Stop MILES | Notary $ | ☐ Adv. Travel $ | ☐ Rush $ | ☐ Copy $ | ☐ Other $ | TOTAL FEES $

TYPE: ☐ Acknowledgment ☐ Jurat ☐ Copy Certification ☐ Oath/Affirmation ☐ Oath of Office ☐ Proof of Execution ☐ Protest ☐ Other

DOCUMENT
- DOC TYPE: ☐ Deed (Grant • Trust Transfer • Gift • Interspousal • Quitclaim • ToD • Warranty) ☐ DOT (Mortgage • Certification • Rev / Irrev • Am / Rest) ☐ Trust ☐ POA (General / Limited • Durable / Springing) ☐ POAH (AHCD • Living Will) ☐ Agreement (Compliance-E&O • Correction) ☐ Affidavit (Borrower • Occupancy • Ownership • Refi • Survey • Debts & Liens • Name-Signature-ID • Marital • Death • Will) ☐ Other (Vehicle Title • Safe Deposit Box)
- DOC DATE: J F M A M J J A S O N D ,   DOC TITLE or TYPE   # OF PAGES   ☐ Inspect/Copy Request   Entry X-Ref #

☐ **SATISFACTORY EVIDENCE** ☐ Driver's License / Passport / State ID / Military / Government / Tribal / Inmate / Other ID *or* ☐ Credible Witness(es)

SIGNER: SIGNER's NAME | ☐ For | ADDRESS | ☐ Non-Public | ☐ Capacity # | ☐ Voluntary | ☐ Proper ID | ISSUED | SIGNATURE ☐ (oath / affirmation, if any) ☐ (by Mark)
PHONE C / H / W / | *or* ☐ MISC | | | AGENCY | ☐ CA DMV | ☐ US State Dept | EXPIRES

CW #1: #1 WITNESS's NAME | ☐ P/Known | ADDRESS | ☐ Non-Public | ☐ Driver's License ☐ Passport ☐ Other ID # | ISSUED | SIGNATURE ☐ (after oath / affirmation)
PHONE C / H / W / | *or* ☐ MISC | | | AGENCY ☐ CA DMV ☐ US State Dept | EXPIRES | ❶

CW #2: #2 WITNESS's NAME | ☐ P/Known | ADDRESS | ☐ Non-Public | ☐ Driver's License ☐ Passport ☐ Other ID # | ISSUED | SIGNATURE ☐ (after oath / affirmation)
PHONE C / H / W / | *or* ☐ MISC | | | AGENCY ☐ CA DMV ☐ US State Dept | EXPIRES | ❷

Fingerprint (R T I M R P L)

NOTARY NAME (printed): _____   COMMISSION #: _____

Entry 17

SERVICE

DATE	TIME	am	ADDRESS	☐ Signer's	☐ Office	NOTES	☐ Stop	MILES	Notary	☐ Adv. Travel	☐ Rush	☐ Copy	☐ Other	TOTAL FEES
- -20	:	pm							$	$	$	$	$	$

TYPE ☐ Acknowledgment ☐ Jurat ☐ Copy Certification ☐ Oath/Affirmation ☐ Oath of Office ☐ Proof of Execution ☐ Protest ☐ Other

R T I M R P L **Fingerprint**

DOCUMENT

DOC TYPE ☐ Deed   ☐ DOT   ☐ Trust   ☐ POA   ☐ POAH   ☐ Agreement   ☐ Affidavit   ☐ Other
Grant • Trust Transfer • Gift | Mortgage | Certification | General / Limited | AHCD | Compliance-E&O | Borrower • Occupancy • Ownership • Refi • Survey | Vehicle Title
Interspousal • Quitclaim • ToD • Warranty | Rev / Irrev • Am / Rest | Durable / Springing | Living Will | Correction | Debts & Liens • Name-Signature-ID • Marital • Death • Will | Safe Deposit Box

DOC DATE J F M A M J   J A S O N D   ,   DOC TITLE or TYPE   # OF PAGES ☐ Inspect/Copy Request   Entry X-Ref #

☐ **SATISFACTORY EVIDENCE** ☐ Driver's License / Passport / State ID / Military / Government / Tribal / Inmate / Other ID **or** ☐ Credible Witness(es)

SIGNER

SIGNER's NAME	☐ For	ADDRESS	☐ Non-Public	☐ Capacity	☐ Voluntary	☐ Proper ID	ISSUED	SIGNATURE	☐ (oath / affirmation, if any)	☐ (by Mark)
				#						
PHONE C / H / W	or ☐ MISC			AGENCY	☐ CA DMV	☐ US State Dept	EXPIRES	➡		

CW #1

#1 WITNESS's NAME	☐ P/Known	ADDRESS	☐ Non-Public	☐ Driver's License	☐ Passport	☐ Other ID	ISSUED	SIGNATURE	☐ (after oath / affirmation)
				#					
PHONE C / H / W	or ☐ MISC			AGENCY	☐ CA DMV	☐ US State Dept	EXPIRES	❶	

CW #2

#2 WITNESS's NAME	☐ P/Known	ADDRESS	☐ Non-Public	☐ Driver's License	☐ Passport	☐ Other ID	ISSUED	SIGNATURE	☐ (after oath / affirmation)
				#					
PHONE C / H / W	or ☐ MISC			AGENCY	☐ CA DMV	☐ US State Dept	EXPIRES	❷	

Entry 18

SERVICE

DATE	TIME	am	ADDRESS	☐ Signer's	☐ Office	NOTES	☐ Stop	MILES	Notary	☐ Adv. Travel	☐ Rush	☐ Copy	☐ Other	TOTAL FEES
- -20	:	pm							$	$	$	$	$	$

TYPE ☐ Acknowledgment ☐ Jurat ☐ Copy Certification ☐ Oath/Affirmation ☐ Oath of Office ☐ Proof of Execution ☐ Protest ☐ Other

R T I M R P L **Fingerprint**

DOCUMENT

DOC TYPE ☐ Deed   ☐ DOT   ☐ Trust   ☐ POA   ☐ POAH   ☐ Agreement   ☐ Affidavit   ☐ Other
Grant • Trust Transfer • Gift | Mortgage | Certification | General / Limited | AHCD | Compliance-E&O | Borrower • Occupancy • Ownership • Refi • Survey | Vehicle Title
Interspousal • Quitclaim • ToD • Warranty | Rev / Irrev • Am / Rest | Durable / Springing | Living Will | Correction | Debts & Liens • Name-Signature-ID • Marital • Death • Will | Safe Deposit Box

DOC DATE J F M A M J   J A S O N D   ,   DOC TITLE or TYPE   # OF PAGES ☐ Inspect/Copy Request   Entry X-Ref #

☐ **SATISFACTORY EVIDENCE** ☐ Driver's License / Passport / State ID / Military / Government / Tribal / Inmate / Other ID **or** ☐ Credible Witness(es)

SIGNER

SIGNER's NAME	☐ For	ADDRESS	☐ Non-Public	☐ Capacity	☐ Voluntary	☐ Proper ID	ISSUED	SIGNATURE	☐ (oath / affirmation, if any)	☐ (by Mark)
				#						
PHONE C / H / W	or ☐ MISC			AGENCY	☐ CA DMV	☐ US State Dept	EXPIRES	➡		

CW #1

#1 WITNESS's NAME	☐ P/Known	ADDRESS	☐ Non-Public	☐ Driver's License	☐ Passport	☐ Other ID	ISSUED	SIGNATURE	☐ (after oath / affirmation)
				#					
PHONE C / H / W	or ☐ MISC			AGENCY	☐ CA DMV	☐ US State Dept	EXPIRES	❶	

CW #2

#2 WITNESS's NAME	☐ P/Known	ADDRESS	☐ Non-Public	☐ Driver's License	☐ Passport	☐ Other ID	ISSUED	SIGNATURE	☐ (after oath / affirmation)
				#					
PHONE C / H / W	or ☐ MISC			AGENCY	☐ CA DMV	☐ US State Dept	EXPIRES	❷	

NOTARY NAME (printed): _____ COMMISSION #: _____

Entry 19

SERVICE | DATE: _ - _ -20__ | TIME: __:__ am/pm | ADDRESS ☐ Signer's ☐ Office | NOTES | ☐ Stop | MILES $__ | Notary $__ | ☐ Adv. Travel $__ | ☐ Rush $__ | ☐ Copy $__ | ☐ Other $__ | TOTAL FEES $__

TYPE: ☐ Acknowledgment ☐ Jurat ☐ Copy Certification ☐ Oath/Affirmation ☐ Oath of Office ☐ Proof of Execution ☐ Protest ☐ Other

DOCUMENT

DOC TYPE: ☐ Deed (Grant • Trust Transfer • Gift • Interspousal • Quitclaim • ToD • Warranty) ☐ DOT (Mortgage) ☐ Trust (Certification • Rev / Irrev • Am / Rest) ☐ POA (General / Limited • Durable / Springing) ☐ POAH (AHCD • Living Will) ☐ Agreement (Compliance-E&O • Correction) ☐ Affidavit (Borrower • Occupancy • Ownership • Refi • Survey • Debts & Liens • Name-Signature-ID • Marital • Death • Will) ☐ Other (Vehicle Title • Safe Deposit Box)

DOC DATE: J F M A M J J A S O N D , ____ DOC TITLE or TYPE: _____ # OF PAGES: __ ☐ Inspect/Copy Request Entry X-Ref #: __

Fingerprint R T I M R P L

☐ **SATISFACTORY EVIDENCE** ☐ Driver's License / Passport / State ID / Military / Government / Tribal / Inmate / Other ID **or** ☐ Credible Witness(es)

SIGNER

SIGNER's NAME: _____ ☐ For ADDRESS: _____ ☐ Non-Public ☐ Capacity ☐ Voluntary ☐ Proper ID ISSUED: __ SIGNATURE: __ ☐ (oath / affirmation, if any) ☐ (by Mark)
PHONE C/H/W: __ / __ or ☐ MISC #: __ AGENCY: __ ☐ CA DMV ☐ US State Dept EXPIRES: __ →

CW #1

#1 WITNESS's NAME: _____ ☐ P/Known ADDRESS: _____ ☐ Non-Public ☐ Driver's License ☐ Passport ☐ Other ID ISSUED: __ SIGNATURE: __ ☐ (after oath / affirmation)
PHONE C/H/W: __ / __ or ☐ MISC #: __ AGENCY: __ ☐ CA DMV ☐ US State Dept EXPIRES: __ ❶

CW #2

#2 WITNESS's NAME: _____ ☐ P/Known ADDRESS: _____ ☐ Non-Public ☐ Driver's License ☐ Passport ☐ Other ID ISSUED: __ SIGNATURE: __ ☐ (after oath / affirmation)
PHONE C/H/W: __ / __ or ☐ MISC #: __ AGENCY: __ ☐ CA DMV ☐ US State Dept EXPIRES: __ ❷

Entry 20

SERVICE | DATE: _ - _ -20__ | TIME: __:__ am/pm | ADDRESS ☐ Signer's ☐ Office | NOTES | ☐ Stop | MILES $__ | Notary $__ | ☐ Adv. Travel $__ | ☐ Rush $__ | ☐ Copy $__ | ☐ Other $__ | TOTAL FEES $__

TYPE: ☐ Acknowledgment ☐ Jurat ☐ Copy Certification ☐ Oath/Affirmation ☐ Oath of Office ☐ Proof of Execution ☐ Protest ☐ Other

DOCUMENT

DOC TYPE: ☐ Deed (Grant • Trust Transfer • Gift • Interspousal • Quitclaim • ToD • Warranty) ☐ DOT (Mortgage) ☐ Trust (Certification • Rev / Irrev • Am / Rest) ☐ POA (General / Limited • Durable / Springing) ☐ POAH (AHCD • Living Will) ☐ Agreement (Compliance-E&O • Correction) ☐ Affidavit (Borrower • Occupancy • Ownership • Refi • Survey • Debts & Liens • Name-Signature-ID • Marital • Death • Will) ☐ Other (Vehicle Title • Safe Deposit Box)

DOC DATE: J F M A M J J A S O N D , ____ DOC TITLE or TYPE: _____ # OF PAGES: __ ☐ Inspect/Copy Request Entry X-Ref #: __

Fingerprint R T I M R P L

☐ **SATISFACTORY EVIDENCE** ☐ Driver's License / Passport / State ID / Military / Government / Tribal / Inmate / Other ID **or** ☐ Credible Witness(es)

SIGNER

SIGNER's NAME: _____ ☐ For ADDRESS: _____ ☐ Non-Public ☐ Capacity ☐ Voluntary ☐ Proper ID ISSUED: __ SIGNATURE: __ ☐ (oath / affirmation, if any) ☐ (by Mark)
PHONE C/H/W: __ / __ or ☐ MISC #: __ AGENCY: __ ☐ CA DMV ☐ US State Dept EXPIRES: __ →

CW #1

#1 WITNESS's NAME: _____ ☐ P/Known ADDRESS: _____ ☐ Non-Public ☐ Driver's License ☐ Passport ☐ Other ID ISSUED: __ SIGNATURE: __ ☐ (after oath / affirmation)
PHONE C/H/W: __ / __ or ☐ MISC #: __ AGENCY: __ ☐ CA DMV ☐ US State Dept EXPIRES: __ ❶

CW #2

#2 WITNESS's NAME: _____ ☐ P/Known ADDRESS: _____ ☐ Non-Public ☐ Driver's License ☐ Passport ☐ Other ID ISSUED: __ SIGNATURE: __ ☐ (after oath / affirmation)
PHONE C/H/W: __ / __ or ☐ MISC #: __ AGENCY: __ ☐ CA DMV ☐ US State Dept EXPIRES: __ ❷

NOTARY NAME (printed):   COMMISSION #:

Entry 21

SERVICE	DATE - -20	TIME : am pm	ADDRESS	☐ Signer's ☐ Office NOTES	☐ Stop	MILES	Notary ☐ Adv. Travel ☐ Rush ☐ Copy ☐ Other TOTAL FEES	**21**

$ $ $ $ $ $

TYPE ☐ Acknowledgment ☐ Jurat ☐ Copy Certification ☐ Oath/Affirmation ☐ Oath of Office ☐ Proof of Execution ☐ Protest ☐ Other

R Fingerprint

DOCUMENT

DOC TYPE ☐ Deed ☐ DOT ☐ Trust ☐ POA ☐ POAH ☐ Agreement ☐ Affidavit ☐ Other
Grant • Trust Transfer • Gift | Mortgage | Certification | General / Limited | AHCD | Compliance-E&O | Borrower • Occupancy • Ownership • Refi • Survey | Vehicle Title
Interspousal • Quitclaim • ToD • Warranty | Rev / Irrev • Am / Rest | Durable / Springing | Living Will | Correction | Debts & Liens • Name-Signature-ID • Marital • Death • Will | Safe Deposit Box

T I M R P L

DOC DATE J F M A M J J A S O N D   , | DOC TITLE or TYPE | # OF PAGES ☐ Inspect/Copy Request
Entry X-Ref #

☐ **SATISFACTORY EVIDENCE** ☐ Driver's License / Passport / State ID / Military / Government / Tribal / Inmate / Other ID **or** ☐ Credible Witness(es)

SIGNER	SIGNER's NAME ☐ For	ADDRESS	☐ Non-Public	☐ Capacity # ☐ Voluntary ☐ Proper ID	ISSUED	SIGNATURE ☐ (oath / affirmation, if any) ☐ (by Mark)
	PHONE C / H / W or ☐ MISC /			AGENCY ☐ CA DMV ☐ US State Dept	EXPIRES	➡

CW #1	#1 WITNESS's NAME ☐ P/Known	ADDRESS	☐ Non-Public	☐ Driver's License ☐ Passport ☐ Other ID #	ISSUED	SIGNATURE ☐ (after oath / affirmation)
	PHONE C / H / W or ☐ MISC /			AGENCY ☐ CA DMV ☐ US State Dept	EXPIRES	❶

CW #2	#2 WITNESS's NAME ☐ P/Known	ADDRESS	☐ Non-Public	☐ Driver's License ☐ Passport ☐ Other ID #	ISSUED	SIGNATURE ☐ (after oath / affirmation)
	PHONE C / H / W or ☐ MISC /			AGENCY ☐ CA DMV ☐ US State Dept	EXPIRES	❷

Entry 22

SERVICE	DATE - -20	TIME : am pm	ADDRESS	☐ Signer's ☐ Office NOTES	☐ Stop	MILES	Notary ☐ Adv. Travel ☐ Rush ☐ Copy ☐ Other TOTAL FEES	**22**

$ $ $ $ $ $

TYPE ☐ Acknowledgment ☐ Jurat ☐ Copy Certification ☐ Oath/Affirmation ☐ Oath of Office ☐ Proof of Execution ☐ Protest ☐ Other

R Fingerprint

DOCUMENT

DOC TYPE ☐ Deed ☐ DOT ☐ Trust ☐ POA ☐ POAH ☐ Agreement ☐ Affidavit ☐ Other
Grant • Trust Transfer • Gift | Mortgage | Certification | General / Limited | AHCD | Compliance-E&O | Borrower • Occupancy • Ownership • Refi • Survey | Vehicle Title
Interspousal • Quitclaim • ToD • Warranty | Rev / Irrev • Am / Rest | Durable / Springing | Living Will | Correction | Debts & Liens • Name-Signature-ID • Marital • Death • Will | Safe Deposit Box

T I M R P

DOC DATE J F M A M J J A S O N D   , | DOC TITLE or TYPE | # OF PAGES ☐ Inspect/Copy Request
Entry X-Ref #

☐ **SATISFACTORY EVIDENCE** ☐ Driver's License / Passport / State ID / Military / Government / Tribal / Inmate / Other ID **or** ☐ Credible Witness(es) L

SIGNER	SIGNER's NAME ☐ For	ADDRESS	☐ Non-Public	☐ Capacity # ☐ Voluntary ☐ Proper ID	ISSUED	SIGNATURE ☐ (oath / affirmation, if any) ☐ (by Mark)
	PHONE C / H / W or ☐ MISC /			AGENCY ☐ CA DMV ☐ US State Dept	EXPIRES	➡

CW #1	#1 WITNESS's NAME ☐ P/Known	ADDRESS	☐ Non-Public	☐ Driver's License ☐ Passport ☐ Other ID #	ISSUED	SIGNATURE ☐ (after oath / affirmation)
	PHONE C / H / W or ☐ MISC /			AGENCY ☐ CA DMV ☐ US State Dept	EXPIRES	❶

CW #2	#2 WITNESS's NAME ☐ P/Known	ADDRESS	☐ Non-Public	☐ Driver's License ☐ Passport ☐ Other ID #	ISSUED	SIGNATURE ☐ (after oath / affirmation)
	PHONE C / H / W or ☐ MISC /			AGENCY ☐ CA DMV ☐ US State Dept	EXPIRES	❷

NOTARY NAME (printed):   COMMISSION #:

Entry 23

SERVICE
- DATE: - -20 | TIME: : am/pm | ADDRESS | ☐ Signer's ☐ Office | NOTES | ☐ Stop | MILES | Notary $ | ☐ Adv. Travel $ | ☐ Rush $ | ☐ Copy $ | ☐ Other $ | TOTAL FEES $
- TYPE: ☐ Acknowledgment ☐ Jurat ☐ Copy Certification ☐ Oath/Affirmation ☐ Oath of Office ☐ Proof of Execution ☐ Protest ☐ Other

DOCUMENT
- DOC TYPE: ☐ Deed (Grant • Trust Transfer • Gift • Interspousal • Quitclaim • ToD • Warranty) ☐ DOT (Mortgage • Certification • Rev / Irrev • Am / Rest) ☐ Trust ☐ POA (General / Limited • Durable / Springing) ☐ POAH (AHCD • Living Will) ☐ Agreement ☐ Affidavit (Compliance-E&O • Borrower • Occupancy • Ownership • Refi • Survey • Correction • Debts & Liens • Name-Signature-ID • Marital • Death • Will) ☐ Other (Vehicle Title • Safe Deposit Box)
- DOC DATE: J F M A M J J A S O N D , | DOC TITLE or TYPE | # OF PAGES | ☐ Inspect/Copy Request | Entry X-Ref #

R T I M R P L Fingerprint

☐ **SATISFACTORY EVIDENCE** ☐ Driver's License / Passport / State ID / Military / Government / Tribal / Inmate / Other ID *or* ☐ Credible Witness(es)

SIGNER
- SIGNER's NAME | ☐ For | ADDRESS | ☐ Non-Public | ☐ Capacity # | ☐ Voluntary | ☐ Proper ID | ISSUED | SIGNATURE | ☐ (oath / affirmation, if any) | ☐ (by Mark)
- PHONE C / H / W / | *or* ☐ MISC | | | AGENCY | ☐ CA DMV | ☐ US State Dept | EXPIRES | ➡

CW #1
- #1 WITNESS's NAME | ☐ P/Known | ADDRESS | ☐ Non-Public | ☐ Driver's License ☐ Passport ☐ Other ID # | ISSUED | SIGNATURE | ☐ (after oath / affirmation)
- PHONE C / H / W / | *or* ☐ MISC | | AGENCY ☐ CA DMV ☐ US State Dept | EXPIRES | ❶

CW #2
- #2 WITNESS's NAME | ☐ P/Known | ADDRESS | ☐ Non-Public | ☐ Driver's License ☐ Passport ☐ Other ID # | ISSUED | SIGNATURE | ☐ (after oath / affirmation)
- PHONE C / H / W / | *or* ☐ MISC | | AGENCY ☐ CA DMV ☐ US State Dept | EXPIRES | ❷

Entry 24

SERVICE
- DATE: - -20 | TIME: : am/pm | ADDRESS | ☐ Signer's ☐ Office | NOTES | ☐ Stop | MILES | Notary $ | ☐ Adv. Travel $ | ☐ Rush $ | ☐ Copy $ | ☐ Other $ | TOTAL FEES $
- TYPE: ☐ Acknowledgment ☐ Jurat ☐ Copy Certification ☐ Oath/Affirmation ☐ Oath of Office ☐ Proof of Execution ☐ Protest ☐ Other

DOCUMENT
- DOC TYPE: ☐ Deed (Grant • Trust Transfer • Gift • Interspousal • Quitclaim • ToD • Warranty) ☐ DOT (Mortgage • Certification • Rev / Irrev • Am / Rest) ☐ Trust ☐ POA (General / Limited • Durable / Springing) ☐ POAH (AHCD • Living Will) ☐ Agreement ☐ Affidavit (Compliance-E&O • Borrower • Occupancy • Ownership • Refi • Survey • Correction • Debts & Liens • Name-Signature-ID • Marital • Death • Will) ☐ Other (Vehicle Title • Safe Deposit Box)
- DOC DATE: J F M A M J J A S O N D , | DOC TITLE or TYPE | # OF PAGES | ☐ Inspect/Copy Request | Entry X-Ref #

R T I M R P L Fingerprint

☐ **SATISFACTORY EVIDENCE** ☐ Driver's License / Passport / State ID / Military / Government / Tribal / Inmate / Other ID *or* ☐ Credible Witness(es)

SIGNER
- SIGNER's NAME | ☐ For | ADDRESS | ☐ Non-Public | ☐ Capacity # | ☐ Voluntary | ☐ Proper ID | ISSUED | SIGNATURE | ☐ (oath / affirmation, if any) | ☐ (by Mark)
- PHONE C / H / W / | *or* ☐ MISC | | AGENCY ☐ CA DMV ☐ US State Dept | EXPIRES | ➡

CW #1
- #1 WITNESS's NAME | ☐ P/Known | ADDRESS | ☐ Non-Public | ☐ Driver's License ☐ Passport ☐ Other ID # | ISSUED | SIGNATURE | ☐ (after oath / affirmation)
- PHONE C / H / W / | *or* ☐ MISC | | AGENCY ☐ CA DMV ☐ US State Dept | EXPIRES | ❶

CW #2
- #2 WITNESS's NAME | ☐ P/Known | ADDRESS | ☐ Non-Public | ☐ Driver's License ☐ Passport ☐ Other ID # | ISSUED | SIGNATURE | ☐ (after oath / affirmation)
- PHONE C / H / W / | *or* ☐ MISC | | AGENCY ☐ CA DMV ☐ US State Dept | EXPIRES | ❷

NOTARY NAME (printed):   COMMISSION #:

Entry 25

SERVICE | DATE – -20 | TIME : am/pm | ADDRESS ☐ Signer's ☐ Office | NOTES | ☐ Stop | MILES | Notary $ ☐ Adv. Travel $ ☐ Rush $ ☐ Copy $ ☐ Other $ TOTAL FEES $

TYPE ☐ Acknowledgment ☐ Jurat ☐ Copy Certification ☐ Oath/Affirmation ☐ Oath of Office ☐ Proof of Execution ☐ Protest ☐ Other

R T I M R P L   **Fingerprint**

DOCUMENT

DOC TYPE ☐ Deed ☐ DOT ☐ Trust ☐ POA ☐ POAH ☐ Agreement ☐ Affidavit ☐ Other

Grant • Trust Transfer • Gift   Mortgage   Certification   General / Limited   AHCD   Compliance-E&O   Borrower • Occupancy • Ownership • Refi • Survey   Vehicle Title

Interspousal • Quitclaim • ToD • Warranty   Rev / Irrev • Am / Rest   Durable / Springing   Living Will   Correction   Debts & Liens • Name-Signature-ID • Marital • Death • Will   Safe Deposit Box

DOC DATE   J F M A M J   J A S O N D ,   DOC TITLE or TYPE   # OF PAGES   ☐ Inspect/Copy Request   Entry X-Ref #

☐ **SATISFACTORY EVIDENCE** ☐ Driver's License / Passport / State ID / Military / Government / Tribal / Inmate / Other ID   *or*   ☐ Credible Witness(es)

SIGNER

SIGNER's NAME ☐ For | ADDRESS ☐ Non-Public | ☐ Capacity ☐ Voluntary ☐ Proper ID | ISSUED # | SIGNATURE ☐ *(oath / affirmation, if any)* ☐ *(by Mark)*

PHONE C / H / W   *or* ☐ MISC / | AGENCY ☐ CA DMV ☐ US State Dept | EXPIRES | ➡

CW #1

#1 WITNESS's NAME ☐ P/Known | ADDRESS ☐ Non-Public | ☐ Driver's License ☐ Passport ☐ Other ID | ISSUED # | SIGNATURE ☐ *(after oath / affirmation)*

PHONE C / H / W   *or* ☐ MISC / | AGENCY ☐ CA DMV ☐ US State Dept | EXPIRES | ❶

CW #2

#2 WITNESS's NAME ☐ P/Known | ADDRESS ☐ Non-Public | ☐ Driver's License ☐ Passport ☐ Other ID | ISSUED # | SIGNATURE ☐ *(after oath / affirmation)*

PHONE C / H / W   *or* ☐ MISC / | AGENCY ☐ CA DMV ☐ US State Dept | EXPIRES | ❷

Entry 26

SERVICE | DATE – -20 | TIME : am/pm | ADDRESS ☐ Signer's ☐ Office | NOTES | ☐ Stop | MILES | Notary $ ☐ Adv. Travel $ ☐ Rush $ ☐ Copy $ ☐ Other $ TOTAL FEES $

TYPE ☐ Acknowledgment ☐ Jurat ☐ Copy Certification ☐ Oath/Affirmation ☐ Oath of Office ☐ Proof of Execution ☐ Protest ☐ Other

R T I M R P L   **Fingerprint**

DOCUMENT

DOC TYPE ☐ Deed ☐ DOT ☐ Trust ☐ POA ☐ POAH ☐ Agreement ☐ Affidavit ☐ Other

Grant • Trust Transfer • Gift   Mortgage   Certification   General / Limited   AHCD   Compliance-E&O   Borrower • Occupancy • Ownership • Refi • Survey   Vehicle Title

Interspousal • Quitclaim • ToD • Warranty   Rev / Irrev • Am / Rest   Durable / Springing   Living Will   Correction   Debts & Liens • Name-Signature-ID • Marital • Death • Will   Safe Deposit Box

DOC DATE   J F M A M J   J A S O N D ,   DOC TITLE or TYPE   # OF PAGES   ☐ Inspect/Copy Request   Entry X-Ref #

☐ **SATISFACTORY EVIDENCE** ☐ Driver's License / Passport / State ID / Military / Government / Tribal / Inmate / Other ID   *or*   ☐ Credible Witness(es)

SIGNER

SIGNER's NAME ☐ For | ADDRESS ☐ Non-Public | ☐ Capacity ☐ Voluntary ☐ Proper ID | ISSUED # | SIGNATURE ☐ *(oath / affirmation, if any)* ☐ *(by Mark)*

PHONE C / H / W   *or* ☐ MISC / | AGENCY ☐ CA DMV ☐ US State Dept | EXPIRES | ➡

CW #1

#1 WITNESS's NAME ☐ P/Known | ADDRESS ☐ Non-Public | ☐ Driver's License ☐ Passport ☐ Other ID | ISSUED # | SIGNATURE ☐ *(after oath / affirmation)*

PHONE C / H / W   *or* ☐ MISC / | AGENCY ☐ CA DMV ☐ US State Dept | EXPIRES | ❶

CW #2

#2 WITNESS's NAME ☐ P/Known | ADDRESS ☐ Non-Public | ☐ Driver's License ☐ Passport ☐ Other ID | ISSUED # | SIGNATURE ☐ *(after oath / affirmation)*

PHONE C / H / W   *or* ☐ MISC / | AGENCY ☐ CA DMV ☐ US State Dept | EXPIRES | ❷

NOTARY NAME (printed):   COMMISSION #:

Entry 27

SERVICE — DATE: - -20 | TIME: : am/pm | ADDRESS ☐ Signer's ☐ Office | NOTES | ☐ Stop | MILES | Notary $ | ☐ Adv. Travel $ | ☐ Rush $ | ☐ Copy $ | ☐ Other $ | TOTAL FEES $

TYPE: ☐ Acknowledgment ☐ Jurat ☐ Copy Certification ☐ Oath/Affirmation ☐ Oath of Office ☐ Proof of Execution ☐ Protest ☐ Other   **Fingerprint** (R T I M R P L)

DOCUMENT — DOC TYPE: ☐ Deed (Grant • Trust Transfer • Gift • Interspousal • Quitclaim • ToD • Warranty) ☐ DOT (Mortgage) ☐ Trust (Certification • Rev/Irrev • Am/Rest) ☐ POA (General/Limited • Durable/Springing) ☐ POAH (AHCD • Living Will) ☐ Agreement (Compliance-E&O • Correction) ☐ Affidavit (Borrower • Occupancy • Ownership • Refi • Survey • Debts & Liens • Name-Signature-ID • Marital • Death • Will) ☐ Other (Vehicle Title • Safe Deposit Box)

DOC DATE: J F M A M J / J A S O N D ,   DOC TITLE or TYPE: # OF PAGES: ☐ Inspect/Copy Request   Entry X-Ref #

☐ **SATISFACTORY EVIDENCE** ☐ Driver's License / Passport / State ID / Military / Government / Tribal / Inmate / Other ID   *or*   ☐ Credible Witness(es)

SIGNER — SIGNER's NAME | ☐ For | ADDRESS | ☐ Non-Public | ☐ Capacity # | ☐ Voluntary | ☐ Proper ID | ISSUED | SIGNATURE ☐ (oath/affirmation, if any) ☐ (by Mark)
PHONE C/H/W / | *or* ☐ MISC | | | AGENCY | ☐ CA DMV | ☐ US State Dept | EXPIRES | ➡

CW #1 — #1 WITNESS's NAME | ☐ P/Known | ADDRESS | ☐ Non-Public | ☐ Driver's License | ☐ Passport | ☐ Other ID | ISSUED | SIGNATURE ☐ (after oath/affirmation)
PHONE C/H/W / | *or* ☐ MISC | | | AGENCY | ☐ CA DMV | ☐ US State Dept | EXPIRES | ❶

CW #2 — #2 WITNESS's NAME | ☐ P/Known | ADDRESS | ☐ Non-Public | ☐ Driver's License | ☐ Passport | ☐ Other ID | ISSUED | SIGNATURE ☐ (after oath/affirmation)
PHONE C/H/W / | *or* ☐ MISC | | | AGENCY | ☐ CA DMV | ☐ US State Dept | EXPIRES | ❷

Entry 28

SERVICE — DATE: - -20 | TIME: : am/pm | ADDRESS ☐ Signer's ☐ Office | NOTES | ☐ Stop | MILES | Notary $ | ☐ Adv. Travel $ | ☐ Rush $ | ☐ Copy $ | ☐ Other $ | TOTAL FEES $

TYPE: ☐ Acknowledgment ☐ Jurat ☐ Copy Certification ☐ Oath/Affirmation ☐ Oath of Office ☐ Proof of Execution ☐ Protest ☐ Other   **Fingerprint** (R T I M R P L)

DOCUMENT — DOC TYPE: ☐ Deed (Grant • Trust Transfer • Gift • Interspousal • Quitclaim • ToD • Warranty) ☐ DOT (Mortgage) ☐ Trust (Certification • Rev/Irrev • Am/Rest) ☐ POA (General/Limited • Durable/Springing) ☐ POAH (AHCD • Living Will) ☐ Agreement (Compliance-E&O • Correction) ☐ Affidavit (Borrower • Occupancy • Ownership • Refi • Survey • Debts & Liens • Name-Signature-ID • Marital • Death • Will) ☐ Other (Vehicle Title • Safe Deposit Box)

DOC DATE: J F M A M J / J A S O N D ,   DOC TITLE or TYPE: # OF PAGES: ☐ Inspect/Copy Request   Entry X-Ref #

☐ **SATISFACTORY EVIDENCE** ☐ Driver's License / Passport / State ID / Military / Government / Tribal / Inmate / Other ID   *or*   ☐ Credible Witness(es)

SIGNER — SIGNER's NAME | ☐ For | ADDRESS | ☐ Non-Public | ☐ Capacity # | ☐ Voluntary | ☐ Proper ID | ISSUED | SIGNATURE ☐ (oath/affirmation, if any) ☐ (by Mark)
PHONE C/H/W / | *or* ☐ MISC | | | AGENCY | ☐ CA DMV | ☐ US State Dept | EXPIRES | ➡

CW #1 — #1 WITNESS's NAME | ☐ P/Known | ADDRESS | ☐ Non-Public | ☐ Driver's License | ☐ Passport | ☐ Other ID | ISSUED | SIGNATURE ☐ (after oath/affirmation)
PHONE C/H/W / | *or* ☐ MISC | | | AGENCY | ☐ CA DMV | ☐ US State Dept | EXPIRES | ❶

CW #2 — #2 WITNESS's NAME | ☐ P/Known | ADDRESS | ☐ Non-Public | ☐ Driver's License | ☐ Passport | ☐ Other ID | ISSUED | SIGNATURE ☐ (after oath/affirmation)
PHONE C/H/W / | *or* ☐ MISC | | | AGENCY | ☐ CA DMV | ☐ US State Dept | EXPIRES | ❷

NOTARY NAME (printed):   COMMISSION #:

Entry 29

| SERVICE | DATE - -20 | TIME : am pm | ADDRESS | ☐ Signer's | ☐ Office | NOTES | ☐ Stop | MILES | Notary $ | ☐ Adv. Travel $ | ☐ Rush $ | ☐ Copy $ | ☐ Other $ | TOTAL FEES $ | **29** |

TYPE ☐ Acknowledgment ☐ Jurat ☐ Copy Certification ☐ Oath/Affirmation ☐ Oath of Office ☐ Proof of Execution ☐ Protest ☐ Other

R   **Fingerprint**

DOCUMENT

DOC TYPE ☐ Deed ☐ DOT ☐ Trust ☐ POA ☐ POAH ☐ Agreement ☐ Affidavit ☐ Other

Grant • Trust Transfer • Gift   Mortgage   Certification   General / Limited   AHCD   Compliance-E&O   Borrower • Occupancy • Ownership • Refi • Survey   Vehicle Title

Interspousal • Quitclaim • ToD • Warranty   Rev / Irrev • Am / Rest   Durable / Springing   Living Will   Correction   Debts & Liens • Name-Signature-ID • Marital • Death • Will   Safe Deposit Box

DOC DATE J F M A M J   J A S O N D   ,   DOC TITLE or TYPE   # OF PAGES   ☐ Inspect/Copy Request   Entry X-Ref #

T I M R P L

☐ **SATISFACTORY EVIDENCE** ☐ Driver's License / Passport / State ID / Military / Government / Tribal / Inmate / Other ID *or* ☐ Credible Witness(es)

SIGNER

| SIGNER's NAME | ☐ For | ADDRESS | ☐ Non-Public | ☐ Capacity | ☐ Voluntary | ☐ Proper ID | ISSUED # | SIGNATURE | ☐ (oath / affirmation, if any) | ☐ (by Mark) |

PHONE C / H / W   *or* ☐ MISC   AGENCY   ☐ CA DMV   ☐ US State Dept   EXPIRES   ➡

CW #1

| #1 WITNESS's NAME | ☐ P/Known | ADDRESS | ☐ Non-Public | ☐ Driver's License | ☐ Passport | ☐ Other ID | ISSUED # | SIGNATURE | ☐ (after oath / affirmation) |

PHONE C / H / W   *or* ☐ MISC   AGENCY   ☐ CA DMV   ☐ US State Dept   EXPIRES   ❶

CW #2

| #2 WITNESS's NAME | ☐ P/Known | ADDRESS | ☐ Non-Public | ☐ Driver's License | ☐ Passport | ☐ Other ID | ISSUED # | SIGNATURE | ☐ (after oath / affirmation) |

PHONE C / H / W   *or* ☐ MISC   AGENCY   ☐ CA DMV   ☐ US State Dept   EXPIRES   ❷

Entry 30

| SERVICE | DATE - -20 | TIME : am pm | ADDRESS | ☐ Signer's | ☐ Office | NOTES | ☐ Stop | MILES | Notary $ | ☐ Adv. Travel $ | ☐ Rush $ | ☐ Copy $ | ☐ Other $ | TOTAL FEES $ | **30** |

TYPE ☐ Acknowledgment ☐ Jurat ☐ Copy Certification ☐ Oath/Affirmation ☐ Oath of Office ☐ Proof of Execution ☐ Protest ☐ Other

R   **Fingerprint**

DOCUMENT

DOC TYPE ☐ Deed ☐ DOT ☐ Trust ☐ POA ☐ POAH ☐ Agreement ☐ Affidavit ☐ Other

Grant • Trust Transfer • Gift   Mortgage   Certification   General / Limited   AHCD   Compliance-E&O   Borrower • Occupancy • Ownership • Refi • Survey   Vehicle Title

Interspousal • Quitclaim • ToD • Warranty   Rev / Irrev • Am / Rest   Durable / Springing   Living Will   Correction   Debts & Liens • Name-Signature-ID • Marital • Death • Will   Safe Deposit Box

DOC DATE J F M A M J   J A S O N D   ,   DOC TITLE or TYPE   # OF PAGES   ☐ Inspect/Copy Request   Entry X-Ref #

T I M R P L

☐ **SATISFACTORY EVIDENCE** ☐ Driver's License / Passport / State ID / Military / Government / Tribal / Inmate / Other ID *or* ☐ Credible Witness(es)

SIGNER

| SIGNER's NAME | ☐ For | ADDRESS | ☐ Non-Public | ☐ Capacity | ☐ Voluntary | ☐ Proper ID | ISSUED # | SIGNATURE | ☐ (oath / affirmation, if any) | ☐ (by Mark) |

PHONE C / H / W   *or* ☐ MISC   AGENCY   ☐ CA DMV   ☐ US State Dept   EXPIRES   ➡

CW #1

| #1 WITNESS's NAME | ☐ P/Known | ADDRESS | ☐ Non-Public | ☐ Driver's License | ☐ Passport | ☐ Other ID | ISSUED # | SIGNATURE | ☐ (after oath / affirmation) |

PHONE C / H / W   *or* ☐ MISC   AGENCY   ☐ CA DMV   ☐ US State Dept   EXPIRES   ❶

CW #2

| #2 WITNESS's NAME | ☐ P/Known | ADDRESS | ☐ Non-Public | ☐ Driver's License | ☐ Passport | ☐ Other ID | ISSUED # | SIGNATURE | ☐ (after oath / affirmation) |

PHONE C / H / W   *or* ☐ MISC   AGENCY   ☐ CA DMV   ☐ US State Dept   EXPIRES   ❷

NOTARY NAME (printed):   COMMISSION #:

Entry 31

SERVICE — DATE - -20 | TIME : am/pm | ADDRESS ☐ Signer's ☐ Office | NOTES | ☐ Stop | MILES | Notary $ | ☐ Adv. Travel $ | ☐ Rush $ | ☐ Copy $ | ☐ Other $ | TOTAL FEES $

TYPE ☐ Acknowledgment ☐ Jurat ☐ Copy Certification ☐ Oath/Affirmation ☐ Oath of Office ☐ Proof of Execution ☐ Protest ☐ Other

DOCUMENT —
DOC TYPE ☐ Deed | ☐ DOT | ☐ Trust | ☐ POA | ☐ POAH | ☐ Agreement | ☐ Affidavit | ☐ Other
Grant • Trust Transfer • Gift | Mortgage | Certification | General / Limited | AHCD | Compliance-E&O | Borrower • Occupancy • Ownership • Refi • Survey | Vehicle Title
Interspousal • Quitclaim • ToD • Warranty | Rev / Irrev • Am / Rest | Durable / Springing | Living Will | Correction | Debts & Liens • Name-Signature-ID • Marital • Death • Will | Safe Deposit Box

DOC DATE J F M A M J J A S O N D ,   DOC TITLE or TYPE   # OF PAGES ☐ Inspect/Copy Request   Entry X-Ref #

☐ **SATISFACTORY EVIDENCE** ☐ Driver's License / Passport / State ID / Military / Government / Tribal / Inmate / Other ID *or* ☐ Credible Witness(es)

SIGNER — SIGNER's NAME | ☐ For | ADDRESS | ☐ Non-Public | ☐ Capacity # | ☐ Voluntary | ☐ Proper ID | ISSUED | SIGNATURE ☐ (oath / affirmation, if any) ☐ (by Mark)
PHONE C / H / W / | *or* ☐ MISC | | | AGENCY | ☐ CA DMV | ☐ US State Dept | EXPIRES | ➡

CW #1 — #1 WITNESS's NAME | ☐ P/Known | ADDRESS | ☐ Non-Public | ☐ Driver's License # | ☐ Passport | ☐ Other ID | ISSUED | SIGNATURE ☐ (after oath / affirmation)
PHONE C / H / W / | *or* ☐ MISC | | | AGENCY | ☐ CA DMV | ☐ US State Dept | EXPIRES | ❶

CW #2 — #2 WITNESS's NAME | ☐ P/Known | ADDRESS | ☐ Non-Public | ☐ Driver's License # | ☐ Passport | ☐ Other ID | ISSUED | SIGNATURE ☐ (after oath / affirmation)
PHONE C / H / W / | *or* ☐ MISC | | | AGENCY | ☐ CA DMV | ☐ US State Dept | EXPIRES | ❷

R T I M R P L   **Fingerprint**

Entry 32

SERVICE — DATE - -20 | TIME : am/pm | ADDRESS ☐ Signer's ☐ Office | NOTES | ☐ Stop | MILES | Notary $ | ☐ Adv. Travel $ | ☐ Rush $ | ☐ Copy $ | ☐ Other $ | TOTAL FEES $

TYPE ☐ Acknowledgment ☐ Jurat ☐ Copy Certification ☐ Oath/Affirmation ☐ Oath of Office ☐ Proof of Execution ☐ Protest ☐ Other

DOCUMENT —
DOC TYPE ☐ Deed | ☐ DOT | ☐ Trust | ☐ POA | ☐ POAH | ☐ Agreement | ☐ Affidavit | ☐ Other
Grant • Trust Transfer • Gift | Mortgage | Certification | General / Limited | AHCD | Compliance-E&O | Borrower • Occupancy • Ownership • Refi • Survey | Vehicle Title
Interspousal • Quitclaim • ToD • Warranty | Rev / Irrev • Am / Rest | Durable / Springing | Living Will | Correction | Debts & Liens • Name-Signature-ID • Marital • Death • Will | Safe Deposit Box

DOC DATE J F M A M J J A S O N D ,   DOC TITLE or TYPE   # OF PAGES ☐ Inspect/Copy Request   Entry X-Ref #

☐ **SATISFACTORY EVIDENCE** ☐ Driver's License / Passport / State ID / Military / Government / Tribal / Inmate / Other ID *or* ☐ Credible Witness(es)

SIGNER — SIGNER's NAME | ☐ For | ADDRESS | ☐ Non-Public | ☐ Capacity # | ☐ Voluntary | ☐ Proper ID | ISSUED | SIGNATURE ☐ (oath / affirmation, if any) ☐ (by Mark)
PHONE C / H / W / | *or* ☐ MISC | | | AGENCY | ☐ CA DMV | ☐ US State Dept | EXPIRES | ➡

CW #1 — #1 WITNESS's NAME | ☐ P/Known | ADDRESS | ☐ Non-Public | ☐ Driver's License # | ☐ Passport | ☐ Other ID | ISSUED | SIGNATURE ☐ (after oath / affirmation)
PHONE C / H / W / | *or* ☐ MISC | | | AGENCY | ☐ CA DMV | ☐ US State Dept | EXPIRES | ❶

CW #2 — #2 WITNESS's NAME | ☐ P/Known | ADDRESS | ☐ Non-Public | ☐ Driver's License # | ☐ Passport | ☐ Other ID | ISSUED | SIGNATURE ☐ (after oath / affirmation)
PHONE C / H / W / | *or* ☐ MISC | | | AGENCY | ☐ CA DMV | ☐ US State Dept | EXPIRES | ❷

R T I M R P L   **Fingerprint**

NOTARY NAME (printed):   COMMISSION #:

Entry 33

SERVICE	DATE ___ - ___ -20___ TIME ___:___ am/pm ADDRESS ☐ Signer's ☐ Office NOTES ☐ Stop MILES Notary ☐ Adv. Travel ☐ Rush ☐ Copy ☐ Other TOTAL FEES $ ___ $ ___ $ ___ $ ___ $ ___ $ ___ **33**

TYPE ☐ Acknowledgment ☐ Jurat ☐ Copy Certification ☐ Oath/Affirmation ☐ Oath of Office ☐ Proof of Execution ☐ Protest ☐ Other   R | **Fingerprint**

DOCUMENT

DOC TYPE ☐ Deed ☐ DOT ☐ Trust ☐ POA ☐ POAH ☐ Agreement ☐ Affidavit ☐ Other

Grant • Trust Transfer • Gift   Mortgage   Certification   General / Limited   AHCD   Compliance-E&O   Borrower • Occupancy • Ownership • Refi • Survey   Vehicle Title
Interspousal • Quitclaim • ToD • Warranty   Rev / Irrev • Am / Rest   Durable / Springing   Living Will   Correction   Debts & Liens • Name-Signature-ID • Marital • Death • Will   Safe Deposit Box

DOC DATE J F M A M J   DOC TITLE or TYPE   # OF PAGES ☐ Inspect/Copy Request
          J A S O N D ,   Entry X-Ref #

T I M R P

☐ **SATISFACTORY EVIDENCE** ☐ Driver's License / Passport / State ID / Military / Government / Tribal / Inmate / Other ID **or** ☐ Credible Witness(es)   L

	SIGNER's NAME	☐ For	ADDRESS	☐ Non-Public	☐ Capacity	☐ Voluntary	☐ Proper ID	ISSUED	SIGNATURE	☐ (oath / affirmation, if any)	☐ (by Mark)
SIGNER					#						
	PHONE C / H / W	or ☐ MISC			AGENCY	☐ CA DMV	☐ US State Dept	EXPIRES	➡		

	#1 WITNESS's NAME	☐ P/Known	ADDRESS	☐ Non-Public	☐ Driver's License	☐ Passport	☐ Other ID	ISSUED	SIGNATURE	☐ (after oath / affirmation)
CW #1					#					
	PHONE C / H / W	or ☐ MISC			AGENCY	☐ CA DMV	☐ US State Dept	EXPIRES	❶	

	#2 WITNESS's NAME	☐ P/Known	ADDRESS	☐ Non-Public	☐ Driver's License	☐ Passport	☐ Other ID	ISSUED	SIGNATURE	☐ (after oath / affirmation)
CW #2					#					
	PHONE C / H / W	or ☐ MISC			AGENCY	☐ CA DMV	☐ US State Dept	EXPIRES	❷	

Entry 34

SERVICE	DATE ___ - ___ -20___ TIME ___:___ am/pm ADDRESS ☐ Signer's ☐ Office NOTES ☐ Stop MILES Notary ☐ Adv. Travel ☐ Rush ☐ Copy ☐ Other TOTAL FEES $ ___ $ ___ $ ___ $ ___ $ ___ $ ___ **34**

TYPE ☐ Acknowledgment ☐ Jurat ☐ Copy Certification ☐ Oath/Affirmation ☐ Oath of Office ☐ Proof of Execution ☐ Protest ☐ Other   R | **Fingerprint**

DOCUMENT

DOC TYPE ☐ Deed ☐ DOT ☐ Trust ☐ POA ☐ POAH ☐ Agreement ☐ Affidavit ☐ Other

Grant • Trust Transfer • Gift   Mortgage   Certification   General / Limited   AHCD   Compliance-E&O   Borrower • Occupancy • Ownership • Refi • Survey   Vehicle Title
Interspousal • Quitclaim • ToD • Warranty   Rev / Irrev • Am / Rest   Durable / Springing   Living Will   Correction   Debts & Liens • Name-Signature-ID • Marital • Death • Will   Safe Deposit Box

DOC DATE J F M A M J   DOC TITLE or TYPE   # OF PAGES ☐ Inspect/Copy Request
          J A S O N D ,   Entry X-Ref #

T I M R P

☐ **SATISFACTORY EVIDENCE** ☐ Driver's License / Passport / State ID / Military / Government / Tribal / Inmate / Other ID **or** ☐ Credible Witness(es)   L

	SIGNER's NAME	☐ For	ADDRESS	☐ Non-Public	☐ Capacity	☐ Voluntary	☐ Proper ID	ISSUED	SIGNATURE	☐ (oath / affirmation, if any)	☐ (by Mark)
SIGNER					#						
	PHONE C / H / W	or ☐ MISC			AGENCY	☐ CA DMV	☐ US State Dept	EXPIRES	➡		

	#1 WITNESS's NAME	☐ P/Known	ADDRESS	☐ Non-Public	☐ Driver's License	☐ Passport	☐ Other ID	ISSUED	SIGNATURE	☐ (after oath / affirmation)
CW #1					#					
	PHONE C / H / W	or ☐ MISC			AGENCY	☐ CA DMV	☐ US State Dept	EXPIRES	❶	

	#2 WITNESS's NAME	☐ P/Known	ADDRESS	☐ Non-Public	☐ Driver's License	☐ Passport	☐ Other ID	ISSUED	SIGNATURE	☐ (after oath / affirmation)
CW #2					#					
	PHONE C / H / W	or ☐ MISC			AGENCY	☐ CA DMV	☐ US State Dept	EXPIRES	❷	

NOTARY NAME (printed): COMMISSION #:

Entry 35

SERVICE — DATE: - -20 | TIME: : am/pm | ADDRESS | ☐ Signer's ☐ Office | NOTES | ☐ Stop | MILES | Notary $ | ☐ Adv. Travel $ | ☐ Rush $ | ☐ Copy $ | ☐ Other $ | TOTAL FEES $

TYPE: ☐ Acknowledgment ☐ Jurat ☐ Copy Certification ☐ Oath/Affirmation ☐ Oath of Office ☐ Proof of Execution ☐ Protest ☐ Other

DOCUMENT
- DOC TYPE: ☐ Deed (Grant • Trust Transfer • Gift • Interspousal • Quitclaim • ToD • Warranty) ☐ DOT (Mortgage • Rev / Irrev • Am / Rest) ☐ Trust (Certification • Durable / Springing) ☐ POA (General / Limited) ☐ POAH (AHCD • Living Will) ☐ Agreement (Compliance-E&O • Correction) ☐ Affidavit (Borrower • Occupancy • Ownership • Refi • Survey • Debts & Liens • Name-Signature-ID • Marital • Death • Will) ☐ Other (Vehicle Title • Safe Deposit Box)
- DOC DATE: J F M A M J J A S O N D , | DOC TITLE or TYPE | # OF PAGES | ☐ Inspect/Copy Request | Entry X-Ref #

Fingerprint R T I M R P L

☐ **SATISFACTORY EVIDENCE** ☐ Driver's License / Passport / State ID / Military / Government / Tribal / Inmate / Other ID *or* ☐ Credible Witness(es)

SIGNER
- SIGNER's NAME | ☐ For | ADDRESS | ☐ Non-Public | ☐ Capacity # | ☐ Voluntary | ☐ Proper ID | ISSUED | SIGNATURE | ☐ (oath / affirmation, if any) | ☐ (by Mark)
- PHONE C / H / W / | *or* ☐ MISC | | | AGENCY | ☐ CA DMV | ☐ US State Dept | EXPIRES | ➡

CW #1
- #1 WITNESS's NAME | ☐ P/Known | ADDRESS | ☐ Non-Public | ☐ Driver's License | ☐ Passport | ☐ Other ID | ISSUED | SIGNATURE | ☐ (after oath / affirmation)
- PHONE C / H / W / | *or* ☐ MISC | # | | AGENCY | ☐ CA DMV | ☐ US State Dept | EXPIRES | ❶

CW #2
- #2 WITNESS's NAME | ☐ P/Known | ADDRESS | ☐ Non-Public | ☐ Driver's License | ☐ Passport | ☐ Other ID | ISSUED | SIGNATURE | ☐ (after oath / affirmation)
- PHONE C / H / W / | *or* ☐ MISC | # | | AGENCY | ☐ CA DMV | ☐ US State Dept | EXPIRES | ❷

Entry 36

SERVICE — DATE: - -20 | TIME: : am/pm | ADDRESS | ☐ Signer's ☐ Office | NOTES | ☐ Stop | MILES | Notary $ | ☐ Adv. Travel $ | ☐ Rush $ | ☐ Copy $ | ☐ Other $ | TOTAL FEES $

TYPE: ☐ Acknowledgment ☐ Jurat ☐ Copy Certification ☐ Oath/Affirmation ☐ Oath of Office ☐ Proof of Execution ☐ Protest ☐ Other

DOCUMENT
- DOC TYPE: ☐ Deed (Grant • Trust Transfer • Gift • Interspousal • Quitclaim • ToD • Warranty) ☐ DOT (Mortgage • Rev / Irrev • Am / Rest) ☐ Trust (Certification • Durable / Springing) ☐ POA (General / Limited) ☐ POAH (AHCD • Living Will) ☐ Agreement (Compliance-E&O • Correction) ☐ Affidavit (Borrower • Occupancy • Ownership • Refi • Survey • Debts & Liens • Name-Signature-ID • Marital • Death • Will) ☐ Other (Vehicle Title • Safe Deposit Box)
- DOC DATE: J F M A M J J A S O N D , | DOC TITLE or TYPE | # OF PAGES | ☐ Inspect/Copy Request | Entry X-Ref #

Fingerprint R T I M R P L

☐ **SATISFACTORY EVIDENCE** ☐ Driver's License / Passport / State ID / Military / Government / Tribal / Inmate / Other ID *or* ☐ Credible Witness(es)

SIGNER
- SIGNER's NAME | ☐ For | ADDRESS | ☐ Non-Public | ☐ Capacity # | ☐ Voluntary | ☐ Proper ID | ISSUED | SIGNATURE | ☐ (oath / affirmation, if any) | ☐ (by Mark)
- PHONE C / H / W / | *or* ☐ MISC | | | AGENCY | ☐ CA DMV | ☐ US State Dept | EXPIRES | ➡

CW #1
- #1 WITNESS's NAME | ☐ P/Known | ADDRESS | ☐ Non-Public | ☐ Driver's License | ☐ Passport | ☐ Other ID | ISSUED | SIGNATURE | ☐ (after oath / affirmation)
- PHONE C / H / W / | *or* ☐ MISC | # | | AGENCY | ☐ CA DMV | ☐ US State Dept | EXPIRES | ❶

CW #2
- #2 WITNESS's NAME | ☐ P/Known | ADDRESS | ☐ Non-Public | ☐ Driver's License | ☐ Passport | ☐ Other ID | ISSUED | SIGNATURE | ☐ (after oath / affirmation)
- PHONE C / H / W / | *or* ☐ MISC | # | | AGENCY | ☐ CA DMV | ☐ US State Dept | EXPIRES | ❷

NOTARY NAME (printed):   **COMMISSION #:**

Entry 37

| SERVICE | DATE - -20 | TIME : am pm | ADDRESS ☐ Signer's ☐ Office NOTES | ☐ Stop | MILES | Notary $ | ☐ Adv. Travel $ | ☐ Rush $ | ☐ Copy $ | ☐ Other $ | TOTAL FEES $ | **37** |

TYPE ☐ Acknowledgment ☐ Jurat ☐ Copy Certification ☐ Oath/Affirmation ☐ Oath of Office ☐ Proof of Execution ☐ Protest ☐ Other   **R**   **Fingerprint**

DOCUMENT

DOC TYPE	☐ Deed	☐ DOT	☐ Trust	☐ POA	☐ POAH	☐ Agreement	☐ Affidavit	☐ Other	T
	Grant • Trust Transfer • Gift	Mortgage	Certification	General / Limited	AHCD	Compliance-E&O	Borrower • Occupancy • Ownership • Refi • Survey	Vehicle Title	I
	Interspousal • Quitclaim • ToD • Warranty	Rev / Irrev • Am / Rest	Durable / Springing	Living Will		Correction	Debts & Liens • Name-Signature-ID • Marital • Death • Will	Safe Deposit Box	M

DOC DATE J F M A M J / J A S O N D ,   DOC TITLE or TYPE   # OF PAGES ☐ Inspect/Copy Request   Entry X-Ref #   **R / P / L**

☐ **SATISFACTORY EVIDENCE** ☐ Driver's License / Passport / State ID / Military / Government / Tribal / Inmate / Other ID **or** ☐ Credible Witness(es)

SIGNER	SIGNER's NAME ☐ For	ADDRESS	☐ Non-Public	☐ Capacity # ☐ Voluntary ☐ Proper ID	ISSUED	SIGNATURE ☐ (oath / affirmation, if any) ☐ (by Mark)
	PHONE C / H / W or ☐ MISC /			AGENCY ☐ CA DMV ☐ US State Dept	EXPIRES	➡

CW #1	#1 WITNESS's NAME ☐ P/Known	ADDRESS	☐ Non-Public	☐ Driver's License ☐ Passport ☐ Other ID #	ISSUED	SIGNATURE ☐ (after oath / affirmation)
	PHONE C / H / W or ☐ MISC /			AGENCY ☐ CA DMV ☐ US State Dept	EXPIRES	❶

CW #2	#2 WITNESS's NAME ☐ P/Known	ADDRESS	☐ Non-Public	☐ Driver's License ☐ Passport ☐ Other ID #	ISSUED	SIGNATURE ☐ (after oath / affirmation)
	PHONE C / H / W or ☐ MISC /			AGENCY ☐ CA DMV ☐ US State Dept	EXPIRES	❷

Entry 38

| SERVICE | DATE - -20 | TIME : am pm | ADDRESS ☐ Signer's ☐ Office NOTES | ☐ Stop | MILES | Notary $ | ☐ Adv. Travel $ | ☐ Rush $ | ☐ Copy $ | ☐ Other $ | TOTAL FEES $ | **38** |

TYPE ☐ Acknowledgment ☐ Jurat ☐ Copy Certification ☐ Oath/Affirmation ☐ Oath of Office ☐ Proof of Execution ☐ Protest ☐ Other   **R**   **Fingerprint**

DOCUMENT

DOC TYPE	☐ Deed	☐ DOT	☐ Trust	☐ POA	☐ POAH	☐ Agreement	☐ Affidavit	☐ Other	T
	Grant • Trust Transfer • Gift	Mortgage	Certification	General / Limited	AHCD	Compliance-E&O	Borrower • Occupancy • Ownership • Refi • Survey	Vehicle Title	I
	Interspousal • Quitclaim • ToD • Warranty	Rev / Irrev • Am / Rest	Durable / Springing	Living Will		Correction	Debts & Liens • Name-Signature-ID • Marital • Death • Will	Safe Deposit Box	M

DOC DATE J F M A M J / J A S O N D ,   DOC TITLE or TYPE   # OF PAGES ☐ Inspect/Copy Request   Entry X-Ref #   **R / P**

☐ **SATISFACTORY EVIDENCE** ☐ Driver's License / Passport / State ID / Military / Government / Tribal / Inmate / Other ID **or** ☐ Credible Witness(es)   **L**

SIGNER	SIGNER's NAME ☐ For	ADDRESS	☐ Non-Public	☐ Capacity # ☐ Voluntary ☐ Proper ID	ISSUED	SIGNATURE ☐ (oath / affirmation, if any) ☐ (by Mark)
	PHONE C / H / W or ☐ MISC /			AGENCY ☐ CA DMV ☐ US State Dept	EXPIRES	➡

CW #1	#1 WITNESS's NAME ☐ P/Known	ADDRESS	☐ Non-Public	☐ Driver's License ☐ Passport ☐ Other ID #	ISSUED	SIGNATURE ☐ (after oath / affirmation)
	PHONE C / H / W or ☐ MISC /			AGENCY ☐ CA DMV ☐ US State Dept	EXPIRES	❶

CW #2	#2 WITNESS's NAME ☐ P/Known	ADDRESS	☐ Non-Public	☐ Driver's License ☐ Passport ☐ Other ID #	ISSUED	SIGNATURE ☐ (after oath / affirmation)
	PHONE C / H / W or ☐ MISC /			AGENCY ☐ CA DMV ☐ US State Dept	EXPIRES	❷

NOTARY NAME (printed):   COMMISSION #:

Entry 39

SERVICE — DATE: - -20 | TIME: : am/pm | ADDRESS | ☐ Signer's ☐ Office | NOTES | ☐ Stop | MILES $ | Notary $ | ☐ Adv. Travel $ | ☐ Rush $ | ☐ Copy $ | ☐ Other | TOTAL FEES $

TYPE: ☐ Acknowledgment ☐ Jurat ☐ Copy Certification ☐ Oath/Affirmation ☐ Oath of Office ☐ Proof of Execution ☐ Protest ☐ Other   R T I M R P L   **Fingerprint**

DOCUMENT — DOC TYPE: ☐ Deed (Grant • Trust Transfer • Gift • Interspousal • Quitclaim • ToD • Warranty) ☐ DOT (Mortgage • Certification • Rev / Irrev • Am / Rest) ☐ Trust (Durable / Springing) ☐ POA (General / Limited) ☐ POAH (AHCD • Living Will) ☐ Agreement (Compliance-E&O • Correction) ☐ Affidavit (Borrower • Occupancy • Ownership • Refi • Survey • Debts & Liens • Name-Signature-ID • Marital • Death • Will) ☐ Other (Vehicle Title • Safe Deposit Box)

DOC DATE: J F M A M J / J A S O N D ,   DOC TITLE or TYPE   # OF PAGES   ☐ Inspect/Copy Request   Entry X-Ref #

☐ **SATISFACTORY EVIDENCE** ☐ Driver's License / Passport / State ID / Military / Government / Tribal / Inmate / Other ID **or** ☐ Credible Witness(es)

SIGNER — SIGNER's NAME | ☐ For | ADDRESS | ☐ Non-Public | ☐ Capacity # | ☐ Voluntary | ☐ Proper ID | ISSUED | SIGNATURE ☐ (oath / affirmation, if any) ☐ (by Mark)
PHONE C/H/W / | or ☐ MISC | | | AGENCY | ☐ CA DMV | ☐ US State Dept | EXPIRES | ➡

CW #1 — #1 WITNESS's NAME | ☐ P/Known | ADDRESS | ☐ Non-Public | ☐ Driver's License # | ☐ Passport | ☐ Other ID | ISSUED | SIGNATURE ☐ (after oath / affirmation)
PHONE C/H/W / | or ☐ MISC | | | AGENCY | ☐ CA DMV | ☐ US State Dept | EXPIRES | ❶

CW #2 — #2 WITNESS's NAME | ☐ P/Known | ADDRESS | ☐ Non-Public | ☐ Driver's License # | ☐ Passport | ☐ Other ID | ISSUED | SIGNATURE ☐ (after oath / affirmation)
PHONE C/H/W / | or ☐ MISC | | | AGENCY | ☐ CA DMV | ☐ US State Dept | EXPIRES | ❷

Entry 40

SERVICE — DATE: - -20 | TIME: : am/pm | ADDRESS | ☐ Signer's ☐ Office | NOTES | ☐ Stop | MILES $ | Notary $ | ☐ Adv. Travel $ | ☐ Rush $ | ☐ Copy $ | ☐ Other | TOTAL FEES $

TYPE: ☐ Acknowledgment ☐ Jurat ☐ Copy Certification ☐ Oath/Affirmation ☐ Oath of Office ☐ Proof of Execution ☐ Protest ☐ Other   R T I M R P L   **Fingerprint**

DOCUMENT — DOC TYPE: ☐ Deed (Grant • Trust Transfer • Gift • Interspousal • Quitclaim • ToD • Warranty) ☐ DOT (Mortgage • Certification • Rev / Irrev • Am / Rest) ☐ Trust (Durable / Springing) ☐ POA (General / Limited) ☐ POAH (AHCD • Living Will) ☐ Agreement (Compliance-E&O • Correction) ☐ Affidavit (Borrower • Occupancy • Ownership • Refi • Survey • Debts & Liens • Name-Signature-ID • Marital • Death • Will) ☐ Other (Vehicle Title • Safe Deposit Box)

DOC DATE: J F M A M J / J A S O N D ,   DOC TITLE or TYPE   # OF PAGES   ☐ Inspect/Copy Request   Entry X-Ref #

☐ **SATISFACTORY EVIDENCE** ☐ Driver's License / Passport / State ID / Military / Government / Tribal / Inmate / Other ID **or** ☐ Credible Witness(es)

SIGNER — SIGNER's NAME | ☐ For | ADDRESS | ☐ Non-Public | ☐ Capacity # | ☐ Voluntary | ☐ Proper ID | ISSUED | SIGNATURE ☐ (oath / affirmation, if any) ☐ (by Mark)
PHONE C/H/W / | or ☐ MISC | | | AGENCY | ☐ CA DMV | ☐ US State Dept | EXPIRES | ➡

CW #1 — #1 WITNESS's NAME | ☐ P/Known | ADDRESS | ☐ Non-Public | ☐ Driver's License # | ☐ Passport | ☐ Other ID | ISSUED | SIGNATURE ☐ (after oath / affirmation)
PHONE C/H/W / | or ☐ MISC | | | AGENCY | ☐ CA DMV | ☐ US State Dept | EXPIRES | ❶

CW #2 — #2 WITNESS's NAME | ☐ P/Known | ADDRESS | ☐ Non-Public | ☐ Driver's License # | ☐ Passport | ☐ Other ID | ISSUED | SIGNATURE ☐ (after oath / affirmation)
PHONE C/H/W / | or ☐ MISC | | | AGENCY | ☐ CA DMV | ☐ US State Dept | EXPIRES | ❷

NOTARY NAME (printed):   COMMISSION #:

Entry 41

SERVICE — DATE - -20 · TIME : am pm · ADDRESS ☐ Signer's ☐ Office · NOTES · ☐ Stop · MILES · Notary ☐ Adv. Travel ☐ Rush ☐ Copy ☐ Other · TOTAL FEES · $ $ $ $ $ $

TYPE ☐ Acknowledgment ☐ Jurat ☐ Copy Certification ☐ Oath/Affirmation ☐ Oath of Office ☐ Proof of Execution ☐ Protest ☐ Other

R T I M R P L — **Fingerprint**

DOCUMENT

DOC TYPE ☐ Deed ☐ DOT ☐ Trust ☐ POA ☐ POAH ☐ Agreement ☐ Affidavit ☐ Other
- Deed: Grant • Trust Transfer • Gift / Interspousal • Quitclaim • ToD • Warranty
- DOT: Mortgage
- Trust: Certification / Rev / Irrev • Am / Rest
- POA: General / Limited / Durable / Springing
- POAH: AHCD / Living Will
- Agreement: Compliance-E&O / Correction
- Affidavit: Borrower • Occupancy • Ownership • Refi • Survey / Debts & Liens • Name-Signature-ID • Marital • Death • Will
- Other: Vehicle Title / Safe Deposit Box

DOC DATE J F M A M J J A S O N D , · DOC TITLE or TYPE · # OF PAGES ☐ Inspect/Copy Request · Entry X-Ref #

☐ **SATISFACTORY EVIDENCE** ☐ Driver's License / Passport / State ID / Military / Government / Tribal / Inmate / Other ID **or** ☐ Credible Witness(es)

SIGNER
SIGNER's NAME ☐ For · ADDRESS ☐ Non-Public ☐ Capacity ☐ Voluntary ☐ Proper ID · ISSUED # · SIGNATURE ☐ (oath / affirmation, if any) ☐ (by Mark)
PHONE C / H / W _or_ ☐ MISC / · AGENCY ☐ CA DMV ☐ US State Dept · EXPIRES · ➡

CW #1
#1 WITNESS's NAME ☐ P/Known · ADDRESS ☐ Non-Public ☐ Driver's License ☐ Passport ☐ Other ID · ISSUED # · SIGNATURE ☐ (after oath / affirmation)
PHONE C / H / W _or_ ☐ MISC / · AGENCY ☐ CA DMV ☐ US State Dept · EXPIRES · ❶

CW #2
#2 WITNESS's NAME ☐ P/Known · ADDRESS ☐ Non-Public ☐ Driver's License ☐ Passport ☐ Other ID · ISSUED # · SIGNATURE ☐ (after oath / affirmation)
PHONE C / H / W _or_ ☐ MISC / · AGENCY ☐ CA DMV ☐ US State Dept · EXPIRES · ❷

Entry 42

SERVICE — DATE - -20 · TIME : am pm · ADDRESS ☐ Signer's ☐ Office · NOTES · ☐ Stop · MILES · Notary ☐ Adv. Travel ☐ Rush ☐ Copy ☐ Other · TOTAL FEES · $ $ $ $ $ $

TYPE ☐ Acknowledgment ☐ Jurat ☐ Copy Certification ☐ Oath/Affirmation ☐ Oath of Office ☐ Proof of Execution ☐ Protest ☐ Other

R T I M R P L — **Fingerprint**

DOCUMENT

DOC TYPE ☐ Deed ☐ DOT ☐ Trust ☐ POA ☐ POAH ☐ Agreement ☐ Affidavit ☐ Other
- Deed: Grant • Trust Transfer • Gift / Interspousal • Quitclaim • ToD • Warranty
- DOT: Mortgage
- Trust: Certification / Rev / Irrev • Am / Rest
- POA: General / Limited / Durable / Springing
- POAH: AHCD / Living Will
- Agreement: Compliance-E&O / Correction
- Affidavit: Borrower • Occupancy • Ownership • Refi • Survey / Debts & Liens • Name-Signature-ID • Marital • Death • Will
- Other: Vehicle Title / Safe Deposit Box

DOC DATE J F M A M J J A S O N D , · DOC TITLE or TYPE · # OF PAGES ☐ Inspect/Copy Request · Entry X-Ref #

☐ **SATISFACTORY EVIDENCE** ☐ Driver's License / Passport / State ID / Military / Government / Tribal / Inmate / Other ID **or** ☐ Credible Witness(es)

SIGNER
SIGNER's NAME ☐ For · ADDRESS ☐ Non-Public ☐ Capacity ☐ Voluntary ☐ Proper ID · ISSUED # · SIGNATURE ☐ (oath / affirmation, if any) ☐ (by Mark)
PHONE C / H / W _or_ ☐ MISC / · AGENCY ☐ CA DMV ☐ US State Dept · EXPIRES · ➡

CW #1
#1 WITNESS's NAME ☐ P/Known · ADDRESS ☐ Non-Public ☐ Driver's License ☐ Passport ☐ Other ID · ISSUED # · SIGNATURE ☐ (after oath / affirmation)
PHONE C / H / W _or_ ☐ MISC / · AGENCY ☐ CA DMV ☐ US State Dept · EXPIRES · ❶

CW #2
#2 WITNESS's NAME ☐ P/Known · ADDRESS ☐ Non-Public ☐ Driver's License ☐ Passport ☐ Other ID · ISSUED # · SIGNATURE ☐ (after oath / affirmation)
PHONE C / H / W _or_ ☐ MISC / · AGENCY ☐ CA DMV ☐ US State Dept · EXPIRES · ❷

NOTARY NAME (printed):   COMMISSION #:

Entry 43

SERVICE — DATE: - -20 | TIME: : am/pm | ADDRESS | ☐ Signer's ☐ Office | NOTES | ☐ Stop | MILES | Notary $ | ☐ Adv. Travel $ | ☐ Rush $ | ☐ Copy $ | ☐ Other $ | TOTAL FEES $

TYPE: ☐ Acknowledgment ☐ Jurat ☐ Copy Certification ☐ Oath/Affirmation ☐ Oath of Office ☐ Proof of Execution ☐ Protest ☐ Other

DOCUMENT — DOC TYPE: ☐ Deed (Grant • Trust Transfer • Gift • Interspousal • Quitclaim • ToD • Warranty) ☐ DOT (Mortgage) ☐ Trust (Certification • Rev / Irrev • Am / Rest) ☐ POA (General / Limited • Durable / Springing) ☐ POAH (AHCD • Living Will) ☐ Agreement (Compliance-E&O • Correction) ☐ Affidavit (Borrower • Occupancy • Ownership • Refi • Survey • Debts & Liens • Name-Signature-ID • Marital • Death • Will) ☐ Other (Vehicle Title • Safe Deposit Box)

DOC DATE: J F M A M J / J A S O N D ,   DOC TITLE or TYPE   # OF PAGES   ☐ Inspect/Copy Request   Entry X-Ref #

Fingerprint: R T I M R P L

☐ **SATISFACTORY EVIDENCE** ☐ Driver's License / Passport / State ID / Military / Government / Tribal / Inmate / Other ID   *or*   ☐ Credible Witness(es)

SIGNER — SIGNER's NAME | ☐ For | ADDRESS | ☐ Non-Public | ☐ Capacity # | ☐ Voluntary | ☐ Proper ID | ISSUED | SIGNATURE | ☐ (oath / affirmation, if any) | ☐ (by Mark)
PHONE C / H / W   *or* ☐ MISC   AGENCY   ☐ CA DMV ☐ US State Dept   EXPIRES

CW #1 — #1 WITNESS's NAME | ☐ P/Known | ADDRESS | ☐ Non-Public | ☐ Driver's License # | ☐ Passport | ☐ Other ID | ISSUED | SIGNATURE | ☐ (after oath / affirmation)
PHONE C / H / W   *or* ☐ MISC   AGENCY   ☐ CA DMV ☐ US State Dept   EXPIRES   ❶

CW #2 — #2 WITNESS's NAME | ☐ P/Known | ADDRESS | ☐ Non-Public | ☐ Driver's License # | ☐ Passport | ☐ Other ID | ISSUED | SIGNATURE | ☐ (after oath / affirmation)
PHONE C / H / W   *or* ☐ MISC   AGENCY   ☐ CA DMV ☐ US State Dept   EXPIRES   ❷

Entry 44

SERVICE — DATE: - -20 | TIME: : am/pm | ADDRESS | ☐ Signer's ☐ Office | NOTES | ☐ Stop | MILES | Notary $ | ☐ Adv. Travel $ | ☐ Rush $ | ☐ Copy $ | ☐ Other $ | TOTAL FEES $

TYPE: ☐ Acknowledgment ☐ Jurat ☐ Copy Certification ☐ Oath/Affirmation ☐ Oath of Office ☐ Proof of Execution ☐ Protest ☐ Other

DOCUMENT — DOC TYPE: ☐ Deed (Grant • Trust Transfer • Gift • Interspousal • Quitclaim • ToD • Warranty) ☐ DOT (Mortgage) ☐ Trust (Certification • Rev / Irrev • Am / Rest) ☐ POA (General / Limited • Durable / Springing) ☐ POAH (AHCD • Living Will) ☐ Agreement (Compliance-E&O • Correction) ☐ Affidavit (Borrower • Occupancy • Ownership • Refi • Survey • Debts & Liens • Name-Signature-ID • Marital • Death • Will) ☐ Other (Vehicle Title • Safe Deposit Box)

DOC DATE: J F M A M J / J A S O N D ,   DOC TITLE or TYPE   # OF PAGES   ☐ Inspect/Copy Request   Entry X-Ref #

Fingerprint: R T I M R P L

☐ **SATISFACTORY EVIDENCE** ☐ Driver's License / Passport / State ID / Military / Government / Tribal / Inmate / Other ID   *or*   ☐ Credible Witness(es)

SIGNER — SIGNER's NAME | ☐ For | ADDRESS | ☐ Non-Public | ☐ Capacity # | ☐ Voluntary | ☐ Proper ID | ISSUED | SIGNATURE | ☐ (oath / affirmation, if any) | ☐ (by Mark)
PHONE C / H / W   *or* ☐ MISC   AGENCY   ☐ CA DMV ☐ US State Dept   EXPIRES

CW #1 — #1 WITNESS's NAME | ☐ P/Known | ADDRESS | ☐ Non-Public | ☐ Driver's License # | ☐ Passport | ☐ Other ID | ISSUED | SIGNATURE | ☐ (after oath / affirmation)
PHONE C / H / W   *or* ☐ MISC   AGENCY   ☐ CA DMV ☐ US State Dept   EXPIRES   ❶

CW #2 — #2 WITNESS's NAME | ☐ P/Known | ADDRESS | ☐ Non-Public | ☐ Driver's License # | ☐ Passport | ☐ Other ID | ISSUED | SIGNATURE | ☐ (after oath / affirmation)
PHONE C / H / W   *or* ☐ MISC   AGENCY   ☐ CA DMV ☐ US State Dept   EXPIRES   ❷

NOTARY NAME (printed):   COMMISSION #:

Entry 45

SERVICE	DATE - -20	TIME : am / pm	ADDRESS	☐ Signer's ☐ Office	NOTES	☐ Stop	MILES	Notary ☐ Adv. Travel ☐ Rush ☐ Copy ☐ Other	TOTAL FEES

$ $ $ $ $ $

45

TYPE ☐ Acknowledgment ☐ Jurat ☐ Copy Certification ☐ Oath/Affirmation ☐ Oath of Office ☐ Proof of Execution ☐ Protest ☐ Other   R   **Fingerprint**

DOCUMENT

DOC TYPE ☐ Deed   ☐ DOT   ☐ Trust   ☐ POA   ☐ POAH   ☐ Agreement   ☐ Affidavit   ☐ Other

Grant • Trust Transfer • Gift   Mortgage   Certification   General / Limited   AHCD   Compliance-E&O   Borrower • Occupancy • Ownership • Refi • Survey   Vehicle Title

Interspousal • Quitclaim • ToD • Warranty   Rev / Irrev • Am / Rest   Durable / Springing   Living Will   Correction   Debts & Liens • Name-Signature-ID • Marital • Death • Will   Safe Deposit Box

DOC DATE   J F M A M J   J A S O N D   ,   DOC TITLE or TYPE   # OF PAGES ☐ Inspect/Copy Request   Entry X-Ref #

T I M R P L

☐ **SATISFACTORY EVIDENCE** ☐ Driver's License / Passport / State ID / Military / Government / Tribal / Inmate / Other ID   *or*   ☐ Credible Witness(es)

SIGNER	SIGNER's NAME	☐ For	ADDRESS	☐ Non-Public	☐ Capacity ☐ Voluntary ☐ Proper ID	ISSUED	SIGNATURE ☐ (oath / affirmation, if any) ☐ (by Mark)

PHONE C / H / W   *or* ☐ MISC   /   AGENCY ☐ CA DMV ☐ US State Dept EXPIRES   ➡

CW #1	#1 WITNESS's NAME	☐ P/Known	ADDRESS	☐ Non-Public	☐ Driver's License ☐ Passport ☐ Other ID	ISSUED	SIGNATURE ☐ (after oath / affirmation)

#

PHONE C / H / W   *or* ☐ MISC   /   AGENCY ☐ CA DMV ☐ US State Dept EXPIRES   ❶

CW #2	#2 WITNESS's NAME	☐ P/Known	ADDRESS	☐ Non-Public	☐ Driver's License ☐ Passport ☐ Other ID	ISSUED	SIGNATURE ☐ (after oath / affirmation)

#

PHONE C / H / W   *or* ☐ MISC   /   AGENCY ☐ CA DMV ☐ US State Dept EXPIRES   ❷

Entry 46

SERVICE	DATE - -20	TIME : am / pm	ADDRESS	☐ Signer's ☐ Office	NOTES	☐ Stop	MILES	Notary ☐ Adv. Travel ☐ Rush ☐ Copy ☐ Other	TOTAL FEES

$ $ $ $ $ $

46

TYPE ☐ Acknowledgment ☐ Jurat ☐ Copy Certification ☐ Oath/Affirmation ☐ Oath of Office ☐ Proof of Execution ☐ Protest ☐ Other   R   **Fingerprint**

DOCUMENT

DOC TYPE ☐ Deed   ☐ DOT   ☐ Trust   ☐ POA   ☐ POAH   ☐ Agreement   ☐ Affidavit   ☐ Other

Grant • Trust Transfer • Gift   Mortgage   Certification   General / Limited   AHCD   Compliance-E&O   Borrower • Occupancy • Ownership • Refi • Survey   Vehicle Title

Interspousal • Quitclaim • ToD • Warranty   Rev / Irrev • Am / Rest   Durable / Springing   Living Will   Correction   Debts & Liens • Name-Signature-ID • Marital • Death • Will   Safe Deposit Box

DOC DATE   J F M A M J   J A S O N D   ,   DOC TITLE or TYPE   # OF PAGES ☐ Inspect/Copy Request   Entry X-Ref #

T I M R P L

☐ **SATISFACTORY EVIDENCE** ☐ Driver's License / Passport / State ID / Military / Government / Tribal / Inmate / Other ID   *or*   ☐ Credible Witness(es)

SIGNER	SIGNER's NAME	☐ For	ADDRESS	☐ Non-Public	☐ Capacity ☐ Voluntary ☐ Proper ID	ISSUED	SIGNATURE ☐ (oath / affirmation, if any) ☐ (by Mark)

#

PHONE C / H / W   *or* ☐ MISC   /   AGENCY ☐ CA DMV ☐ US State Dept EXPIRES   ➡

CW #1	#1 WITNESS's NAME	☐ P/Known	ADDRESS	☐ Non-Public	☐ Driver's License ☐ Passport ☐ Other ID	ISSUED	SIGNATURE ☐ (after oath / affirmation)

#

PHONE C / H / W   *or* ☐ MISC   /   AGENCY ☐ CA DMV ☐ US State Dept EXPIRES   ❶

CW #2	#2 WITNESS's NAME	☐ P/Known	ADDRESS	☐ Non-Public	☐ Driver's License ☐ Passport ☐ Other ID	ISSUED	SIGNATURE ☐ (after oath / affirmation)

#

PHONE C / H / W   *or* ☐ MISC   /   AGENCY ☐ CA DMV ☐ US State Dept EXPIRES   ❷

NOTARY NAME (printed):   COMMISSION #:

Entry 47

SERVICE — DATE __-__-20__ | TIME __:__ am/pm | ADDRESS | ☐ Signer's ☐ Office | NOTES | ☐ Stop | MILES | Notary $ | ☐ Adv. Travel $ | ☐ Rush $ | ☐ Copy $ | ☐ Other $ | TOTAL FEES $

TYPE: ☐ Acknowledgment ☐ Jurat ☐ Copy Certification ☐ Oath/Affirmation ☐ Oath of Office ☐ Proof of Execution ☐ Protest ☐ Other

DOCUMENT — DOC TYPE:
- ☐ Deed — Grant • Trust Transfer • Gift • Interspousal • Quitclaim • ToD • Warranty
- ☐ DOT — Mortgage • Certification • Rev / Irrev • Am / Rest
- ☐ Trust — Certification • Rev / Irrev • Am / Rest
- ☐ POA — General / Limited • Durable / Springing
- ☐ POAH — AHCD • Living Will
- ☐ Agreement — Compliance-E&O • Correction
- ☐ Affidavit — Borrower • Occupancy • Ownership • Refi • Survey • Debts & Liens • Name-Signature-ID • Marital • Death • Will
- ☐ Other — Vehicle Title • Safe Deposit Box

DOC DATE: J F M A M J J A S O N D , ____ | DOC TITLE or TYPE | # OF PAGES | ☐ Inspect/Copy Request | Entry X-Ref #

☐ **SATISFACTORY EVIDENCE** ☐ Driver's License / Passport / State ID / Military / Government / Tribal / Inmate / Other ID **or** ☐ Credible Witness(es)

SIGNER — SIGNER's NAME | ☐ For | ADDRESS | ☐ Non-Public | ☐ Capacity # | ☐ Voluntary | ☐ Proper ID | ISSUED | SIGNATURE | ☐ (oath / affirmation, if any) | ☐ (by Mark)
PHONE C / H / W ____ / ____ | **or** ☐ MISC | | | AGENCY | ☐ CA DMV | ☐ US State Dept | EXPIRES | ➡

CW #1 — #1 WITNESS's NAME | ☐ P/Known | ADDRESS | ☐ Non-Public | ☐ Driver's License ☐ Passport ☐ Other ID # | ISSUED | SIGNATURE | ☐ (after oath / affirmation)
PHONE C / H / W ____ / ____ | **or** ☐ MISC | | | AGENCY ☐ CA DMV ☐ US State Dept | EXPIRES | ❶

CW #2 — #2 WITNESS's NAME | ☐ P/Known | ADDRESS | ☐ Non-Public | ☐ Driver's License ☐ Passport ☐ Other ID # | ISSUED | SIGNATURE | ☐ (after oath / affirmation)
PHONE C / H / W ____ / ____ | **or** ☐ MISC | | | AGENCY ☐ CA DMV ☐ US State Dept | EXPIRES | ❷

R T I M R P L — **Fingerprint**

Entry 48

SERVICE — DATE __-__-20__ | TIME __:__ am/pm | ADDRESS | ☐ Signer's ☐ Office | NOTES | ☐ Stop | MILES | Notary $ | ☐ Adv. Travel $ | ☐ Rush $ | ☐ Copy $ | ☐ Other $ | TOTAL FEES $

TYPE: ☐ Acknowledgment ☐ Jurat ☐ Copy Certification ☐ Oath/Affirmation ☐ Oath of Office ☐ Proof of Execution ☐ Protest ☐ Other

DOCUMENT — DOC TYPE:
- ☐ Deed — Grant • Trust Transfer • Gift • Interspousal • Quitclaim • ToD • Warranty
- ☐ DOT — Mortgage • Rev / Irrev • Am / Rest
- ☐ Trust — Certification • Rev / Irrev • Am / Rest
- ☐ POA — General / Limited • Durable / Springing
- ☐ POAH — AHCD • Living Will
- ☐ Agreement — Compliance-E&O • Correction
- ☐ Affidavit — Borrower • Occupancy • Ownership • Refi • Survey • Debts & Liens • Name-Signature-ID • Marital • Death • Will
- ☐ Other — Vehicle Title • Safe Deposit Box

DOC DATE: J F M A M J J A S O N D , ____ | DOC TITLE or TYPE | # OF PAGES | ☐ Inspect/Copy Request | Entry X-Ref #

☐ **SATISFACTORY EVIDENCE** ☐ Driver's License / Passport / State ID / Military / Government / Tribal / Inmate / Other ID **or** ☐ Credible Witness(es)

SIGNER — SIGNER's NAME | ☐ For | ADDRESS | ☐ Non-Public | ☐ Capacity # | ☐ Voluntary | ☐ Proper ID | ISSUED | SIGNATURE | ☐ (oath / affirmation, if any) | ☐ (by Mark)
PHONE C / H / W ____ / ____ | **or** ☐ MISC | | | AGENCY ☐ CA DMV ☐ US State Dept | EXPIRES | ➡

CW #1 — #1 WITNESS's NAME | ☐ P/Known | ADDRESS | ☐ Non-Public | ☐ Driver's License ☐ Passport ☐ Other ID # | ISSUED | SIGNATURE | ☐ (after oath / affirmation)
PHONE C / H / W ____ / ____ | **or** ☐ MISC | | | AGENCY ☐ CA DMV ☐ US State Dept | EXPIRES | ❶

CW #2 — #2 WITNESS's NAME | ☐ P/Known | ADDRESS | ☐ Non-Public | ☐ Driver's License ☐ Passport ☐ Other ID # | ISSUED | SIGNATURE | ☐ (after oath / affirmation)
PHONE C / H / W ____ / ____ | **or** ☐ MISC | | | AGENCY ☐ CA DMV ☐ US State Dept | EXPIRES | ❷

R T I M R P L — **Fingerprint**

NOTARY NAME (printed):   COMMISSION #:

Entry 49

SERVICE — DATE − −20   TIME : am/pm   ADDRESS   ☐ Signer's   ☐ Office   NOTES   ☐ Stop   MILES   Notary ☐ Adv. Travel ☐ Rush ☐ Copy ☐ Other   TOTAL FEES $ $ $ $ $ $ **49**

TYPE   ☐ Acknowledgment   ☐ Jurat   ☐ Copy Certification   ☐ Oath/Affirmation   ☐ Oath of Office   ☐ Proof of Execution   ☐ Protest   ☐ Other   R   **Fingerprint**

DOCUMENT — DOC TYPE   ☐ Deed   ☐ DOT   ☐ Trust   ☐ POA   ☐ POAH   ☐ Agreement   ☐ Affidavit   ☐ Other   T I M R P

Grant • Trust Transfer • Gift   Mortgage   Certification   General / Limited   AHCD   Compliance-E&O   Borrower • Occupancy • Ownership • Refi • Survey   Vehicle Title

Interspousal • Quitclaim • ToD • Warranty   Rev / Irrev • Am / Rest   Durable / Springing   Living Will   Correction   Debts & Liens • Name-Signature-ID • Marital • Death • Will   Safe Deposit Box

DOC DATE   J F M A M J   DOC TITLE or TYPE   # OF PAGES   ☐ Inspect/Copy Request

J A S O N D   ,   Entry X-Ref #

☐ **SATISFACTORY EVIDENCE** ☐ Driver's License / Passport / State ID / Military / Government / Tribal / Inmate / Other ID   *or*   ☐ Credible Witness(es)   L

SIGNER — SIGNER's NAME   ☐ For   ADDRESS   ☐ Non-Public   ☐ Capacity   ☐ Voluntary   ☐ Proper ID   ISSUED   #   SIGNATURE   ☐ *(oath / affirmation, if any)*   ☐ *(by Mark)*

PHONE C / H / W   *or* ☐ MISC   /   AGENCY   ☐ CA DMV   ☐ US State Dept   EXPIRES   ➡

CW #1 — #1 WITNESS's NAME   ☐ P/Known   ADDRESS   ☐ Non-Public   ☐ Driver's License   ☐ Passport   ☐ Other ID   ISSUED   #   SIGNATURE   ☐ *(after oath / affirmation)*

PHONE C / H / W   *or* ☐ MISC   /   AGENCY   ☐ CA DMV   ☐ US State Dept   EXPIRES   ❶

CW #2 — #2 WITNESS's NAME   ☐ P/Known   ADDRESS   ☐ Non-Public   ☐ Driver's License   ☐ Passport   ☐ Other ID   ISSUED   #   SIGNATURE   ☐ *(after oath / affirmation)*

PHONE C / H / W   *or* ☐ MISC   /   AGENCY   ☐ CA DMV   ☐ US State Dept   EXPIRES   ❷

Entry 50

SERVICE — DATE − −20   TIME : am/pm   ADDRESS   ☐ Signer's   ☐ Office   NOTES   ☐ Stop   MILES   Notary ☐ Adv. Travel ☐ Rush ☐ Copy ☐ Other   TOTAL FEES $ $ $ $ $ $ **50**

TYPE   ☐ Acknowledgment   ☐ Jurat   ☐ Copy Certification   ☐ Oath/Affirmation   ☐ Oath of Office   ☐ Proof of Execution   ☐ Protest   ☐ Other   R   **Fingerprint**

DOCUMENT — DOC TYPE   ☐ Deed   ☐ DOT   ☐ Trust   ☐ POA   ☐ POAH   ☐ Agreement   ☐ Affidavit   ☐ Other   T I M R P

Grant • Trust Transfer • Gift   Mortgage   Certification   General / Limited   AHCD   Compliance-E&O   Borrower • Occupancy • Ownership • Refi • Survey   Vehicle Title

Interspousal • Quitclaim • ToD • Warranty   Rev / Irrev • Am / Rest   Durable / Springing   Living Will   Correction   Debts & Liens • Name-Signature-ID • Marital • Death • Will   Safe Deposit Box

DOC DATE   J F M A M J   DOC TITLE or TYPE   # OF PAGES   ☐ Inspect/Copy Request

J A S O N D   ,   Entry X-Ref #

☐ **SATISFACTORY EVIDENCE** ☐ Driver's License / Passport / State ID / Military / Government / Tribal / Inmate / Other ID   *or*   ☐ Credible Witness(es)   L

SIGNER — SIGNER's NAME   ☐ For   ADDRESS   ☐ Non-Public   ☐ Capacity   ☐ Voluntary   ☐ Proper ID   ISSUED   #   SIGNATURE   ☐ *(oath / affirmation, if any)*   ☐ *(by Mark)*

PHONE C / H / W   *or* ☐ MISC   /   AGENCY   ☐ CA DMV   ☐ US State Dept   EXPIRES   ➡

CW #1 — #1 WITNESS's NAME   ☐ P/Known   ADDRESS   ☐ Non-Public   ☐ Driver's License   ☐ Passport   ☐ Other ID   ISSUED   #   SIGNATURE   ☐ *(after oath / affirmation)*

PHONE C / H / W   *or* ☐ MISC   /   AGENCY   ☐ CA DMV   ☐ US State Dept   EXPIRES   ❶

CW #2 — #2 WITNESS's NAME   ☐ P/Known   ADDRESS   ☐ Non-Public   ☐ Driver's License   ☐ Passport   ☐ Other ID   ISSUED   #   SIGNATURE   ☐ *(after oath / affirmation)*

PHONE C / H / W   *or* ☐ MISC   /   AGENCY   ☐ CA DMV   ☐ US State Dept   EXPIRES   ❷

NOTARY NAME (printed): _____ **COMMISSION #:** _____

Entry 51

| SERVICE | DATE __-__-20__ | TIME __:__ am/pm | ADDRESS ☐ Signer's ☐ Office | NOTES | ☐ Stop MILES | Notary $ | ☐ Adv. Travel $ | ☐ Rush $ | ☐ Copy $ | ☐ Other $ | TOTAL FEES $ |

TYPE: ☐ Acknowledgment ☐ Jurat ☐ Copy Certification ☐ Oath/Affirmation ☐ Oath of Office ☐ Proof of Execution ☐ Protest ☐ Other

Fingerprint — R T I M R P L

DOCUMENT
DOC TYPE: ☐ Deed (Grant • Trust Transfer • Gift • Interspousal • Quitclaim • ToD • Warranty) ☐ DOT (Mortgage) ☐ Trust (Certification • Rev / Irrev • Am / Rest) ☐ POA (General / Limited • Durable / Springing) ☐ POAH (AHCD • Living Will) ☐ Agreement (Compliance-E&O • Correction) ☐ Affidavit (Borrower • Occupancy • Ownership • Refi • Survey • Debts & Liens • Name-Signature-ID • Marital • Death • Will) ☐ Other (Vehicle Title • Safe Deposit Box)

DOC DATE: J F M A M J J A S O N D , ____ **DOC TITLE or TYPE:** _____ **# OF PAGES:** ____ ☐ Inspect/Copy Request **Entry X-Ref #:** ____

☐ **SATISFACTORY EVIDENCE** ☐ Driver's License / Passport / State ID / Military / Government / Tribal / Inmate / Other ID **or** ☐ Credible Witness(es)

SIGNER
- SIGNER's NAME ____ ☐ For ADDRESS ____ ☐ Non-Public # ____ ☐ Capacity ☐ Voluntary ☐ Proper ID ISSUED ____ SIGNATURE ____ ☐ (oath / affirmation, if any) ☐ (by Mark)
- PHONE C / H / W ____ / ____ or ☐ MISC AGENCY ____ ☐ CA DMV ☐ US State Dept EXPIRES ____ ➡

CW #1
- #1 WITNESS's NAME ____ ☐ P/Known ADDRESS ____ ☐ Non-Public # ____ ☐ Driver's License ☐ Passport ☐ Other ID ISSUED ____ SIGNATURE ____ ☐ (after oath / affirmation)
- PHONE C / H / W ____ / ____ or ☐ MISC AGENCY ____ ☐ CA DMV ☐ US State Dept EXPIRES ____ ❶

CW #2
- #2 WITNESS's NAME ____ ☐ P/Known ADDRESS ____ ☐ Non-Public # ____ ☐ Driver's License ☐ Passport ☐ Other ID ISSUED ____ SIGNATURE ____ ☐ (after oath / affirmation)
- PHONE C / H / W ____ / ____ or ☐ MISC AGENCY ____ ☐ CA DMV ☐ US State Dept EXPIRES ____ ❷

Entry 52

| SERVICE | DATE __-__-20__ | TIME __:__ am/pm | ADDRESS ☐ Signer's ☐ Office | NOTES | ☐ Stop MILES | Notary $ | ☐ Adv. Travel $ | ☐ Rush $ | ☐ Copy $ | ☐ Other $ | TOTAL FEES $ |

TYPE: ☐ Acknowledgment ☐ Jurat ☐ Copy Certification ☐ Oath/Affirmation ☐ Oath of Office ☐ Proof of Execution ☐ Protest ☐ Other

Fingerprint — R T I M R P L

DOCUMENT
DOC TYPE: ☐ Deed (Grant • Trust Transfer • Gift • Interspousal • Quitclaim • ToD • Warranty) ☐ DOT (Mortgage) ☐ Trust (Certification • Rev / Irrev • Am / Rest) ☐ POA (General / Limited • Durable / Springing) ☐ POAH (AHCD • Living Will) ☐ Agreement (Compliance-E&O • Correction) ☐ Affidavit (Borrower • Occupancy • Ownership • Refi • Survey • Debts & Liens • Name-Signature-ID • Marital • Death • Will) ☐ Other (Vehicle Title • Safe Deposit Box)

DOC DATE: J F M A M J J A S O N D , ____ **DOC TITLE or TYPE:** _____ **# OF PAGES:** ____ ☐ Inspect/Copy Request **Entry X-Ref #:** ____

☐ **SATISFACTORY EVIDENCE** ☐ Driver's License / Passport / State ID / Military / Government / Tribal / Inmate / Other ID **or** ☐ Credible Witness(es)

SIGNER
- SIGNER's NAME ____ ☐ For ADDRESS ____ ☐ Non-Public # ____ ☐ Capacity ☐ Voluntary ☐ Proper ID ISSUED ____ SIGNATURE ____ ☐ (oath / affirmation, if any) ☐ (by Mark)
- PHONE C / H / W ____ / ____ or ☐ MISC AGENCY ____ ☐ CA DMV ☐ US State Dept EXPIRES ____ ➡

CW #1
- #1 WITNESS's NAME ____ ☐ P/Known ADDRESS ____ ☐ Non-Public # ____ ☐ Driver's License ☐ Passport ☐ Other ID ISSUED ____ SIGNATURE ____ ☐ (after oath / affirmation)
- PHONE C / H / W ____ / ____ or ☐ MISC AGENCY ____ ☐ CA DMV ☐ US State Dept EXPIRES ____ ❶

CW #2
- #2 WITNESS's NAME ____ ☐ P/Known ADDRESS ____ ☐ Non-Public # ____ ☐ Driver's License ☐ Passport ☐ Other ID ISSUED ____ SIGNATURE ____ ☐ (after oath / affirmation)
- PHONE C / H / W ____ / ____ or ☐ MISC AGENCY ____ ☐ CA DMV ☐ US State Dept EXPIRES ____ ❷

NOTARY NAME (printed):   COMMISSION #:

53

SERVICE

DATE	TIME	am	ADDRESS	☐ Signer's	☐ Office	NOTES	☐ Stop	MILES	Notary	☐ Adv. Travel	☐ Rush	☐ Copy	☐ Other	TOTAL FEES
- -20	:	pm							$	$		$	$	$	$

TYPE ☐ Acknowledgment ☐ Jurat ☐ Copy Certification ☐ Oath/Affirmation ☐ Oath of Office ☐ Proof of Execution ☐ Protest ☐ Other

R Fingerprint

DOCUMENT

DOC TYPE ☐ Deed ☐ DOT ☐ Trust ☐ POA ☐ POAH ☐ Agreement ☐ Affidavit ☐ Other
Grant • Trust Transfer • Gift | Mortgage | Certification | General / Limited | AHCD | Compliance-E&O | Borrower • Occupancy • Ownership • Refi • Survey | Vehicle Title
Interspousal • Quitclaim • ToD • Warranty | Rev / Irrev • Am / Rest | Durable / Springing | Living Will | Correction | Debts & Liens • Name-Signature-ID • Marital • Death • Will | Safe Deposit Box

DOC DATE J F M A M J   DOC TITLE or TYPE   # OF PAGES ☐ Inspect/Copy Request
       J A S O N D   ,   Entry X-Ref #

T I M R P

☐ **SATISFACTORY EVIDENCE** ☐ Driver's License / Passport / State ID / Military / Government / Tribal / Inmate / Other ID **or** ☐ Credible Witness(es)   L

SIGNER

SIGNER's NAME   ☐ For   ADDRESS   ☐ Non-Public ☐ Capacity ☐ Voluntary ☐ Proper ID ISSUED   SIGNATURE ☐ (oath / affirmation, if any) ☐ (by Mark)
                                                 #

PHONE C / H / W   or ☐ MISC   AGENCY   ☐ CA DMV   ☐ US State Dept   EXPIRES   ➡
     /

CW #1

#1 WITNESS's NAME   ☐ P/Known   ADDRESS   ☐ Non-Public ☐ Driver's License ☐ Passport ☐ Other ID ISSUED   SIGNATURE ☐ (after oath / affirmation)
                                                 #

PHONE C / H / W   or ☐ MISC   AGENCY   ☐ CA DMV   ☐ US State Dept   EXPIRES   ❶
     /

CW #2

#2 WITNESS's NAME   ☐ P/Known   ADDRESS   ☐ Non-Public ☐ Driver's License ☐ Passport ☐ Other ID ISSUED   SIGNATURE ☐ (after oath / affirmation)
                                                 #

PHONE C / H / W   or ☐ MISC   AGENCY   ☐ CA DMV   ☐ US State Dept   EXPIRES   ❷
     /

54

SERVICE

DATE	TIME	am	ADDRESS	☐ Signer's	☐ Office	NOTES	☐ Stop	MILES	Notary	☐ Adv. Travel	☐ Rush	☐ Copy	☐ Other	TOTAL FEES
- -20	:	pm							$	$		$	$	$	$

TYPE ☐ Acknowledgment ☐ Jurat ☐ Copy Certification ☐ Oath/Affirmation ☐ Oath of Office ☐ Proof of Execution ☐ Protest ☐ Other

R Fingerprint

DOCUMENT

DOC TYPE ☐ Deed ☐ DOT ☐ Trust ☐ POA ☐ POAH ☐ Agreement ☐ Affidavit ☐ Other
Grant • Trust Transfer • Gift | Mortgage | Certification | General / Limited | AHCD | Compliance-E&O | Borrower • Occupancy • Ownership • Refi • Survey | Vehicle Title
Interspousal • Quitclaim • ToD • Warranty | Rev / Irrev • Am / Rest | Durable / Springing | Living Will | Correction | Debts & Liens • Name-Signature-ID • Marital • Death • Will | Safe Deposit Box

DOC DATE J F M A M J   DOC TITLE or TYPE   # OF PAGES ☐ Inspect/Copy Request
       J A S O N D   ,   Entry X-Ref #

T I M R P

☐ **SATISFACTORY EVIDENCE** ☐ Driver's License / Passport / State ID / Military / Government / Tribal / Inmate / Other ID **or** ☐ Credible Witness(es)   L

SIGNER

SIGNER's NAME   ☐ For   ADDRESS   ☐ Non-Public ☐ Capacity ☐ Voluntary ☐ Proper ID ISSUED   SIGNATURE ☐ (oath / affirmation, if any) ☐ (by Mark)
                                                 #

PHONE C / H / W   or ☐ MISC   AGENCY   ☐ CA DMV   ☐ US State Dept   EXPIRES   ➡
     /

CW #1

#1 WITNESS's NAME   ☐ P/Known   ADDRESS   ☐ Non-Public ☐ Driver's License ☐ Passport ☐ Other ID ISSUED   SIGNATURE ☐ (after oath / affirmation)
                                                 #

PHONE C / H / W   or ☐ MISC   AGENCY   ☐ CA DMV   ☐ US State Dept   EXPIRES   ❶
     /

CW #2

#2 WITNESS's NAME   ☐ P/Known   ADDRESS   ☐ Non-Public ☐ Driver's License ☐ Passport ☐ Other ID ISSUED   SIGNATURE ☐ (after oath / affirmation)
                                                 #

PHONE C / H / W   or ☐ MISC   AGENCY   ☐ CA DMV   ☐ US State Dept   EXPIRES   ❷
     /

NOTARY NAME (printed): _____   COMMISSION #: _____

Entry 55

SERVICE — DATE: __-__-20__ TIME: __:__ am/pm ADDRESS: _____ ☐ Signer's ☐ Office NOTES: _____ ☐ Stop MILES: ___ Notary $___ Adv. Travel $___ ☐ Rush $___ ☐ Copy $___ ☐ Other $___ TOTAL FEES $___

TYPE: ☐ Acknowledgment ☐ Jurat ☐ Copy Certification ☐ Oath/Affirmation ☐ Oath of Office ☐ Proof of Execution ☐ Protest ☐ Other

DOCUMENT — DOC TYPE:
- ☐ Deed — Grant • Trust Transfer • Gift • Interspousal • Quitclaim • ToD • Warranty
- ☐ DOT — Mortgage • Rev / Irrev • Am / Rest
- ☐ Trust — Certification
- ☐ POA — General / Limited • Durable / Springing
- ☐ POAH — AHCD • Living Will
- ☐ Agreement — Compliance-E&O • Correction
- ☐ Affidavit — Borrower • Occupancy • Ownership • Refi • Survey • Debts & Liens • Name-Signature-ID • Marital • Death • Will
- ☐ Other — Vehicle Title • Safe Deposit Box

DOC DATE: J F M A M J J A S O N D , ____   DOC TITLE or TYPE: _____   # OF PAGES: ___   ☐ Inspect/Copy Request   Entry X-Ref #: ___

☐ **SATISFACTORY EVIDENCE** ☐ Driver's License / Passport / State ID / Military / Government / Tribal / Inmate / Other ID *or* ☐ Credible Witness(es)

SIGNER — SIGNER's NAME: _____ ☐ For ADDRESS: _____ ☐ Non-Public ☐ Capacity ☐ Voluntary ☐ Proper ID ISSUED: ___ SIGNATURE ☐ (oath / affirmation, if any) ☐ (by Mark)
PHONE C / H / W: ___/___ *or* ☐ MISC: ___ #: ___ AGENCY: ___ ☐ CA DMV ☐ US State Dept EXPIRES: ___ ➡

CW #1 — #1 WITNESS's NAME: _____ ☐ P/Known ADDRESS: _____ ☐ Non-Public ☐ Driver's License ☐ Passport ☐ Other ID ISSUED: ___ SIGNATURE ☐ (after oath / affirmation)
PHONE C / H / W: ___/___ *or* ☐ MISC: ___ #: ___ AGENCY: ___ ☐ CA DMV ☐ US State Dept EXPIRES: ___ ❶

CW #2 — #2 WITNESS's NAME: _____ ☐ P/Known ADDRESS: _____ ☐ Non-Public ☐ Driver's License ☐ Passport ☐ Other ID ISSUED: ___ SIGNATURE ☐ (after oath / affirmation)
PHONE C / H / W: ___/___ *or* ☐ MISC: ___ #: ___ AGENCY: ___ ☐ CA DMV ☐ US State Dept EXPIRES: ___ ❷

Fingerprint — R T I M R P L

Entry 56

SERVICE — DATE: __-__-20__ TIME: __:__ am/pm ADDRESS: _____ ☐ Signer's ☐ Office NOTES: _____ ☐ Stop MILES: ___ Notary $___ Adv. Travel $___ ☐ Rush $___ ☐ Copy $___ ☐ Other $___ TOTAL FEES $___

TYPE: ☐ Acknowledgment ☐ Jurat ☐ Copy Certification ☐ Oath/Affirmation ☐ Oath of Office ☐ Proof of Execution ☐ Protest ☐ Other

DOCUMENT — DOC TYPE:
- ☐ Deed — Grant • Trust Transfer • Gift • Interspousal • Quitclaim • ToD • Warranty
- ☐ DOT — Mortgage • Rev / Irrev • Am / Rest
- ☐ Trust — Certification
- ☐ POA — General / Limited • Durable / Springing
- ☐ POAH — AHCD • Living Will
- ☐ Agreement — Compliance-E&O • Correction
- ☐ Affidavit — Borrower • Occupancy • Ownership • Refi • Survey • Debts & Liens • Name-Signature-ID • Marital • Death • Will
- ☐ Other — Vehicle Title • Safe Deposit Box

DOC DATE: J F M A M J J A S O N D , ____   DOC TITLE or TYPE: _____   # OF PAGES: ___   ☐ Inspect/Copy Request   Entry X-Ref #: ___

☐ **SATISFACTORY EVIDENCE** ☐ Driver's License / Passport / State ID / Military / Government / Tribal / Inmate / Other ID *or* ☐ Credible Witness(es)

SIGNER — SIGNER's NAME: _____ ☐ For ADDRESS: _____ ☐ Non-Public ☐ Capacity ☐ Voluntary ☐ Proper ID ISSUED: ___ SIGNATURE ☐ (oath / affirmation, if any) ☐ (by Mark)
PHONE C / H / W: ___/___ *or* ☐ MISC: ___ #: ___ AGENCY: ___ ☐ CA DMV ☐ US State Dept EXPIRES: ___ ➡

CW #1 — #1 WITNESS's NAME: _____ ☐ P/Known ADDRESS: _____ ☐ Non-Public ☐ Driver's License ☐ Passport ☐ Other ID ISSUED: ___ SIGNATURE ☐ (after oath / affirmation)
PHONE C / H / W: ___/___ *or* ☐ MISC: ___ #: ___ AGENCY: ___ ☐ CA DMV ☐ US State Dept EXPIRES: ___ ❶

CW #2 — #2 WITNESS's NAME: _____ ☐ P/Known ADDRESS: _____ ☐ Non-Public ☐ Driver's License ☐ Passport ☐ Other ID ISSUED: ___ SIGNATURE ☐ (after oath / affirmation)
PHONE C / H / W: ___/___ *or* ☐ MISC: ___ #: ___ AGENCY: ___ ☐ CA DMV ☐ US State Dept EXPIRES: ___ ❷

Fingerprint — R T I M R P L

NOTARY NAME (printed): _____   COMMISSION #: _____

Entry 57

| SERVICE | DATE __ - __ -20__ | TIME __:__ ☐am ☐pm | ADDRESS ☐ Signer's ☐ Office | NOTES | ☐ Stop | MILES | Notary $ | ☐ Adv. Travel $ | ☐ Rush $ | ☐ Copy $ | ☐ Other $ | TOTAL FEES $ | **57** |

TYPE: ☐ Acknowledgment ☐ Jurat ☐ Copy Certification ☐ Oath/Affirmation ☐ Oath of Office ☐ Proof of Execution ☐ Protest ☐ Other

Fingerprint   R T I M R P L

DOCUMENT

DOC TYPE	☐ Deed	☐ DOT	☐ Trust	☐ POA	☐ POAH	☐ Agreement		☐ Affidavit	☐ Other
	Grant • Trust Transfer • Gift	Mortgage	Certification	General / Limited	AHCD	Compliance-E&O	Borrower • Occupancy • Ownership • Refi • Survey		Vehicle Title
	Interspousal • Quitclaim • ToD • Warranty	Rev / Irrev • Am / Rest	Durable / Springing	Living Will		Correction	Debts & Liens • Name-Signature-ID • Marital • Death • Will		Safe Deposit Box

DOC DATE J F M A M J J A S O N D , ____   DOC TITLE or TYPE ____   # OF PAGES ____ ☐ Inspect/Copy Request   Entry X-Ref # ____

☐ **SATISFACTORY EVIDENCE** ☐ Driver's License / Passport / State ID / Military / Government / Tribal / Inmate / Other ID   **or**   ☐ Credible Witness(es)

SIGNER

| SIGNER's NAME | ☐ For | ADDRESS | ☐ Non-Public | ☐ Capacity | ☐ Voluntary | ☐ Proper ID | ISSUED # | SIGNATURE ☐ (oath / affirmation, if any) ☐ (by Mark) |
| PHONE C / H / W ____ / ____ | or ☐ MISC | | | AGENCY | ☐ CA DMV | ☐ US State Dept | EXPIRES | ➤ |

CW #1

| #1 WITNESS's NAME | ☐ P/Known | ADDRESS | ☐ Non-Public | ☐ Driver's License | ☐ Passport | ☐ Other ID | ISSUED # | SIGNATURE ☐ (after oath / affirmation) |
| PHONE C / H / W ____ / ____ | or ☐ MISC | | | AGENCY | ☐ CA DMV | ☐ US State Dept | EXPIRES | ❶ |

CW #2

| #2 WITNESS's NAME | ☐ P/Known | ADDRESS | ☐ Non-Public | ☐ Driver's License | ☐ Passport | ☐ Other ID | ISSUED # | SIGNATURE ☐ (after oath / affirmation) |
| PHONE C / H / W ____ / ____ | or ☐ MISC | | | AGENCY | ☐ CA DMV | ☐ US State Dept | EXPIRES | ❷ |

Entry 58

| SERVICE | DATE __ - __ -20__ | TIME __:__ ☐am ☐pm | ADDRESS ☐ Signer's ☐ Office | NOTES | ☐ Stop | MILES | Notary $ | ☐ Adv. Travel $ | ☐ Rush $ | ☐ Copy $ | ☐ Other $ | TOTAL FEES $ | **58** |

TYPE: ☐ Acknowledgment ☐ Jurat ☐ Copy Certification ☐ Oath/Affirmation ☐ Oath of Office ☐ Proof of Execution ☐ Protest ☐ Other

Fingerprint   R T I M R P L

DOCUMENT

DOC TYPE	☐ Deed	☐ DOT	☐ Trust	☐ POA	☐ POAH	☐ Agreement		☐ Affidavit	☐ Other
	Grant • Trust Transfer • Gift	Mortgage	Certification	General / Limited	AHCD	Compliance-E&O	Borrower • Occupancy • Ownership • Refi • Survey		Vehicle Title
	Interspousal • Quitclaim • ToD • Warranty	Rev / Irrev • Am / Rest	Durable / Springing	Living Will		Correction	Debts & Liens • Name-Signature-ID • Marital • Death • Will		Safe Deposit Box

DOC DATE J F M A M J J A S O N D , ____   DOC TITLE or TYPE ____   # OF PAGES ____ ☐ Inspect/Copy Request   Entry X-Ref # ____

☐ **SATISFACTORY EVIDENCE** ☐ Driver's License / Passport / State ID / Military / Government / Tribal / Inmate / Other ID   **or**   ☐ Credible Witness(es)

SIGNER

| SIGNER's NAME | ☐ For | ADDRESS | ☐ Non-Public | ☐ Capacity | ☐ Voluntary | ☐ Proper ID | ISSUED # | SIGNATURE ☐ (oath / affirmation, if any) ☐ (by Mark) |
| PHONE C / H / W ____ / ____ | or ☐ MISC | | | AGENCY | ☐ CA DMV | ☐ US State Dept | EXPIRES | ➤ |

CW #1

| #1 WITNESS's NAME | ☐ P/Known | ADDRESS | ☐ Non-Public | ☐ Driver's License | ☐ Passport | ☐ Other ID | ISSUED # | SIGNATURE ☐ (after oath / affirmation) |
| PHONE C / H / W ____ / ____ | or ☐ MISC | | | AGENCY | ☐ CA DMV | ☐ US State Dept | EXPIRES | ❶ |

CW #2

| #2 WITNESS's NAME | ☐ P/Known | ADDRESS | ☐ Non-Public | ☐ Driver's License | ☐ Passport | ☐ Other ID | ISSUED # | SIGNATURE ☐ (after oath / affirmation) |
| PHONE C / H / W ____ / ____ | or ☐ MISC | | | AGENCY | ☐ CA DMV | ☐ US State Dept | EXPIRES | ❷ |

NOTARY NAME (printed):   COMMISSION #:

Entry 59

SERVICE — DATE - -20 | TIME : am/pm | ADDRESS | ☐ Signer's ☐ Office | NOTES | ☐ Stop MILES | Notary $ | ☐ Adv. Travel $ | ☐ Rush $ | ☐ Copy $ | ☐ Other $ | TOTAL FEES $

TYPE: ☐ Acknowledgment ☐ Jurat ☐ Copy Certification ☐ Oath/Affirmation ☐ Oath of Office ☐ Proof of Execution ☐ Protest ☐ Other   **Fingerprint** R

DOCUMENT — DOC TYPE: ☐ Deed ☐ DOT ☐ Trust ☐ POA ☐ POAH ☐ Agreement ☐ Affidavit ☐ Other
Grant • Trust Transfer • Gift | Mortgage | Certification | General / Limited | AHCD | Compliance-E&O | Borrower • Occupancy • Ownership • Refi • Survey | Vehicle Title
Interspousal • Quitclaim • ToD • Warranty | Rev / Irrev • Am / Rest | Durable / Springing | Living Will | Correction | Debts & Liens • Name-Signature-ID • Marital • Death • Will | Safe Deposit Box

DOC DATE: J F M A M J J A S O N D ,   DOC TITLE or TYPE   # OF PAGES   ☐ Inspect/Copy Request   Entry X-Ref #

☐ **SATISFACTORY EVIDENCE** ☐ Driver's License / Passport / State ID / Military / Government / Tribal / Inmate / Other ID   *or*   ☐ Credible Witness(es)   T I M R P L

SIGNER — SIGNER's NAME | ☐ For | ADDRESS | ☐ Non-Public | ☐ Capacity # | ☐ Voluntary | ☐ Proper ID | ISSUED | SIGNATURE ☐ (oath / affirmation, if any) ☐ (by Mark)
PHONE C / H / W / | *or* ☐ MISC | | | AGENCY | ☐ CA DMV | ☐ US State Dept | EXPIRES | ➡

CW #1 — #1 WITNESS's NAME | ☐ P/Known | ADDRESS | ☐ Non-Public | ☐ Driver's License | ☐ Passport | ☐ Other ID | ISSUED | SIGNATURE ☐ (after oath / affirmation)
PHONE C / H / W / | *or* ☐ MISC | | | AGENCY | ☐ CA DMV | ☐ US State Dept | EXPIRES | ❶

CW #2 — #2 WITNESS's NAME | ☐ P/Known | ADDRESS | ☐ Non-Public | ☐ Driver's License | ☐ Passport | ☐ Other ID | ISSUED | SIGNATURE ☐ (after oath / affirmation)
PHONE C / H / W / | *or* ☐ MISC | | | AGENCY | ☐ CA DMV | ☐ US State Dept | EXPIRES | ❷

Entry 60

SERVICE — DATE - -20 | TIME : am/pm | ADDRESS | ☐ Signer's ☐ Office | NOTES | ☐ Stop MILES | Notary $ | ☐ Adv. Travel $ | ☐ Rush $ | ☐ Copy $ | ☐ Other $ | TOTAL FEES $

TYPE: ☐ Acknowledgment ☐ Jurat ☐ Copy Certification ☐ Oath/Affirmation ☐ Oath of Office ☐ Proof of Execution ☐ Protest ☐ Other   **Fingerprint** R

DOCUMENT — DOC TYPE: ☐ Deed ☐ DOT ☐ Trust ☐ POA ☐ POAH ☐ Agreement ☐ Affidavit ☐ Other
Grant • Trust Transfer • Gift | Mortgage | Certification | General / Limited | AHCD | Compliance-E&O | Borrower • Occupancy • Ownership • Refi • Survey | Vehicle Title
Interspousal • Quitclaim • ToD • Warranty | Rev / Irrev • Am / Rest | Durable / Springing | Living Will | Correction | Debts & Liens • Name-Signature-ID • Marital • Death • Will | Safe Deposit Box

DOC DATE: J F M A M J J A S O N D ,   DOC TITLE or TYPE   # OF PAGES   ☐ Inspect/Copy Request   Entry X-Ref #

☐ **SATISFACTORY EVIDENCE** ☐ Driver's License / Passport / State ID / Military / Government / Tribal / Inmate / Other ID   *or*   ☐ Credible Witness(es)   T I M R P L

SIGNER — SIGNER's NAME | ☐ For | ADDRESS | ☐ Non-Public | ☐ Capacity # | ☐ Voluntary | ☐ Proper ID | ISSUED | SIGNATURE ☐ (oath / affirmation, if any) ☐ (by Mark)
PHONE C / H / W / | *or* ☐ MISC | | | AGENCY | ☐ CA DMV | ☐ US State Dept | EXPIRES | ➡

CW #1 — #1 WITNESS's NAME | ☐ P/Known | ADDRESS | ☐ Non-Public | ☐ Driver's License | ☐ Passport | ☐ Other ID | ISSUED | SIGNATURE ☐ (after oath / affirmation)
PHONE C / H / W / | *or* ☐ MISC | | | AGENCY | ☐ CA DMV | ☐ US State Dept | EXPIRES | ❶

CW #2 — #2 WITNESS's NAME | ☐ P/Known | ADDRESS | ☐ Non-Public | ☐ Driver's License | ☐ Passport | ☐ Other ID | ISSUED | SIGNATURE ☐ (after oath / affirmation)
PHONE C / H / W / | *or* ☐ MISC | | | AGENCY | ☐ CA DMV | ☐ US State Dept | EXPIRES | ❷

NOTARY NAME (printed):   COMMISSION #:

61

SERVICE

DATE	TIME	am	ADDRESS	☐ Signer's	☐ Office	NOTES	☐ Stop	MILES	Notary	☐ Adv. Travel	☐ Rush	☐ Copy	☐ Other	TOTAL FEES
- -20	:	pm							$	$	$	$	$	$

TYPE   ☐ Acknowledgment   ☐ Jurat   ☐ Copy Certification   ☐ Oath/Affirmation   ☐ Oath of Office   ☐ Proof of Execution   ☐ Protest   ☐ Other

R   **Fingerprint**

DOCUMENT

DOC TYPE   ☐ Deed   ☐ DOT   ☐ Trust   ☐ POA   ☐ POAH   ☐ Agreement   ☐ Affidavit   ☐ Other

Grant • Trust Transfer • Gift   Mortgage   Certification   General / Limited   AHCD   Compliance-E&O   Borrower • Occupancy • Ownership • Refi • Survey   Vehicle Title

Interspousal • Quitclaim • ToD • Warranty   Rev / Irrev • Am / Rest   Durable / Springing   Living Will   Correction   Debts & Liens • Name-Signature-ID • Marital • Death • Will   Safe Deposit Box

T I M R P

DOC DATE J F M A M J J A S O N D ,	DOC TITLE or TYPE	# OF PAGES	☐ Inspect/Copy Request
			Entry X-Ref #

L

☐ **SATISFACTORY EVIDENCE**   ☐ Driver's License / Passport / State ID / Military / Government / Tribal / Inmate / Other ID   *or*   ☐ Credible Witness(es)

SIGNER

SIGNER's NAME	☐ For	ADDRESS	☐ Non-Public	☐ Capacity	☐ Voluntary	☐ Proper ID	ISSUED	SIGNATURE	☐ (oath / affirmation, if any)	☐ (by Mark)
				#						
PHONE C / H / W *or* ☐ MISC				AGENCY	☐ CA DMV	☐ US State Dept	EXPIRES	➡		
/										

CW #1

#1 WITNESS's NAME	☐ P/Known	ADDRESS	☐ Non-Public	☐ Driver's License	☐ Passport	☐ Other ID	ISSUED	SIGNATURE	☐ (after oath / affirmation)
				#					
PHONE C / H / W *or* ☐ MISC				AGENCY	☐ CA DMV	☐ US State Dept	EXPIRES	❶	
/									

CW #2

#2 WITNESS's NAME	☐ P/Known	ADDRESS	☐ Non-Public	☐ Driver's License	☐ Passport	☐ Other ID	ISSUED	SIGNATURE	☐ (after oath / affirmation)
				#					
PHONE C / H / W *or* ☐ MISC				AGENCY	☐ CA DMV	☐ US State Dept	EXPIRES	❷	
/									

62

SERVICE

DATE	TIME	am	ADDRESS	☐ Signer's	☐ Office	NOTES	☐ Stop	MILES	Notary	☐ Adv. Travel	☐ Rush	☐ Copy	☐ Other	TOTAL FEES
- -20	:	pm							$	$	$	$	$	$

TYPE   ☐ Acknowledgment   ☐ Jurat   ☐ Copy Certification   ☐ Oath/Affirmation   ☐ Oath of Office   ☐ Proof of Execution   ☐ Protest   ☐ Other

R   **Fingerprint**

DOCUMENT

DOC TYPE   ☐ Deed   ☐ DOT   ☐ Trust   ☐ POA   ☐ POAH   ☐ Agreement   ☐ Affidavit   ☐ Other

Grant • Trust Transfer • Gift   Mortgage   Certification   General / Limited   AHCD   Compliance-E&O   Borrower • Occupancy • Ownership • Refi • Survey   Vehicle Title

Interspousal • Quitclaim • ToD • Warranty   Rev / Irrev • Am / Rest   Durable / Springing   Living Will   Correction   Debts & Liens • Name-Signature-ID • Marital • Death • Will   Safe Deposit Box

T I M R P

DOC DATE J F M A M J J A S O N D ,	DOC TITLE or TYPE	# OF PAGES	☐ Inspect/Copy Request
			Entry X-Ref #

L

☐ **SATISFACTORY EVIDENCE**   ☐ Driver's License / Passport / State ID / Military / Government / Tribal / Inmate / Other ID   *or*   ☐ Credible Witness(es)

SIGNER

SIGNER's NAME	☐ For	ADDRESS	☐ Non-Public	☐ Capacity	☐ Voluntary	☐ Proper ID	ISSUED	SIGNATURE	☐ (oath / affirmation, if any)	☐ (by Mark)
				#						
PHONE C / H / W *or* ☐ MISC				AGENCY	☐ CA DMV	☐ US State Dept	EXPIRES	➡		
/										

CW #1

#1 WITNESS's NAME	☐ P/Known	ADDRESS	☐ Non-Public	☐ Driver's License	☐ Passport	☐ Other ID	ISSUED	SIGNATURE	☐ (after oath / affirmation)
				#					
PHONE C / H / W *or* ☐ MISC				AGENCY	☐ CA DMV	☐ US State Dept	EXPIRES	❶	
/									

CW #2

#2 WITNESS's NAME	☐ P/Known	ADDRESS	☐ Non-Public	☐ Driver's License	☐ Passport	☐ Other ID	ISSUED	SIGNATURE	☐ (after oath / affirmation)
				#					
PHONE C / H / W *or* ☐ MISC				AGENCY	☐ CA DMV	☐ US State Dept	EXPIRES	❷	
/									

NOTARY NAME (printed): COMMISSION #:

Entry 63

SERVICE — DATE: - -20 TIME: : am/pm ADDRESS ☐ Signer's ☐ Office NOTES ☐ Stop MILES Notary $ ☐ Adv. Travel $ ☐ Rush $ ☐ Copy $ ☐ Other $ TOTAL FEES $

TYPE ☐ Acknowledgment ☐ Jurat ☐ Copy Certification ☐ Oath/Affirmation ☐ Oath of Office ☐ Proof of Execution ☐ Protest ☐ Other

Fingerprint R T I M R P L

DOCUMENT
DOC TYPE ☐ Deed ☐ DOT ☐ Trust ☐ POA ☐ POAH ☐ Agreement ☐ Affidavit ☐ Other
Grant • Trust Transfer • Gift | Mortgage | Certification | General / Limited | AHCD | Compliance-E&O | Borrower • Occupancy • Ownership • Refi • Survey | Vehicle Title
Interspousal • Quitclaim • ToD • Warranty | Rev / Irrev • Am / Rest | Durable / Springing | Living Will | Correction | Debts & Liens • Name-Signature-ID • Marital • Death • Will | Safe Deposit Box

DOC DATE J F M A M J J A S O N D , DOC TITLE or TYPE   # OF PAGES ☐ Inspect/Copy Request Entry X-Ref #

☐ **SATISFACTORY EVIDENCE** ☐ Driver's License / Passport / State ID / Military / Government / Tribal / Inmate / Other ID *or* ☐ Credible Witness(es)

SIGNER
SIGNER's NAME ☐ For ADDRESS ☐ Non-Public ☐ Capacity ☐ Voluntary ☐ Proper ID ISSUED # SIGNATURE ☐ (oath / affirmation, if any) ☐ (by Mark)
PHONE C / H / W / *or* ☐ MISC AGENCY ☐ CA DMV ☐ US State Dept EXPIRES ➤

CW #1
#1 WITNESS's NAME ☐ P/Known ADDRESS ☐ Non-Public ☐ Driver's License ☐ Passport ☐ Other ID ISSUED # SIGNATURE ☐ (after oath / affirmation)
PHONE C / H / W / *or* ☐ MISC AGENCY ☐ CA DMV ☐ US State Dept EXPIRES ❶

CW #2
#2 WITNESS's NAME ☐ P/Known ADDRESS ☐ Non-Public ☐ Driver's License ☐ Passport ☐ Other ID ISSUED # SIGNATURE ☐ (after oath / affirmation)
PHONE C / H / W / *or* ☐ MISC AGENCY ☐ CA DMV ☐ US State Dept EXPIRES ❷

Entry 64

SERVICE — DATE: - -20 TIME: : am/pm ADDRESS ☐ Signer's ☐ Office NOTES ☐ Stop MILES Notary $ ☐ Adv. Travel $ ☐ Rush $ ☐ Copy $ ☐ Other $ TOTAL FEES $

TYPE ☐ Acknowledgment ☐ Jurat ☐ Copy Certification ☐ Oath/Affirmation ☐ Oath of Office ☐ Proof of Execution ☐ Protest ☐ Other

Fingerprint R T I M R P L

DOCUMENT
DOC TYPE ☐ Deed ☐ DOT ☐ Trust ☐ POA ☐ POAH ☐ Agreement ☐ Affidavit ☐ Other
Grant • Trust Transfer • Gift | Mortgage | Certification | General / Limited | AHCD | Compliance-E&O | Borrower • Occupancy • Ownership • Refi • Survey | Vehicle Title
Interspousal • Quitclaim • ToD • Warranty | Rev / Irrev • Am / Rest | Durable / Springing | Living Will | Correction | Debts & Liens • Name-Signature-ID • Marital • Death • Will | Safe Deposit Box

DOC DATE J F M A M J J A S O N D , DOC TITLE or TYPE   # OF PAGES ☐ Inspect/Copy Request Entry X-Ref #

☐ **SATISFACTORY EVIDENCE** ☐ Driver's License / Passport / State ID / Military / Government / Tribal / Inmate / Other ID *or* ☐ Credible Witness(es)

SIGNER
SIGNER's NAME ☐ For ADDRESS ☐ Non-Public ☐ Capacity ☐ Voluntary ☐ Proper ID ISSUED # SIGNATURE ☐ (oath / affirmation, if any) ☐ (by Mark)
PHONE C / H / W / *or* ☐ MISC AGENCY ☐ CA DMV ☐ US State Dept EXPIRES ➤

CW #1
#1 WITNESS's NAME ☐ P/Known ADDRESS ☐ Non-Public ☐ Driver's License ☐ Passport ☐ Other ID ISSUED # SIGNATURE ☐ (after oath / affirmation)
PHONE C / H / W / *or* ☐ MISC AGENCY ☐ CA DMV ☐ US State Dept EXPIRES ❶

CW #2
#2 WITNESS's NAME ☐ P/Known ADDRESS ☐ Non-Public ☐ Driver's License ☐ Passport ☐ Other ID ISSUED # SIGNATURE ☐ (after oath / affirmation)
PHONE C / H / W / *or* ☐ MISC AGENCY ☐ CA DMV ☐ US State Dept EXPIRES ❷

NOTARY NAME (printed):   COMMISSION #:

Entry 65

SERVICE

DATE - -20   TIME : am/pm   ADDRESS ☐ Signer's ☐ Office   NOTES   ☐ Stop   MILES   Notary ☐ Adv. Travel ☐ Rush ☐ Copy ☐ Other   TOTAL FEES $ $ $ $ $ $

TYPE ☐ Acknowledgment ☐ Jurat ☐ Copy Certification ☐ Oath/Affirmation ☐ Oath of Office ☐ Proof of Execution ☐ Protest ☐ Other

R T I M R P L   **Fingerprint**

DOCUMENT

DOC TYPE	☐ Deed	☐ DOT	☐ Trust	☐ POA	☐ POAH	☐ Agreement		☐ Affidavit	☐ Other
	Grant • Trust Transfer • Gift	Mortgage	Certification	General / Limited	AHCD	Compliance-E&O	Borrower • Occupancy • Ownership • Refi • Survey		Vehicle Title
	Interspousal • Quitclaim • ToD • Warranty	Rev / Irrev • Am / Rest	Durable / Springing	Living Will		Correction	Debts & Liens • Name-Signature-ID • Marital • Death • Will		Safe Deposit Box

DOC DATE J F M A M J J A S O N D ,   DOC TITLE or TYPE   # OF PAGES ☐ Inspect/Copy Request   Entry X-Ref #

☐ **SATISFACTORY EVIDENCE** ☐ Driver's License / Passport / State ID / Military / Government / Tribal / Inmate / Other ID   **or**   ☐ Credible Witness(es)

SIGNER

SIGNER's NAME ☐ For   ADDRESS ☐ Non-Public ☐ Capacity ☐ Voluntary ☐ Proper ID   ISSUED #   SIGNATURE ☐ (oath / affirmation, if any) ☐ (by Mark)

PHONE C / H / W   or ☐ MISC   AGENCY ☐ CA DMV ☐ US State Dept   EXPIRES   ➤

CW #1

#1 WITNESS's NAME ☐ P/Known   ADDRESS ☐ Non-Public ☐ Driver's License ☐ Passport ☐ Other ID   ISSUED #   SIGNATURE ☐ (after oath / affirmation)

PHONE C / H / W   or ☐ MISC   AGENCY ☐ CA DMV ☐ US State Dept   EXPIRES   ❶

CW #2

#2 WITNESS's NAME ☐ P/Known   ADDRESS ☐ Non-Public ☐ Driver's License ☐ Passport ☐ Other ID   ISSUED #   SIGNATURE ☐ (after oath / affirmation)

PHONE C / H / W   or ☐ MISC   AGENCY ☐ CA DMV ☐ US State Dept   EXPIRES   ❷

Entry 66

SERVICE

DATE - -20   TIME : am/pm   ADDRESS ☐ Signer's ☐ Office   NOTES   ☐ Stop   MILES   Notary ☐ Adv. Travel ☐ Rush ☐ Copy ☐ Other   TOTAL FEES $ $ $ $ $ $

TYPE ☐ Acknowledgment ☐ Jurat ☐ Copy Certification ☐ Oath/Affirmation ☐ Oath of Office ☐ Proof of Execution ☐ Protest ☐ Other

R T I M R P L   **Fingerprint**

DOCUMENT

DOC TYPE	☐ Deed	☐ DOT	☐ Trust	☐ POA	☐ POAH	☐ Agreement		☐ Affidavit	☐ Other
	Grant • Trust Transfer • Gift	Mortgage	Certification	General / Limited	AHCD	Compliance-E&O	Borrower • Occupancy • Ownership • Refi • Survey		Vehicle Title
	Interspousal • Quitclaim • ToD • Warranty	Rev / Irrev • Am / Rest	Durable / Springing	Living Will		Correction	Debts & Liens • Name-Signature-ID • Marital • Death • Will		Safe Deposit Box

DOC DATE J F M A M J J A S O N D ,   DOC TITLE or TYPE   # OF PAGES ☐ Inspect/Copy Request   Entry X-Ref #

☐ **SATISFACTORY EVIDENCE** ☐ Driver's License / Passport / State ID / Military / Government / Tribal / Inmate / Other ID   **or**   ☐ Credible Witness(es)

SIGNER

SIGNER's NAME ☐ For   ADDRESS ☐ Non-Public ☐ Capacity ☐ Voluntary ☐ Proper ID   ISSUED #   SIGNATURE ☐ (oath / affirmation, if any) ☐ (by Mark)

PHONE C / H / W   or ☐ MISC   AGENCY ☐ CA DMV ☐ US State Dept   EXPIRES   ➤

CW #1

#1 WITNESS's NAME ☐ P/Known   ADDRESS ☐ Non-Public ☐ Driver's License ☐ Passport ☐ Other ID   ISSUED #   SIGNATURE ☐ (after oath / affirmation)

PHONE C / H / W   or ☐ MISC   AGENCY ☐ CA DMV ☐ US State Dept   EXPIRES   ❶

CW #2

#2 WITNESS's NAME ☐ P/Known   ADDRESS ☐ Non-Public ☐ Driver's License ☐ Passport ☐ Other ID   ISSUED #   SIGNATURE ☐ (after oath / affirmation)

PHONE C / H / W   or ☐ MISC   AGENCY ☐ CA DMV ☐ US State Dept   EXPIRES   ❷

NOTARY NAME (printed):   COMMISSION #:

Entry 67

SERVICE
- DATE: - -20
- TIME: : am/pm
- ADDRESS: ☐ Signer's ☐ Office
- NOTES:
- ☐ Stop MILES | Notary $ | ☐ Adv. Travel $ | ☐ Rush $ | ☐ Copy $ | ☐ Other $ | TOTAL FEES $

TYPE: ☐ Acknowledgment ☐ Jurat ☐ Copy Certification ☐ Oath/Affirmation ☐ Oath of Office ☐ Proof of Execution ☐ Protest ☐ Other

Fingerprint R T I M R P L

DOCUMENT
- DOC TYPE: ☐ Deed (Grant • Trust Transfer • Gift • Interspousal • Quitclaim • ToD • Warranty) ☐ DOT (Mortgage) ☐ Trust (Certification • Rev / Irrev • Am / Rest) ☐ POA (General / Limited • Durable / Springing) ☐ POAH (AHCD • Living Will) ☐ Agreement (Compliance-E&O • Correction) ☐ Affidavit (Borrower • Occupancy • Ownership • Refi • Survey • Debts & Liens • Name-Signature-ID • Marital • Death • Will) ☐ Other (Vehicle Title • Safe Deposit Box)
- DOC DATE: J F M A M J / J A S O N D ,
- DOC TITLE or TYPE:
- # OF PAGES: ☐ Inspect/Copy Request
- Entry X-Ref #:

☐ **SATISFACTORY EVIDENCE** ☐ Driver's License / Passport / State ID / Military / Government / Tribal / Inmate / Other ID *or* ☐ Credible Witness(es)

SIGNER
- SIGNER's NAME | ☐ For | ADDRESS | ☐ Non-Public | ☐ Capacity # | ☐ Voluntary | ☐ Proper ID | ISSUED | SIGNATURE ☐ (oath / affirmation, if any) ☐ (by Mark)
- PHONE C / H / W / | *or* ☐ MISC | AGENCY | ☐ CA DMV | ☐ US State Dept | EXPIRES

CW #1
- #1 WITNESS's NAME | ☐ P/Known | ADDRESS | ☐ Non-Public | ☐ Driver's License | ☐ Passport | ☐ Other ID | ISSUED | SIGNATURE ☐ (after oath / affirmation)
- PHONE C / H / W / | *or* ☐ MISC | AGENCY | ☐ CA DMV | ☐ US State Dept | EXPIRES | ❶

CW #2
- #2 WITNESS's NAME | ☐ P/Known | ADDRESS | ☐ Non-Public | ☐ Driver's License | ☐ Passport | ☐ Other ID | ISSUED | SIGNATURE ☐ (after oath / affirmation)
- PHONE C / H / W / | *or* ☐ MISC | AGENCY | ☐ CA DMV | ☐ US State Dept | EXPIRES | ❷

Entry 68

SERVICE
- DATE: - -20
- TIME: : am/pm
- ADDRESS: ☐ Signer's ☐ Office
- NOTES:
- ☐ Stop MILES | Notary $ | ☐ Adv. Travel $ | ☐ Rush $ | ☐ Copy $ | ☐ Other $ | TOTAL FEES $

TYPE: ☐ Acknowledgment ☐ Jurat ☐ Copy Certification ☐ Oath/Affirmation ☐ Oath of Office ☐ Proof of Execution ☐ Protest ☐ Other

Fingerprint R T I M R P L

DOCUMENT
- DOC TYPE: ☐ Deed (Grant • Trust Transfer • Gift • Interspousal • Quitclaim • ToD • Warranty) ☐ DOT (Mortgage) ☐ Trust (Certification • Rev / Irrev • Am / Rest) ☐ POA (General / Limited • Durable / Springing) ☐ POAH (AHCD • Living Will) ☐ Agreement (Compliance-E&O • Correction) ☐ Affidavit (Borrower • Occupancy • Ownership • Refi • Survey • Debts & Liens • Name-Signature-ID • Marital • Death • Will) ☐ Other (Vehicle Title • Safe Deposit Box)
- DOC DATE: J F M A M J / J A S O N D ,
- DOC TITLE or TYPE:
- # OF PAGES: ☐ Inspect/Copy Request
- Entry X-Ref #:

☐ **SATISFACTORY EVIDENCE** ☐ Driver's License / Passport / State ID / Military / Government / Tribal / Inmate / Other ID *or* ☐ Credible Witness(es)

SIGNER
- SIGNER's NAME | ☐ For | ADDRESS | ☐ Non-Public | ☐ Capacity # | ☐ Voluntary | ☐ Proper ID | ISSUED | SIGNATURE ☐ (oath / affirmation, if any) ☐ (by Mark)
- PHONE C / H / W / | *or* ☐ MISC | AGENCY | ☐ CA DMV | ☐ US State Dept | EXPIRES

CW #1
- #1 WITNESS's NAME | ☐ P/Known | ADDRESS | ☐ Non-Public | ☐ Driver's License | ☐ Passport | ☐ Other ID | ISSUED | SIGNATURE ☐ (after oath / affirmation)
- PHONE C / H / W / | *or* ☐ MISC | AGENCY | ☐ CA DMV | ☐ US State Dept | EXPIRES | ❶

CW #2
- #2 WITNESS's NAME | ☐ P/Known | ADDRESS | ☐ Non-Public | ☐ Driver's License | ☐ Passport | ☐ Other ID | ISSUED | SIGNATURE ☐ (after oath / affirmation)
- PHONE C / H / W / | *or* ☐ MISC | AGENCY | ☐ CA DMV | ☐ US State Dept | EXPIRES | ❷

NOTARY NAME (printed):   **COMMISSION #:**

Entry 69

| SERVICE | DATE `-  -20` | TIME `:` am pm | ADDRESS ☐ Signer's ☐ Office | NOTES | ☐ Stop | MILES | Notary $ | ☐ Adv. Travel $ | ☐ Rush $ | ☐ Copy $ | ☐ Other $ | TOTAL FEES $ | **69** |

TYPE ☐ Acknowledgment ☐ Jurat ☐ Copy Certification ☐ Oath/Affirmation ☐ Oath of Office ☐ Proof of Execution ☐ Protest ☐ Other

R | **Fingerprint**

DOCUMENT

DOC TYPE ☐ Deed ☐ DOT ☐ Trust ☐ POA ☐ POAH ☐ Agreement ☐ Affidavit ☐ Other

Grant • Trust Transfer • Gift | Mortgage | Certification | General / Limited | AHCD | Compliance-E&O | Borrower • Occupancy • Ownership • Refi • Survey | Vehicle Title
Interspousal • Quitclaim • ToD • Warranty | Rev / Irrev • Am / Rest | Durable / Springing | Living Will | Correction | Debts & Liens • Name-Signature-ID • Marital • Death • Will | Safe Deposit Box

DOC DATE J F M A M J / J A S O N D ,

DOC TITLE or TYPE   **# OF PAGES** ☐ Inspect/Copy Request   Entry X-Ref #

T I M R P L

☐ **SATISFACTORY EVIDENCE** ☐ Driver's License / Passport / State ID / Military / Government / Tribal / Inmate / Other ID   **or**   ☐ Credible Witness(es)

SIGNER

| SIGNER's NAME | ☐ For | ADDRESS | ☐ Non-Public | ☐ Capacity ☐ Voluntary ☐ Proper ID | ISSUED | SIGNATURE ☐ (oath / affirmation, if any) ☐ (by Mark) |
| PHONE C / H / W   / | **or** ☐ MISC | | | # AGENCY ☐ CA DMV ☐ US State Dept | EXPIRES | ➡ |

CW #1

| #1 WITNESS's NAME | ☐ P/Known | ADDRESS | ☐ Non-Public | ☐ Driver's License ☐ Passport ☐ Other ID | ISSUED | SIGNATURE ☐ (after oath / affirmation) |
| PHONE C / H / W   / | **or** ☐ MISC | | | # AGENCY ☐ CA DMV ☐ US State Dept | EXPIRES | ❶ |

CW #2

| #2 WITNESS's NAME | ☐ P/Known | ADDRESS | ☐ Non-Public | ☐ Driver's License ☐ Passport ☐ Other ID | ISSUED | SIGNATURE ☐ (after oath / affirmation) |
| PHONE C / H / W   / | **or** ☐ MISC | | | # AGENCY ☐ CA DMV ☐ US State Dept | EXPIRES | ❷ |

Entry 70

| SERVICE | DATE `-  -20` | TIME `:` am pm | ADDRESS ☐ Signer's ☐ Office | NOTES | ☐ Stop | MILES | Notary $ | ☐ Adv. Travel $ | ☐ Rush $ | ☐ Copy $ | ☐ Other $ | TOTAL FEES $ | **70** |

TYPE ☐ Acknowledgment ☐ Jurat ☐ Copy Certification ☐ Oath/Affirmation ☐ Oath of Office ☐ Proof of Execution ☐ Protest ☐ Other

R | **Fingerprint**

DOCUMENT

DOC TYPE ☐ Deed ☐ DOT ☐ Trust ☐ POA ☐ POAH ☐ Agreement ☐ Affidavit ☐ Other

Grant • Trust Transfer • Gift | Mortgage | Certification | General / Limited | AHCD | Compliance-E&O | Borrower • Occupancy • Ownership • Refi • Survey | Vehicle Title
Interspousal • Quitclaim • ToD • Warranty | Rev / Irrev • Am / Rest | Durable / Springing | Living Will | Correction | Debts & Liens • Name-Signature-ID • Marital • Death • Will | Safe Deposit Box

DOC DATE J F M A M J / J A S O N D ,

DOC TITLE or TYPE   **# OF PAGES** ☐ Inspect/Copy Request   Entry X-Ref #

T I M R P L

☐ **SATISFACTORY EVIDENCE** ☐ Driver's License / Passport / State ID / Military / Government / Tribal / Inmate / Other ID   **or**   ☐ Credible Witness(es)

SIGNER

| SIGNER's NAME | ☐ For | ADDRESS | ☐ Non-Public | ☐ Capacity ☐ Voluntary ☐ Proper ID | ISSUED | SIGNATURE ☐ (oath / affirmation, if any) ☐ (by Mark) |
| PHONE C / H / W   / | **or** ☐ MISC | | | # AGENCY ☐ CA DMV ☐ US State Dept | EXPIRES | ➡ |

CW #1

| #1 WITNESS's NAME | ☐ P/Known | ADDRESS | ☐ Non-Public | ☐ Driver's License ☐ Passport ☐ Other ID | ISSUED | SIGNATURE ☐ (after oath / affirmation) |
| PHONE C / H / W   / | **or** ☐ MISC | | | # AGENCY ☐ CA DMV ☐ US State Dept | EXPIRES | ❶ |

CW #2

| #2 WITNESS's NAME | ☐ P/Known | ADDRESS | ☐ Non-Public | ☐ Driver's License ☐ Passport ☐ Other ID | ISSUED | SIGNATURE ☐ (after oath / affirmation) |
| PHONE C / H / W   / | **or** ☐ MISC | | | # AGENCY ☐ CA DMV ☐ US State Dept | EXPIRES | ❷ |

NOTARY NAME (printed):   COMMISSION #:

Entry 71

SERVICE — DATE: - -20 | TIME: : am/pm | ADDRESS | ☐ Signer's ☐ Office | NOTES | ☐ Stop | MILES | Notary $ | ☐ Adv. Travel $ | ☐ Rush $ | ☐ Copy $ | ☐ Other $ | TOTAL FEES $

TYPE: ☐ Acknowledgment ☐ Jurat ☐ Copy Certification ☐ Oath/Affirmation ☐ Oath of Office ☐ Proof of Execution ☐ Protest ☐ Other   R T I M R P L   **Fingerprint**

DOCUMENT
DOC TYPE: ☐ Deed (Grant • Trust Transfer • Gift / Interspousal • Quitclaim • ToD • Warranty) ☐ DOT (Mortgage / Rev / Irrev • Am / Rest) ☐ Trust (Certification / Durable / Springing) ☐ POA (General / Limited) ☐ POAH (AHCD / Living Will) ☐ Agreement (Compliance-E&O / Correction) ☐ Affidavit (Borrower • Occupancy • Ownership • Refi • Survey / Debts & Liens • Name-Signature-ID • Marital • Death • Will) ☐ Other (Vehicle Title / Safe Deposit Box)

DOC DATE: J F M A M J J A S O N D ,   DOC TITLE or TYPE   # OF PAGES   ☐ Inspect/Copy Request   Entry X-Ref #

☐ **SATISFACTORY EVIDENCE** ☐ Driver's License / Passport / State ID / Military / Government / Tribal / Inmate / Other ID **or** ☐ Credible Witness(es)

SIGNER: SIGNER's NAME | ☐ For | ADDRESS | ☐ Non-Public | ☐ Capacity | ☐ Voluntary | ☐ Proper ID | ISSUED # | SIGNATURE ☐ (oath / affirmation, if any) ☐ (by Mark)
PHONE C / H / W / | or ☐ MISC | | | AGENCY | ☐ CA DMV | ☐ US State Dept | EXPIRES | ➡

CW #1: #1 WITNESS's NAME | ☐ P/Known | ADDRESS | ☐ Non-Public | ☐ Driver's License | ☐ Passport | ☐ Other ID | ISSUED # | SIGNATURE ☐ (after oath / affirmation)
PHONE C / H / W / | or ☐ MISC | | | AGENCY | ☐ CA DMV | ☐ US State Dept | EXPIRES | ❶

CW #2: #2 WITNESS's NAME | ☐ P/Known | ADDRESS | ☐ Non-Public | ☐ Driver's License | ☐ Passport | ☐ Other ID | ISSUED # | SIGNATURE ☐ (after oath / affirmation)
PHONE C / H / W / | or ☐ MISC | | | AGENCY | ☐ CA DMV | ☐ US State Dept | EXPIRES | ❷

Entry 72

SERVICE — DATE: - -20 | TIME: : am/pm | ADDRESS | ☐ Signer's ☐ Office | NOTES | ☐ Stop | MILES | Notary $ | ☐ Adv. Travel $ | ☐ Rush $ | ☐ Copy $ | ☐ Other $ | TOTAL FEES $

TYPE: ☐ Acknowledgment ☐ Jurat ☐ Copy Certification ☐ Oath/Affirmation ☐ Oath of Office ☐ Proof of Execution ☐ Protest ☐ Other   R T I M R P L   **Fingerprint**

DOCUMENT
DOC TYPE: ☐ Deed (Grant • Trust Transfer • Gift / Interspousal • Quitclaim • ToD • Warranty) ☐ DOT (Mortgage / Rev / Irrev • Am / Rest) ☐ Trust (Certification / Durable / Springing) ☐ POA (General / Limited) ☐ POAH (AHCD / Living Will) ☐ Agreement (Compliance-E&O / Correction) ☐ Affidavit (Borrower • Occupancy • Ownership • Refi • Survey / Debts & Liens • Name-Signature-ID • Marital • Death • Will) ☐ Other (Vehicle Title / Safe Deposit Box)

DOC DATE: J F M A M J J A S O N D ,   DOC TITLE or TYPE   # OF PAGES   ☐ Inspect/Copy Request   Entry X-Ref #

☐ **SATISFACTORY EVIDENCE** ☐ Driver's License / Passport / State ID / Military / Government / Tribal / Inmate / Other ID **or** ☐ Credible Witness(es)

SIGNER: SIGNER's NAME | ☐ For | ADDRESS | ☐ Non-Public | ☐ Capacity | ☐ Voluntary | ☐ Proper ID | ISSUED # | SIGNATURE ☐ (oath / affirmation, if any) ☐ (by Mark)
PHONE C / H / W / | or ☐ MISC | | | AGENCY | ☐ CA DMV | ☐ US State Dept | EXPIRES | ➡

CW #1: #1 WITNESS's NAME | ☐ P/Known | ADDRESS | ☐ Non-Public | ☐ Driver's License | ☐ Passport | ☐ Other ID | ISSUED # | SIGNATURE ☐ (after oath / affirmation)
PHONE C / H / W / | or ☐ MISC | | | AGENCY | ☐ CA DMV | ☐ US State Dept | EXPIRES | ❶

CW #2: #2 WITNESS's NAME | ☐ P/Known | ADDRESS | ☐ Non-Public | ☐ Driver's License | ☐ Passport | ☐ Other ID | ISSUED # | SIGNATURE ☐ (after oath / affirmation)
PHONE C / H / W / | or ☐ MISC | | | AGENCY | ☐ CA DMV | ☐ US State Dept | EXPIRES | ❷

NOTARY NAME (printed): _____ **COMMISSION #:** _____

Entry 73

SERVICE	DATE __ - __ -20__	TIME __ : __ am/pm	ADDRESS	☐ Signer's ☐ Office	NOTES	☐ Stop	MILES	Notary $	☐ Adv. Travel $	☐ Rush $	☐ Copy $	☐ Other $	TOTAL FEES $	**73**

TYPE ☐ Acknowledgment ☐ Jurat ☐ Copy Certification ☐ Oath/Affirmation ☐ Oath of Office ☐ Proof of Execution ☐ Protest ☐ Other

Fingerprint — R T I M R P L

DOCUMENT

DOC TYPE ☐ Deed (Grant • Trust Transfer • Gift • Interspousal • Quitclaim • ToD • Warranty) ☐ DOT (Mortgage • Rev / Irrev • Am / Rest) ☐ Trust (Certification) ☐ POA (General / Limited • Durable / Springing) ☐ POAH (AHCD • Living Will) ☐ Agreement (Compliance-E&O • Correction) ☐ Affidavit (Borrower • Occupancy • Ownership • Refi • Survey • Debts & Liens • Name-Signature-ID • Marital • Death • Will) ☐ Other (Vehicle Title • Safe Deposit Box)

DOC DATE J F M A M J J A S O N D , _____ **DOC TITLE or TYPE** _____ **# OF PAGES** _____ ☐ Inspect/Copy Request **Entry X-Ref #** _____

☐ **SATISFACTORY EVIDENCE** ☐ Driver's License / Passport / State ID / Military / Government / Tribal / Inmate / Other ID **or** ☐ Credible Witness(es)

SIGNER

SIGNER's NAME _____ ☐ For | ADDRESS _____ ☐ Non-Public | ☐ Capacity ☐ Voluntary ☐ Proper ID | ISSUED # _____ | SIGNATURE ☐ (oath / affirmation, if any) ☐ (by Mark)

PHONE C / H / W ___/___ **or** ☐ MISC | AGENCY ☐ CA DMV ☐ US State Dept | EXPIRES _____ | ➡

CW #1

#1 WITNESS's NAME _____ ☐ P/Known | ADDRESS _____ ☐ Non-Public | ☐ Driver's License ☐ Passport ☐ Other ID | ISSUED # _____ | SIGNATURE ☐ (after oath / affirmation)

PHONE C / H / W ___/___ **or** ☐ MISC | AGENCY ☐ CA DMV ☐ US State Dept | EXPIRES _____ | ❶

CW #2

#2 WITNESS's NAME _____ ☐ P/Known | ADDRESS _____ ☐ Non-Public | ☐ Driver's License ☐ Passport ☐ Other ID | ISSUED # _____ | SIGNATURE ☐ (after oath / affirmation)

PHONE C / H / W ___/___ **or** ☐ MISC | AGENCY ☐ CA DMV ☐ US State Dept | EXPIRES _____ | ❷

Entry 74

SERVICE	DATE __ - __ -20__	TIME __ : __ am/pm	ADDRESS	☐ Signer's ☐ Office	NOTES	☐ Stop	MILES	Notary $	☐ Adv. Travel $	☐ Rush $	☐ Copy $	☐ Other $	TOTAL FEES $	**74**

TYPE ☐ Acknowledgment ☐ Jurat ☐ Copy Certification ☐ Oath/Affirmation ☐ Oath of Office ☐ Proof of Execution ☐ Protest ☐ Other

Fingerprint — R T I M R P L

DOCUMENT

DOC TYPE ☐ Deed (Grant • Trust Transfer • Gift • Interspousal • Quitclaim • ToD • Warranty) ☐ DOT (Mortgage • Rev / Irrev • Am / Rest) ☐ Trust (Certification) ☐ POA (General / Limited • Durable / Springing) ☐ POAH (AHCD • Living Will) ☐ Agreement (Compliance-E&O • Correction) ☐ Affidavit (Borrower • Occupancy • Ownership • Refi • Survey • Debts & Liens • Name-Signature-ID • Marital • Death • Will) ☐ Other (Vehicle Title • Safe Deposit Box)

DOC DATE J F M A M J J A S O N D , _____ **DOC TITLE or TYPE** _____ **# OF PAGES** _____ ☐ Inspect/Copy Request **Entry X-Ref #** _____

☐ **SATISFACTORY EVIDENCE** ☐ Driver's License / Passport / State ID / Military / Government / Tribal / Inmate / Other ID **or** ☐ Credible Witness(es)

SIGNER

SIGNER's NAME _____ ☐ For | ADDRESS _____ ☐ Non-Public | ☐ Capacity ☐ Voluntary ☐ Proper ID | ISSUED # _____ | SIGNATURE ☐ (oath / affirmation, if any) ☐ (by Mark)

PHONE C / H / W ___/___ **or** ☐ MISC | AGENCY ☐ CA DMV ☐ US State Dept | EXPIRES _____ | ➡

CW #1

#1 WITNESS's NAME _____ ☐ P/Known | ADDRESS _____ ☐ Non-Public | ☐ Driver's License ☐ Passport ☐ Other ID | ISSUED # _____ | SIGNATURE ☐ (after oath / affirmation)

PHONE C / H / W ___/___ **or** ☐ MISC | AGENCY ☐ CA DMV ☐ US State Dept | EXPIRES _____ | ❶

CW #2

#2 WITNESS's NAME _____ ☐ P/Known | ADDRESS _____ ☐ Non-Public | ☐ Driver's License ☐ Passport ☐ Other ID | ISSUED # _____ | SIGNATURE ☐ (after oath / affirmation)

PHONE C / H / W ___/___ **or** ☐ MISC | AGENCY ☐ CA DMV ☐ US State Dept | EXPIRES _____ | ❷

Entry 75

NOTARY NAME (printed): _____ **COMMISSION #:** _____

SERVICE
- DATE: __-__-20__
- TIME: __:__ ☐ am ☐ pm
- ADDRESS: ☐ Signer's ☐ Office
- NOTES: ☐ Stop MILES ____
- Notary $____ ☐ Adv. Travel $____ ☐ Rush $____ ☐ Copy $____ ☐ Other $____ **TOTAL FEES** $____

TYPE: ☐ Acknowledgment ☐ Jurat ☐ Copy Certification ☐ Oath/Affirmation ☐ Oath of Office ☐ Proof of Execution ☐ Protest ☐ Other

Fingerprint — R T I M R P L

DOCUMENT
- DOC TYPE: ☐ Deed (Grant • Trust Transfer • Gift • Interspousal • Quitclaim • ToD • Warranty) ☐ DOT (Mortgage) ☐ Trust (Certification • Rev/Irrev • Am/Rest) ☐ POA (General/Limited • Durable/Springing) ☐ POAH (AHCD • Living Will) ☐ Agreement (Compliance-E&O • Correction) ☐ Affidavit (Borrower • Occupancy • Ownership • Refi • Survey • Debts & Liens • Name-Signature-ID • Marital • Death • Will) ☐ Other (Vehicle Title • Safe Deposit Box)
- DOC DATE: J F M A M J J A S O N D , ____
- DOC TITLE or TYPE: _____
- # OF PAGES: ____ ☐ Inspect/Copy Request
- Entry X-Ref #: ____

☐ **SATISFACTORY EVIDENCE** ☐ Driver's License / Passport / State ID / Military / Government / Tribal / Inmate / Other ID *or* ☐ Credible Witness(es)

SIGNER
- SIGNER's NAME: _____ ☐ For
- ADDRESS: _____ ☐ Non-Public
- ☐ Capacity ☐ Voluntary ☐ Proper ID
- ISSUED: ____ #____
- SIGNATURE: _____ ☐ (oath / affirmation, if any) ☐ (by Mark)
- PHONE C/H/W: ___/___ or ☐ MISC
- AGENCY: ____ ☐ CA DMV ☐ US State Dept EXPIRES: ____

CW #1
- #1 WITNESS's NAME: _____ ☐ P/Known
- ADDRESS: _____ ☐ Non-Public
- ☐ Driver's License ☐ Passport ☐ Other ID ISSUED: ____ #____
- SIGNATURE: _____ ☐ (after oath / affirmation)
- PHONE C/H/W: ___/___ or ☐ MISC
- AGENCY: ____ ☐ CA DMV ☐ US State Dept EXPIRES: ____ ❶

CW #2
- #2 WITNESS's NAME: _____ ☐ P/Known
- ADDRESS: _____ ☐ Non-Public
- ☐ Driver's License ☐ Passport ☐ Other ID ISSUED: ____ #____
- SIGNATURE: _____ ☐ (after oath / affirmation)
- PHONE C/H/W: ___/___ or ☐ MISC
- AGENCY: ____ ☐ CA DMV ☐ US State Dept EXPIRES: ____ ❷

Entry 76

SERVICE
- DATE: __-__-20__
- TIME: __:__ ☐ am ☐ pm
- ADDRESS: ☐ Signer's ☐ Office
- NOTES: ☐ Stop MILES ____
- Notary $____ ☐ Adv. Travel $____ ☐ Rush $____ ☐ Copy $____ ☐ Other $____ **TOTAL FEES** $____

TYPE: ☐ Acknowledgment ☐ Jurat ☐ Copy Certification ☐ Oath/Affirmation ☐ Oath of Office ☐ Proof of Execution ☐ Protest ☐ Other

Fingerprint — R T I M R P L

DOCUMENT
- DOC TYPE: ☐ Deed (Grant • Trust Transfer • Gift • Interspousal • Quitclaim • ToD • Warranty) ☐ DOT (Mortgage) ☐ Trust (Certification • Rev/Irrev • Am/Rest) ☐ POA (General/Limited • Durable/Springing) ☐ POAH (AHCD • Living Will) ☐ Agreement (Compliance-E&O • Correction) ☐ Affidavit (Borrower • Occupancy • Ownership • Refi • Survey • Debts & Liens • Name-Signature-ID • Marital • Death • Will) ☐ Other (Vehicle Title • Safe Deposit Box)
- DOC DATE: J F M A M J J A S O N D , ____
- DOC TITLE or TYPE: _____
- # OF PAGES: ____ ☐ Inspect/Copy Request
- Entry X-Ref #: ____

☐ **SATISFACTORY EVIDENCE** ☐ Driver's License / Passport / State ID / Military / Government / Tribal / Inmate / Other ID *or* ☐ Credible Witness(es)

SIGNER
- SIGNER's NAME: _____ ☐ For
- ADDRESS: _____ ☐ Non-Public
- ☐ Capacity ☐ Voluntary ☐ Proper ID
- ISSUED: ____ #____
- SIGNATURE: _____ ☐ (oath / affirmation, if any) ☐ (by Mark)
- PHONE C/H/W: ___/___ or ☐ MISC
- AGENCY: ____ ☐ CA DMV ☐ US State Dept EXPIRES: ____

CW #1
- #1 WITNESS's NAME: _____ ☐ P/Known
- ADDRESS: _____ ☐ Non-Public
- ☐ Driver's License ☐ Passport ☐ Other ID ISSUED: ____ #____
- SIGNATURE: _____ ☐ (after oath / affirmation)
- PHONE C/H/W: ___/___ or ☐ MISC
- AGENCY: ____ ☐ CA DMV ☐ US State Dept EXPIRES: ____ ❶

CW #2
- #2 WITNESS's NAME: _____ ☐ P/Known
- ADDRESS: _____ ☐ Non-Public
- ☐ Driver's License ☐ Passport ☐ Other ID ISSUED: ____ #____
- SIGNATURE: _____ ☐ (after oath / affirmation)
- PHONE C/H/W: ___/___ or ☐ MISC
- AGENCY: ____ ☐ CA DMV ☐ US State Dept EXPIRES: ____ ❷

NOTARY NAME (printed):   COMMISSION #:

Entry 77

SERVICE

DATE	TIME	am pm	ADDRESS	☐ Signer's	☐ Office	NOTES	☐ Stop	MILES	Notary	☐ Adv. Travel	☐ Rush	☐ Copy	☐ Other	TOTAL FEES
- -20	:								$	$	$	$	$	$

TYPE ☐ Acknowledgment ☐ Jurat ☐ Copy Certification ☐ Oath/Affirmation ☐ Oath of Office ☐ Proof of Execution ☐ Protest ☐ Other

DOCUMENT

DOC TYPE ☐ Deed ☐ DOT ☐ Trust ☐ POA ☐ POAH ☐ Agreement ☐ Affidavit ☐ Other

Grant • Trust Transfer • Gift   Mortgage   Certification   General / Limited   AHCD   Compliance-E&O   Borrower • Occupancy • Ownership • Refi • Survey   Vehicle Title
Interspousal • Quitclaim • ToD • Warranty   Rev / Irrev • Am / Rest   Durable / Springing   Living Will   Correction   Debts & Liens • Name-Signature-ID • Marital • Death • Will   Safe Deposit Box

DOC DATE J F M A M J J A S O N D ,   DOC TITLE or TYPE   # OF PAGES ☐ Inspect/Copy Request   Entry X-Ref #

☐ **SATISFACTORY EVIDENCE** ☐ Driver's License / Passport / State ID / Military / Government / Tribal / Inmate / Other ID *or* ☐ Credible Witness(es)

SIGNER

SIGNER's NAME   ☐ For ADDRESS   ☐ Non-Public ☐ Capacity # ☐ Voluntary ☐ Proper ID ISSUED   SIGNATURE ☐ (oath / affirmation, if any) ☐ (by Mark)

PHONE C / H / W   *or* ☐ MISC   AGENCY ☐ CA DMV ☐ US State Dept EXPIRES   ➡

CW #1

#1 WITNESS's NAME   ☐ P/Known ADDRESS   ☐ Non-Public ☐ Driver's License # ☐ Passport ☐ Other ID ISSUED   SIGNATURE ☐ (after oath / affirmation)

PHONE C / H / W   *or* ☐ MISC   AGENCY ☐ CA DMV ☐ US State Dept EXPIRES   ❶

CW #2

#2 WITNESS's NAME   ☐ P/Known ADDRESS   ☐ Non-Public ☐ Driver's License # ☐ Passport ☐ Other ID ISSUED   SIGNATURE ☐ (after oath / affirmation)

PHONE C / H / W   *or* ☐ MISC   AGENCY ☐ CA DMV ☐ US State Dept EXPIRES   ❷

Fingerprint   R T I M R P L

Entry 78

SERVICE

DATE	TIME	am pm	ADDRESS	☐ Signer's	☐ Office	NOTES	☐ Stop	MILES	Notary	☐ Adv. Travel	☐ Rush	☐ Copy	☐ Other	TOTAL FEES
- -20	:								$	$	$	$	$	$

TYPE ☐ Acknowledgment ☐ Jurat ☐ Copy Certification ☐ Oath/Affirmation ☐ Oath of Office ☐ Proof of Execution ☐ Protest ☐ Other

DOCUMENT

DOC TYPE ☐ Deed ☐ DOT ☐ Trust ☐ POA ☐ POAH ☐ Agreement ☐ Affidavit ☐ Other

Grant • Trust Transfer • Gift   Mortgage   Certification   General / Limited   AHCD   Compliance-E&O   Borrower • Occupancy • Ownership • Refi • Survey   Vehicle Title
Interspousal • Quitclaim • ToD • Warranty   Rev / Irrev • Am / Rest   Durable / Springing   Living Will   Correction   Debts & Liens • Name-Signature-ID • Marital • Death • Will   Safe Deposit Box

DOC DATE J F M A M J J A S O N D ,   DOC TITLE or TYPE   # OF PAGES ☐ Inspect/Copy Request   Entry X-Ref #

☐ **SATISFACTORY EVIDENCE** ☐ Driver's License / Passport / State ID / Military / Government / Tribal / Inmate / Other ID *or* ☐ Credible Witness(es)

SIGNER

SIGNER's NAME   ☐ For ADDRESS   ☐ Non-Public ☐ Capacity # ☐ Voluntary ☐ Proper ID ISSUED   SIGNATURE ☐ (oath / affirmation, if any) ☐ (by Mark)

PHONE C / H / W   *or* ☐ MISC   AGENCY ☐ CA DMV ☐ US State Dept EXPIRES   ➡

CW #1

#1 WITNESS's NAME   ☐ P/Known ADDRESS   ☐ Non-Public ☐ Driver's License # ☐ Passport ☐ Other ID ISSUED   SIGNATURE ☐ (after oath / affirmation)

PHONE C / H / W   *or* ☐ MISC   AGENCY ☐ CA DMV ☐ US State Dept EXPIRES   ❶

CW #2

#2 WITNESS's NAME   ☐ P/Known ADDRESS   ☐ Non-Public ☐ Driver's License # ☐ Passport ☐ Other ID ISSUED   SIGNATURE ☐ (after oath / affirmation)

PHONE C / H / W   *or* ☐ MISC   AGENCY ☐ CA DMV ☐ US State Dept EXPIRES   ❷

Fingerprint   R T I M R P L

NOTARY NAME (printed): COMMISSION #:

Entry 79

SERVICE
- DATE: - -20
- TIME: : am/pm
- ADDRESS: ☐ Signer's ☐ Office
- NOTES
- ☐ Stop MILES: $____
- Notary: $____ ☐ Adv. Travel: $____ ☐ Rush: $____ ☐ Copy: $____ ☐ Other: $____ TOTAL FEES: $____
- TYPE: ☐ Acknowledgment ☐ Jurat ☐ Copy Certification ☐ Oath/Affirmation ☐ Oath of Office ☐ Proof of Execution ☐ Protest ☐ Other

DOCUMENT
- DOC TYPE: ☐ Deed (Grant • Trust Transfer • Gift • Interspousal • Quitclaim • ToD • Warranty) ☐ DOT (Mortgage • Certification • Rev / Irrev • Am / Rest) ☐ Trust ☐ POA (General / Limited • Durable / Springing) ☐ POAH (AHCD • Living Will) ☐ Agreement (Compliance-E&O • Correction) ☐ Affidavit (Borrower • Occupancy • Ownership • Refi • Survey • Debts & Liens • Name-Signature-ID • Marital • Death • Will) ☐ Other (Vehicle Title • Safe Deposit Box)
- DOC DATE: J F M A M J J A S O N D ,
- DOC TITLE or TYPE:
- # OF PAGES:
- ☐ Inspect/Copy Request
- Entry X-Ref #:

Fingerprint: R T I M R P L

☐ **SATISFACTORY EVIDENCE** ☐ Driver's License / Passport / State ID / Military / Government / Tribal / Inmate / Other ID **or** ☐ Credible Witness(es)

SIGNER
- SIGNER's NAME ☐ For | ADDRESS ☐ Non-Public | ☐ Capacity ☐ Voluntary ☐ Proper ID | ISSUED # | SIGNATURE ☐ (oath / affirmation, if any) ☐ (by Mark)
- PHONE C / H / W   or ☐ MISC | AGENCY ☐ CA DMV ☐ US State Dept | EXPIRES | ➤

CW #1
- #1 WITNESS's NAME ☐ P/Known | ADDRESS ☐ Non-Public | ☐ Driver's License ☐ Passport ☐ Other ID | ISSUED # | SIGNATURE ☐ (after oath / affirmation)
- PHONE C / H / W or ☐ MISC | AGENCY ☐ CA DMV ☐ US State Dept | EXPIRES | ❶

CW #2
- #2 WITNESS's NAME ☐ P/Known | ADDRESS ☐ Non-Public | ☐ Driver's License ☐ Passport ☐ Other ID | ISSUED # | SIGNATURE ☐ (after oath / affirmation)
- PHONE C / H / W or ☐ MISC | AGENCY ☐ CA DMV ☐ US State Dept | EXPIRES | ❷

Entry 80

SERVICE
- DATE: - -20
- TIME: : am/pm
- ADDRESS: ☐ Signer's ☐ Office
- NOTES
- ☐ Stop MILES: $____
- Notary: $____ ☐ Adv. Travel: $____ ☐ Rush: $____ ☐ Copy: $____ ☐ Other: $____ TOTAL FEES: $____
- TYPE: ☐ Acknowledgment ☐ Jurat ☐ Copy Certification ☐ Oath/Affirmation ☐ Oath of Office ☐ Proof of Execution ☐ Protest ☐ Other

DOCUMENT
- DOC TYPE: ☐ Deed (Grant • Trust Transfer • Gift • Interspousal • Quitclaim • ToD • Warranty) ☐ DOT (Mortgage • Certification • Rev / Irrev • Am / Rest) ☐ Trust ☐ POA (General / Limited • Durable / Springing) ☐ POAH (AHCD • Living Will) ☐ Agreement (Compliance-E&O • Correction) ☐ Affidavit (Borrower • Occupancy • Ownership • Refi • Survey • Debts & Liens • Name-Signature-ID • Marital • Death • Will) ☐ Other (Vehicle Title • Safe Deposit Box)
- DOC DATE: J F M A M J J A S O N D ,
- DOC TITLE or TYPE:
- # OF PAGES:
- ☐ Inspect/Copy Request
- Entry X-Ref #:

Fingerprint: R T I M R P L

☐ **SATISFACTORY EVIDENCE** ☐ Driver's License / Passport / State ID / Military / Government / Tribal / Inmate / Other ID **or** ☐ Credible Witness(es)

SIGNER
- SIGNER's NAME ☐ For | ADDRESS ☐ Non-Public | ☐ Capacity ☐ Voluntary ☐ Proper ID | ISSUED # | SIGNATURE ☐ (oath / affirmation, if any) ☐ (by Mark)
- PHONE C / H / W   or ☐ MISC | AGENCY ☐ CA DMV ☐ US State Dept | EXPIRES | ➤

CW #1
- #1 WITNESS's NAME ☐ P/Known | ADDRESS ☐ Non-Public | ☐ Driver's License ☐ Passport ☐ Other ID | ISSUED # | SIGNATURE ☐ (after oath / affirmation)
- PHONE C / H / W or ☐ MISC | AGENCY ☐ CA DMV ☐ US State Dept | EXPIRES | ❶

CW #2
- #2 WITNESS's NAME ☐ P/Known | ADDRESS ☐ Non-Public | ☐ Driver's License ☐ Passport ☐ Other ID | ISSUED # | SIGNATURE ☐ (after oath / affirmation)
- PHONE C / H / W or ☐ MISC | AGENCY ☐ CA DMV ☐ US State Dept | EXPIRES | ❷

NOTARY NAME (printed): _____ COMMISSION #: _____

Entry 81

SERVICE	DATE __ - __ -20__	TIME __:__ ☐ am ☐ pm	ADDRESS ☐ Signer's ☐ Office	NOTES	☐ Stop	MILES	Notary ☐ Adv. Travel ☐ Rush ☐ Copy ☐ Other TOTAL FEES

$ ___ $ ___ $ ___ $ ___ $ ___ $ ___   **81**

TYPE ☐ Acknowledgment ☐ Jurat ☐ Copy Certification ☐ Oath/Affirmation ☐ Oath of Office ☐ Proof of Execution ☐ Protest ☐ Other

DOCUMENT

DOC TYPE ☐ Deed ☐ DOT ☐ Trust ☐ POA ☐ POAH ☐ Agreement ☐ Affidavit ☐ Other

Grant • Trust Transfer • Gift | Mortgage | Certification | General / Limited | AHCD | Compliance-E&O | Borrower • Occupancy • Ownership • Refi • Survey | Vehicle Title

Interspousal • Quitclaim • ToD • Warranty | Rev / Irrev • Am / Rest | Durable / Springing | Living Will | Correction | Debts & Liens • Name-Signature-ID • Marital • Death • Will | Safe Deposit Box

DOC DATE J F M A M J J A S O N D , ____ | **DOC TITLE or TYPE** ____ | **# OF PAGES** ☐ Inspect/Copy Request   Entry X-Ref #

R T I M R P L — Fingerprint

☐ **SATISFACTORY EVIDENCE** ☐ Driver's License / Passport / State ID / Military / Government / Tribal / Inmate / Other ID **or** ☐ Credible Witness(es)

SIGNER

SIGNER's NAME ____ ☐ For | ADDRESS ____ ☐ Non-Public | ☐ Capacity ☐ Voluntary ☐ Proper ID # ____ | ISSUED ____ | SIGNATURE ☐ (oath / affirmation, if any) ☐ (by Mark)

PHONE C / H / W ____ **or** ☐ MISC | AGENCY ☐ CA DMV ☐ US State Dept | EXPIRES ____ ➡

CW #1

#1 WITNESS's NAME ____ ☐ P/Known | ADDRESS ____ ☐ Non-Public | ☐ Driver's License ☐ Passport ☐ Other ID # ____ | ISSUED ____ | SIGNATURE ☐ (after oath / affirmation)

PHONE C / H / W ____ **or** ☐ MISC | AGENCY ☐ CA DMV ☐ US State Dept | EXPIRES ____ ❶

CW #2

#2 WITNESS's NAME ____ ☐ P/Known | ADDRESS ____ ☐ Non-Public | ☐ Driver's License ☐ Passport ☐ Other ID # ____ | ISSUED ____ | SIGNATURE ☐ (after oath / affirmation)

PHONE C / H / W ____ **or** ☐ MISC | AGENCY ☐ CA DMV ☐ US State Dept | EXPIRES ____ ❷

Entry 82

SERVICE	DATE __ - __ -20__	TIME __:__ ☐ am ☐ pm	ADDRESS ☐ Signer's ☐ Office	NOTES	☐ Stop	MILES	Notary ☐ Adv. Travel ☐ Rush ☐ Copy ☐ Other TOTAL FEES

$ ___ $ ___ $ ___ $ ___ $ ___ $ ___   **82**

TYPE ☐ Acknowledgment ☐ Jurat ☐ Copy Certification ☐ Oath/Affirmation ☐ Oath of Office ☐ Proof of Execution ☐ Protest ☐ Other

DOCUMENT

DOC TYPE ☐ Deed ☐ DOT ☐ Trust ☐ POA ☐ POAH ☐ Agreement ☐ Affidavit ☐ Other

Grant • Trust Transfer • Gift | Mortgage | Certification | General / Limited | AHCD | Compliance-E&O | Borrower • Occupancy • Ownership • Refi • Survey | Vehicle Title

Interspousal • Quitclaim • ToD • Warranty | Rev / Irrev • Am / Rest | Durable / Springing | Living Will | Correction | Debts & Liens • Name-Signature-ID • Marital • Death • Will | Safe Deposit Box

DOC DATE J F M A M J J A S O N D , ____ | **DOC TITLE or TYPE** ____ | **# OF PAGES** ☐ Inspect/Copy Request   Entry X-Ref #

R T I M R P L — Fingerprint

☐ **SATISFACTORY EVIDENCE** ☐ Driver's License / Passport / State ID / Military / Government / Tribal / Inmate / Other ID **or** ☐ Credible Witness(es)

SIGNER

SIGNER's NAME ____ ☐ For | ADDRESS ____ ☐ Non-Public | ☐ Capacity ☐ Voluntary ☐ Proper ID # ____ | ISSUED ____ | SIGNATURE ☐ (oath / affirmation, if any) ☐ (by Mark)

PHONE C / H / W ____ **or** ☐ MISC | AGENCY ☐ CA DMV ☐ US State Dept | EXPIRES ____ ➡

CW #1

#1 WITNESS's NAME ____ ☐ P/Known | ADDRESS ____ ☐ Non-Public | ☐ Driver's License ☐ Passport ☐ Other ID # ____ | ISSUED ____ | SIGNATURE ☐ (after oath / affirmation)

PHONE C / H / W ____ **or** ☐ MISC | AGENCY ☐ CA DMV ☐ US State Dept | EXPIRES ____ ❶

CW #2

#2 WITNESS's NAME ____ ☐ P/Known | ADDRESS ____ ☐ Non-Public | ☐ Driver's License ☐ Passport ☐ Other ID # ____ | ISSUED ____ | SIGNATURE ☐ (after oath / affirmation)

PHONE C / H / W ____ **or** ☐ MISC | AGENCY ☐ CA DMV ☐ US State Dept | EXPIRES ____ ❷

Entry 83

NOTARY NAME (printed): _____ **COMMISSION #:** _____

SERVICE — DATE: __-__-20__ | TIME: __:__ am/pm | ADDRESS: ☐ Signer's ☐ Office | NOTES: ☐ Stop | MILES | Notary $__ | Adv. Travel $__ | ☐ Rush $__ | ☐ Copy $__ | ☐ Other $__ | TOTAL FEES $__

TYPE: ☐ Acknowledgment ☐ Jurat ☐ Copy Certification ☐ Oath/Affirmation ☐ Oath of Office ☐ Proof of Execution ☐ Protest ☐ Other

DOCUMENT
- DOC TYPE: ☐ Deed (Grant • Trust Transfer • Gift • Interspousal • Quitclaim • ToD • Warranty) ☐ DOT (Mortgage) ☐ Trust (Certification • Rev / Irrev • Am / Rest) ☐ POA (General / Limited • Durable / Springing) ☐ POAH (AHCD • Living Will) ☐ Agreement (Compliance-E&O • Correction) ☐ Affidavit (Borrower • Occupancy • Ownership • Refi • Survey • Debts & Liens • Name-Signature-ID • Marital • Death • Will) ☐ Other (Vehicle Title • Safe Deposit Box)
- DOC DATE: J F M A M J J A S O N D , ____ | DOC TITLE or TYPE: _____ | # OF PAGES: __ | ☐ Inspect/Copy Request | Entry X-Ref #: __

☐ **SATISFACTORY EVIDENCE** ☐ Driver's License / Passport / State ID / Military / Government / Tribal / Inmate / Other ID   *or*   ☐ Credible Witness(es)

SIGNER — SIGNER's NAME: ___ ☐ For | ADDRESS: ___ ☐ Non-Public # ___ | ☐ Capacity ☐ Voluntary ☐ Proper ID | ISSUED | SIGNATURE ☐ (oath / affirmation, if any) ☐ (by Mark) | PHONE C / H / W: ___ / ___ *or* ☐ MISC | AGENCY ☐ CA DMV ☐ US State Dept | EXPIRES ➡

CW #1 — #1 WITNESS's NAME: ___ ☐ P/Known | ADDRESS ___ ☐ Non-Public # ___ | ☐ Driver's License ☐ Passport ☐ Other ID | ISSUED | SIGNATURE ☐ (after oath / affirmation) | PHONE C / H / W: ___ / ___ *or* ☐ MISC | AGENCY ☐ CA DMV ☐ US State Dept | EXPIRES ❶

CW #2 — #2 WITNESS's NAME: ___ ☐ P/Known | ADDRESS ___ ☐ Non-Public # ___ | ☐ Driver's License ☐ Passport ☐ Other ID | ISSUED | SIGNATURE ☐ (after oath / affirmation) | PHONE C / H / W: ___ / ___ *or* ☐ MISC | AGENCY ☐ CA DMV ☐ US State Dept | EXPIRES ❷

Fingerprint — R T I M R P L

Entry 84

SERVICE — DATE: __-__-20__ | TIME: __:__ am/pm | ADDRESS: ☐ Signer's ☐ Office | NOTES: ☐ Stop | MILES | Notary $__ | Adv. Travel $__ | ☐ Rush $__ | ☐ Copy $__ | ☐ Other $__ | TOTAL FEES $__

TYPE: ☐ Acknowledgment ☐ Jurat ☐ Copy Certification ☐ Oath/Affirmation ☐ Oath of Office ☐ Proof of Execution ☐ Protest ☐ Other

DOCUMENT
- DOC TYPE: ☐ Deed (Grant • Trust Transfer • Gift • Interspousal • Quitclaim • ToD • Warranty) ☐ DOT (Mortgage) ☐ Trust (Certification • Rev / Irrev • Am / Rest) ☐ POA (General / Limited • Durable / Springing) ☐ POAH (AHCD • Living Will) ☐ Agreement (Compliance-E&O • Correction) ☐ Affidavit (Borrower • Occupancy • Ownership • Refi • Survey • Debts & Liens • Name-Signature-ID • Marital • Death • Will) ☐ Other (Vehicle Title • Safe Deposit Box)
- DOC DATE: J F M A M J J A S O N D , ____ | DOC TITLE or TYPE: _____ | # OF PAGES: __ | ☐ Inspect/Copy Request | Entry X-Ref #: __

☐ **SATISFACTORY EVIDENCE** ☐ Driver's License / Passport / State ID / Military / Government / Tribal / Inmate / Other ID   *or*   ☐ Credible Witness(es)

SIGNER — SIGNER's NAME: ___ ☐ For | ADDRESS: ___ ☐ Non-Public # ___ | ☐ Capacity ☐ Voluntary ☐ Proper ID | ISSUED | SIGNATURE ☐ (oath / affirmation, if any) ☐ (by Mark) | PHONE C / H / W: ___ / ___ *or* ☐ MISC | AGENCY ☐ CA DMV ☐ US State Dept | EXPIRES ➡

CW #1 — #1 WITNESS's NAME: ___ ☐ P/Known | ADDRESS ___ ☐ Non-Public # ___ | ☐ Driver's License ☐ Passport ☐ Other ID | ISSUED | SIGNATURE ☐ (after oath / affirmation) | PHONE C / H / W: ___ / ___ *or* ☐ MISC | AGENCY ☐ CA DMV ☐ US State Dept | EXPIRES ❶

CW #2 — #2 WITNESS's NAME: ___ ☐ P/Known | ADDRESS ___ ☐ Non-Public # ___ | ☐ Driver's License ☐ Passport ☐ Other ID | ISSUED | SIGNATURE ☐ (after oath / affirmation) | PHONE C / H / W: ___ / ___ *or* ☐ MISC | AGENCY ☐ CA DMV ☐ US State Dept | EXPIRES ❷

Fingerprint — R T I M R P L

NOTARY NAME (printed):   COMMISSION #:

85

SERVICE	DATE - -20	TIME : am / pm	ADDRESS	☐ Signer's ☐ Office	NOTES	☐ Stop	MILES	Notary	☐ Adv. Travel	☐ Rush	☐ Copy	☐ Other	TOTAL FEES
							$	$	$	$	$		$

TYPE   ☐ Acknowledgment   ☐ Jurat   ☐ Copy Certification   ☐ Oath/Affirmation   ☐ Oath of Office   ☐ Proof of Execution   ☐ Protest   ☐ Other

Fingerprint   R / T / I / M / R / P / L

DOCUMENT

DOC TYPE   ☐ Deed   ☐ DOT   ☐ Trust   ☐ POA   ☐ POAH   ☐ Agreement   ☐ Affidavit   ☐ Other
Grant • Trust Transfer • Gift   Mortgage   Certification   General / Limited   AHCD   Compliance-E&O   Borrower • Occupancy • Ownership • Refi • Survey   Vehicle Title
Interspousal • Quitclaim • ToD • Warranty   Rev / Irrev • Am / Rest   Durable / Springing   Living Will   Correction   Debts & Liens • Name-Signature-ID • Marital • Death • Will   Safe Deposit Box

DOC DATE   J F M A M J   J A S O N D   , | DOC TITLE or TYPE | # OF PAGES   ☐ Inspect/Copy Request   Entry X-Ref #

☐ **SATISFACTORY EVIDENCE** ☐ Driver's License / Passport / State ID / Military / Government / Tribal / Inmate / Other ID   *or*   ☐ Credible Witness(es)

SIGNER	SIGNER's NAME	☐ For	ADDRESS	☐ Non-Public	☐ Capacity ☐ Voluntary ☐ Proper ID #	ISSUED	SIGNATURE ☐ (oath / affirmation, if any) ☐ (by Mark)
	PHONE C / H / W *or* ☐ MISC				AGENCY ☐ CA DMV ☐ US State Dept	EXPIRES	➡

CW #1	#1 WITNESS's NAME	☐ P/Known	ADDRESS	☐ Non-Public	☐ Driver's License ☐ Passport ☐ Other ID #	ISSUED	SIGNATURE ☐ (after oath / affirmation)
	PHONE C / H / W *or* ☐ MISC				AGENCY ☐ CA DMV ☐ US State Dept	EXPIRES	❶

CW #2	#2 WITNESS's NAME	☐ P/Known	ADDRESS	☐ Non-Public	☐ Driver's License ☐ Passport ☐ Other ID #	ISSUED	SIGNATURE ☐ (after oath / affirmation)
	PHONE C / H / W *or* ☐ MISC				AGENCY ☐ CA DMV ☐ US State Dept	EXPIRES	❷

86

SERVICE	DATE - -20	TIME : am / pm	ADDRESS	☐ Signer's ☐ Office	NOTES	☐ Stop	MILES	Notary	☐ Adv. Travel	☐ Rush	☐ Copy	☐ Other	TOTAL FEES
							$	$	$	$	$		$

TYPE   ☐ Acknowledgment   ☐ Jurat   ☐ Copy Certification   ☐ Oath/Affirmation   ☐ Oath of Office   ☐ Proof of Execution   ☐ Protest   ☐ Other

Fingerprint   R / T / I / M / R / P / L

DOCUMENT

DOC TYPE   ☐ Deed   ☐ DOT   ☐ Trust   ☐ POA   ☐ POAH   ☐ Agreement   ☐ Affidavit   ☐ Other
Grant • Trust Transfer • Gift   Mortgage   Certification   General / Limited   AHCD   Compliance-E&O   Borrower • Occupancy • Ownership • Refi • Survey   Vehicle Title
Interspousal • Quitclaim • ToD • Warranty   Rev / Irrev • Am / Rest   Durable / Springing   Living Will   Correction   Debts & Liens • Name-Signature-ID • Marital • Death • Will   Safe Deposit Box

DOC DATE   J F M A M J   J A S O N D   , | DOC TITLE or TYPE | # OF PAGES   ☐ Inspect/Copy Request   Entry X-Ref #

☐ **SATISFACTORY EVIDENCE** ☐ Driver's License / Passport / State ID / Military / Government / Tribal / Inmate / Other ID   *or*   ☐ Credible Witness(es)

SIGNER	SIGNER's NAME	☐ For	ADDRESS	☐ Non-Public	☐ Capacity ☐ Voluntary ☐ Proper ID #	ISSUED	SIGNATURE ☐ (oath / affirmation, if any) ☐ (by Mark)
	PHONE C / H / W *or* ☐ MISC				AGENCY ☐ CA DMV ☐ US State Dept	EXPIRES	➡

CW #1	#1 WITNESS's NAME	☐ P/Known	ADDRESS	☐ Non-Public	☐ Driver's License ☐ Passport ☐ Other ID #	ISSUED	SIGNATURE ☐ (after oath / affirmation)
	PHONE C / H / W *or* ☐ MISC				AGENCY ☐ CA DMV ☐ US State Dept	EXPIRES	❶

CW #2	#2 WITNESS's NAME	☐ P/Known	ADDRESS	☐ Non-Public	☐ Driver's License ☐ Passport ☐ Other ID #	ISSUED	SIGNATURE ☐ (after oath / affirmation)
	PHONE C / H / W *or* ☐ MISC				AGENCY ☐ CA DMV ☐ US State Dept	EXPIRES	❷

NOTARY NAME (printed): _____   COMMISSION #: _____

Entry 87

SERVICE — DATE: __-__-20__ TIME: __:__ am/pm ADDRESS: _____ ☐ Signer's ☐ Office NOTES: _____ ☐ Stop MILES: ___ Notary $___ ☐ Adv. Travel $___ ☐ Rush $___ ☐ Copy $___ ☐ Other $___ TOTAL FEES $___

TYPE: ☐ Acknowledgment ☐ Jurat ☐ Copy Certification ☐ Oath/Affirmation ☐ Oath of Office ☐ Proof of Execution ☐ Protest ☐ Other

DOCUMENT
- DOC TYPE: ☐ Deed (Grant • Trust Transfer • Gift • Interspousal • Quitclaim • ToD • Warranty) ☐ DOT (Mortgage • Certification • Rev / Irrev • Am / Rest) ☐ Trust ☐ POA (General / Limited • Durable / Springing) ☐ POAH (AHCD • Living Will) ☐ Agreement (Compliance-E&O • Correction) ☐ Affidavit (Borrower • Occupancy • Ownership • Refi • Survey • Debts & Liens • Name-Signature-ID • Marital • Death • Will) ☐ Other (Vehicle Title • Safe Deposit Box)
- DOC DATE: J F M A M J J A S O N D , ____   DOC TITLE or TYPE: _____   # OF PAGES: ___   ☐ Inspect/Copy Request   Entry X-Ref #: ___

R T I M R P L Fingerprint

☐ **SATISFACTORY EVIDENCE** ☐ Driver's License / Passport / State ID / Military / Government / Tribal / Inmate / Other ID **or** ☐ Credible Witness(es)

SIGNER — SIGNER's NAME: _____ ☐ For ADDRESS: _____ ☐ Non-Public ☐ Capacity ☐ Voluntary ☐ Proper ID ISSUED: ___ SIGNATURE ☐ (oath / affirmation, if any) ☐ (by Mark)
PHONE C/H/W: ___/___ or ☐ MISC #___ AGENCY: ___ ☐ CA DMV ☐ US State Dept EXPIRES: ___ ➡

CW #1 — #1 WITNESS's NAME: _____ ☐ P/Known ADDRESS: _____ ☐ Non-Public ☐ Driver's License ☐ Passport ☐ Other ID ISSUED: ___ SIGNATURE ☐ (after oath / affirmation)
PHONE C/H/W: ___/___ or ☐ MISC #___ AGENCY: ___ ☐ CA DMV ☐ US State Dept EXPIRES: ___ ❶

CW #2 — #2 WITNESS's NAME: _____ ☐ P/Known ADDRESS: _____ ☐ Non-Public ☐ Driver's License ☐ Passport ☐ Other ID ISSUED: ___ SIGNATURE ☐ (after oath / affirmation)
PHONE C/H/W: ___/___ or ☐ MISC #___ AGENCY: ___ ☐ CA DMV ☐ US State Dept EXPIRES: ___ ❷

Entry 88

SERVICE — DATE: __-__-20__ TIME: __:__ am/pm ADDRESS: _____ ☐ Signer's ☐ Office NOTES: _____ ☐ Stop MILES: ___ Notary $___ ☐ Adv. Travel $___ ☐ Rush $___ ☐ Copy $___ ☐ Other $___ TOTAL FEES $___

TYPE: ☐ Acknowledgment ☐ Jurat ☐ Copy Certification ☐ Oath/Affirmation ☐ Oath of Office ☐ Proof of Execution ☐ Protest ☐ Other

DOCUMENT
- DOC TYPE: ☐ Deed (Grant • Trust Transfer • Gift • Interspousal • Quitclaim • ToD • Warranty) ☐ DOT (Mortgage • Certification • Rev / Irrev • Am / Rest) ☐ Trust ☐ POA (General / Limited • Durable / Springing) ☐ POAH (AHCD • Living Will) ☐ Agreement (Compliance-E&O • Correction) ☐ Affidavit (Borrower • Occupancy • Ownership • Refi • Survey • Debts & Liens • Name-Signature-ID • Marital • Death • Will) ☐ Other (Vehicle Title • Safe Deposit Box)
- DOC DATE: J F M A M J J A S O N D , ____   DOC TITLE or TYPE: _____   # OF PAGES: ___   ☐ Inspect/Copy Request   Entry X-Ref #: ___

R T I M R P L Fingerprint

☐ **SATISFACTORY EVIDENCE** ☐ Driver's License / Passport / State ID / Military / Government / Tribal / Inmate / Other ID **or** ☐ Credible Witness(es)

SIGNER — SIGNER's NAME: _____ ☐ For ADDRESS: _____ ☐ Non-Public ☐ Capacity ☐ Voluntary ☐ Proper ID ISSUED: ___ SIGNATURE ☐ (oath / affirmation, if any) ☐ (by Mark)
PHONE C/H/W: ___/___ or ☐ MISC #___ AGENCY: ___ ☐ CA DMV ☐ US State Dept EXPIRES: ___ ➡

CW #1 — #1 WITNESS's NAME: _____ ☐ P/Known ADDRESS: _____ ☐ Non-Public ☐ Driver's License ☐ Passport ☐ Other ID ISSUED: ___ SIGNATURE ☐ (after oath / affirmation)
PHONE C/H/W: ___/___ or ☐ MISC #___ AGENCY: ___ ☐ CA DMV ☐ US State Dept EXPIRES: ___ ❶

CW #2 — #2 WITNESS's NAME: _____ ☐ P/Known ADDRESS: _____ ☐ Non-Public ☐ Driver's License ☐ Passport ☐ Other ID ISSUED: ___ SIGNATURE ☐ (after oath / affirmation)
PHONE C/H/W: ___/___ or ☐ MISC #___ AGENCY: ___ ☐ CA DMV ☐ US State Dept EXPIRES: ___ ❷

NOTARY NAME (printed): _____ COMMISSION #: _____

Entry 89

SERVICE	DATE: - -20	TIME: : am pm	ADDRESS	☐ Signer's ☐ Office	NOTES	☐ Stop	MILES	Notary	☐ Adv. Travel	☐ Rush	☐ Copy	☐ Other	TOTAL FEES	**89**
								$	$		$	$	$ $	

TYPE ☐ Acknowledgment ☐ Jurat ☐ Copy Certification ☐ Oath/Affirmation ☐ Oath of Office ☐ Proof of Execution ☐ Protest ☐ Other

R **Fingerprint**

DOC TYPE ☐ Deed ☐ DOT ☐ Trust ☐ POA ☐ POAH ☐ Agreement ☐ Affidavit ☐ Other

| Grant • Trust Transfer • Gift | Mortgage | Certification | General / Limited | AHCD | Compliance-E&O | Borrower • Occupancy • Ownership • Refi • Survey | Vehicle Title |
| Interspousal • Quitclaim • ToD • Warranty | | Rev / Irrev • Am / Rest | Durable / Springing | Living Will | Correction | Debts & Liens • Name-Signature-ID • Marital • Death • Will | Safe Deposit Box |

DOC DATE J F M A M J J A S O N D ,   DOC TITLE or TYPE   # OF PAGES ☐ Inspect/Copy Request   Entry X-Ref #

T I M R P

☐ **SATISFACTORY EVIDENCE** ☐ Driver's License / Passport / State ID / Military / Government / Tribal / Inmate / Other ID *or* ☐ Credible Witness(es)

L

SIGNER
SIGNER's NAME ☐ For ADDRESS ☐ Non-Public ☐ Capacity ☐ Voluntary ☐ Proper ID ISSUED # SIGNATURE ☐ *(oath / affirmation, if any)* ☐ *(by Mark)*
PHONE C / H / W *or* ☐ MISC / AGENCY ☐ CA DMV ☐ US State Dept EXPIRES ➡

CW #1
#1 WITNESS's NAME ☐ P/Known ADDRESS ☐ Non-Public ☐ Driver's License ☐ Passport ☐ Other ID ISSUED # SIGNATURE ☐ *(after oath / affirmation)*
PHONE C / H / W *or* ☐ MISC / AGENCY ☐ CA DMV ☐ US State Dept EXPIRES ❶

CW #2
#2 WITNESS's NAME ☐ P/Known ADDRESS ☐ Non-Public ☐ Driver's License ☐ Passport ☐ Other ID ISSUED # SIGNATURE ☐ *(after oath / affirmation)*
PHONE C / H / W *or* ☐ MISC / AGENCY ☐ CA DMV ☐ US State Dept EXPIRES ❷

Entry 90

SERVICE	DATE: - -20	TIME: : am pm	ADDRESS	☐ Signer's ☐ Office	NOTES	☐ Stop	MILES	Notary	☐ Adv. Travel	☐ Rush	☐ Copy	☐ Other	TOTAL FEES	**90**
								$	$		$	$	$ $	

TYPE ☐ Acknowledgment ☐ Jurat ☐ Copy Certification ☐ Oath/Affirmation ☐ Oath of Office ☐ Proof of Execution ☐ Protest ☐ Other

R **Fingerprint**

DOC TYPE ☐ Deed ☐ DOT ☐ Trust ☐ POA ☐ POAH ☐ Agreement ☐ Affidavit ☐ Other

| Grant • Trust Transfer • Gift | Mortgage | Certification | General / Limited | AHCD | Compliance-E&O | Borrower • Occupancy • Ownership • Refi • Survey | Vehicle Title |
| Interspousal • Quitclaim • ToD • Warranty | | Rev / Irrev • Am / Rest | Durable / Springing | Living Will | Correction | Debts & Liens • Name-Signature-ID • Marital • Death • Will | Safe Deposit Box |

DOC DATE J F M A M J J A S O N D ,   DOC TITLE or TYPE   # OF PAGES ☐ Inspect/Copy Request   Entry X-Ref #

T I M R P

☐ **SATISFACTORY EVIDENCE** ☐ Driver's License / Passport / State ID / Military / Government / Tribal / Inmate / Other ID *or* ☐ Credible Witness(es)

L

SIGNER
SIGNER's NAME ☐ For ADDRESS ☐ Non-Public ☐ Capacity ☐ Voluntary ☐ Proper ID ISSUED # SIGNATURE ☐ *(oath / affirmation, if any)* ☐ *(by Mark)*
PHONE C / H / W *or* ☐ MISC / AGENCY ☐ CA DMV ☐ US State Dept EXPIRES ➡

CW #1
#1 WITNESS's NAME ☐ P/Known ADDRESS ☐ Non-Public ☐ Driver's License ☐ Passport ☐ Other ID ISSUED # SIGNATURE ☐ *(after oath / affirmation)*
PHONE C / H / W *or* ☐ MISC / AGENCY ☐ CA DMV ☐ US State Dept EXPIRES ❶

CW #2
#2 WITNESS's NAME ☐ P/Known ADDRESS ☐ Non-Public ☐ Driver's License ☐ Passport ☐ Other ID ISSUED # SIGNATURE ☐ *(after oath / affirmation)*
PHONE C / H / W *or* ☐ MISC / AGENCY ☐ CA DMV ☐ US State Dept EXPIRES ❷

NOTARY NAME (printed): COMMISSION #:

Entry 91

| SERVICE | DATE - -20 | TIME : am/pm | ADDRESS | ☐ Signer's ☐ Office | NOTES | ☐ Stop | MILES | Notary $ | ☐ Adv. Travel $ | ☐ Rush $ | ☐ Copy $ | ☐ Other $ | TOTAL FEES $ |

TYPE: ☐ Acknowledgment ☐ Jurat ☐ Copy Certification ☐ Oath/Affirmation ☐ Oath of Office ☐ Proof of Execution ☐ Protest ☐ Other

Fingerprint R T I M R P L

DOC TYPE: ☐ Deed ☐ DOT ☐ Trust ☐ POA ☐ POAH ☐ Agreement ☐ Affidavit ☐ Other
Grant • Trust Transfer • Gift | Mortgage | Certification | General / Limited | AHCD | Compliance-E&O | Borrower • Occupancy • Ownership • Refi • Survey | Vehicle Title
Interspousal • Quitclaim • ToD • Warranty | Rev / Irrev • Am / Rest | Durable / Springing | Living Will | Correction | Debts & Liens • Name-Signature-ID • Marital • Death • Will | Safe Deposit Box

DOC DATE: J F M A M J J A S O N D , | DOC TITLE or TYPE | # OF PAGES | ☐ Inspect/Copy Request | Entry X-Ref #

☐ **SATISFACTORY EVIDENCE** ☐ Driver's License / Passport / State ID / Military / Government / Tribal / Inmate / Other ID *or* ☐ Credible Witness(es)

SIGNER:
- SIGNER's NAME | ☐ For | ADDRESS | ☐ Non-Public | ☐ Capacity # | ☐ Voluntary | ☐ Proper ID | ISSUED | SIGNATURE ☐ (oath / affirmation, if any) ☐ (by Mark)
- PHONE C / H / W / | *or* ☐ MISC | AGENCY | ☐ CA DMV ☐ US State Dept | EXPIRES | ➤

CW #1:
- #1 WITNESS's NAME | ☐ P/Known | ADDRESS | ☐ Non-Public | ☐ Driver's License ☐ Passport ☐ Other ID # | ISSUED | SIGNATURE ☐ (after oath / affirmation)
- PHONE C / H / W / | *or* ☐ MISC | AGENCY | ☐ CA DMV ☐ US State Dept | EXPIRES | ❶

CW #2:
- #2 WITNESS's NAME | ☐ P/Known | ADDRESS | ☐ Non-Public | ☐ Driver's License ☐ Passport ☐ Other ID # | ISSUED | SIGNATURE ☐ (after oath / affirmation)
- PHONE C / H / W / | *or* ☐ MISC | AGENCY | ☐ CA DMV ☐ US State Dept | EXPIRES | ❷

Entry 92

| SERVICE | DATE - -20 | TIME : am/pm | ADDRESS | ☐ Signer's ☐ Office | NOTES | ☐ Stop | MILES | Notary $ | ☐ Adv. Travel $ | ☐ Rush $ | ☐ Copy $ | ☐ Other $ | TOTAL FEES $ |

TYPE: ☐ Acknowledgment ☐ Jurat ☐ Copy Certification ☐ Oath/Affirmation ☐ Oath of Office ☐ Proof of Execution ☐ Protest ☐ Other

Fingerprint R T I M R P L

DOC TYPE: ☐ Deed ☐ DOT ☐ Trust ☐ POA ☐ POAH ☐ Agreement ☐ Affidavit ☐ Other
Grant • Trust Transfer • Gift | Mortgage | Certification | General / Limited | AHCD | Compliance-E&O | Borrower • Occupancy • Ownership • Refi • Survey | Vehicle Title
Interspousal • Quitclaim • ToD • Warranty | Rev / Irrev • Am / Rest | Durable / Springing | Living Will | Correction | Debts & Liens • Name-Signature-ID • Marital • Death • Will | Safe Deposit Box

DOC DATE: J F M A M J J A S O N D , | DOC TITLE or TYPE | # OF PAGES | ☐ Inspect/Copy Request | Entry X-Ref #

☐ **SATISFACTORY EVIDENCE** ☐ Driver's License / Passport / State ID / Military / Government / Tribal / Inmate / Other ID *or* ☐ Credible Witness(es)

SIGNER:
- SIGNER's NAME | ☐ For | ADDRESS | ☐ Non-Public | ☐ Capacity # | ☐ Voluntary | ☐ Proper ID | ISSUED | SIGNATURE ☐ (oath / affirmation, if any) ☐ (by Mark)
- PHONE C / H / W / | *or* ☐ MISC | AGENCY | ☐ CA DMV ☐ US State Dept | EXPIRES | ➤

CW #1:
- #1 WITNESS's NAME | ☐ P/Known | ADDRESS | ☐ Non-Public | ☐ Driver's License ☐ Passport ☐ Other ID # | ISSUED | SIGNATURE ☐ (after oath / affirmation)
- PHONE C / H / W / | *or* ☐ MISC | AGENCY | ☐ CA DMV ☐ US State Dept | EXPIRES | ❶

CW #2:
- #2 WITNESS's NAME | ☐ P/Known | ADDRESS | ☐ Non-Public | ☐ Driver's License ☐ Passport ☐ Other ID # | ISSUED | SIGNATURE ☐ (after oath / affirmation)
- PHONE C / H / W / | *or* ☐ MISC | AGENCY | ☐ CA DMV ☐ US State Dept | EXPIRES | ❷

NOTARY NAME (printed):   **COMMISSION #:**

Entry 93

SERVICE	DATE - -20	TIME : am / pm	ADDRESS ☐ Signer's ☐ Office	NOTES	☐ Stop	MILES	Notary ☐ Adv. Travel ☐ Rush ☐ Copy ☐ Other TOTAL FEES $ $ $ $ $ $	**93**

R | **Fingerprint**

TYPE ☐ Acknowledgment ☐ Jurat ☐ Copy Certification ☐ Oath/Affirmation ☐ Oath of Office ☐ Proof of Execution ☐ Protest ☐ Other

DOCUMENT

DOC TYPE ☐ Deed ☐ DOT ☐ Trust ☐ POA ☐ POAH ☐ Agreement ☐ Affidavit ☐ Other

Grant • Trust Transfer • Gift | Mortgage | Certification | General / Limited | AHCD | Compliance-E&O | Borrower • Occupancy • Ownership • Refi • Survey | Vehicle Title
Interspousal • Quitclaim • ToD • Warranty | Rev / Irrev • Am / Rest | Durable / Springing | Living Will | Correction | Debts & Liens • Name-Signature-ID • Marital • Death • Will | Safe Deposit Box

DOC DATE J F M A M J   J A S O N D ,   **DOC TITLE or TYPE**   **# OF PAGES** ☐ Inspect/Copy Request   Entry X-Ref #

T I M R P L

☐ **SATISFACTORY EVIDENCE** ☐ Driver's License / Passport / State ID / Military / Government / Tribal / Inmate / Other ID *or* ☐ Credible Witness(es)

SIGNER

SIGNER's NAME	☐ For	ADDRESS	☐ Non-Public	☐ Capacity ☐ Voluntary ☐ Proper ID	ISSUED	SIGNATURE ☐ (oath / affirmation, if any) ☐ (by Mark)
#						
PHONE C / H / W *or* ☐ MISC			AGENCY ☐ CA DMV ☐ US State Dept	EXPIRES	➡

CW #1

#1 WITNESS's NAME	☐ P/Known	ADDRESS	☐ Non-Public	☐ Driver's License ☐ Passport ☐ Other ID	ISSUED	SIGNATURE ☐ (after oath / affirmation)
#						
PHONE C / H / W *or* ☐ MISC			AGENCY ☐ CA DMV ☐ US State Dept	EXPIRES	❶

CW #2

#2 WITNESS's NAME	☐ P/Known	ADDRESS	☐ Non-Public	☐ Driver's License ☐ Passport ☐ Other ID	ISSUED	SIGNATURE ☐ (after oath / affirmation)
#						
PHONE C / H / W *or* ☐ MISC			AGENCY ☐ CA DMV ☐ US State Dept	EXPIRES	❷

Entry 94

SERVICE	DATE - -20	TIME : am / pm	ADDRESS ☐ Signer's ☐ Office	NOTES	☐ Stop	MILES	Notary ☐ Adv. Travel ☐ Rush ☐ Copy ☐ Other TOTAL FEES $ $ $ $ $ $	**94**

R | **Fingerprint**

TYPE ☐ Acknowledgment ☐ Jurat ☐ Copy Certification ☐ Oath/Affirmation ☐ Oath of Office ☐ Proof of Execution ☐ Protest ☐ Other

DOCUMENT

DOC TYPE ☐ Deed ☐ DOT ☐ Trust ☐ POA ☐ POAH ☐ Agreement ☐ Affidavit ☐ Other

Grant • Trust Transfer • Gift | Mortgage | Certification | General / Limited | AHCD | Compliance-E&O | Borrower • Occupancy • Ownership • Refi • Survey | Vehicle Title
Interspousal • Quitclaim • ToD • Warranty | Rev / Irrev • Am / Rest | Durable / Springing | Living Will | Correction | Debts & Liens • Name-Signature-ID • Marital • Death • Will | Safe Deposit Box

DOC DATE J F M A M J   J A S O N D ,   **DOC TITLE or TYPE**   **# OF PAGES** ☐ Inspect/Copy Request   Entry X-Ref #

T I M R P L

☐ **SATISFACTORY EVIDENCE** ☐ Driver's License / Passport / State ID / Military / Government / Tribal / Inmate / Other ID *or* ☐ Credible Witness(es)

SIGNER

SIGNER's NAME	☐ For	ADDRESS	☐ Non-Public	☐ Capacity ☐ Voluntary ☐ Proper ID	ISSUED	SIGNATURE ☐ (oath / affirmation, if any) ☐ (by Mark)
#						
PHONE C / H / W *or* ☐ MISC			AGENCY ☐ CA DMV ☐ US State Dept	EXPIRES	➡

CW #1

#1 WITNESS's NAME	☐ P/Known	ADDRESS	☐ Non-Public	☐ Driver's License ☐ Passport ☐ Other ID	ISSUED	SIGNATURE ☐ (after oath / affirmation)
#						
PHONE C / H / W *or* ☐ MISC			AGENCY ☐ CA DMV ☐ US State Dept	EXPIRES	❶

CW #2

#2 WITNESS's NAME	☐ P/Known	ADDRESS	☐ Non-Public	☐ Driver's License ☐ Passport ☐ Other ID	ISSUED	SIGNATURE ☐ (after oath / affirmation)
#						
PHONE C / H / W *or* ☐ MISC			AGENCY ☐ CA DMV ☐ US State Dept	EXPIRES	❷

NOTARY NAME (printed): COMMISSION #:

Entry 95

SERVICE — DATE: - -20 | TIME: : am/pm | ADDRESS | ☐ Signer's ☐ Office | NOTES | ☐ Stop | MILES | Notary $ | ☐ Adv. Travel $ | ☐ Rush $ | ☐ Copy $ | ☐ Other $ | TOTAL FEES $

TYPE: ☐ Acknowledgment ☐ Jurat ☐ Copy Certification ☐ Oath/Affirmation ☐ Oath of Office ☐ Proof of Execution ☐ Protest ☐ Other

DOCUMENT
DOC TYPE: ☐ Deed ☐ DOT ☐ Trust ☐ POA ☐ POAH ☐ Agreement ☐ Affidavit ☐ Other
Grant • Trust Transfer • Gift | Mortgage | Certification | General / Limited | AHCD | Compliance-E&O | Borrower • Occupancy • Ownership • Refi • Survey | Vehicle Title
Interspousal • Quitclaim • ToD • Warranty | Rev / Irrev • Am / Rest | Durable / Springing | Living Will | Correction | Debts & Liens • Name-Signature-ID • Marital • Death • Will | Safe Deposit Box

DOC DATE: J F M A M J / J A S O N D , | DOC TITLE or TYPE | # OF PAGES | ☐ Inspect/Copy Request | Entry X-Ref #

R T I M R P L | **Fingerprint**

☐ **SATISFACTORY EVIDENCE** ☐ Driver's License / Passport / State ID / Military / Government / Tribal / Inmate / Other ID *or* ☐ Credible Witness(es)

SIGNER
SIGNER's NAME | ☐ For | ADDRESS | ☐ Non-Public | ☐ Capacity # | ☐ Voluntary | ☐ Proper ID | ISSUED | SIGNATURE | ☐ (oath / affirmation, if any) | ☐ (by Mark)
PHONE C / H / W / | *or* ☐ MISC | | | AGENCY | ☐ CA DMV | ☐ US State Dept | EXPIRES | ➡

CW #1
#1 WITNESS's NAME | ☐ P/Known | ADDRESS | ☐ Non-Public | ☐ Driver's License ☐ Passport ☐ Other ID # | ISSUED | SIGNATURE | ☐ (after oath / affirmation)
PHONE C / H / W / | *or* ☐ MISC | | | AGENCY | ☐ CA DMV | ☐ US State Dept | EXPIRES | ❶

CW #2
#2 WITNESS's NAME | ☐ P/Known | ADDRESS | ☐ Non-Public | ☐ Driver's License ☐ Passport ☐ Other ID # | ISSUED | SIGNATURE | ☐ (after oath / affirmation)
PHONE C / H / W / | *or* ☐ MISC | | | AGENCY | ☐ CA DMV | ☐ US State Dept | EXPIRES | ❷

Entry 96

SERVICE — DATE: - -20 | TIME: : am/pm | ADDRESS | ☐ Signer's ☐ Office | NOTES | ☐ Stop | MILES | Notary $ | ☐ Adv. Travel $ | ☐ Rush $ | ☐ Copy $ | ☐ Other $ | TOTAL FEES $

TYPE: ☐ Acknowledgment ☐ Jurat ☐ Copy Certification ☐ Oath/Affirmation ☐ Oath of Office ☐ Proof of Execution ☐ Protest ☐ Other

DOCUMENT
DOC TYPE: ☐ Deed ☐ DOT ☐ Trust ☐ POA ☐ POAH ☐ Agreement ☐ Affidavit ☐ Other
Grant • Trust Transfer • Gift | Mortgage | Certification | General / Limited | AHCD | Compliance-E&O | Borrower • Occupancy • Ownership • Refi • Survey | Vehicle Title
Interspousal • Quitclaim • ToD • Warranty | Rev / Irrev • Am / Rest | Durable / Springing | Living Will | Correction | Debts & Liens • Name-Signature-ID • Marital • Death • Will | Safe Deposit Box

DOC DATE: J F M A M J / J A S O N D , | DOC TITLE or TYPE | # OF PAGES | ☐ Inspect/Copy Request | Entry X-Ref #

R T I M R P L | **Fingerprint**

☐ **SATISFACTORY EVIDENCE** ☐ Driver's License / Passport / State ID / Military / Government / Tribal / Inmate / Other ID *or* ☐ Credible Witness(es)

SIGNER
SIGNER's NAME | ☐ For | ADDRESS | ☐ Non-Public | ☐ Capacity # | ☐ Voluntary | ☐ Proper ID | ISSUED | SIGNATURE | ☐ (oath / affirmation, if any) | ☐ (by Mark)
PHONE C / H / W / | *or* ☐ MISC | | | AGENCY | ☐ CA DMV | ☐ US State Dept | EXPIRES | ➡

CW #1
#1 WITNESS's NAME | ☐ P/Known | ADDRESS | ☐ Non-Public | ☐ Driver's License ☐ Passport ☐ Other ID # | ISSUED | SIGNATURE | ☐ (after oath / affirmation)
PHONE C / H / W / | *or* ☐ MISC | | | AGENCY | ☐ CA DMV | ☐ US State Dept | EXPIRES | ❶

CW #2
#2 WITNESS's NAME | ☐ P/Known | ADDRESS | ☐ Non-Public | ☐ Driver's License ☐ Passport ☐ Other ID # | ISSUED | SIGNATURE | ☐ (after oath / affirmation)
PHONE C / H / W / | *or* ☐ MISC | | | AGENCY | ☐ CA DMV | ☐ US State Dept | EXPIRES | ❷

NOTARY NAME (printed): _____   COMMISSION #: _____

Entry 97

SERVICE	DATE - -20	TIME :	am pm	ADDRESS	☐ Signer's	☐ Office	NOTES	☐ Stop	MILES	Notary ☐ Adv. Travel ☐ Rush ☐ Copy ☐ Other	TOTAL FEES
								$	$	$ $ $ $	$

TYPE ☐ Acknowledgment ☐ Jurat ☐ Copy Certification ☐ Oath/Affirmation ☐ Oath of Office ☐ Proof of Execution ☐ Protest ☐ Other

R T I M R P L   **Fingerprint**

DOCUMENT

DOC TYPE ☐ Deed   ☐ DOT   ☐ Trust   ☐ POA   ☐ POAH   ☐ Agreement   ☐ Affidavit   ☐ Other

Grant • Trust Transfer • Gift   Mortgage   Certification   General / Limited   AHCD   Compliance-E&O   Borrower • Occupancy • Ownership • Refi • Survey   Vehicle Title
Interspousal • Quitclaim • ToD • Warranty   Rev / Irrev • Am / Rest   Durable / Springing   Living Will   Correction   Debts & Liens • Name-Signature-ID • Marital • Death • Will   Safe Deposit Box

DOC DATE   J F M A M J   J A S O N D   ,   DOC TITLE or TYPE   # OF PAGES   ☐ Inspect/Copy Request   Entry X-Ref #

☐ **SATISFACTORY EVIDENCE** ☐ Driver's License / Passport / State ID / Military / Government / Tribal / Inmate / Other ID   *or*   ☐ Credible Witness(es)

SIGNER

SIGNER's NAME   ☐ For   ADDRESS   ☐ Non-Public   ☐ Capacity   ☐ Voluntary   ☐ Proper ID   ISSUED #   SIGNATURE   ☐ *(oath / affirmation, if any)*   ☐ *(by Mark)*
PHONE C / H / W   *or* ☐ MISC   /   AGENCY   ☐ CA DMV   ☐ US State Dept   EXPIRES   ➤

CW #1

#1 WITNESS's NAME   ☐ P/Known   ADDRESS   ☐ Non-Public   ☐ Driver's License   ☐ Passport   ☐ Other ID   ISSUED #   SIGNATURE   ☐ *(after oath / affirmation)*
PHONE C / H / W   *or* ☐ MISC   /   AGENCY   ☐ CA DMV   ☐ US State Dept   EXPIRES   ❶

CW #2

#2 WITNESS's NAME   ☐ P/Known   ADDRESS   ☐ Non-Public   ☐ Driver's License   ☐ Passport   ☐ Other ID   ISSUED #   SIGNATURE   ☐ *(after oath / affirmation)*
PHONE C / H / W   *or* ☐ MISC   /   AGENCY   ☐ CA DMV   ☐ US State Dept   EXPIRES   ❷

Entry 98

SERVICE	DATE - -20	TIME :	am pm	ADDRESS	☐ Signer's	☐ Office	NOTES	☐ Stop	MILES	Notary ☐ Adv. Travel ☐ Rush ☐ Copy ☐ Other	TOTAL FEES
								$	$	$ $ $ $	$

TYPE ☐ Acknowledgment ☐ Jurat ☐ Copy Certification ☐ Oath/Affirmation ☐ Oath of Office ☐ Proof of Execution ☐ Protest ☐ Other

R T I M R P L   **Fingerprint**

DOCUMENT

DOC TYPE ☐ Deed   ☐ DOT   ☐ Trust   ☐ POA   ☐ POAH   ☐ Agreement   ☐ Affidavit   ☐ Other

Grant • Trust Transfer • Gift   Mortgage   Certification   General / Limited   AHCD   Compliance-E&O   Borrower • Occupancy • Ownership • Refi • Survey   Vehicle Title
Interspousal • Quitclaim • ToD • Warranty   Rev / Irrev • Am / Rest   Durable / Springing   Living Will   Correction   Debts & Liens • Name-Signature-ID • Marital • Death • Will   Safe Deposit Box

DOC DATE   J F M A M J   J A S O N D   ,   DOC TITLE or TYPE   # OF PAGES   ☐ Inspect/Copy Request   Entry X-Ref #

☐ **SATISFACTORY EVIDENCE** ☐ Driver's License / Passport / State ID / Military / Government / Tribal / Inmate / Other ID   *or*   ☐ Credible Witness(es)

SIGNER

SIGNER's NAME   ☐ For   ADDRESS   ☐ Non-Public   ☐ Capacity   ☐ Voluntary   ☐ Proper ID   ISSUED #   SIGNATURE   ☐ *(oath / affirmation, if any)*   ☐ *(by Mark)*
PHONE C / H / W   *or* ☐ MISC   /   AGENCY   ☐ CA DMV   ☐ US State Dept   EXPIRES   ➤

CW #1

#1 WITNESS's NAME   ☐ P/Known   ADDRESS   ☐ Non-Public   ☐ Driver's License   ☐ Passport   ☐ Other ID   ISSUED #   SIGNATURE   ☐ *(after oath / affirmation)*
PHONE C / H / W   *or* ☐ MISC   /   AGENCY   ☐ CA DMV   ☐ US State Dept   EXPIRES   ❶

CW #2

#2 WITNESS's NAME   ☐ P/Known   ADDRESS   ☐ Non-Public   ☐ Driver's License   ☐ Passport   ☐ Other ID   ISSUED #   SIGNATURE   ☐ *(after oath / affirmation)*
PHONE C / H / W   *or* ☐ MISC   /   AGENCY   ☐ CA DMV   ☐ US State Dept   EXPIRES   ❷

NOTARY NAME (printed):   COMMISSION #:

Entry 99

SERVICE — DATE: - -20   TIME: : am/pm   ADDRESS ☐ Signer's ☐ Office   NOTES   ☐ Stop   MILES   Notary $ ☐ Adv. Travel $ ☐ Rush $ ☐ Copy $ ☐ Other $ TOTAL FEES $

TYPE: ☐ Acknowledgment ☐ Jurat ☐ Copy Certification ☐ Oath/Affirmation ☐ Oath of Office ☐ Proof of Execution ☐ Protest ☐ Other

DOCUMENT — DOC TYPE: ☐ Deed (Grant • Trust Transfer • Gift / Interspousal • Quitclaim • ToD • Warranty) ☐ DOT (Mortgage) ☐ Trust (Certification / Rev / Irrev • Am / Rest) ☐ POA (General / Limited / Durable / Springing) ☐ POAH (AHCD / Living Will) ☐ Agreement (Compliance-E&O / Correction) ☐ Affidavit (Borrower • Occupancy • Ownership • Refi • Survey / Debts & Liens • Name-Signature-ID • Marital • Death • Will) ☐ Other (Vehicle Title / Safe Deposit Box)

DOC DATE: J F M A M J J A S O N D ,   DOC TITLE or TYPE   # OF PAGES   ☐ Inspect/Copy Request   Entry X-Ref #

☐ **SATISFACTORY EVIDENCE** ☐ Driver's License / Passport / State ID / Military / Government / Tribal / Inmate / Other ID   *or*   ☐ Credible Witness(es)

SIGNER — SIGNER's NAME   ☐ For   ADDRESS   ☐ Non-Public   ☐ Capacity #   ☐ Voluntary   ☐ Proper ID   ISSUED   SIGNATURE   ☐ (oath / affirmation, if any)   ☐ (by Mark)
PHONE C / H / W   /   *or* ☐ MISC   AGENCY   ☐ CA DMV   ☐ US State Dept   EXPIRES

CW #1 — #1 WITNESS's NAME   ☐ P/Known   ADDRESS   ☐ Non-Public   ☐ Driver's License   ☐ Passport   ☐ Other ID   ISSUED   SIGNATURE   ☐ (after oath / affirmation)
PHONE C / H / W   /   *or* ☐ MISC   AGENCY   ☐ CA DMV   ☐ US State Dept   EXPIRES   ❶

CW #2 — #2 WITNESS's NAME   ☐ P/Known   ADDRESS   ☐ Non-Public   ☐ Driver's License   ☐ Passport   ☐ Other ID   ISSUED   SIGNATURE   ☐ (after oath / affirmation)
PHONE C / H / W   /   *or* ☐ MISC   AGENCY   ☐ CA DMV   ☐ US State Dept   EXPIRES   ❷

Fingerprint (R T I M R P L)

Entry 100

SERVICE — DATE: - -20   TIME: : am/pm   ADDRESS ☐ Signer's ☐ Office   NOTES   ☐ Stop   MILES   Notary $ ☐ Adv. Travel $ ☐ Rush $ ☐ Copy $ ☐ Other $ TOTAL FEES $

TYPE: ☐ Acknowledgment ☐ Jurat ☐ Copy Certification ☐ Oath/Affirmation ☐ Oath of Office ☐ Proof of Execution ☐ Protest ☐ Other

DOCUMENT — DOC TYPE: ☐ Deed (Grant • Trust Transfer • Gift / Interspousal • Quitclaim • ToD • Warranty) ☐ DOT (Mortgage) ☐ Trust (Certification / Rev / Irrev • Am / Rest) ☐ POA (General / Limited / Durable / Springing) ☐ POAH (AHCD / Living Will) ☐ Agreement (Compliance-E&O / Correction) ☐ Affidavit (Borrower • Occupancy • Ownership • Refi • Survey / Debts & Liens • Name-Signature-ID • Marital • Death • Will) ☐ Other (Vehicle Title / Safe Deposit Box)

DOC DATE: J F M A M J J A S O N D ,   DOC TITLE or TYPE   # OF PAGES   ☐ Inspect/Copy Request   Entry X-Ref #

☐ **SATISFACTORY EVIDENCE** ☐ Driver's License / Passport / State ID / Military / Government / Tribal / Inmate / Other ID   *or*   ☐ Credible Witness(es)

SIGNER — SIGNER's NAME   ☐ For   ADDRESS   ☐ Non-Public   ☐ Capacity #   ☐ Voluntary   ☐ Proper ID   ISSUED   SIGNATURE   ☐ (oath / affirmation, if any)   ☐ (by Mark)
PHONE C / H / W   /   *or* ☐ MISC   AGENCY   ☐ CA DMV   ☐ US State Dept   EXPIRES

CW #1 — #1 WITNESS's NAME   ☐ P/Known   ADDRESS   ☐ Non-Public   ☐ Driver's License   ☐ Passport   ☐ Other ID   ISSUED   SIGNATURE   ☐ (after oath / affirmation)
PHONE C / H / W   /   *or* ☐ MISC   AGENCY   ☐ CA DMV   ☐ US State Dept   EXPIRES   ❶

CW #2 — #2 WITNESS's NAME   ☐ P/Known   ADDRESS   ☐ Non-Public   ☐ Driver's License   ☐ Passport   ☐ Other ID   ISSUED   SIGNATURE   ☐ (after oath / affirmation)
PHONE C / H / W   /   *or* ☐ MISC   AGENCY   ☐ CA DMV   ☐ US State Dept   EXPIRES   ❷

Fingerprint (R T I M R P L)

NOTARY NAME (printed):   **COMMISSION #:**

101

SERVICE	DATE - -20	TIME : am / pm	ADDRESS ☐ Signer's ☐ Office	NOTES	☐ Stop	MILES	Notary ☐ Adv. Travel ☐ Rush ☐ Copy ☐ Other	TOTAL FEES
					$ $		$ $	$ $

	TYPE ☐ Acknowledgment ☐ Jurat ☐ Copy Certification ☐ Oath/Affirmation ☐ Oath of Office ☐ Proof of Execution ☐ Protest ☐ Other

R	**Fingerprint**
T	
I	
M	
R	
P	
L	

DOCUMENT

DOC TYPE ☐ Deed ☐ DOT ☐ Trust ☐ POA ☐ POAH ☐ Agreement ☐ Affidavit ☐ Other

Grant • Trust Transfer • Gift   Mortgage   Certification   General / Limited   AHCD   Compliance-E&O   Borrower • Occupancy • Ownership • Refi • Survey   Vehicle Title

Interspousal • Quitclaim • ToD • Warranty   Rev / Irrev • Am / Rest   Durable / Springing   Living Will   Correction   Debts & Liens • Name-Signature-ID • Marital • Death • Will   Safe Deposit Box

DOC DATE J F M A M J J A S O N D ,   DOC TITLE or TYPE   # OF PAGES   ☐ Inspect/Copy Request   Entry X-Ref #

☐ **SATISFACTORY EVIDENCE** ☐ Driver's License / Passport / State ID / Military / Government / Tribal / Inmate / Other ID *or* ☐ Credible Witness(es)

SIGNER

SIGNER's NAME	☐ For	ADDRESS	☐ Non-Public	☐ Capacity ☐ Voluntary ☐ Proper ID #	ISSUED	SIGNATURE ☐ (oath / affirmation, if any) ☐ (by Mark)
PHONE C / H / W /	*or* ☐ MISC			AGENCY ☐ CA DMV ☐ US State Dept	EXPIRES	➡

CW #1

#1 WITNESS's NAME	☐ P/Known	ADDRESS	☐ Non-Public	☐ Driver's License ☐ Passport ☐ Other ID #	ISSUED	SIGNATURE ☐ (after oath / affirmation)
PHONE C / H / W /	*or* ☐ MISC			AGENCY ☐ CA DMV ☐ US State Dept	EXPIRES	❶

CW #2

#2 WITNESS's NAME	☐ P/Known	ADDRESS	☐ Non-Public	☐ Driver's License ☐ Passport ☐ Other ID #	ISSUED	SIGNATURE ☐ (after oath / affirmation)
PHONE C / H / W /	*or* ☐ MISC			AGENCY ☐ CA DMV ☐ US State Dept	EXPIRES	❷

102

SERVICE	DATE - -20	TIME : am / pm	ADDRESS ☐ Signer's ☐ Office	NOTES	☐ Stop	MILES	Notary ☐ Adv. Travel ☐ Rush ☐ Copy ☐ Other	TOTAL FEES
					$ $		$ $	$ $

	TYPE ☐ Acknowledgment ☐ Jurat ☐ Copy Certification ☐ Oath/Affirmation ☐ Oath of Office ☐ Proof of Execution ☐ Protest ☐ Other

R	**Fingerprint**
T	
I	
M	
R	
P	
L	

DOCUMENT

DOC TYPE ☐ Deed ☐ DOT ☐ Trust ☐ POA ☐ POAH ☐ Agreement ☐ Affidavit ☐ Other

Grant • Trust Transfer • Gift   Mortgage   Certification   General / Limited   AHCD   Compliance-E&O   Borrower • Occupancy • Ownership • Refi • Survey   Vehicle Title

Interspousal • Quitclaim • ToD • Warranty   Rev / Irrev • Am / Rest   Durable / Springing   Living Will   Correction   Debts & Liens • Name-Signature-ID • Marital • Death • Will   Safe Deposit Box

DOC DATE J F M A M J J A S O N D ,   DOC TITLE or TYPE   # OF PAGES   ☐ Inspect/Copy Request   Entry X-Ref #

☐ **SATISFACTORY EVIDENCE** ☐ Driver's License / Passport / State ID / Military / Government / Tribal / Inmate / Other ID *or* ☐ Credible Witness(es)

SIGNER

SIGNER's NAME	☐ For	ADDRESS	☐ Non-Public	☐ Capacity ☐ Voluntary ☐ Proper ID #	ISSUED	SIGNATURE ☐ (oath / affirmation, if any) ☐ (by Mark)
PHONE C / H / W /	*or* ☐ MISC			AGENCY ☐ CA DMV ☐ US State Dept	EXPIRES	➡

CW #1

#1 WITNESS's NAME	☐ P/Known	ADDRESS	☐ Non-Public	☐ Driver's License ☐ Passport ☐ Other ID #	ISSUED	SIGNATURE ☐ (after oath / affirmation)
PHONE C / H / W /	*or* ☐ MISC			AGENCY ☐ CA DMV ☐ US State Dept	EXPIRES	❶

CW #2

#2 WITNESS's NAME	☐ P/Known	ADDRESS	☐ Non-Public	☐ Driver's License ☐ Passport ☐ Other ID #	ISSUED	SIGNATURE ☐ (after oath / affirmation)
PHONE C / H / W /	*or* ☐ MISC			AGENCY ☐ CA DMV ☐ US State Dept	EXPIRES	❷

NOTARY NAME (printed):   COMMISSION #:

Entry 103

SERVICE — DATE: - -20   TIME: : am/pm   ADDRESS ☐ Signer's ☐ Office   NOTES   ☐ Stop   MILES   Notary $ ☐ Adv. Travel $ ☐ Rush $ ☐ Copy $ ☐ Other $ TOTAL FEES $

TYPE: ☐ Acknowledgment   ☐ Jurat   ☐ Copy Certification   ☐ Oath/Affirmation   ☐ Oath of Office   ☐ Proof of Execution   ☐ Protest   ☐ Other

DOCUMENT — DOC TYPE: ☐ Deed (Grant • Trust Transfer • Gift • Interspousal • Quitclaim • ToD • Warranty)   ☐ DOT (Mortgage • Rev / Irrev • Am / Rest)   ☐ Trust (Certification)   ☐ POA (General / Limited • Durable / Springing)   ☐ POAH (AHCD • Living Will)   ☐ Agreement (Compliance-E&O • Correction)   ☐ Affidavit (Borrower • Occupancy • Ownership • Refi • Survey • Debts & Liens • Name-Signature-ID • Marital • Death • Will)   ☐ Other (Vehicle Title • Safe Deposit Box)

DOC DATE: J F M A M J J A S O N D ,   DOC TITLE or TYPE   # OF PAGES   ☐ Inspect/Copy Request   Entry X-Ref #

Fingerprint R T I M R P L

☐ **SATISFACTORY EVIDENCE** ☐ Driver's License / Passport / State ID / Military / Government / Tribal / Inmate / Other ID   *or*   ☐ Credible Witness(es)

SIGNER — SIGNER's NAME   ☐ For   ADDRESS   ☐ Non-Public   ☐ Capacity   ☐ Voluntary   ☐ Proper ID   ISSUED #   SIGNATURE   ☐ (oath / affirmation, if any)   ☐ (by Mark)
PHONE C / H / W /   *or* ☐ MISC   AGENCY   ☐ CA DMV   ☐ US State Dept   EXPIRES   ➔

CW #1 — #1 WITNESS's NAME   ☐ P/Known   ADDRESS   ☐ Non-Public   ☐ Driver's License   ☐ Passport   ☐ Other ID   ISSUED #   SIGNATURE   ☐ (after oath / affirmation)
PHONE C / H / W /   *or* ☐ MISC   AGENCY   ☐ CA DMV   ☐ US State Dept   EXPIRES   ❶

CW #2 — #2 WITNESS's NAME   ☐ P/Known   ADDRESS   ☐ Non-Public   ☐ Driver's License   ☐ Passport   ☐ Other ID   ISSUED #   SIGNATURE   ☐ (after oath / affirmation)
PHONE C / H / W /   *or* ☐ MISC   AGENCY   ☐ CA DMV   ☐ US State Dept   EXPIRES   ❷

Entry 104

SERVICE — DATE: - -20   TIME: : am/pm   ADDRESS ☐ Signer's ☐ Office   NOTES   ☐ Stop   MILES   Notary $ ☐ Adv. Travel $ ☐ Rush $ ☐ Copy $ ☐ Other $ TOTAL FEES $

TYPE: ☐ Acknowledgment   ☐ Jurat   ☐ Copy Certification   ☐ Oath/Affirmation   ☐ Oath of Office   ☐ Proof of Execution   ☐ Protest   ☐ Other

DOCUMENT — DOC TYPE: ☐ Deed (Grant • Trust Transfer • Gift • Interspousal • Quitclaim • ToD • Warranty)   ☐ DOT (Mortgage • Rev / Irrev • Am / Rest)   ☐ Trust (Certification)   ☐ POA (General / Limited • Durable / Springing)   ☐ POAH (AHCD • Living Will)   ☐ Agreement (Compliance-E&O • Correction)   ☐ Affidavit (Borrower • Occupancy • Ownership • Refi • Survey • Debts & Liens • Name-Signature-ID • Marital • Death • Will)   ☐ Other (Vehicle Title • Safe Deposit Box)

DOC DATE: J F M A M J J A S O N D ,   DOC TITLE or TYPE   # OF PAGES   ☐ Inspect/Copy Request   Entry X-Ref #

Fingerprint R T I M R P L

☐ **SATISFACTORY EVIDENCE** ☐ Driver's License / Passport / State ID / Military / Government / Tribal / Inmate / Other ID   *or*   ☐ Credible Witness(es)

SIGNER — SIGNER's NAME   ☐ For   ADDRESS   ☐ Non-Public   ☐ Capacity   ☐ Voluntary   ☐ Proper ID   ISSUED #   SIGNATURE   ☐ (oath / affirmation, if any)   ☐ (by Mark)
PHONE C / H / W /   *or* ☐ MISC   AGENCY   ☐ CA DMV   ☐ US State Dept   EXPIRES   ➔

CW #1 — #1 WITNESS's NAME   ☐ P/Known   ADDRESS   ☐ Non-Public   ☐ Driver's License   ☐ Passport   ☐ Other ID   ISSUED #   SIGNATURE   ☐ (after oath / affirmation)
PHONE C / H / W /   *or* ☐ MISC   AGENCY   ☐ CA DMV   ☐ US State Dept   EXPIRES   ❶

CW #2 — #2 WITNESS's NAME   ☐ P/Known   ADDRESS   ☐ Non-Public   ☐ Driver's License   ☐ Passport   ☐ Other ID   ISSUED #   SIGNATURE   ☐ (after oath / affirmation)
PHONE C / H / W /   *or* ☐ MISC   AGENCY   ☐ CA DMV   ☐ US State Dept   EXPIRES   ❷

NOTARY NAME (printed):   COMMISSION #:

Entry 105

SERVICE

DATE ___ - ___ -20___ TIME ___ : ___ am/pm ADDRESS ☐ Signer's ☐ Office NOTES ☐ Stop MILES Notary ☐ Adv. Travel ☐ Rush ☐ Copy ☐ Other TOTAL FEES
$ ___ $ ___ $ ___ $ ___ $ ___ $ ___

TYPE ☐ Acknowledgment ☐ Jurat ☐ Copy Certification ☐ Oath/Affirmation ☐ Oath of Office ☐ Proof of Execution ☐ Protest ☐ Other

Fingerprint

DOCUMENT

DOC TYPE ☐ Deed ☐ DOT ☐ Trust ☐ POA ☐ POAH ☐ Agreement ☐ Affidavit ☐ Other
Grant • Trust Transfer • Gift | Mortgage | Certification | General / Limited | AHCD | Compliance-E&O | Borrower • Occupancy • Ownership • Refi • Survey | Vehicle Title
Interspousal • Quitclaim • ToD • Warranty | Rev / Irrev • Am / Rest | Durable / Springing | Living Will | Correction | Debts & Liens • Name-Signature-ID • Marital • Death • Will | Safe Deposit Box

DOC DATE J F M A M J J A S O N D , ___   DOC TITLE or TYPE ___   # OF PAGES ___ ☐ Inspect/Copy Request   Entry X-Ref # ___

R T I M R P L

☐ **SATISFACTORY EVIDENCE** ☐ Driver's License / Passport / State ID / Military / Government / Tribal / Inmate / Other ID **or** ☐ Credible Witness(es)

SIGNER

SIGNER's NAME ☐ For ADDRESS ☐ Non-Public ☐ Capacity ☐ Voluntary ☐ Proper ID ISSUED # ___ SIGNATURE ☐ (oath / affirmation, if any) ☐ (by Mark)
PHONE C / H / W ___ or ☐ MISC ___   AGENCY ☐ CA DMV ☐ US State Dept EXPIRES ➜

CW #1

#1 WITNESS's NAME ☐ P/Known ADDRESS ☐ Non-Public ☐ Driver's License ☐ Passport ☐ Other ID ISSUED # ___ SIGNATURE ☐ (after oath / affirmation)
PHONE C / H / W ___ or ☐ MISC ___   AGENCY ☐ CA DMV ☐ US State Dept EXPIRES ❶

CW #2

#2 WITNESS's NAME ☐ P/Known ADDRESS ☐ Non-Public ☐ Driver's License ☐ Passport ☐ Other ID ISSUED # ___ SIGNATURE ☐ (after oath / affirmation)
PHONE C / H / W ___ or ☐ MISC ___   AGENCY ☐ CA DMV ☐ US State Dept EXPIRES ❷

Entry 106

SERVICE

DATE ___ - ___ -20___ TIME ___ : ___ am/pm ADDRESS ☐ Signer's ☐ Office NOTES ☐ Stop MILES Notary ☐ Adv. Travel ☐ Rush ☐ Copy ☐ Other TOTAL FEES
$ ___ $ ___ $ ___ $ ___ $ ___ $ ___

TYPE ☐ Acknowledgment ☐ Jurat ☐ Copy Certification ☐ Oath/Affirmation ☐ Oath of Office ☐ Proof of Execution ☐ Protest ☐ Other

Fingerprint

DOCUMENT

DOC TYPE ☐ Deed ☐ DOT ☐ Trust ☐ POA ☐ POAH ☐ Agreement ☐ Affidavit ☐ Other
Grant • Trust Transfer • Gift | Mortgage | Certification | General / Limited | AHCD | Compliance-E&O | Borrower • Occupancy • Ownership • Refi • Survey | Vehicle Title
Interspousal • Quitclaim • ToD • Warranty | Rev / Irrev • Am / Rest | Durable / Springing | Living Will | Correction | Debts & Liens • Name-Signature-ID • Marital • Death • Will | Safe Deposit Box

DOC DATE J F M A M J J A S O N D , ___   DOC TITLE or TYPE ___   # OF PAGES ___ ☐ Inspect/Copy Request   Entry X-Ref # ___

R T I M R P L

☐ **SATISFACTORY EVIDENCE** ☐ Driver's License / Passport / State ID / Military / Government / Tribal / Inmate / Other ID **or** ☐ Credible Witness(es)

SIGNER

SIGNER's NAME ☐ For ADDRESS ☐ Non-Public ☐ Capacity ☐ Voluntary ☐ Proper ID ISSUED # ___ SIGNATURE ☐ (oath / affirmation, if any) ☐ (by Mark)
PHONE C / H / W ___ or ☐ MISC ___   AGENCY ☐ CA DMV ☐ US State Dept EXPIRES ➜

CW #1

#1 WITNESS's NAME ☐ P/Known ADDRESS ☐ Non-Public ☐ Driver's License ☐ Passport ☐ Other ID ISSUED # ___ SIGNATURE ☐ (after oath / affirmation)
PHONE C / H / W ___ or ☐ MISC ___   AGENCY ☐ CA DMV ☐ US State Dept EXPIRES ❶

CW #2

#2 WITNESS's NAME ☐ P/Known ADDRESS ☐ Non-Public ☐ Driver's License ☐ Passport ☐ Other ID ISSUED # ___ SIGNATURE ☐ (after oath / affirmation)
PHONE C / H / W ___ or ☐ MISC ___   AGENCY ☐ CA DMV ☐ US State Dept EXPIRES ❷

NOTARY NAME (printed): COMMISSION #:

Entry 107

SERVICE — DATE: - -20 | TIME: : am/pm | ADDRESS | ☐ Signer's ☐ Office | NOTES | ☐ Stop | MILES | Notary $ | ☐ Adv. Travel $ | ☐ Rush $ | ☐ Copy $ | ☐ Other $ | TOTAL FEES $

TYPE: ☐ Acknowledgment ☐ Jurat ☐ Copy Certification ☐ Oath/Affirmation ☐ Oath of Office ☐ Proof of Execution ☐ Protest ☐ Other

DOCUMENT

DOC TYPE:
- ☐ Deed — Grant • Trust Transfer • Gift • Interspousal • Quitclaim • ToD • Warranty
- ☐ DOT — Mortgage
- ☐ Trust — Certification • Rev / Irrev • Am / Rest
- ☐ POA — General / Limited • Durable / Springing
- ☐ POAH — AHCD • Living Will
- ☐ Agreement — Compliance-E&O • Correction
- ☐ Affidavit — Borrower • Occupancy • Ownership • Refi • Survey • Debts & Liens • Name-Signature-ID • Marital • Death • Will
- ☐ Other — Vehicle Title • Safe Deposit Box

DOC DATE: J F M A M J J A S O N D , | DOC TITLE or TYPE | # OF PAGES | ☐ Inspect/Copy Request | Entry X-Ref #

☐ **SATISFACTORY EVIDENCE** ☐ Driver's License / Passport / State ID / Military / Government / Tribal / Inmate / Other ID *or* ☐ Credible Witness(es)

SIGNER: SIGNER's NAME | ☐ For | ADDRESS | ☐ Non-Public | ☐ Capacity # | ☐ Voluntary | ☐ Proper ID | ISSUED | SIGNATURE | ☐ (oath / affirmation, if any) | ☐ (by Mark)
PHONE C / H / W / | *or* ☐ MISC | | | AGENCY | ☐ CA DMV | ☐ US State Dept | EXPIRES | ➡

CW #1: #1 WITNESS's NAME | ☐ P/Known | ADDRESS | ☐ Non-Public | ☐ Driver's License | ☐ Passport | ☐ Other ID | ISSUED | SIGNATURE | ☐ (after oath / affirmation)
PHONE C / H / W / | *or* ☐ MISC | | | AGENCY | ☐ CA DMV | ☐ US State Dept | EXPIRES | ❶

CW #2: #2 WITNESS's NAME | ☐ P/Known | ADDRESS | ☐ Non-Public | ☐ Driver's License | ☐ Passport | ☐ Other ID | ISSUED | SIGNATURE | ☐ (after oath / affirmation)
PHONE C / H / W / | *or* ☐ MISC | | | AGENCY | ☐ CA DMV | ☐ US State Dept | EXPIRES | ❷

Fingerprint — R T I M R P L

Entry 108

SERVICE — DATE: - -20 | TIME: : am/pm | ADDRESS | ☐ Signer's ☐ Office | NOTES | ☐ Stop | MILES | Notary $ | ☐ Adv. Travel $ | ☐ Rush $ | ☐ Copy $ | ☐ Other $ | TOTAL FEES $

TYPE: ☐ Acknowledgment ☐ Jurat ☐ Copy Certification ☐ Oath/Affirmation ☐ Oath of Office ☐ Proof of Execution ☐ Protest ☐ Other

DOCUMENT

DOC TYPE:
- ☐ Deed — Grant • Trust Transfer • Gift • Interspousal • Quitclaim • ToD • Warranty
- ☐ DOT — Mortgage
- ☐ Trust — Certification • Rev / Irrev • Am / Rest
- ☐ POA — General / Limited • Durable / Springing
- ☐ POAH — AHCD • Living Will
- ☐ Agreement — Compliance-E&O • Correction
- ☐ Affidavit — Borrower • Occupancy • Ownership • Refi • Survey • Debts & Liens • Name-Signature-ID • Marital • Death • Will
- ☐ Other — Vehicle Title • Safe Deposit Box

DOC DATE: J F M A M J J A S O N D , | DOC TITLE or TYPE | # OF PAGES | ☐ Inspect/Copy Request | Entry X-Ref #

☐ **SATISFACTORY EVIDENCE** ☐ Driver's License / Passport / State ID / Military / Government / Tribal / Inmate / Other ID *or* ☐ Credible Witness(es)

SIGNER: SIGNER's NAME | ☐ For | ADDRESS | ☐ Non-Public | ☐ Capacity # | ☐ Voluntary | ☐ Proper ID | ISSUED | SIGNATURE | ☐ (oath / affirmation, if any) | ☐ (by Mark)
PHONE C / H / W / | *or* ☐ MISC | | | AGENCY | ☐ CA DMV | ☐ US State Dept | EXPIRES | ➡

CW #1: #1 WITNESS's NAME | ☐ P/Known | ADDRESS | ☐ Non-Public | ☐ Driver's License | ☐ Passport | ☐ Other ID | ISSUED | SIGNATURE | ☐ (after oath / affirmation)
PHONE C / H / W / | *or* ☐ MISC | | | AGENCY | ☐ CA DMV | ☐ US State Dept | EXPIRES | ❶

CW #2: #2 WITNESS's NAME | ☐ P/Known | ADDRESS | ☐ Non-Public | ☐ Driver's License | ☐ Passport | ☐ Other ID | ISSUED | SIGNATURE | ☐ (after oath / affirmation)
PHONE C / H / W / | *or* ☐ MISC | | | AGENCY | ☐ CA DMV | ☐ US State Dept | EXPIRES | ❷

Fingerprint — R T I M R P L

NOTARY NAME (printed):   COMMISSION #:

109

SERVICE

DATE   -   -20   TIME   :   am / pm   ADDRESS   ☐ Signer's   ☐ Office   NOTES   ☐ Stop   MILES   Notary ☐ Adv. Travel ☐ Rush ☐ Copy ☐ Other   TOTAL FEES $ $ $ $ $ $

TYPE   ☐ Acknowledgment   ☐ Jurat   ☐ Copy Certification   ☐ Oath/Affirmation   ☐ Oath of Office   ☐ Proof of Execution   ☐ Protest   ☐ Other

Fingerprint   R T I M R P L

DOCUMENT

DOC TYPE   ☐ Deed   ☐ DOT   ☐ Trust   ☐ POA   ☐ POAH   ☐ Agreement   ☐ Affidavit   ☐ Other

Grant • Trust Transfer • Gift   Mortgage   Certification   General / Limited   AHCD   Compliance-E&O   Borrower • Occupancy • Ownership • Refi • Survey   Vehicle Title

Interspousal • Quitclaim • ToD • Warranty   Rev / Irrev • Am / Rest   Durable / Springing   Living Will   Correction   Debts & Liens • Name-Signature-ID • Marital • Death • Will   Safe Deposit Box

DOC DATE   J F M A M J   J A S O N D   ,   DOC TITLE or TYPE   # OF PAGES   ☐ Inspect/Copy Request   Entry X-Ref #

☐ **SATISFACTORY EVIDENCE** ☐ Driver's License / Passport / State ID / Military / Government / Tribal / Inmate / Other ID   *or*   ☐ Credible Witness(es)

SIGNER

SIGNER's NAME   ☐ For   ADDRESS   ☐ Non-Public   ☐ Capacity   ☐ Voluntary   ☐ Proper ID   ISSUED #   SIGNATURE   ☐ (oath / affirmation, if any)   ☐ (by Mark)

PHONE C / H / W   *or* ☐ MISC   AGENCY   ☐ CA DMV   ☐ US State Dept   EXPIRES   ➡

CW #1

#1 WITNESS's NAME   ☐ P/Known   ADDRESS   ☐ Non-Public   ☐ Driver's License   ☐ Passport   ☐ Other ID   ISSUED #   SIGNATURE   ☐ (after oath / affirmation)

PHONE C / H / W   *or* ☐ MISC   AGENCY   ☐ CA DMV   ☐ US State Dept   EXPIRES   ❶

CW #2

#2 WITNESS's NAME   ☐ P/Known   ADDRESS   ☐ Non-Public   ☐ Driver's License   ☐ Passport   ☐ Other ID   ISSUED #   SIGNATURE   ☐ (after oath / affirmation)

PHONE C / H / W   *or* ☐ MISC   AGENCY   ☐ CA DMV   ☐ US State Dept   EXPIRES   ❷

110

SERVICE

DATE   -   -20   TIME   :   am / pm   ADDRESS   ☐ Signer's   ☐ Office   NOTES   ☐ Stop   MILES   Notary ☐ Adv. Travel ☐ Rush ☐ Copy ☐ Other   TOTAL FEES $ $ $ $ $ $

TYPE   ☐ Acknowledgment   ☐ Jurat   ☐ Copy Certification   ☐ Oath/Affirmation   ☐ Oath of Office   ☐ Proof of Execution   ☐ Protest   ☐ Other

Fingerprint   R T I M R P L

DOCUMENT

DOC TYPE   ☐ Deed   ☐ DOT   ☐ Trust   ☐ POA   ☐ POAH   ☐ Agreement   ☐ Affidavit   ☐ Other

Grant • Trust Transfer • Gift   Mortgage   Certification   General / Limited   AHCD   Compliance-E&O   Borrower • Occupancy • Ownership • Refi • Survey   Vehicle Title

Interspousal • Quitclaim • ToD • Warranty   Rev / Irrev • Am / Rest   Durable / Springing   Living Will   Correction   Debts & Liens • Name-Signature-ID • Marital • Death • Will   Safe Deposit Box

DOC DATE   J F M A M J   J A S O N D   ,   DOC TITLE or TYPE   # OF PAGES   ☐ Inspect/Copy Request   Entry X-Ref #

☐ **SATISFACTORY EVIDENCE** ☐ Driver's License / Passport / State ID / Military / Government / Tribal / Inmate / Other ID   *or*   ☐ Credible Witness(es)

SIGNER

SIGNER's NAME   ☐ For   ADDRESS   ☐ Non-Public   ☐ Capacity   ☐ Voluntary   ☐ Proper ID   ISSUED #   SIGNATURE   ☐ (oath / affirmation, if any)   ☐ (by Mark)

PHONE C / H / W   *or* ☐ MISC   AGENCY   ☐ CA DMV   ☐ US State Dept   EXPIRES   ➡

CW #1

#1 WITNESS's NAME   ☐ P/Known   ADDRESS   ☐ Non-Public   ☐ Driver's License   ☐ Passport   ☐ Other ID   ISSUED #   SIGNATURE   ☐ (after oath / affirmation)

PHONE C / H / W   *or* ☐ MISC   AGENCY   ☐ CA DMV   ☐ US State Dept   EXPIRES   ❶

CW #2

#2 WITNESS's NAME   ☐ P/Known   ADDRESS   ☐ Non-Public   ☐ Driver's License   ☐ Passport   ☐ Other ID   ISSUED #   SIGNATURE   ☐ (after oath / affirmation)

PHONE C / H / W   *or* ☐ MISC   AGENCY   ☐ CA DMV   ☐ US State Dept   EXPIRES   ❷

NOTARY NAME (printed):   COMMISSION #:

Entry 111

SERVICE — DATE: - -20 | TIME: : am/pm | ADDRESS ☐ Signer's ☐ Office | NOTES | ☐ Stop | MILES | Notary $ | ☐ Adv. Travel $ | ☐ Rush $ | ☐ Copy $ | ☐ Other $ | TOTAL FEES $

TYPE: ☐ Acknowledgment ☐ Jurat ☐ Copy Certification ☐ Oath/Affirmation ☐ Oath of Office ☐ Proof of Execution ☐ Protest ☐ Other   **Fingerprint** (R T I M R P L)

DOCUMENT — DOC TYPE: ☐ Deed (Grant • Trust Transfer • Gift • Interspousal • Quitclaim • ToD • Warranty) ☐ DOT (Mortgage • Certification • Rev / Irrev • Am / Rest) ☐ Trust ☐ POA (General / Limited • Durable / Springing) ☐ POAH (AHCD • Living Will) ☐ Agreement (Compliance-E&O • Correction) ☐ Affidavit (Borrower • Occupancy • Ownership • Refi • Survey • Debts & Liens • Name-Signature-ID • Marital • Death • Will) ☐ Other (Vehicle Title • Safe Deposit Box)

DOC DATE: J F M A M J J A S O N D ,   DOC TITLE or TYPE: # OF PAGES: ☐ Inspect/Copy Request   Entry X-Ref #:

☐ **SATISFACTORY EVIDENCE** ☐ Driver's License / Passport / State ID / Military / Government / Tribal / Inmate / Other ID *or* ☐ Credible Witness(es)

SIGNER — SIGNER's NAME | ☐ For | ADDRESS | ☐ Non-Public | ☐ Capacity # | ☐ Voluntary | ☐ Proper ID | ISSUED | SIGNATURE ☐ (oath / affirmation, if any) ☐ (by Mark)
PHONE C / H / W / | *or* ☐ MISC | | | AGENCY | ☐ CA DMV | ☐ US State Dept | EXPIRES | ➤

CW #1 — #1 WITNESS's NAME | ☐ P/Known | ADDRESS | ☐ Non-Public | ☐ Driver's License # | ☐ Passport | ☐ Other ID | ISSUED | SIGNATURE ☐ (after oath / affirmation)
PHONE C / H / W / | *or* ☐ MISC | | | AGENCY | ☐ CA DMV | ☐ US State Dept | EXPIRES | ❶

CW #2 — #2 WITNESS's NAME | ☐ P/Known | ADDRESS | ☐ Non-Public | ☐ Driver's License # | ☐ Passport | ☐ Other ID | ISSUED | SIGNATURE ☐ (after oath / affirmation)
PHONE C / H / W / | *or* ☐ MISC | | | AGENCY | ☐ CA DMV | ☐ US State Dept | EXPIRES | ❷

Entry 112

SERVICE — DATE: - -20 | TIME: : am/pm | ADDRESS ☐ Signer's ☐ Office | NOTES | ☐ Stop | MILES | Notary $ | ☐ Adv. Travel $ | ☐ Rush $ | ☐ Copy $ | ☐ Other $ | TOTAL FEES $

TYPE: ☐ Acknowledgment ☐ Jurat ☐ Copy Certification ☐ Oath/Affirmation ☐ Oath of Office ☐ Proof of Execution ☐ Protest ☐ Other   **Fingerprint** (R T I M R P L)

DOCUMENT — DOC TYPE: ☐ Deed (Grant • Trust Transfer • Gift • Interspousal • Quitclaim • ToD • Warranty) ☐ DOT (Mortgage • Certification • Rev / Irrev • Am / Rest) ☐ Trust ☐ POA (General / Limited • Durable / Springing) ☐ POAH (AHCD • Living Will) ☐ Agreement (Compliance-E&O • Correction) ☐ Affidavit (Borrower • Occupancy • Ownership • Refi • Survey • Debts & Liens • Name-Signature-ID • Marital • Death • Will) ☐ Other (Vehicle Title • Safe Deposit Box)

DOC DATE: J F M A M J J A S O N D ,   DOC TITLE or TYPE: # OF PAGES: ☐ Inspect/Copy Request   Entry X-Ref #:

☐ **SATISFACTORY EVIDENCE** ☐ Driver's License / Passport / State ID / Military / Government / Tribal / Inmate / Other ID *or* ☐ Credible Witness(es)

SIGNER — SIGNER's NAME | ☐ For | ADDRESS | ☐ Non-Public | ☐ Capacity # | ☐ Voluntary | ☐ Proper ID | ISSUED | SIGNATURE ☐ (oath / affirmation, if any) ☐ (by Mark)
PHONE C / H / W / | *or* ☐ MISC | | | AGENCY | ☐ CA DMV | ☐ US State Dept | EXPIRES | ➤

CW #1 — #1 WITNESS's NAME | ☐ P/Known | ADDRESS | ☐ Non-Public | ☐ Driver's License # | ☐ Passport | ☐ Other ID | ISSUED | SIGNATURE ☐ (after oath / affirmation)
PHONE C / H / W / | *or* ☐ MISC | | | AGENCY | ☐ CA DMV | ☐ US State Dept | EXPIRES | ❶

CW #2 — #2 WITNESS's NAME | ☐ P/Known | ADDRESS | ☐ Non-Public | ☐ Driver's License # | ☐ Passport | ☐ Other ID | ISSUED | SIGNATURE ☐ (after oath / affirmation)
PHONE C / H / W / | *or* ☐ MISC | | | AGENCY | ☐ CA DMV | ☐ US State Dept | EXPIRES | ❷

NOTARY NAME (printed): _____   COMMISSION #: _____

113

| SERVICE | DATE   -   -20___ | TIME ___:___ □ am □ pm | ADDRESS ___ | □ Signer's □ Office | NOTES | □ Stop | MILES | Notary $ | □ Adv. Travel $ | □ Rush | □ Copy $ | □ Other $ | TOTAL FEES $ |

| TYPE | □ Acknowledgment □ Jurat □ Copy Certification □ Oath/Affirmation □ Oath of Office □ Proof of Execution □ Protest □ Other |

R   **Fingerprint**

DOCUMENT

DOC TYPE □ Deed □ DOT □ Trust □ POA □ POAH □ Agreement □ Affidavit □ Other

Grant • Trust Transfer • Gift   Mortgage   Certification   General / Limited   AHCD   Compliance-E&O   Borrower • Occupancy • Ownership • Refi • Survey   Vehicle Title

Interspousal • Quitclaim • ToD • Warranty   Rev / Irrev • Am / Rest   Durable / Springing   Living Will   Correction   Debts & Liens • Name-Signature-ID • Marital • Death • Will   Safe Deposit Box

DOC DATE   J F M A M J   J A S O N D   ,   DOC TITLE or TYPE   # OF PAGES   □ Inspect/Copy Request   Entry X-Ref #

T I M R P L

□ **SATISFACTORY EVIDENCE** □ Driver's License / Passport / State ID / Military / Government / Tribal / Inmate / Other ID   *or*   □ Credible Witness(es)

SIGNER

SIGNER's NAME   □ For   ADDRESS   □ Non-Public □ Capacity □ Voluntary □ Proper ID   ISSUED #   SIGNATURE □ (oath / affirmation, if any) □ (by Mark)

PHONE C / H / W   *or* □ MISC   /   AGENCY □ CA DMV □ US State Dept EXPIRES   ➡

CW #1

#1 WITNESS's NAME □ P/Known   ADDRESS   □ Non-Public □ Driver's License □ Passport □ Other ID   ISSUED #   SIGNATURE □ (after oath / affirmation)

PHONE C / H / W   *or* □ MISC   /   AGENCY □ CA DMV □ US State Dept EXPIRES   ❶

CW #2

#2 WITNESS's NAME □ P/Known   ADDRESS   □ Non-Public □ Driver's License □ Passport □ Other ID   ISSUED #   SIGNATURE □ (after oath / affirmation)

PHONE C / H / W   *or* □ MISC   /   AGENCY □ CA DMV □ US State Dept EXPIRES   ❷

114

| SERVICE | DATE   -   -20___ | TIME ___:___ □ am □ pm | ADDRESS ___ | □ Signer's □ Office | NOTES | □ Stop | MILES | Notary $ | □ Adv. Travel $ | □ Rush | □ Copy $ | □ Other $ | TOTAL FEES $ |

| TYPE | □ Acknowledgment □ Jurat □ Copy Certification □ Oath/Affirmation □ Oath of Office □ Proof of Execution □ Protest □ Other |

R   **Fingerprint**

DOCUMENT

DOC TYPE □ Deed □ DOT □ Trust □ POA □ POAH □ Agreement □ Affidavit □ Other

Grant • Trust Transfer • Gift   Mortgage   Certification   General / Limited   AHCD   Compliance-E&O   Borrower • Occupancy • Ownership • Refi • Survey   Vehicle Title

Interspousal • Quitclaim • ToD • Warranty   Rev / Irrev • Am / Rest   Durable / Springing   Living Will   Correction   Debts & Liens • Name-Signature-ID • Marital • Death • Will   Safe Deposit Box

DOC DATE   J F M A M J   J A S O N D   ,   DOC TITLE or TYPE   # OF PAGES   □ Inspect/Copy Request   Entry X-Ref #

T I M R P L

□ **SATISFACTORY EVIDENCE** □ Driver's License / Passport / State ID / Military / Government / Tribal / Inmate / Other ID   *or*   □ Credible Witness(es)

SIGNER

SIGNER's NAME   □ For   ADDRESS   □ Non-Public □ Capacity □ Voluntary □ Proper ID   ISSUED #   SIGNATURE □ (oath / affirmation, if any) □ (by Mark)

PHONE C / H / W   *or* □ MISC   /   AGENCY □ CA DMV □ US State Dept EXPIRES   ➡

CW #1

#1 WITNESS's NAME □ P/Known   ADDRESS   □ Non-Public □ Driver's License □ Passport □ Other ID   ISSUED #   SIGNATURE □ (after oath / affirmation)

PHONE C / H / W   *or* □ MISC   /   AGENCY □ CA DMV □ US State Dept EXPIRES   ❶

CW #2

#2 WITNESS's NAME □ P/Known   ADDRESS   □ Non-Public □ Driver's License □ Passport □ Other ID   ISSUED #   SIGNATURE □ (after oath / affirmation)

PHONE C / H / W   *or* □ MISC   /   AGENCY □ CA DMV □ US State Dept EXPIRES   ❷

NOTARY NAME (printed):   **COMMISSION #:**

Entry 115

SERVICE	DATE	TIME	ADDRESS	☐ Signer's ☐ Office	NOTES	☐ Stop MILES	Notary	☐ Adv. Travel	☐ Rush	☐ Copy	☐ Other	TOTAL FEES
	- -20	: am/pm				$	$		$	$	$	$

TYPE ☐ Acknowledgment ☐ Jurat ☐ Copy Certification ☐ Oath/Affirmation ☐ Oath of Office ☐ Proof of Execution ☐ Protest ☐ Other   **Fingerprint (R)**

DOCUMENT

DOC TYPE ☐ Deed ☐ DOT ☐ Trust ☐ POA ☐ POAH ☐ Agreement ☐ Affidavit ☐ Other
Grant • Trust Transfer • Gift | Mortgage | Certification | General / Limited | AHCD | Compliance-E&O | Borrower • Occupancy • Ownership • Refi • Survey | Vehicle Title
Interspousal • Quitclaim • ToD • Warranty | Rev / Irrev • Am / Rest | Durable / Springing | Living Will | Correction | Debts & Liens • Name-Signature-ID • Marital • Death • Will | Safe Deposit Box

DOC DATE J F M A M J J A S O N D ,   **DOC TITLE or TYPE**   **# OF PAGES**   ☐ Inspect/Copy Request   **Entry X-Ref #**

☐ **SATISFACTORY EVIDENCE** ☐ Driver's License / Passport / State ID / Military / Government / Tribal / Inmate / Other ID **or** ☐ Credible Witness(es)

SIGNER
- SIGNER's NAME | ☐ For | ADDRESS | ☐ Non-Public | ☐ Capacity | ☐ Voluntary | ☐ Proper ID | ISSUED # | SIGNATURE ☐ (oath / affirmation, if any) ☐ (by Mark)
- PHONE C / H / W | or ☐ MISC | | | AGENCY | ☐ CA DMV | ☐ US State Dept | EXPIRES | →

CW #1
- #1 WITNESS's NAME | ☐ P/Known | ADDRESS | ☐ Non-Public | ☐ Driver's License ☐ Passport ☐ Other ID | ISSUED # | SIGNATURE ☐ (after oath / affirmation)
- PHONE C / H / W | or ☐ MISC | | | AGENCY | ☐ CA DMV | ☐ US State Dept | EXPIRES | ❶

CW #2
- #2 WITNESS's NAME | ☐ P/Known | ADDRESS | ☐ Non-Public | ☐ Driver's License ☐ Passport ☐ Other ID | ISSUED # | SIGNATURE ☐ (after oath / affirmation)
- PHONE C / H / W | or ☐ MISC | | | AGENCY | ☐ CA DMV | ☐ US State Dept | EXPIRES | ❷

Entry 116

SERVICE	DATE	TIME	ADDRESS	☐ Signer's ☐ Office	NOTES	☐ Stop MILES	Notary	☐ Adv. Travel	☐ Rush	☐ Copy	☐ Other	TOTAL FEES
	- -20	: am/pm				$	$		$	$	$	$

TYPE ☐ Acknowledgment ☐ Jurat ☐ Copy Certification ☐ Oath/Affirmation ☐ Oath of Office ☐ Proof of Execution ☐ Protest ☐ Other   **Fingerprint (R)**

DOC TYPE ☐ Deed ☐ DOT ☐ Trust ☐ POA ☐ POAH ☐ Agreement ☐ Affidavit ☐ Other
Grant • Trust Transfer • Gift | Mortgage | Certification | General / Limited | AHCD | Compliance-E&O | Borrower • Occupancy • Ownership • Refi • Survey | Vehicle Title
Interspousal • Quitclaim • ToD • Warranty | Rev / Irrev • Am / Rest | Durable / Springing | Living Will | Correction | Debts & Liens • Name-Signature-ID • Marital • Death • Will | Safe Deposit Box

DOC DATE J F M A M J J A S O N D ,   **DOC TITLE or TYPE**   **# OF PAGES**   ☐ Inspect/Copy Request   **Entry X-Ref #**

☐ **SATISFACTORY EVIDENCE** ☐ Driver's License / Passport / State ID / Military / Government / Tribal / Inmate / Other ID **or** ☐ Credible Witness(es)

SIGNER
- SIGNER's NAME | ☐ For | ADDRESS | ☐ Non-Public | ☐ Capacity | ☐ Voluntary | ☐ Proper ID | ISSUED # | SIGNATURE ☐ (oath / affirmation, if any) ☐ (by Mark)
- PHONE C / H / W | or ☐ MISC | | | AGENCY | ☐ CA DMV | ☐ US State Dept | EXPIRES | →

CW #1
- #1 WITNESS's NAME | ☐ P/Known | ADDRESS | ☐ Non-Public | ☐ Driver's License ☐ Passport ☐ Other ID | ISSUED # | SIGNATURE ☐ (after oath / affirmation)
- PHONE C / H / W | or ☐ MISC | | | AGENCY | ☐ CA DMV | ☐ US State Dept | EXPIRES | ❶

CW #2
- #2 WITNESS's NAME | ☐ P/Known | ADDRESS | ☐ Non-Public | ☐ Driver's License ☐ Passport ☐ Other ID | ISSUED # | SIGNATURE ☐ (after oath / affirmation)
- PHONE C / H / W | or ☐ MISC | | | AGENCY | ☐ CA DMV | ☐ US State Dept | EXPIRES | ❷

NOTARY NAME (printed):   COMMISSION #:

Entry 117

SERVICE						
DATE - -20	TIME : am / pm	ADDRESS	☐ Signer's ☐ Office	NOTES	☐ Stop MILES Notary ☐ Adv. Travel ☐ Rush ☐ Copy ☐ Other TOTAL FEES $ $ $ $ $ $	117

TYPE ☐ Acknowledgment ☐ Jurat ☐ Copy Certification ☐ Oath/Affirmation ☐ Oath of Office ☐ Proof of Execution ☐ Protest ☐ Other

R	Fingerprint
T	
I	
M	
R	
P	
L	

DOCUMENT

DOC TYPE ☐ Deed ☐ DOT ☐ Trust ☐ POA ☐ POAH ☐ Agreement ☐ Affidavit ☐ Other

Grant • Trust Transfer • Gift   Mortgage   Certification   General / Limited   AHCD   Compliance-E&O   Borrower • Occupancy • Ownership • Refi • Survey   Vehicle Title

Interspousal • Quitclaim • ToD • Warranty   Rev / Irrev • Am / Rest   Durable / Springing   Living Will   Correction   Debts & Liens • Name-Signature-ID • Marital • Death • Will   Safe Deposit Box

DOC DATE   J F M A M J   J A S O N D   ,   DOC TITLE or TYPE   # OF PAGES   ☐ Inspect/Copy Request   Entry X-Ref #

☐ **SATISFACTORY EVIDENCE** ☐ Driver's License / Passport / State ID / Military / Government / Tribal / Inmate / Other ID   *or*   ☐ Credible Witness(es)

SIGNER

SIGNER's NAME   ☐ For   ADDRESS   ☐ Non-Public   ☐ Capacity   ☐ Voluntary   ☐ Proper ID   ISSUED #   SIGNATURE ☐ *(oath / affirmation, if any)* ☐ *(by Mark)*

PHONE C / H / W   /   *or* ☐ MISC   AGENCY   ☐ CA DMV   ☐ US State Dept   EXPIRES   ➡

CW #1

#1 WITNESS's NAME   ☐ P/Known   ADDRESS   ☐ Non-Public   ☐ Driver's License ☐ Passport ☐ Other ID   ISSUED #   SIGNATURE ☐ *(after oath / affirmation)*

PHONE C / H / W   /   *or* ☐ MISC   AGENCY   ☐ CA DMV   ☐ US State Dept   EXPIRES   ❶

CW #2

#2 WITNESS's NAME   ☐ P/Known   ADDRESS   ☐ Non-Public   ☐ Driver's License ☐ Passport ☐ Other ID   ISSUED #   SIGNATURE ☐ *(after oath / affirmation)*

PHONE C / H / W   /   *or* ☐ MISC   AGENCY   ☐ CA DMV   ☐ US State Dept   EXPIRES   ❷

Entry 118

SERVICE						
DATE - -20	TIME : am / pm	ADDRESS	☐ Signer's ☐ Office	NOTES	☐ Stop MILES Notary ☐ Adv. Travel ☐ Rush ☐ Copy ☐ Other TOTAL FEES $ $ $ $ $ $	118

TYPE ☐ Acknowledgment ☐ Jurat ☐ Copy Certification ☐ Oath/Affirmation ☐ Oath of Office ☐ Proof of Execution ☐ Protest ☐ Other

R	Fingerprint
T	
I	
M	
R	
P	
L	

DOCUMENT

DOC TYPE ☐ Deed ☐ DOT ☐ Trust ☐ POA ☐ POAH ☐ Agreement ☐ Affidavit ☐ Other

Grant • Trust Transfer • Gift   Mortgage   Certification   General / Limited   AHCD   Compliance-E&O   Borrower • Occupancy • Ownership • Refi • Survey   Vehicle Title

Interspousal • Quitclaim • ToD • Warranty   Rev / Irrev • Am / Rest   Durable / Springing   Living Will   Correction   Debts & Liens • Name-Signature-ID • Marital • Death • Will   Safe Deposit Box

DOC DATE   J F M A M J   J A S O N D   ,   DOC TITLE or TYPE   # OF PAGES   ☐ Inspect/Copy Request   Entry X-Ref #

☐ **SATISFACTORY EVIDENCE** ☐ Driver's License / Passport / State ID / Military / Government / Tribal / Inmate / Other ID   *or*   ☐ Credible Witness(es)

SIGNER

SIGNER's NAME   ☐ For   ADDRESS   ☐ Non-Public   ☐ Capacity   ☐ Voluntary   ☐ Proper ID   ISSUED #   SIGNATURE ☐ *(oath / affirmation, if any)* ☐ *(by Mark)*

PHONE C / H / W   /   *or* ☐ MISC   AGENCY   ☐ CA DMV   ☐ US State Dept   EXPIRES   ➡

CW #1

#1 WITNESS's NAME   ☐ P/Known   ADDRESS   ☐ Non-Public   ☐ Driver's License ☐ Passport ☐ Other ID   ISSUED #   SIGNATURE ☐ *(after oath / affirmation)*

PHONE C / H / W   /   *or* ☐ MISC   AGENCY   ☐ CA DMV   ☐ US State Dept   EXPIRES   ❶

CW #2

#2 WITNESS's NAME   ☐ P/Known   ADDRESS   ☐ Non-Public   ☐ Driver's License ☐ Passport ☐ Other ID   ISSUED #   SIGNATURE ☐ *(after oath / affirmation)*

PHONE C / H / W   /   *or* ☐ MISC   AGENCY   ☐ CA DMV   ☐ US State Dept   EXPIRES   ❷

NOTARY NAME (printed):   COMMISSION #:

Entry 119

SERVICE — DATE: - -20 | TIME: : am/pm | ADDRESS ☐ Signer's ☐ Office | NOTES | ☐ Stop | MILES | Notary $ | ☐ Adv. Travel $ | ☐ Rush $ | ☐ Copy $ | ☐ Other $ | TOTAL FEES $

TYPE: ☐ Acknowledgment ☐ Jurat ☐ Copy Certification ☐ Oath/Affirmation ☐ Oath of Office ☐ Proof of Execution ☐ Protest ☐ Other   **Fingerprint** (R T I M R P L)

DOCUMENT — DOC TYPE: ☐ Deed (Grant • Trust Transfer • Gift • Interspousal • Quitclaim • ToD • Warranty) ☐ DOT (Mortgage • Rev / Irrev • Am / Rest) ☐ Trust (Certification) ☐ POA (General / Limited • Durable / Springing) ☐ POAH (AHCD • Living Will) ☐ Agreement (Compliance-E&O • Correction) ☐ Affidavit (Borrower • Occupancy • Ownership • Refi • Survey • Debts & Liens • Name-Signature-ID • Marital • Death • Will) ☐ Other (Vehicle Title • Safe Deposit Box)

DOC DATE: J F M A M J J A S O N D ,   DOC TITLE or TYPE: # OF PAGES: ☐ Inspect/Copy Request   Entry X-Ref #:

☐ **SATISFACTORY EVIDENCE** ☐ Driver's License / Passport / State ID / Military / Government / Tribal / Inmate / Other ID   *or*   ☐ Credible Witness(es)

SIGNER — SIGNER's NAME | ☐ For | ADDRESS | ☐ Non-Public | ☐ Capacity # | ☐ Voluntary | ☐ Proper ID | ISSUED | SIGNATURE ☐ (oath / affirmation, if any) ☐ (by Mark)
PHONE C / H / W / | *or* ☐ MISC | | | AGENCY | ☐ CA DMV | ☐ US State Dept | EXPIRES | ➤

CW #1 — #1 WITNESS's NAME | ☐ P/Known | ADDRESS | ☐ Non-Public | ☐ Driver's License # | ☐ Passport | ☐ Other ID | ISSUED | SIGNATURE ☐ (after oath / affirmation)
PHONE C / H / W / | *or* ☐ MISC | | | AGENCY | ☐ CA DMV | ☐ US State Dept | EXPIRES | ❶

CW #2 — #2 WITNESS's NAME | ☐ P/Known | ADDRESS | ☐ Non-Public | ☐ Driver's License # | ☐ Passport | ☐ Other ID | ISSUED | SIGNATURE ☐ (after oath / affirmation)
PHONE C / H / W / | *or* ☐ MISC | | | AGENCY | ☐ CA DMV | ☐ US State Dept | EXPIRES | ❷

Entry 120

SERVICE — DATE: - -20 | TIME: : am/pm | ADDRESS ☐ Signer's ☐ Office | NOTES | ☐ Stop | MILES | Notary $ | ☐ Adv. Travel $ | ☐ Rush $ | ☐ Copy $ | ☐ Other $ | TOTAL FEES $

TYPE: ☐ Acknowledgment ☐ Jurat ☐ Copy Certification ☐ Oath/Affirmation ☐ Oath of Office ☐ Proof of Execution ☐ Protest ☐ Other   **Fingerprint** (R T I M R P L)

DOCUMENT — DOC TYPE: ☐ Deed (Grant • Trust Transfer • Gift • Interspousal • Quitclaim • ToD • Warranty) ☐ DOT (Mortgage • Rev / Irrev • Am / Rest) ☐ Trust (Certification) ☐ POA (General / Limited • Durable / Springing) ☐ POAH (AHCD • Living Will) ☐ Agreement (Compliance-E&O • Correction) ☐ Affidavit (Borrower • Occupancy • Ownership • Refi • Survey • Debts & Liens • Name-Signature-ID • Marital • Death • Will) ☐ Other (Vehicle Title • Safe Deposit Box)

DOC DATE: J F M A M J J A S O N D ,   DOC TITLE or TYPE: # OF PAGES: ☐ Inspect/Copy Request   Entry X-Ref #:

☐ **SATISFACTORY EVIDENCE** ☐ Driver's License / Passport / State ID / Military / Government / Tribal / Inmate / Other ID   *or*   ☐ Credible Witness(es)

SIGNER — SIGNER's NAME | ☐ For | ADDRESS | ☐ Non-Public | ☐ Capacity # | ☐ Voluntary | ☐ Proper ID | ISSUED | SIGNATURE ☐ (oath / affirmation, if any) ☐ (by Mark)
PHONE C / H / W / | *or* ☐ MISC | | | AGENCY | ☐ CA DMV | ☐ US State Dept | EXPIRES | ➤

CW #1 — #1 WITNESS's NAME | ☐ P/Known | ADDRESS | ☐ Non-Public | ☐ Driver's License # | ☐ Passport | ☐ Other ID | ISSUED | SIGNATURE ☐ (after oath / affirmation)
PHONE C / H / W / | *or* ☐ MISC | | | AGENCY | ☐ CA DMV | ☐ US State Dept | EXPIRES | ❶

CW #2 — #2 WITNESS's NAME | ☐ P/Known | ADDRESS | ☐ Non-Public | ☐ Driver's License # | ☐ Passport | ☐ Other ID | ISSUED | SIGNATURE ☐ (after oath / affirmation)
PHONE C / H / W / | *or* ☐ MISC | | | AGENCY | ☐ CA DMV | ☐ US State Dept | EXPIRES | ❷

NOTARY NAME (printed):   COMMISSION #:

Entry 121

SERVICE

DATE: - -20   TIME: :   am / pm   ADDRESS   ☐ Signer's   ☐ Office   NOTES   ☐ Stop   MILES   Notary ☐   Adv. Travel ☐   Rush ☐   Copy ☐   Other ☐   TOTAL FEES $ $ $ $ $ $

TYPE: ☐ Acknowledgment   ☐ Jurat   ☐ Copy Certification   ☐ Oath/Affirmation   ☐ Oath of Office   ☐ Proof of Execution   ☐ Protest   ☐ Other

R T I M R P L   **Fingerprint**

DOCUMENT

DOC TYPE   ☐ Deed   ☐ DOT   ☐ Trust   ☐ POA   ☐ POAH   ☐ Agreement   ☐ Affidavit   ☐ Other

Grant • Trust Transfer • Gift   Mortgage   Certification   General / Limited   AHCD   Compliance-E&O   Borrower • Occupancy • Ownership • Refi • Survey   Vehicle Title

Interspousal • Quitclaim • ToD • Warranty   Rev / Irrev • Am / Rest   Durable / Springing   Living Will   Correction   Debts & Liens • Name-Signature-ID • Marital • Death • Will   Safe Deposit Box

DOC DATE   J F M A M J   J A S O N D   ,   DOC TITLE or TYPE   # OF PAGES   ☐ Inspect/Copy Request   Entry X-Ref #

☐ **SATISFACTORY EVIDENCE** ☐ Driver's License / Passport / State ID / Military / Government / Tribal / Inmate / Other ID   *or*   ☐ Credible Witness(es)

SIGNER

SIGNER's NAME   ☐ For   ADDRESS   ☐ Non-Public   ☐ Capacity   ☐ Voluntary   ☐ Proper ID   ISSUED #   SIGNATURE   ☐ *(oath / affirmation, if any)*   ☐ (by Mark)

PHONE C / H / W   /   *or* ☐ MISC   AGENCY   ☐ CA DMV   ☐ US State Dept   EXPIRES   ➡

CW #1

#1 WITNESS's NAME   ☐ P/Known   ADDRESS   ☐ Non-Public   ☐ Driver's License   ☐ Passport   ☐ Other ID   ISSUED #   SIGNATURE   ☐ *(after oath / affirmation)*

PHONE C / H / W   /   *or* ☐ MISC   AGENCY   ☐ CA DMV   ☐ US State Dept   EXPIRES   ❶

CW #2

#2 WITNESS's NAME   ☐ P/Known   ADDRESS   ☐ Non-Public   ☐ Driver's License   ☐ Passport   ☐ Other ID   ISSUED #   SIGNATURE   ☐ *(after oath / affirmation)*

PHONE C / H / W   /   *or* ☐ MISC   AGENCY   ☐ CA DMV   ☐ US State Dept   EXPIRES   ❷

Entry 122

SERVICE

DATE: - -20   TIME: :   am / pm   ADDRESS   ☐ Signer's   ☐ Office   NOTES   ☐ Stop   MILES   Notary ☐   Adv. Travel ☐   Rush ☐   Copy ☐   Other ☐   TOTAL FEES $ $ $ $ $ $

TYPE: ☐ Acknowledgment   ☐ Jurat   ☐ Copy Certification   ☐ Oath/Affirmation   ☐ Oath of Office   ☐ Proof of Execution   ☐ Protest   ☐ Other

R T I M R P L   **Fingerprint**

DOCUMENT

DOC TYPE   ☐ Deed   ☐ DOT   ☐ Trust   ☐ POA   ☐ POAH   ☐ Agreement   ☐ Affidavit   ☐ Other

Grant • Trust Transfer • Gift   Mortgage   Certification   General / Limited   AHCD   Compliance-E&O   Borrower • Occupancy • Ownership • Refi • Survey   Vehicle Title

Interspousal • Quitclaim • ToD • Warranty   Rev / Irrev • Am / Rest   Durable / Springing   Living Will   Correction   Debts & Liens • Name-Signature-ID • Marital • Death • Will   Safe Deposit Box

DOC DATE   J F M A M J   J A S O N D   ,   DOC TITLE or TYPE   # OF PAGES   ☐ Inspect/Copy Request   Entry X-Ref #

☐ **SATISFACTORY EVIDENCE** ☐ Driver's License / Passport / State ID / Military / Government / Tribal / Inmate / Other ID   *or*   ☐ Credible Witness(es)

SIGNER

SIGNER's NAME   ☐ For   ADDRESS   ☐ Non-Public   ☐ Capacity   ☐ Voluntary   ☐ Proper ID   ISSUED #   SIGNATURE   ☐ *(oath / affirmation, if any)*   ☐ (by Mark)

PHONE C / H / W   /   *or* ☐ MISC   AGENCY   ☐ CA DMV   ☐ US State Dept   EXPIRES   ➡

CW #1

#1 WITNESS's NAME   ☐ P/Known   ADDRESS   ☐ Non-Public   ☐ Driver's License   ☐ Passport   ☐ Other ID   ISSUED #   SIGNATURE   ☐ *(after oath / affirmation)*

PHONE C / H / W   /   *or* ☐ MISC   AGENCY   ☐ CA DMV   ☐ US State Dept   EXPIRES   ❶

CW #2

#2 WITNESS's NAME   ☐ P/Known   ADDRESS   ☐ Non-Public   ☐ Driver's License   ☐ Passport   ☐ Other ID   ISSUED #   SIGNATURE   ☐ *(after oath / affirmation)*

PHONE C / H / W   /   *or* ☐ MISC   AGENCY   ☐ CA DMV   ☐ US State Dept   EXPIRES   ❷

NOTARY NAME (printed): COMMISSION #:

Entry 123

SERVICE
- DATE: - -20
- TIME: : am/pm
- ADDRESS
- ☐ Signer's ☐ Office NOTES
- ☐ Stop MILES
- Notary $ ☐ Adv. Travel $ ☐ Rush $ ☐ Copy $ ☐ Other $ TOTAL FEES $

TYPE: ☐ Acknowledgment ☐ Jurat ☐ Copy Certification ☐ Oath/Affirmation ☐ Oath of Office ☐ Proof of Execution ☐ Protest ☐ Other

DOCUMENT
- DOC TYPE: ☐ Deed ☐ DOT ☐ Trust ☐ POA ☐ POAH ☐ Agreement ☐ Affidavit ☐ Other
  - Grant • Trust Transfer • Gift | Mortgage | Certification | General / Limited | AHCD | Compliance-E&O | Borrower • Occupancy • Ownership • Refi • Survey | Vehicle Title
  - Interspousal • Quitclaim • ToD • Warranty | Rev / Irrev • Am / Rest | Durable / Springing | Living Will | Correction | Debts & Liens • Name-Signature-ID • Marital • Death • Will | Safe Deposit Box
- DOC DATE: J F M A M J J A S O N D ,
- DOC TITLE or TYPE
- # OF PAGES
- ☐ Inspect/Copy Request
- Entry X-Ref #

Fingerprint R T I M R P L

☐ **SATISFACTORY EVIDENCE** ☐ Driver's License / Passport / State ID / Military / Government / Tribal / Inmate / Other ID *or* ☐ Credible Witness(es)

SIGNER
- SIGNER's NAME | ☐ For | ADDRESS | ☐ Non-Public | ☐ Capacity # | ☐ Voluntary | ☐ Proper ID | ISSUED | SIGNATURE | ☐ (oath / affirmation, if any) ☐ (by Mark)
- PHONE C / H / W / | *or* ☐ MISC | | | AGENCY | ☐ CA DMV | ☐ US State Dept | EXPIRES | ➡

CW #1
- #1 WITNESS's NAME | ☐ P/Known | ADDRESS | ☐ Non-Public | ☐ Driver's License # | ☐ Passport | ☐ Other ID | ISSUED | SIGNATURE | ☐ (after oath / affirmation)
- PHONE C / H / W / | *or* ☐ MISC | | | AGENCY | ☐ CA DMV | ☐ US State Dept | EXPIRES | ❶

CW #2
- #2 WITNESS's NAME | ☐ P/Known | ADDRESS | ☐ Non-Public | ☐ Driver's License # | ☐ Passport | ☐ Other ID | ISSUED | SIGNATURE | ☐ (after oath / affirmation)
- PHONE C / H / W / | *or* ☐ MISC | | | AGENCY | ☐ CA DMV | ☐ US State Dept | EXPIRES | ❷

Entry 124

SERVICE
- DATE: - -20
- TIME: : am/pm
- ADDRESS
- ☐ Signer's ☐ Office NOTES
- ☐ Stop MILES
- Notary $ ☐ Adv. Travel $ ☐ Rush $ ☐ Copy $ ☐ Other $ TOTAL FEES $

TYPE: ☐ Acknowledgment ☐ Jurat ☐ Copy Certification ☐ Oath/Affirmation ☐ Oath of Office ☐ Proof of Execution ☐ Protest ☐ Other

DOCUMENT
- DOC TYPE: ☐ Deed ☐ DOT ☐ Trust ☐ POA ☐ POAH ☐ Agreement ☐ Affidavit ☐ Other
  - Grant • Trust Transfer • Gift | Mortgage | Certification | General / Limited | AHCD | Compliance-E&O | Borrower • Occupancy • Ownership • Refi • Survey | Vehicle Title
  - Interspousal • Quitclaim • ToD • Warranty | Rev / Irrev • Am / Rest | Durable / Springing | Living Will | Correction | Debts & Liens • Name-Signature-ID • Marital • Death • Will | Safe Deposit Box
- DOC DATE: J F M A M J J A S O N D ,
- DOC TITLE or TYPE
- # OF PAGES
- ☐ Inspect/Copy Request
- Entry X-Ref #

Fingerprint R T I M R P L

☐ **SATISFACTORY EVIDENCE** ☐ Driver's License / Passport / State ID / Military / Government / Tribal / Inmate / Other ID *or* ☐ Credible Witness(es)

SIGNER
- SIGNER's NAME | ☐ For | ADDRESS | ☐ Non-Public | ☐ Capacity # | ☐ Voluntary | ☐ Proper ID | ISSUED | SIGNATURE | ☐ (oath / affirmation, if any) ☐ (by Mark)
- PHONE C / H / W / | *or* ☐ MISC | | | AGENCY | ☐ CA DMV | ☐ US State Dept | EXPIRES | ➡

CW #1
- #1 WITNESS's NAME | ☐ P/Known | ADDRESS | ☐ Non-Public | ☐ Driver's License # | ☐ Passport | ☐ Other ID | ISSUED | SIGNATURE | ☐ (after oath / affirmation)
- PHONE C / H / W / | *or* ☐ MISC | | | AGENCY | ☐ CA DMV | ☐ US State Dept | EXPIRES | ❶

CW #2
- #2 WITNESS's NAME | ☐ P/Known | ADDRESS | ☐ Non-Public | ☐ Driver's License # | ☐ Passport | ☐ Other ID | ISSUED | SIGNATURE | ☐ (after oath / affirmation)
- PHONE C / H / W / | *or* ☐ MISC | | | AGENCY | ☐ CA DMV | ☐ US State Dept | EXPIRES | ❷

NOTARY NAME (printed):   COMMISSION #:

Entry 125

SERVICE

DATE   -   -20   TIME   :   am pm   ADDRESS   ☐ Signer's   ☐ Office   NOTES   ☐ Stop   MILES   Notary   ☐ Adv. Travel   ☐ Rush   ☐ Copy   ☐ Other   TOTAL FEES

$ $ $ $ $ $

TYPE   ☐ Acknowledgment   ☐ Jurat   ☐ Copy Certification   ☐ Oath/Affirmation   ☐ Oath of Office   ☐ Proof of Execution   ☐ Protest   ☐ Other   R   **Fingerprint**

DOCUMENT

DOC TYPE   ☐ Deed   ☐ DOT   ☐ Trust   ☐ POA   ☐ POAH   ☐ Agreement   ☐ Affidavit   ☐ Other

Grant • Trust Transfer • Gift   Mortgage   Certification   General / Limited   AHCD   Compliance-E&O   Borrower • Occupancy • Ownership • Refi • Survey   Vehicle Title

Interspousal • Quitclaim • ToD • Warranty   Rev / Irrev • Am / Rest   Durable / Springing   Living Will   Correction   Debts & Liens • Name-Signature-ID • Marital • Death • Will   Safe Deposit Box

DOC DATE   J F M A M J   J A S O N D   ,   DOC TITLE or TYPE   # OF PAGES   ☐ Inspect/Copy Request   Entry X-Ref #

T I M R P L

☐ **SATISFACTORY EVIDENCE**   ☐ Driver's License / Passport / State ID / Military / Government / Tribal / Inmate / Other ID   *or*   ☐ Credible Witness(es)

SIGNER

SIGNER's NAME   ☐ For   ADDRESS   ☐ Non-Public   ☐ Capacity   ☐ Voluntary   ☐ Proper ID   ISSUED   SIGNATURE   ☐ (oath / affirmation, if any)   ☐ (by Mark)

#

PHONE C / H / W   *or* ☐ MISC   AGENCY   ☐ CA DMV   ☐ US State Dept   EXPIRES   ➡

CW #1

#1 WITNESS's NAME   ☐ P/Known   ADDRESS   ☐ Non-Public   ☐ Driver's License   ☐ Passport   ☐ Other ID   ISSUED   SIGNATURE   ☐ (after oath / affirmation)

#

PHONE C / H / W   *or* ☐ MISC   AGENCY   ☐ CA DMV   ☐ US State Dept   EXPIRES   ❶

CW #2

#2 WITNESS's NAME   ☐ P/Known   ADDRESS   ☐ Non-Public   ☐ Driver's License   ☐ Passport   ☐ Other ID   ISSUED   SIGNATURE   ☐ (after oath / affirmation)

#

PHONE C / H / W   *or* ☐ MISC   AGENCY   ☐ CA DMV   ☐ US State Dept   EXPIRES   ❷

Entry 126

SERVICE

DATE   -   -20   TIME   :   am pm   ADDRESS   ☐ Signer's   ☐ Office   NOTES   ☐ Stop   MILES   Notary   ☐ Adv. Travel   ☐ Rush   ☐ Copy   ☐ Other   TOTAL FEES

$ $ $ $ $ $

TYPE   ☐ Acknowledgment   ☐ Jurat   ☐ Copy Certification   ☐ Oath/Affirmation   ☐ Oath of Office   ☐ Proof of Execution   ☐ Protest   ☐ Other   R   **Fingerprint**

DOCUMENT

DOC TYPE   ☐ Deed   ☐ DOT   ☐ Trust   ☐ POA   ☐ POAH   ☐ Agreement   ☐ Affidavit   ☐ Other

Grant • Trust Transfer • Gift   Mortgage   Certification   General / Limited   AHCD   Compliance-E&O   Borrower • Occupancy • Ownership • Refi • Survey   Vehicle Title

Interspousal • Quitclaim • ToD • Warranty   Rev / Irrev • Am / Rest   Durable / Springing   Living Will   Correction   Debts & Liens • Name-Signature-ID • Marital • Death • Will   Safe Deposit Box

DOC DATE   J F M A M J   J A S O N D   ,   DOC TITLE or TYPE   # OF PAGES   ☐ Inspect/Copy Request   Entry X-Ref #

T I M R P L

☐ **SATISFACTORY EVIDENCE**   ☐ Driver's License / Passport / State ID / Military / Government / Tribal / Inmate / Other ID   *or*   ☐ Credible Witness(es)

SIGNER

SIGNER's NAME   ☐ For   ADDRESS   ☐ Non-Public   ☐ Capacity   ☐ Voluntary   ☐ Proper ID   ISSUED   SIGNATURE   ☐ (oath / affirmation, if any)   ☐ (by Mark)

#

PHONE C / H / W   *or* ☐ MISC   AGENCY   ☐ CA DMV   ☐ US State Dept   EXPIRES   ➡

CW #1

#1 WITNESS's NAME   ☐ P/Known   ADDRESS   ☐ Non-Public   ☐ Driver's License   ☐ Passport   ☐ Other ID   ISSUED   SIGNATURE   ☐ (after oath / affirmation)

#

PHONE C / H / W   *or* ☐ MISC   AGENCY   ☐ CA DMV   ☐ US State Dept   EXPIRES   ❶

CW #2

#2 WITNESS's NAME   ☐ P/Known   ADDRESS   ☐ Non-Public   ☐ Driver's License   ☐ Passport   ☐ Other ID   ISSUED   SIGNATURE   ☐ (after oath / affirmation)

#

PHONE C / H / W   *or* ☐ MISC   AGENCY   ☐ CA DMV   ☐ US State Dept   EXPIRES   ❷

NOTARY NAME (printed): _____ COMMISSION #: _____

Entry 127

SERVICE — DATE: __-__-20__ TIME: __:__ am/pm ADDRESS: ☐ Signer's ☐ Office NOTES: _____ ☐ Stop MILES $___ Notary $___ ☐ Adv. Travel $___ ☐ Rush $___ ☐ Copy $___ ☐ Other $___ TOTAL FEES $___

TYPE: ☐ Acknowledgment ☐ Jurat ☐ Copy Certification ☐ Oath/Affirmation ☐ Oath of Office ☐ Proof of Execution ☐ Protest ☐ Other

DOCUMENT — DOC TYPE: ☐ Deed (Grant • Trust Transfer • Gift • Interspousal • Quitclaim • ToD • Warranty) ☐ DOT (Mortgage • Certification • Rev / Irrev • Am / Rest) ☐ Trust ☐ POA (General / Limited • Durable / Springing) ☐ POAH (AHCD • Living Will) ☐ Agreement (Compliance-E&O • Correction) ☐ Affidavit (Borrower • Occupancy • Ownership • Refi • Survey • Debts & Liens • Name-Signature-ID • Marital • Death • Will) ☐ Other (Vehicle Title • Safe Deposit Box)

DOC DATE: J F M A M J J A S O N D , ____ DOC TITLE or TYPE: _____ # OF PAGES: ___ ☐ Inspect/Copy Request Entry X-Ref #: ___

Fingerprint R T I M R P L

☐ **SATISFACTORY EVIDENCE** ☐ Driver's License / Passport / State ID / Military / Government / Tribal / Inmate / Other ID **or** ☐ Credible Witness(es)

SIGNER — SIGNER's NAME: _____ ☐ For ADDRESS: _____ ☐ Non-Public ☐ Capacity ☐ Voluntary ☐ Proper ID ISSUED #: _____ SIGNATURE: _____ ☐ (oath / affirmation, if any) ☐ (by Mark)
PHONE C/H/W: __/__ or ☐ MISC: _____ AGENCY: ☐ CA DMV ☐ US State Dept EXPIRES: _____ ➡

CW #1 — #1 WITNESS's NAME: _____ ☐ P/Known ADDRESS: _____ ☐ Non-Public ☐ Driver's License ☐ Passport ☐ Other ID ISSUED #: _____ SIGNATURE: _____ ☐ (after oath / affirmation)
PHONE C/H/W: __/__ or ☐ MISC: _____ AGENCY: ☐ CA DMV ☐ US State Dept EXPIRES: _____ ❶

CW #2 — #2 WITNESS's NAME: _____ ☐ P/Known ADDRESS: _____ ☐ Non-Public ☐ Driver's License ☐ Passport ☐ Other ID ISSUED #: _____ SIGNATURE: _____ ☐ (after oath / affirmation)
PHONE C/H/W: __/__ or ☐ MISC: _____ AGENCY: ☐ CA DMV ☐ US State Dept EXPIRES: _____ ❷

Entry 128

SERVICE — DATE: __-__-20__ TIME: __:__ am/pm ADDRESS: ☐ Signer's ☐ Office NOTES: _____ ☐ Stop MILES $___ Notary $___ ☐ Adv. Travel $___ ☐ Rush $___ ☐ Copy $___ ☐ Other $___ TOTAL FEES $___

TYPE: ☐ Acknowledgment ☐ Jurat ☐ Copy Certification ☐ Oath/Affirmation ☐ Oath of Office ☐ Proof of Execution ☐ Protest ☐ Other

DOCUMENT — DOC TYPE: ☐ Deed (Grant • Trust Transfer • Gift • Interspousal • Quitclaim • ToD • Warranty) ☐ DOT (Mortgage • Certification • Rev / Irrev • Am / Rest) ☐ Trust ☐ POA (General / Limited • Durable / Springing) ☐ POAH (AHCD • Living Will) ☐ Agreement (Compliance-E&O • Correction) ☐ Affidavit (Borrower • Occupancy • Ownership • Refi • Survey • Debts & Liens • Name-Signature-ID • Marital • Death • Will) ☐ Other (Vehicle Title • Safe Deposit Box)

DOC DATE: J F M A M J J A S O N D , ____ DOC TITLE or TYPE: _____ # OF PAGES: ___ ☐ Inspect/Copy Request Entry X-Ref #: ___

Fingerprint R T I M R P L

☐ **SATISFACTORY EVIDENCE** ☐ Driver's License / Passport / State ID / Military / Government / Tribal / Inmate / Other ID **or** ☐ Credible Witness(es)

SIGNER — SIGNER's NAME: _____ ☐ For ADDRESS: _____ ☐ Non-Public ☐ Capacity ☐ Voluntary ☐ Proper ID ISSUED #: _____ SIGNATURE: _____ ☐ (oath / affirmation, if any) ☐ (by Mark)
PHONE C/H/W: __/__ or ☐ MISC: _____ AGENCY: ☐ CA DMV ☐ US State Dept EXPIRES: _____ ➡

CW #1 — #1 WITNESS's NAME: _____ ☐ P/Known ADDRESS: _____ ☐ Non-Public ☐ Driver's License ☐ Passport ☐ Other ID ISSUED #: _____ SIGNATURE: _____ ☐ (after oath / affirmation)
PHONE C/H/W: __/__ or ☐ MISC: _____ AGENCY: ☐ CA DMV ☐ US State Dept EXPIRES: _____ ❶

CW #2 — #2 WITNESS's NAME: _____ ☐ P/Known ADDRESS: _____ ☐ Non-Public ☐ Driver's License ☐ Passport ☐ Other ID ISSUED #: _____ SIGNATURE: _____ ☐ (after oath / affirmation)
PHONE C/H/W: __/__ or ☐ MISC: _____ AGENCY: ☐ CA DMV ☐ US State Dept EXPIRES: _____ ❷

NOTARY NAME (printed):   COMMISSION #:

Entry 129

SERVICE — DATE - -20 | TIME : am pm | ADDRESS ☐ Signer's ☐ Office | NOTES | ☐ Stop | MILES | Notary ☐ Adv. Travel ☐ Rush ☐ Copy ☐ Other TOTAL FEES | $ $ | $ $ $ $

TYPE ☐ Acknowledgment ☐ Jurat ☐ Copy Certification ☐ Oath/Affirmation ☐ Oath of Office ☐ Proof of Execution ☐ Protest ☐ Other

R   **Fingerprint**

DOCUMENT

DOC TYPE ☐ Deed | ☐ DOT | ☐ Trust | ☐ POA | ☐ POAH | ☐ Agreement | ☐ Affidavit | ☐ Other

Grant • Trust Transfer • Gift | Mortgage | Certification | General / Limited | AHCD | Compliance-E&O | Borrower • Occupancy • Ownership • Refi • Survey | Vehicle Title
Interspousal • Quitclaim • ToD • Warranty | Rev / Irrev • Am / Rest | Durable / Springing | Living Will | Correction | Debts & Liens • Name-Signature-ID • Marital • Death • Will | Safe Deposit Box

T I M R P

DOC DATE J F M A M J J A S O N D , | DOC TITLE or TYPE | # OF PAGES | ☐ Inspect/Copy Request | Entry X-Ref #

☐ **SATISFACTORY EVIDENCE** ☐ Driver's License / Passport / State ID / Military / Government / Tribal / Inmate / Other ID *or* ☐ Credible Witness(es)   L

SIGNER
SIGNER's NAME | ☐ For | ADDRESS | ☐ Non-Public | ☐ Capacity ☐ Voluntary ☐ Proper ID | ISSUED # | SIGNATURE ☐ (oath / affirmation, if any) ☐ (by Mark)
PHONE C / H / W / | *or* ☐ MISC | | | AGENCY ☐ CA DMV ☐ US State Dept | EXPIRES | ➡

CW #1
#1 WITNESS's NAME | ☐ P/Known | ADDRESS | ☐ Non-Public | ☐ Driver's License ☐ Passport ☐ Other ID | ISSUED # | SIGNATURE ☐ (after oath / affirmation)
PHONE C / H / W / | *or* ☐ MISC | | | AGENCY ☐ CA DMV ☐ US State Dept | EXPIRES | ❶

CW #2
#2 WITNESS's NAME | ☐ P/Known | ADDRESS | ☐ Non-Public | ☐ Driver's License ☐ Passport ☐ Other ID | ISSUED # | SIGNATURE ☐ (after oath / affirmation)
PHONE C / H / W / | *or* ☐ MISC | | | AGENCY ☐ CA DMV ☐ US State Dept | EXPIRES | ❷

Entry 130

SERVICE — DATE - -20 | TIME : am pm | ADDRESS ☐ Signer's ☐ Office | NOTES | ☐ Stop | MILES | Notary ☐ Adv. Travel ☐ Rush ☐ Copy ☐ Other TOTAL FEES | $ $ | $ $ $ $

TYPE ☐ Acknowledgment ☐ Jurat ☐ Copy Certification ☐ Oath/Affirmation ☐ Oath of Office ☐ Proof of Execution ☐ Protest ☐ Other

R   **Fingerprint**

DOCUMENT

DOC TYPE ☐ Deed | ☐ DOT | ☐ Trust | ☐ POA | ☐ POAH | ☐ Agreement | ☐ Affidavit | ☐ Other

Grant • Trust Transfer • Gift | Mortgage | Certification | General / Limited | AHCD | Compliance-E&O | Borrower • Occupancy • Ownership • Refi • Survey | Vehicle Title
Interspousal • Quitclaim • ToD • Warranty | Rev / Irrev • Am / Rest | Durable / Springing | Living Will | Correction | Debts & Liens • Name-Signature-ID • Marital • Death • Will | Safe Deposit Box

T I M R P

DOC DATE J F M A M J J A S O N D , | DOC TITLE or TYPE | # OF PAGES | ☐ Inspect/Copy Request | Entry X-Ref #

☐ **SATISFACTORY EVIDENCE** ☐ Driver's License / Passport / State ID / Military / Government / Tribal / Inmate / Other ID *or* ☐ Credible Witness(es)   L

SIGNER
SIGNER's NAME | ☐ For | ADDRESS | ☐ Non-Public | ☐ Capacity ☐ Voluntary ☐ Proper ID | ISSUED # | SIGNATURE ☐ (oath / affirmation, if any) ☐ (by Mark)
PHONE C / H / W / | *or* ☐ MISC | | | AGENCY ☐ CA DMV ☐ US State Dept | EXPIRES | ➡

CW #1
#1 WITNESS's NAME | ☐ P/Known | ADDRESS | ☐ Non-Public | ☐ Driver's License ☐ Passport ☐ Other ID | ISSUED # | SIGNATURE ☐ (after oath / affirmation)
PHONE C / H / W / | *or* ☐ MISC | | | AGENCY ☐ CA DMV ☐ US State Dept | EXPIRES | ❶

CW #2
#2 WITNESS's NAME | ☐ P/Known | ADDRESS | ☐ Non-Public | ☐ Driver's License ☐ Passport ☐ Other ID | ISSUED # | SIGNATURE ☐ (after oath / affirmation)
PHONE C / H / W / | *or* ☐ MISC | | | AGENCY ☐ CA DMV ☐ US State Dept | EXPIRES | ❷

NOTARY NAME (printed): COMMISSION #:

Entry 131

| SERVICE | DATE - -20 | TIME : am/pm | ADDRESS ☐ Signer's ☐ Office | NOTES | ☐ Stop MILES | Notary $ | ☐ Adv. Travel $ | ☐ Rush $ | ☐ Copy $ | ☐ Other $ | TOTAL FEES $ |

TYPE ☐ Acknowledgment ☐ Jurat ☐ Copy Certification ☐ Oath/Affirmation ☐ Oath of Office ☐ Proof of Execution ☐ Protest ☐ Other

DOCUMENT
DOC TYPE ☐ Deed ☐ DOT ☐ Trust ☐ POA ☐ POAH ☐ Agreement ☐ Affidavit ☐ Other
Grant • Trust Transfer • Gift | Mortgage | Certification | General / Limited | AHCD | Compliance-E&O | Borrower • Occupancy • Ownership • Refi • Survey | Vehicle Title
Interspousal • Quitclaim • ToD • Warranty | Rev / Irrev • Am / Rest | Durable / Springing | Living Will | Correction | Debts & Liens • Name-Signature-ID • Marital • Death • Will | Safe Deposit Box

DOC DATE J F M A M J J A S O N D , | DOC TITLE or TYPE | # OF PAGES | ☐ Inspect/Copy Request | Entry X-Ref #

R T I M R P L — Fingerprint

☐ **SATISFACTORY EVIDENCE** ☐ Driver's License / Passport / State ID / Military / Government / Tribal / Inmate / Other ID *or* ☐ Credible Witness(es)

SIGNER
SIGNER's NAME | ☐ For | ADDRESS | ☐ Non-Public | ☐ Capacity | ☐ Voluntary | ☐ Proper ID | ISSUED # | SIGNATURE ☐ (oath / affirmation, if any) ☐ (by Mark)
PHONE C / H / W / | *or* ☐ MISC | | | AGENCY ☐ CA DMV ☐ US State Dept | EXPIRES | ➤

CW #1
#1 WITNESS's NAME | ☐ P/Known | ADDRESS | ☐ Non-Public | ☐ Driver's License ☐ Passport ☐ Other ID | ISSUED # | SIGNATURE ☐ (after oath / affirmation)
PHONE C / H / W / | *or* ☐ MISC | | | AGENCY ☐ CA DMV ☐ US State Dept | EXPIRES | ❶

CW #2
#2 WITNESS's NAME | ☐ P/Known | ADDRESS | ☐ Non-Public | ☐ Driver's License ☐ Passport ☐ Other ID | ISSUED # | SIGNATURE ☐ (after oath / affirmation)
PHONE C / H / W / | *or* ☐ MISC | | | AGENCY ☐ CA DMV ☐ US State Dept | EXPIRES | ❷

Entry 132

| SERVICE | DATE - -20 | TIME : am/pm | ADDRESS ☐ Signer's ☐ Office | NOTES | ☐ Stop MILES | Notary $ | ☐ Adv. Travel $ | ☐ Rush $ | ☐ Copy $ | ☐ Other $ | TOTAL FEES $ |

TYPE ☐ Acknowledgment ☐ Jurat ☐ Copy Certification ☐ Oath/Affirmation ☐ Oath of Office ☐ Proof of Execution ☐ Protest ☐ Other

DOCUMENT
DOC TYPE ☐ Deed ☐ DOT ☐ Trust ☐ POA ☐ POAH ☐ Agreement ☐ Affidavit ☐ Other
Grant • Trust Transfer • Gift | Mortgage | Certification | General / Limited | AHCD | Compliance-E&O | Borrower • Occupancy • Ownership • Refi • Survey | Vehicle Title
Interspousal • Quitclaim • ToD • Warranty | Rev / Irrev • Am / Rest | Durable / Springing | Living Will | Correction | Debts & Liens • Name-Signature-ID • Marital • Death • Will | Safe Deposit Box

DOC DATE J F M A M J J A S O N D , | DOC TITLE or TYPE | # OF PAGES | ☐ Inspect/Copy Request | Entry X-Ref #

R T I M R P L — Fingerprint

☐ **SATISFACTORY EVIDENCE** ☐ Driver's License / Passport / State ID / Military / Government / Tribal / Inmate / Other ID *or* ☐ Credible Witness(es)

SIGNER
SIGNER's NAME | ☐ For | ADDRESS | ☐ Non-Public | ☐ Capacity | ☐ Voluntary | ☐ Proper ID | ISSUED # | SIGNATURE ☐ (oath / affirmation, if any) ☐ (by Mark)
PHONE C / H / W / | *or* ☐ MISC | | | AGENCY ☐ CA DMV ☐ US State Dept | EXPIRES | ➤

CW #1
#1 WITNESS's NAME | ☐ P/Known | ADDRESS | ☐ Non-Public | ☐ Driver's License ☐ Passport ☐ Other ID | ISSUED # | SIGNATURE ☐ (after oath / affirmation)
PHONE C / H / W / | *or* ☐ MISC | | | AGENCY ☐ CA DMV ☐ US State Dept | EXPIRES | ❶

CW #2
#2 WITNESS's NAME | ☐ P/Known | ADDRESS | ☐ Non-Public | ☐ Driver's License ☐ Passport ☐ Other ID | ISSUED # | SIGNATURE ☐ (after oath / affirmation)
PHONE C / H / W / | *or* ☐ MISC | | | AGENCY ☐ CA DMV ☐ US State Dept | EXPIRES | ❷

NOTARY NAME (printed):   COMMISSION #:

Entry 133

SERVICE	DATE `- -20`	TIME `:` am pm	ADDRESS	☐ Signer's	☐ Office	NOTES	☐ Stop	MILES	Notary	☐ Adv. Travel	☐ Rush	☐ Copy	☐ Other	TOTAL FEES	**133**

$ $ $ $ $ $

TYPE ☐ Acknowledgment ☐ Jurat ☐ Copy Certification ☐ Oath/Affirmation ☐ Oath of Office ☐ Proof of Execution ☐ Protest ☐ Other

R	**Fingerprint**
T	
I	
M	
R	
P	
L	

DOCUMENT

DOC TYPE ☐ Deed ☐ DOT ☐ Trust ☐ POA ☐ POAH ☐ Agreement ☐ Affidavit ☐ Other
Grant • Trust Transfer • Gift | Mortgage | Certification | General / Limited | AHCD | Compliance-E&O | Borrower • Occupancy • Ownership • Refi • Survey | Vehicle Title
Interspousal • Quitclaim • ToD • Warranty | Rev / Irrev • Am / Rest | Durable / Springing | Living Will | Correction | Debts & Liens • Name-Signature-ID • Marital • Death • Will | Safe Deposit Box

DOC DATE J F M A M J J A S O N D ,   DOC TITLE or TYPE   # OF PAGES ☐ Inspect/Copy Request   Entry X-Ref #

☐ **SATISFACTORY EVIDENCE** ☐ Driver's License / Passport / State ID / Military / Government / Tribal / Inmate / Other ID *or* ☐ Credible Witness(es)

SIGNER

SIGNER's NAME	☐ For	ADDRESS	☐ Non-Public	☐ Capacity	☐ Voluntary	☐ Proper ID	ISSUED #	SIGNATURE	☐ (oath / affirmation, if any)	☐ (by Mark)
PHONE C / H / W	*or* ☐ MISC			AGENCY	☐ CA DMV	☐ US State Dept	EXPIRES	➡		

CW #1

#1 WITNESS's NAME	☐ P/Known	ADDRESS	☐ Non-Public	☐ Driver's License	☐ Passport	☐ Other ID	ISSUED #	SIGNATURE	☐ (after oath / affirmation)
PHONE C / H / W	*or* ☐ MISC			AGENCY	☐ CA DMV	☐ US State Dept	EXPIRES	❶	

CW #2

#2 WITNESS's NAME	☐ P/Known	ADDRESS	☐ Non-Public	☐ Driver's License	☐ Passport	☐ Other ID	ISSUED #	SIGNATURE	☐ (after oath / affirmation)
PHONE C / H / W	*or* ☐ MISC			AGENCY	☐ CA DMV	☐ US State Dept	EXPIRES	❷	

Entry 134

SERVICE	DATE `- -20`	TIME `:` am pm	ADDRESS	☐ Signer's	☐ Office	NOTES	☐ Stop	MILES	Notary	☐ Adv. Travel	☐ Rush	☐ Copy	☐ Other	TOTAL FEES	**134**

$ $ $ $ $ $

TYPE ☐ Acknowledgment ☐ Jurat ☐ Copy Certification ☐ Oath/Affirmation ☐ Oath of Office ☐ Proof of Execution ☐ Protest ☐ Other

R	**Fingerprint**
T	
I	
M	
R	
P	
L	

DOCUMENT

DOC TYPE ☐ Deed ☐ DOT ☐ Trust ☐ POA ☐ POAH ☐ Agreement ☐ Affidavit ☐ Other
Grant • Trust Transfer • Gift | Mortgage | Certification | General / Limited | AHCD | Compliance-E&O | Borrower • Occupancy • Ownership • Refi • Survey | Vehicle Title
Interspousal • Quitclaim • ToD • Warranty | Rev / Irrev • Am / Rest | Durable / Springing | Living Will | Correction | Debts & Liens • Name-Signature-ID • Marital • Death • Will | Safe Deposit Box

DOC DATE J F M A M J J A S O N D ,   DOC TITLE or TYPE   # OF PAGES ☐ Inspect/Copy Request   Entry X-Ref #

☐ **SATISFACTORY EVIDENCE** ☐ Driver's License / Passport / State ID / Military / Government / Tribal / Inmate / Other ID *or* ☐ Credible Witness(es)

SIGNER

SIGNER's NAME	☐ For	ADDRESS	☐ Non-Public	☐ Capacity	☐ Voluntary	☐ Proper ID	ISSUED #	SIGNATURE	☐ (oath / affirmation, if any)	☐ (by Mark)
PHONE C / H / W	*or* ☐ MISC			AGENCY	☐ CA DMV	☐ US State Dept	EXPIRES	➡		

CW #1

#1 WITNESS's NAME	☐ P/Known	ADDRESS	☐ Non-Public	☐ Driver's License	☐ Passport	☐ Other ID	ISSUED #	SIGNATURE	☐ (after oath / affirmation)
PHONE C / H / W	*or* ☐ MISC			AGENCY	☐ CA DMV	☐ US State Dept	EXPIRES	❶	

CW #2

#2 WITNESS's NAME	☐ P/Known	ADDRESS	☐ Non-Public	☐ Driver's License	☐ Passport	☐ Other ID	ISSUED #	SIGNATURE	☐ (after oath / affirmation)
PHONE C / H / W	*or* ☐ MISC			AGENCY	☐ CA DMV	☐ US State Dept	EXPIRES	❷	

NOTARY NAME (printed): _____ COMMISSION #: _____

Entry 135

SERVICE — DATE: __-__-20__ | TIME: __:__ am/pm | ADDRESS: ☐ Signer's ☐ Office | NOTES ☐ Stop | MILES | Notary $__ ☐ Adv. Travel $__ ☐ Rush $__ ☐ Copy $__ ☐ Other $__ | TOTAL FEES $__

TYPE: ☐ Acknowledgment ☐ Jurat ☐ Copy Certification ☐ Oath/Affirmation ☐ Oath of Office ☐ Proof of Execution ☐ Protest ☐ Other

DOCUMENT
DOC TYPE:
- ☐ Deed — Grant • Trust Transfer • Gift • Interspousal • Quitclaim • ToD • Warranty
- ☐ DOT — Mortgage • Certification • Rev / Irrev • Am / Rest
- ☐ Trust — General / Limited • Durable / Springing
- ☐ POA
- ☐ POAH — AHCD • Living Will
- ☐ Agreement — Compliance-E&O • Correction
- ☐ Affidavit — Borrower • Occupancy • Ownership • Refi • Survey • Debts & Liens • Name-Signature-ID • Marital • Death • Will
- ☐ Other — Vehicle Title • Safe Deposit Box

DOC DATE: J F M A M J / J A S O N D , ____ | DOC TITLE or TYPE: _____ | # OF PAGES: ___ | ☐ Inspect/Copy Request | Entry X-Ref #: ___

Fingerprint: R T I M R P L

☐ **SATISFACTORY EVIDENCE** ☐ Driver's License / Passport / State ID / Military / Government / Tribal / Inmate / Other ID *or* ☐ Credible Witness(es)

SIGNER
- SIGNER's NAME: _____ ☐ For | ADDRESS: _____ ☐ Non-Public | ☐ Capacity | ☐ Voluntary | ☐ Proper ID | ISSUED | SIGNATURE ☐ (oath / affirmation, if any) ☐ (by Mark)
- PHONE C / H / W: ___ / ___ | or ☐ MISC | # | AGENCY ☐ CA DMV ☐ US State Dept | EXPIRES

CW #1
- #1 WITNESS's NAME: _____ ☐ P/Known | ADDRESS: _____ ☐ Non-Public | ☐ Driver's License ☐ Passport ☐ Other ID | ISSUED | SIGNATURE ☐ (after oath / affirmation)
- PHONE C / H / W: ___ / ___ | or ☐ MISC | # | AGENCY ☐ CA DMV ☐ US State Dept | EXPIRES ❶

CW #2
- #2 WITNESS's NAME: _____ ☐ P/Known | ADDRESS: _____ ☐ Non-Public | ☐ Driver's License ☐ Passport ☐ Other ID | ISSUED | SIGNATURE ☐ (after oath / affirmation)
- PHONE C / H / W: ___ / ___ | or ☐ MISC | # | AGENCY ☐ CA DMV ☐ US State Dept | EXPIRES ❷

Entry 136

SERVICE — DATE: __-__-20__ | TIME: __:__ am/pm | ADDRESS: ☐ Signer's ☐ Office | NOTES ☐ Stop | MILES | Notary $__ ☐ Adv. Travel $__ ☐ Rush $__ ☐ Copy $__ ☐ Other $__ | TOTAL FEES $__

TYPE: ☐ Acknowledgment ☐ Jurat ☐ Copy Certification ☐ Oath/Affirmation ☐ Oath of Office ☐ Proof of Execution ☐ Protest ☐ Other

DOCUMENT
DOC TYPE:
- ☐ Deed — Grant • Trust Transfer • Gift • Interspousal • Quitclaim • ToD • Warranty
- ☐ DOT — Mortgage • Certification • Rev / Irrev • Am / Rest
- ☐ Trust — General / Limited • Durable / Springing
- ☐ POA
- ☐ POAH — AHCD • Living Will
- ☐ Agreement — Compliance-E&O • Correction
- ☐ Affidavit — Borrower • Occupancy • Ownership • Refi • Survey • Debts & Liens • Name-Signature-ID • Marital • Death • Will
- ☐ Other — Vehicle Title • Safe Deposit Box

DOC DATE: J F M A M J / J A S O N D , ____ | DOC TITLE or TYPE: _____ | # OF PAGES: ___ | ☐ Inspect/Copy Request | Entry X-Ref #: ___

Fingerprint: R T I M R P L

☐ **SATISFACTORY EVIDENCE** ☐ Driver's License / Passport / State ID / Military / Government / Tribal / Inmate / Other ID *or* ☐ Credible Witness(es)

SIGNER
- SIGNER's NAME: _____ ☐ For | ADDRESS: _____ ☐ Non-Public | ☐ Capacity | ☐ Voluntary | ☐ Proper ID | ISSUED | SIGNATURE ☐ (oath / affirmation, if any) ☐ (by Mark)
- PHONE C / H / W: ___ / ___ | or ☐ MISC | # | AGENCY ☐ CA DMV ☐ US State Dept | EXPIRES

CW #1
- #1 WITNESS's NAME: _____ ☐ P/Known | ADDRESS: _____ ☐ Non-Public | ☐ Driver's License ☐ Passport ☐ Other ID | ISSUED | SIGNATURE ☐ (after oath / affirmation)
- PHONE C / H / W: ___ / ___ | or ☐ MISC | # | AGENCY ☐ CA DMV ☐ US State Dept | EXPIRES ❶

CW #2
- #2 WITNESS's NAME: _____ ☐ P/Known | ADDRESS: _____ ☐ Non-Public | ☐ Driver's License ☐ Passport ☐ Other ID | ISSUED | SIGNATURE ☐ (after oath / affirmation)
- PHONE C / H / W: ___ / ___ | or ☐ MISC | # | AGENCY ☐ CA DMV ☐ US State Dept | EXPIRES ❷

NOTARY NAME (printed):   COMMISSION #:

Entry 137

SERVICE — DATE - -20   TIME :   am / pm   ADDRESS   ☐ Signer's ☐ Office   NOTES   ☐ Stop   MILES   Notary ☐ Adv. Travel ☐ Rush ☐ Copy ☐ Other   TOTAL FEES $ $ $ $ $ $

TYPE ☐ Acknowledgment ☐ Jurat ☐ Copy Certification ☐ Oath/Affirmation ☐ Oath of Office ☐ Proof of Execution ☐ Protest ☐ Other

R T I M R P L — Fingerprint

DOCUMENT

DOC TYPE ☐ Deed ☐ DOT ☐ Trust ☐ POA ☐ POAH ☐ Agreement ☐ Affidavit ☐ Other

Deed	DOT	Trust	POA	POAH	Agreement	Affidavit	Other
Grant • Trust Transfer • Gift	Mortgage	Certification	General / Limited	AHCD	Compliance-E&O	Borrower • Occupancy • Ownership • Refi • Survey	Vehicle Title
Interspousal • Quitclaim • ToD • Warranty		Rev / Irrev • Am / Rest	Durable / Springing	Living Will	Correction	Debts & Liens • Name-Signature-ID • Marital • Death • Will	Safe Deposit Box

DOC DATE J F M A M J J A S O N D ,   DOC TITLE or TYPE   # OF PAGES ☐ Inspect/Copy Request   Entry X-Ref #

☐ **SATISFACTORY EVIDENCE** ☐ Driver's License / Passport / State ID / Military / Government / Tribal / Inmate / Other ID   *or*   ☐ Credible Witness(es)

SIGNER
SIGNER's NAME ☐ For   ADDRESS ☐ Non-Public ☐ Capacity ☐ Voluntary ☐ Proper ID   ISSUED   #   SIGNATURE ☐ (oath / affirmation, if any) ☐ (by Mark)
PHONE C / H / W   *or* ☐ MISC   AGENCY ☐ CA DMV ☐ US State Dept   EXPIRES ➡

CW #1
#1 WITNESS's NAME ☐ P/Known   ADDRESS ☐ Non-Public ☐ Driver's License ☐ Passport ☐ Other ID   ISSUED   #   SIGNATURE ☐ (after oath / affirmation)
PHONE C / H / W   *or* ☐ MISC   AGENCY ☐ CA DMV ☐ US State Dept   EXPIRES ❶

CW #2
#2 WITNESS's NAME ☐ P/Known   ADDRESS ☐ Non-Public ☐ Driver's License ☐ Passport ☐ Other ID   ISSUED   #   SIGNATURE ☐ (after oath / affirmation)
PHONE C / H / W   *or* ☐ MISC   AGENCY ☐ CA DMV ☐ US State Dept   EXPIRES ❷

Entry 138

SERVICE — DATE - -20   TIME :   am / pm   ADDRESS   ☐ Signer's ☐ Office   NOTES   ☐ Stop   MILES   Notary ☐ Adv. Travel ☐ Rush ☐ Copy ☐ Other   TOTAL FEES $ $ $ $ $ $

TYPE ☐ Acknowledgment ☐ Jurat ☐ Copy Certification ☐ Oath/Affirmation ☐ Oath of Office ☐ Proof of Execution ☐ Protest ☐ Other

R T I M R P L — Fingerprint

DOCUMENT

DOC TYPE ☐ Deed ☐ DOT ☐ Trust ☐ POA ☐ POAH ☐ Agreement ☐ Affidavit ☐ Other

Deed	DOT	Trust	POA	POAH	Agreement	Affidavit	Other
Grant • Trust Transfer • Gift	Mortgage	Certification	General / Limited	AHCD	Compliance-E&O	Borrower • Occupancy • Ownership • Refi • Survey	Vehicle Title
Interspousal • Quitclaim • ToD • Warranty		Rev / Irrev • Am / Rest	Durable / Springing	Living Will	Correction	Debts & Liens • Name-Signature-ID • Marital • Death • Will	Safe Deposit Box

DOC DATE J F M A M J J A S O N D ,   DOC TITLE or TYPE   # OF PAGES ☐ Inspect/Copy Request   Entry X-Ref #

☐ **SATISFACTORY EVIDENCE** ☐ Driver's License / Passport / State ID / Military / Government / Tribal / Inmate / Other ID   *or*   ☐ Credible Witness(es)

SIGNER
SIGNER's NAME ☐ For   ADDRESS ☐ Non-Public ☐ Capacity ☐ Voluntary ☐ Proper ID   ISSUED   #   SIGNATURE ☐ (oath / affirmation, if any) ☐ (by Mark)
PHONE C / H / W   *or* ☐ MISC   AGENCY ☐ CA DMV ☐ US State Dept   EXPIRES ➡

CW #1
#1 WITNESS's NAME ☐ P/Known   ADDRESS ☐ Non-Public ☐ Driver's License ☐ Passport ☐ Other ID   ISSUED   #   SIGNATURE ☐ (after oath / affirmation)
PHONE C / H / W   *or* ☐ MISC   AGENCY ☐ CA DMV ☐ US State Dept   EXPIRES ❶

CW #2
#2 WITNESS's NAME ☐ P/Known   ADDRESS ☐ Non-Public ☐ Driver's License ☐ Passport ☐ Other ID   ISSUED   #   SIGNATURE ☐ (after oath / affirmation)
PHONE C / H / W   *or* ☐ MISC   AGENCY ☐ CA DMV ☐ US State Dept   EXPIRES ❷

NOTARY NAME (printed): _____ **COMMISSION #:** _____

Entry 139

SERVICE — DATE: __-__-20__ | TIME: __:__ am/pm | ADDRESS: ☐ Signer's ☐ Office | NOTES: _____ | ☐ Stop | MILES: ___ | Notary $___ | ☐ Adv. Travel $___ | ☐ Rush $___ | ☐ Copy $___ | ☐ Other $___ | TOTAL FEES $___

TYPE: ☐ Acknowledgment ☐ Jurat ☐ Copy Certification ☐ Oath/Affirmation ☐ Oath of Office ☐ Proof of Execution ☐ Protest ☐ Other

DOCUMENT
- DOC TYPE: ☐ Deed (Grant • Trust Transfer • Gift / Interspousal • Quitclaim • ToD • Warranty) ☐ DOT (Mortgage) ☐ Trust (Certification / Rev / Irrev • Am / Rest) ☐ POA (General / Limited / Durable / Springing) ☐ POAH (AHCD / Living Will) ☐ Agreement (Compliance-E&O / Correction) ☐ Affidavit (Borrower • Occupancy • Ownership • Refi • Survey / Debts & Liens • Name-Signature-ID • Marital • Death • Will) ☐ Other (Vehicle Title / Safe Deposit Box)
- DOC DATE: J F M A M J J A S O N D , ____ | DOC TITLE or TYPE: _____ | # OF PAGES: ___ | ☐ Inspect/Copy Request | Entry X-Ref #: ____

R T I M R P L | **Fingerprint**

☐ **SATISFACTORY EVIDENCE** ☐ Driver's License / Passport / State ID / Military / Government / Tribal / Inmate / Other ID *or* ☐ Credible Witness(es)

SIGNER
- SIGNER's NAME: _____ ☐ For | ADDRESS: _____ ☐ Non-Public | ☐ Capacity # ___ | ☐ Voluntary | ☐ Proper ID | ISSUED: ___ | SIGNATURE: ___ ☐ (oath / affirmation, if any) ☐ (by Mark)
- PHONE C / H / W: ___/___ *or* ☐ MISC | AGENCY: ___ ☐ CA DMV ☐ US State Dept | EXPIRES: ___ ➡

CW #1
- #1 WITNESS's NAME: _____ ☐ P/Known | ADDRESS: _____ ☐ Non-Public | ☐ Driver's License ☐ Passport ☐ Other ID | ISSUED: ___ | SIGNATURE: ___ ☐ (after oath / affirmation)
- PHONE C / H / W: ___/___ *or* ☐ MISC | AGENCY: ___ ☐ CA DMV ☐ US State Dept | EXPIRES: ___ ❶

CW #2
- #2 WITNESS's NAME: _____ ☐ P/Known | ADDRESS: _____ ☐ Non-Public | ☐ Driver's License ☐ Passport ☐ Other ID | ISSUED: ___ | SIGNATURE: ___ ☐ (after oath / affirmation)
- PHONE C / H / W: ___/___ *or* ☐ MISC | AGENCY: ___ ☐ CA DMV ☐ US State Dept | EXPIRES: ___ ❷

Entry 140

SERVICE — DATE: __-__-20__ | TIME: __:__ am/pm | ADDRESS: ☐ Signer's ☐ Office | NOTES: _____ | ☐ Stop | MILES: ___ | Notary $___ | ☐ Adv. Travel $___ | ☐ Rush $___ | ☐ Copy $___ | ☐ Other $___ | TOTAL FEES $___

TYPE: ☐ Acknowledgment ☐ Jurat ☐ Copy Certification ☐ Oath/Affirmation ☐ Oath of Office ☐ Proof of Execution ☐ Protest ☐ Other

DOCUMENT
- DOC TYPE: ☐ Deed (Grant • Trust Transfer • Gift / Interspousal • Quitclaim • ToD • Warranty) ☐ DOT (Mortgage) ☐ Trust (Certification / Rev / Irrev • Am / Rest) ☐ POA (General / Limited / Durable / Springing) ☐ POAH (AHCD / Living Will) ☐ Agreement (Compliance-E&O / Correction) ☐ Affidavit (Borrower • Occupancy • Ownership • Refi • Survey / Debts & Liens • Name-Signature-ID • Marital • Death • Will) ☐ Other (Vehicle Title / Safe Deposit Box)
- DOC DATE: J F M A M J J A S O N D , ____ | DOC TITLE or TYPE: _____ | # OF PAGES: ___ | ☐ Inspect/Copy Request | Entry X-Ref #: ____

R T I M R P L | **Fingerprint**

☐ **SATISFACTORY EVIDENCE** ☐ Driver's License / Passport / State ID / Military / Government / Tribal / Inmate / Other ID *or* ☐ Credible Witness(es)

SIGNER
- SIGNER's NAME: _____ ☐ For | ADDRESS: _____ ☐ Non-Public | ☐ Capacity # ___ | ☐ Voluntary | ☐ Proper ID | ISSUED: ___ | SIGNATURE: ___ ☐ (oath / affirmation, if any) ☐ (by Mark)
- PHONE C / H / W: ___/___ *or* ☐ MISC | AGENCY: ___ ☐ CA DMV ☐ US State Dept | EXPIRES: ___ ➡

CW #1
- #1 WITNESS's NAME: _____ ☐ P/Known | ADDRESS: _____ ☐ Non-Public | ☐ Driver's License ☐ Passport ☐ Other ID | ISSUED: ___ | SIGNATURE: ___ ☐ (after oath / affirmation)
- PHONE C / H / W: ___/___ *or* ☐ MISC | AGENCY: ___ ☐ CA DMV ☐ US State Dept | EXPIRES: ___ ❶

CW #2
- #2 WITNESS's NAME: _____ ☐ P/Known | ADDRESS: _____ ☐ Non-Public | ☐ Driver's License ☐ Passport ☐ Other ID | ISSUED: ___ | SIGNATURE: ___ ☐ (after oath / affirmation)
- PHONE C / H / W: ___/___ *or* ☐ MISC | AGENCY: ___ ☐ CA DMV ☐ US State Dept | EXPIRES: ___ ❷

NOTARY NAME (printed):   COMMISSION #:

141

SERVICE

DATE — -20   TIME :   am / pm   ADDRESS   ☐ Signer's   ☐ Office   NOTES   ☐ Stop   MILES   Notary ☐ Adv. Travel ☐ Rush ☐ Copy ☐ Other TOTAL FEES $ $ $ $ $ $

TYPE ☐ Acknowledgment ☐ Jurat ☐ Copy Certification ☐ Oath/Affirmation ☐ Oath of Office ☐ Proof of Execution ☐ Protest ☐ Other

R T I M R P L   **Fingerprint**

DOCUMENT

DOC TYPE ☐ Deed ☐ DOT ☐ Trust ☐ POA ☐ POAH ☐ Agreement ☐ Affidavit ☐ Other

Grant • Trust Transfer • Gift   Mortgage   Certification   General / Limited   AHCD   Compliance-E&O   Borrower • Occupancy • Ownership • Refi • Survey   Vehicle Title

Interspousal • Quitclaim • ToD • Warranty   Rev / Irrev • Am / Rest   Durable / Springing   Living Will   Correction   Debts & Liens • Name-Signature-ID • Marital • Death • Will   Safe Deposit Box

DOC DATE J F M A M J J A S O N D   ,   DOC TITLE or TYPE   # OF PAGES ☐ Inspect/Copy Request   Entry X-Ref #

☐ **SATISFACTORY EVIDENCE** ☐ Driver's License / Passport / State ID / Military / Government / Tribal / Inmate / Other ID   *or*   ☐ Credible Witness(es)

SIGNER

SIGNER's NAME ☐ For   ADDRESS   ☐ Non-Public ☐ Capacity ☐ Voluntary ☐ Proper ID ISSUED   #   SIGNATURE ☐ *(oath / affirmation, if any)* ☐ *(by Mark)*

PHONE C / H / W   *or* ☐ MISC   /   AGENCY ☐ CA DMV ☐ US State Dept EXPIRES   ➡

CW #1

#1 WITNESS's NAME ☐ P/Known   ADDRESS   ☐ Non-Public ☐ Driver's License ☐ Passport ☐ Other ID ISSUED   #   SIGNATURE ☐ *(after oath / affirmation)*

PHONE C / H / W   *or* ☐ MISC   /   AGENCY ☐ CA DMV ☐ US State Dept EXPIRES   ❶

CW #2

#2 WITNESS's NAME ☐ P/Known   ADDRESS   ☐ Non-Public ☐ Driver's License ☐ Passport ☐ Other ID ISSUED   #   SIGNATURE ☐ *(after oath / affirmation)*

PHONE C / H / W   *or* ☐ MISC   /   AGENCY ☐ CA DMV ☐ US State Dept EXPIRES   ❷

142

SERVICE

DATE — -20   TIME :   am / pm   ADDRESS   ☐ Signer's   ☐ Office   NOTES   ☐ Stop   MILES   Notary ☐ Adv. Travel ☐ Rush ☐ Copy ☐ Other TOTAL FEES $ $ $ $ $ $

TYPE ☐ Acknowledgment ☐ Jurat ☐ Copy Certification ☐ Oath/Affirmation ☐ Oath of Office ☐ Proof of Execution ☐ Protest ☐ Other

R T I M R P L   **Fingerprint**

DOCUMENT

DOC TYPE ☐ Deed ☐ DOT ☐ Trust ☐ POA ☐ POAH ☐ Agreement ☐ Affidavit ☐ Other

Grant • Trust Transfer • Gift   Mortgage   Certification   General / Limited   AHCD   Compliance-E&O   Borrower • Occupancy • Ownership • Refi • Survey   Vehicle Title

Interspousal • Quitclaim • ToD • Warranty   Rev / Irrev • Am / Rest   Durable / Springing   Living Will   Correction   Debts & Liens • Name-Signature-ID • Marital • Death • Will   Safe Deposit Box

DOC DATE J F M A M J J A S O N D   ,   DOC TITLE or TYPE   # OF PAGES ☐ Inspect/Copy Request   Entry X-Ref #

☐ **SATISFACTORY EVIDENCE** ☐ Driver's License / Passport / State ID / Military / Government / Tribal / Inmate / Other ID   *or*   ☐ Credible Witness(es)

SIGNER

SIGNER's NAME ☐ For   ADDRESS   ☐ Non-Public ☐ Capacity ☐ Voluntary ☐ Proper ID ISSUED   #   SIGNATURE ☐ *(oath / affirmation, if any)* ☐ *(by Mark)*

PHONE C / H / W   *or* ☐ MISC   /   AGENCY ☐ CA DMV ☐ US State Dept EXPIRES   ➡

CW #1

#1 WITNESS's NAME ☐ P/Known   ADDRESS   ☐ Non-Public ☐ Driver's License ☐ Passport ☐ Other ID ISSUED   #   SIGNATURE ☐ *(after oath / affirmation)*

PHONE C / H / W   *or* ☐ MISC   /   AGENCY ☐ CA DMV ☐ US State Dept EXPIRES   ❶

CW #2

#2 WITNESS's NAME ☐ P/Known   ADDRESS   ☐ Non-Public ☐ Driver's License ☐ Passport ☐ Other ID ISSUED   #   SIGNATURE ☐ *(after oath / affirmation)*

PHONE C / H / W   *or* ☐ MISC   /   AGENCY ☐ CA DMV ☐ US State Dept EXPIRES   ❷

NOTARY NAME (printed): _____ COMMISSION #: _____

Entry 143

SERVICE — DATE: - -20 TIME: : am/pm ADDRESS ☐ Signer's ☐ Office NOTES ☐ Stop MILES Notary $__ ☐ Adv. Travel $__ ☐ Rush $__ ☐ Copy $__ ☐ Other $__ TOTAL FEES $__

TYPE: ☐ Acknowledgment ☐ Jurat ☐ Copy Certification ☐ Oath/Affirmation ☐ Oath of Office ☐ Proof of Execution ☐ Protest ☐ Other

DOCUMENT — DOC TYPE: ☐ Deed (Grant • Trust Transfer • Gift • Interspousal • Quitclaim • ToD • Warranty) ☐ DOT (Mortgage • Rev / Irrev • Am / Rest) ☐ Trust (Certification) ☐ POA (General / Limited • Durable / Springing) ☐ POAH (AHCD • Living Will) ☐ Agreement (Compliance-E&O • Correction) ☐ Affidavit (Borrower • Occupancy • Ownership • Refi • Survey • Debts & Liens • Name-Signature-ID • Marital • Death • Will) ☐ Other (Vehicle Title • Safe Deposit Box)

DOC DATE: J F M A M J / J A S O N D , ___ DOC TITLE or TYPE: ___ # OF PAGES: ___ ☐ Inspect/Copy Request Entry X-Ref #: ___

Fingerprint R T I M R P L

☐ **SATISFACTORY EVIDENCE** ☐ Driver's License / Passport / State ID / Military / Government / Tribal / Inmate / Other ID *or* ☐ Credible Witness(es)

SIGNER — SIGNER's NAME: ___ ☐ For ADDRESS: ___ ☐ Non-Public ☐ Capacity ☐ Voluntary ☐ Proper ID ISSUED # ___ SIGNATURE ___ ☐ (oath / affirmation, if any) ☐ (by Mark)
PHONE C / H / W: ___ / ___ *or* ☐ MISC AGENCY ___ ☐ CA DMV ☐ US State Dept EXPIRES ___ ➔

CW #1 — #1 WITNESS's NAME: ___ ☐ P/Known ADDRESS: ___ ☐ Non-Public ☐ Driver's License ☐ Passport ☐ Other ID ISSUED # ___ SIGNATURE ___ ☐ (after oath / affirmation)
PHONE C / H / W: ___ / ___ *or* ☐ MISC AGENCY ___ ☐ CA DMV ☐ US State Dept EXPIRES ___ ❶

CW #2 — #2 WITNESS's NAME: ___ ☐ P/Known ADDRESS: ___ ☐ Non-Public ☐ Driver's License ☐ Passport ☐ Other ID ISSUED # ___ SIGNATURE ___ ☐ (after oath / affirmation)
PHONE C / H / W: ___ / ___ *or* ☐ MISC AGENCY ___ ☐ CA DMV ☐ US State Dept EXPIRES ___ ❷

Entry 144

SERVICE — DATE: - -20 TIME: : am/pm ADDRESS ☐ Signer's ☐ Office NOTES ☐ Stop MILES Notary $__ ☐ Adv. Travel $__ ☐ Rush $__ ☐ Copy $__ ☐ Other $__ TOTAL FEES $__

TYPE: ☐ Acknowledgment ☐ Jurat ☐ Copy Certification ☐ Oath/Affirmation ☐ Oath of Office ☐ Proof of Execution ☐ Protest ☐ Other

DOCUMENT — DOC TYPE: ☐ Deed (Grant • Trust Transfer • Gift • Interspousal • Quitclaim • ToD • Warranty) ☐ DOT (Mortgage • Rev / Irrev • Am / Rest) ☐ Trust (Certification) ☐ POA (General / Limited • Durable / Springing) ☐ POAH (AHCD • Living Will) ☐ Agreement (Compliance-E&O • Correction) ☐ Affidavit (Borrower • Occupancy • Ownership • Refi • Survey • Debts & Liens • Name-Signature-ID • Marital • Death • Will) ☐ Other (Vehicle Title • Safe Deposit Box)

DOC DATE: J F M A M J / J A S O N D , ___ DOC TITLE or TYPE: ___ # OF PAGES: ___ ☐ Inspect/Copy Request Entry X-Ref #: ___

Fingerprint R T I M R P L

☐ **SATISFACTORY EVIDENCE** ☐ Driver's License / Passport / State ID / Military / Government / Tribal / Inmate / Other ID *or* ☐ Credible Witness(es)

SIGNER — SIGNER's NAME: ___ ☐ For ADDRESS: ___ ☐ Non-Public ☐ Capacity ☐ Voluntary ☐ Proper ID ISSUED # ___ SIGNATURE ___ ☐ (oath / affirmation, if any) ☐ (by Mark)
PHONE C / H / W: ___ / ___ *or* ☐ MISC AGENCY ___ ☐ CA DMV ☐ US State Dept EXPIRES ___ ➔

CW #1 — #1 WITNESS's NAME: ___ ☐ P/Known ADDRESS: ___ ☐ Non-Public ☐ Driver's License ☐ Passport ☐ Other ID ISSUED # ___ SIGNATURE ___ ☐ (after oath / affirmation)
PHONE C / H / W: ___ / ___ *or* ☐ MISC AGENCY ___ ☐ CA DMV ☐ US State Dept EXPIRES ___ ❶

CW #2 — #2 WITNESS's NAME: ___ ☐ P/Known ADDRESS: ___ ☐ Non-Public ☐ Driver's License ☐ Passport ☐ Other ID ISSUED # ___ SIGNATURE ___ ☐ (after oath / affirmation)
PHONE C / H / W: ___ / ___ *or* ☐ MISC AGENCY ___ ☐ CA DMV ☐ US State Dept EXPIRES ___ ❷

NOTARY NAME (printed): _____ COMMISSION #: _____

Entry 145

| SERVICE | DATE ___ - ___ -20___ | TIME ___:___ am pm | ADDRESS ☐ Signer's ☐ Office | NOTES | ☐ Stop | MILES | Notary ☐ Adv. Travel ☐ Rush ☐ Copy ☐ Other TOTAL FEES $___ $___ $___ $___ $___ $___ | **145** |

TYPE ☐ Acknowledgment ☐ Jurat ☐ Copy Certification ☐ Oath/Affirmation ☐ Oath of Office ☐ Proof of Execution ☐ Protest ☐ Other

DOCUMENT

DOC TYPE ☐ Deed ☐ DOT ☐ Trust ☐ POA ☐ POAH ☐ Agreement ☐ Affidavit ☐ Other
Grant • Trust Transfer • Gift | Mortgage | Certification | General / Limited | AHCD | Compliance-E&O | Borrower • Occupancy • Ownership • Refi • Survey | Vehicle Title
Interspousal • Quitclaim • ToD • Warranty | Rev / Irrev • Am / Rest | Durable / Springing | Living Will | Correction | Debts & Liens • Name-Signature-ID • Marital • Death • Will | Safe Deposit Box

DOC DATE J F M A M J J A S O N D , ___ | DOC TITLE or TYPE _____ | # OF PAGES ___ ☐ Inspect/Copy Request | Entry X-Ref # ___

Fingerprint (R T I M R P L)

☐ **SATISFACTORY EVIDENCE** ☐ Driver's License / Passport / State ID / Military / Government / Tribal / Inmate / Other ID **or** ☐ Credible Witness(es)

SIGNER	SIGNER's NAME ☐ For	ADDRESS ☐ Non-Public	☐ Capacity ☐ Voluntary ☐ Proper ID #	ISSUED	SIGNATURE ☐ (oath / affirmation, if any) ☐ (by Mark)
	PHONE C / H / W ___ / ___ or ☐ MISC		AGENCY ☐ CA DMV ☐ US State Dept	EXPIRES	➡
CW #1	#1 WITNESS's NAME ☐ P/Known	ADDRESS ☐ Non-Public	☐ Driver's License ☐ Passport ☐ Other ID #	ISSUED	SIGNATURE ☐ (after oath / affirmation)
	PHONE C / H / W ___ / ___ or ☐ MISC		AGENCY ☐ CA DMV ☐ US State Dept	EXPIRES	❶
CW #2	#2 WITNESS's NAME ☐ P/Known	ADDRESS ☐ Non-Public	☐ Driver's License ☐ Passport ☐ Other ID #	ISSUED	SIGNATURE ☐ (after oath / affirmation)
	PHONE C / H / W ___ / ___ or ☐ MISC		AGENCY ☐ CA DMV ☐ US State Dept	EXPIRES	❷

Entry 146

| SERVICE | DATE ___ - ___ -20___ | TIME ___:___ am pm | ADDRESS ☐ Signer's ☐ Office | NOTES | ☐ Stop | MILES | Notary ☐ Adv. Travel ☐ Rush ☐ Copy ☐ Other TOTAL FEES $___ $___ $___ $___ $___ $___ | **146** |

TYPE ☐ Acknowledgment ☐ Jurat ☐ Copy Certification ☐ Oath/Affirmation ☐ Oath of Office ☐ Proof of Execution ☐ Protest ☐ Other

DOCUMENT

DOC TYPE ☐ Deed ☐ DOT ☐ Trust ☐ POA ☐ POAH ☐ Agreement ☐ Affidavit ☐ Other
Grant • Trust Transfer • Gift | Mortgage | Certification | General / Limited | AHCD | Compliance-E&O | Borrower • Occupancy • Ownership • Refi • Survey | Vehicle Title
Interspousal • Quitclaim • ToD • Warranty | Rev / Irrev • Am / Rest | Durable / Springing | Living Will | Correction | Debts & Liens • Name-Signature-ID • Marital • Death • Will | Safe Deposit Box

DOC DATE J F M A M J J A S O N D , ___ | DOC TITLE or TYPE _____ | # OF PAGES ___ ☐ Inspect/Copy Request | Entry X-Ref # ___

Fingerprint (R T I M R P L)

☐ **SATISFACTORY EVIDENCE** ☐ Driver's License / Passport / State ID / Military / Government / Tribal / Inmate / Other ID **or** ☐ Credible Witness(es)

SIGNER	SIGNER's NAME ☐ For	ADDRESS ☐ Non-Public	☐ Capacity ☐ Voluntary ☐ Proper ID #	ISSUED	SIGNATURE ☐ (oath / affirmation, if any) ☐ (by Mark)
	PHONE C / H / W ___ / ___ or ☐ MISC		AGENCY ☐ CA DMV ☐ US State Dept	EXPIRES	➡
CW #1	#1 WITNESS's NAME ☐ P/Known	ADDRESS ☐ Non-Public	☐ Driver's License ☐ Passport ☐ Other ID #	ISSUED	SIGNATURE ☐ (after oath / affirmation)
	PHONE C / H / W ___ / ___ or ☐ MISC		AGENCY ☐ CA DMV ☐ US State Dept	EXPIRES	❶
CW #2	#2 WITNESS's NAME ☐ P/Known	ADDRESS ☐ Non-Public	☐ Driver's License ☐ Passport ☐ Other ID #	ISSUED	SIGNATURE ☐ (after oath / affirmation)
	PHONE C / H / W ___ / ___ or ☐ MISC		AGENCY ☐ CA DMV ☐ US State Dept	EXPIRES	❷

NOTARY NAME (printed): COMMISSION #:

Entry 147

SERVICE | DATE - -20 | TIME : am/pm | ADDRESS ☐ Signer's ☐ Office | NOTES | ☐ Stop MILES | Notary $ | ☐ Adv. Travel $ | ☐ Rush $ | ☐ Copy $ | ☐ Other $ | TOTAL FEES $

TYPE: ☐ Acknowledgment ☐ Jurat ☐ Copy Certification ☐ Oath/Affirmation ☐ Oath of Office ☐ Proof of Execution ☐ Protest ☐ Other

DOCUMENT
DOC TYPE: ☐ Deed (Grant • Trust Transfer • Gift, Interspousal • Quitclaim • ToD • Warranty) ☐ DOT (Mortgage) ☐ Trust (Certification, Rev / Irrev • Am / Rest) ☐ POA (General / Limited, Durable / Springing) ☐ POAH (AHCD, Living Will) ☐ Agreement (Compliance-E&O, Correction) ☐ Affidavit (Borrower • Occupancy • Ownership • Refi • Survey, Debts & Liens • Name-Signature-ID • Marital • Death • Will) ☐ Other (Vehicle Title, Safe Deposit Box)

DOC DATE: J F M A M J / J A S O N D , DOC TITLE or TYPE | # OF PAGES | ☐ Inspect/Copy Request | Entry X-Ref #

Fingerprint (R T I M R P L)

☐ SATISFACTORY EVIDENCE ☐ Driver's License / Passport / State ID / Military / Government / Tribal / Inmate / Other ID *or* ☐ Credible Witness(es)

SIGNER: SIGNER's NAME | ☐ For | ADDRESS | ☐ Non-Public | ☐ Capacity # | ☐ Voluntary | ☐ Proper ID | ISSUED | SIGNATURE | ☐ (oath / affirmation, if any) ☐ (by Mark)
PHONE C / H / W / | *or* ☐ MISC | | | AGENCY ☐ CA DMV ☐ US State Dept | EXPIRES

CW #1: #1 WITNESS's NAME | ☐ P/Known | ADDRESS | ☐ Non-Public | ☐ Driver's License ☐ Passport ☐ Other ID # | ISSUED | SIGNATURE | ☐ (after oath / affirmation)
PHONE C / H / W / | *or* ☐ MISC | | | AGENCY ☐ CA DMV ☐ US State Dept | EXPIRES | ❶

CW #2: #2 WITNESS's NAME | ☐ P/Known | ADDRESS | ☐ Non-Public | ☐ Driver's License ☐ Passport ☐ Other ID # | ISSUED | SIGNATURE | ☐ (after oath / affirmation)
PHONE C / H / W / | *or* ☐ MISC | | | AGENCY ☐ CA DMV ☐ US State Dept | EXPIRES | ❷

Entry 148

SERVICE | DATE - -20 | TIME : am/pm | ADDRESS ☐ Signer's ☐ Office | NOTES | ☐ Stop MILES | Notary $ | ☐ Adv. Travel $ | ☐ Rush $ | ☐ Copy $ | ☐ Other $ | TOTAL FEES $

TYPE: ☐ Acknowledgment ☐ Jurat ☐ Copy Certification ☐ Oath/Affirmation ☐ Oath of Office ☐ Proof of Execution ☐ Protest ☐ Other

DOCUMENT
DOC TYPE: ☐ Deed (Grant • Trust Transfer • Gift, Interspousal • Quitclaim • ToD • Warranty) ☐ DOT (Mortgage) ☐ Trust (Certification, Rev / Irrev • Am / Rest) ☐ POA (General / Limited, Durable / Springing) ☐ POAH (AHCD, Living Will) ☐ Agreement (Compliance-E&O, Correction) ☐ Affidavit (Borrower • Occupancy • Ownership • Refi • Survey, Debts & Liens • Name-Signature-ID • Marital • Death • Will) ☐ Other (Vehicle Title, Safe Deposit Box)

DOC DATE: J F M A M J / J A S O N D , DOC TITLE or TYPE | # OF PAGES | ☐ Inspect/Copy Request | Entry X-Ref #

Fingerprint (R T I M R P L)

☐ SATISFACTORY EVIDENCE ☐ Driver's License / Passport / State ID / Military / Government / Tribal / Inmate / Other ID *or* ☐ Credible Witness(es)

SIGNER: SIGNER's NAME | ☐ For | ADDRESS | ☐ Non-Public | ☐ Capacity # | ☐ Voluntary | ☐ Proper ID | ISSUED | SIGNATURE | ☐ (oath / affirmation, if any) ☐ (by Mark)
PHONE C / H / W / | *or* ☐ MISC | | | AGENCY ☐ CA DMV ☐ US State Dept | EXPIRES

CW #1: #1 WITNESS's NAME | ☐ P/Known | ADDRESS | ☐ Non-Public | ☐ Driver's License ☐ Passport ☐ Other ID # | ISSUED | SIGNATURE | ☐ (after oath / affirmation)
PHONE C / H / W / | *or* ☐ MISC | | | AGENCY ☐ CA DMV ☐ US State Dept | EXPIRES | ❶

CW #2: #2 WITNESS's NAME | ☐ P/Known | ADDRESS | ☐ Non-Public | ☐ Driver's License ☐ Passport ☐ Other ID # | ISSUED | SIGNATURE | ☐ (after oath / affirmation)
PHONE C / H / W / | *or* ☐ MISC | | | AGENCY ☐ CA DMV ☐ US State Dept | EXPIRES | ❷

NOTARY NAME (printed):   COMMISSION #:

Entry 149

SERVICE — DATE - -20 | TIME : am/pm | ADDRESS ☐ Signer's ☐ Office | NOTES | ☐ Stop | MILES | Notary $ | ☐ Adv. Travel $ | ☐ Rush | ☐ Copy $ | ☐ Other $ | TOTAL FEES $

TYPE ☐ Acknowledgment ☐ Jurat ☐ Copy Certification ☐ Oath/Affirmation ☐ Oath of Office ☐ Proof of Execution ☐ Protest ☐ Other

R T I M R P L — **Fingerprint**

DOCUMENT
DOC TYPE ☐ Deed ☐ DOT ☐ Trust ☐ POA ☐ POAH ☐ Agreement ☐ Affidavit ☐ Other

Grant • Trust Transfer • Gift | Mortgage | Certification | General / Limited | AHCD | Compliance-E&O | Borrower • Occupancy • Ownership • Refi • Survey | Vehicle Title
Interspousal • Quitclaim • ToD • Warranty | Rev / Irrev • Am / Rest | Durable / Springing | Living Will | Correction | Debts & Liens • Name-Signature-ID • Marital • Death • Will | Safe Deposit Box

DOC DATE J F M A M J J A S O N D , | DOC TITLE or TYPE | # OF PAGES | ☐ Inspect/Copy Request | Entry X-Ref #

☐ **SATISFACTORY EVIDENCE** ☐ Driver's License / Passport / State ID / Military / Government / Tribal / Inmate / Other ID *or* ☐ Credible Witness(es)

SIGNER
SIGNER's NAME | ☐ For | ADDRESS | ☐ Non-Public | ☐ Capacity | ☐ Voluntary | ☐ Proper ID | ISSUED # | SIGNATURE | ☐ (oath / affirmation, if any) | ☐ (by Mark)
PHONE C / H / W / | *or* ☐ MISC | AGENCY | ☐ CA DMV | ☐ US State Dept | EXPIRES | ➡

CW #1
#1 WITNESS's NAME | ☐ P/Known | ADDRESS | ☐ Non-Public | ☐ Driver's License | ☐ Passport | ☐ Other ID | ISSUED # | SIGNATURE | ☐ (after oath / affirmation)
PHONE C / H / W / | *or* ☐ MISC | AGENCY | ☐ CA DMV | ☐ US State Dept | EXPIRES | ❶

CW #2
#2 WITNESS's NAME | ☐ P/Known | ADDRESS | ☐ Non-Public | ☐ Driver's License | ☐ Passport | ☐ Other ID | ISSUED # | SIGNATURE | ☐ (after oath / affirmation)
PHONE C / H / W / | *or* ☐ MISC | AGENCY | ☐ CA DMV | ☐ US State Dept | EXPIRES | ❷

Entry 150

SERVICE — DATE - -20 | TIME : am/pm | ADDRESS ☐ Signer's ☐ Office | NOTES | ☐ Stop | MILES | Notary $ | ☐ Adv. Travel $ | ☐ Rush | ☐ Copy $ | ☐ Other $ | TOTAL FEES $

TYPE ☐ Acknowledgment ☐ Jurat ☐ Copy Certification ☐ Oath/Affirmation ☐ Oath of Office ☐ Proof of Execution ☐ Protest ☐ Other

R T I M R P L — **Fingerprint**

DOCUMENT
DOC TYPE ☐ Deed ☐ DOT ☐ Trust ☐ POA ☐ POAH ☐ Agreement ☐ Affidavit ☐ Other

Grant • Trust Transfer • Gift | Mortgage | Certification | General / Limited | AHCD | Compliance-E&O | Borrower • Occupancy • Ownership • Refi • Survey | Vehicle Title
Interspousal • Quitclaim • ToD • Warranty | Rev / Irrev • Am / Rest | Durable / Springing | Living Will | Correction | Debts & Liens • Name-Signature-ID • Marital • Death • Will | Safe Deposit Box

DOC DATE J F M A M J J A S O N D , | DOC TITLE or TYPE | # OF PAGES | ☐ Inspect/Copy Request | Entry X-Ref #

☐ **SATISFACTORY EVIDENCE** ☐ Driver's License / Passport / State ID / Military / Government / Tribal / Inmate / Other ID *or* ☐ Credible Witness(es)

SIGNER
SIGNER's NAME | ☐ For | ADDRESS | ☐ Non-Public | ☐ Capacity | ☐ Voluntary | ☐ Proper ID | ISSUED # | SIGNATURE | ☐ (oath / affirmation, if any) | ☐ (by Mark)
PHONE C / H / W / | *or* ☐ MISC | AGENCY | ☐ CA DMV | ☐ US State Dept | EXPIRES | ➡

CW #1
#1 WITNESS's NAME | ☐ P/Known | ADDRESS | ☐ Non-Public | ☐ Driver's License | ☐ Passport | ☐ Other ID | ISSUED # | SIGNATURE | ☐ (after oath / affirmation)
PHONE C / H / W / | *or* ☐ MISC | AGENCY | ☐ CA DMV | ☐ US State Dept | EXPIRES | ❶

CW #2
#2 WITNESS's NAME | ☐ P/Known | ADDRESS | ☐ Non-Public | ☐ Driver's License | ☐ Passport | ☐ Other ID | ISSUED # | SIGNATURE | ☐ (after oath / affirmation)
PHONE C / H / W / | *or* ☐ MISC | AGENCY | ☐ CA DMV | ☐ US State Dept | EXPIRES | ❷

NOTARY NAME (printed):   COMMISSION #:

Entry 151

SERVICE — DATE: - -20 | TIME: : am/pm | ADDRESS ☐ Signer's ☐ Office | NOTES | ☐ Stop | MILES | Notary $ | ☐ Adv. Travel $ | ☐ Rush $ | ☐ Copy $ | ☐ Other $ | TOTAL FEES $

TYPE: ☐ Acknowledgment ☐ Jurat ☐ Copy Certification ☐ Oath/Affirmation ☐ Oath of Office ☐ Proof of Execution ☐ Protest ☐ Other   R T I M R P L   **Fingerprint**

DOCUMENT — DOC TYPE: ☐ Deed (Grant • Trust Transfer • Gift / Interspousal • Quitclaim • ToD • Warranty) ☐ DOT (Mortgage / Certification / Rev / Irrev • Am / Rest) ☐ Trust ☐ POA (General / Limited / Durable / Springing) ☐ POAH (AHCD / Living Will) ☐ Agreement (Compliance-E&O / Correction) ☐ Affidavit (Borrower • Occupancy • Ownership • Refi • Survey / Debts & Liens • Name-Signature-ID • Marital • Death • Will) ☐ Other (Vehicle Title / Safe Deposit Box)

DOC DATE: J F M A M J J A S O N D ,   DOC TITLE or TYPE: # OF PAGES: ☐ Inspect/Copy Request   Entry X-Ref #:

☐ **SATISFACTORY EVIDENCE** ☐ Driver's License / Passport / State ID / Military / Government / Tribal / Inmate / Other ID   *or*   ☐ Credible Witness(es)

SIGNER — SIGNER's NAME | ☐ For | ADDRESS | ☐ Non-Public | ☐ Capacity # | ☐ Voluntary | ☐ Proper ID | ISSUED | SIGNATURE ☐ (oath / affirmation, if any) ☐ (by Mark)
PHONE C/H/W: / | *or* ☐ MISC | | | AGENCY | ☐ CA DMV | ☐ US State Dept | EXPIRES | ➡

CW #1 — #1 WITNESS's NAME | ☐ P/Known | ADDRESS | ☐ Non-Public | ☐ Driver's License # | ☐ Passport | ☐ Other ID | ISSUED | SIGNATURE ☐ (after oath / affirmation)
PHONE C/H/W: / | *or* ☐ MISC | | | AGENCY | ☐ CA DMV | ☐ US State Dept | EXPIRES | ❶

CW #2 — #2 WITNESS's NAME | ☐ P/Known | ADDRESS | ☐ Non-Public | ☐ Driver's License # | ☐ Passport | ☐ Other ID | ISSUED | SIGNATURE ☐ (after oath / affirmation)
PHONE C/H/W: / | *or* ☐ MISC | | | AGENCY | ☐ CA DMV | ☐ US State Dept | EXPIRES | ❷

Entry 152

SERVICE — DATE: - -20 | TIME: : am/pm | ADDRESS ☐ Signer's ☐ Office | NOTES | ☐ Stop | MILES | Notary $ | ☐ Adv. Travel $ | ☐ Rush $ | ☐ Copy $ | ☐ Other $ | TOTAL FEES $

TYPE: ☐ Acknowledgment ☐ Jurat ☐ Copy Certification ☐ Oath/Affirmation ☐ Oath of Office ☐ Proof of Execution ☐ Protest ☐ Other   R T I M R P L   **Fingerprint**

DOCUMENT — DOC TYPE: ☐ Deed (Grant • Trust Transfer • Gift / Interspousal • Quitclaim • ToD • Warranty) ☐ DOT (Mortgage / Certification / Rev / Irrev • Am / Rest) ☐ Trust ☐ POA (General / Limited / Durable / Springing) ☐ POAH (AHCD / Living Will) ☐ Agreement (Compliance-E&O / Correction) ☐ Affidavit (Borrower • Occupancy • Ownership • Refi • Survey / Debts & Liens • Name-Signature-ID • Marital • Death • Will) ☐ Other (Vehicle Title / Safe Deposit Box)

DOC DATE: J F M A M J J A S O N D ,   DOC TITLE or TYPE: # OF PAGES: ☐ Inspect/Copy Request   Entry X-Ref #:

☐ **SATISFACTORY EVIDENCE** ☐ Driver's License / Passport / State ID / Military / Government / Tribal / Inmate / Other ID   *or*   ☐ Credible Witness(es)

SIGNER — SIGNER's NAME | ☐ For | ADDRESS | ☐ Non-Public | ☐ Capacity # | ☐ Voluntary | ☐ Proper ID | ISSUED | SIGNATURE ☐ (oath / affirmation, if any) ☐ (by Mark)
PHONE C/H/W: / | *or* ☐ MISC | | | AGENCY | ☐ CA DMV | ☐ US State Dept | EXPIRES | ➡

CW #1 — #1 WITNESS's NAME | ☐ P/Known | ADDRESS | ☐ Non-Public | ☐ Driver's License # | ☐ Passport | ☐ Other ID | ISSUED | SIGNATURE ☐ (after oath / affirmation)
PHONE C/H/W: / | *or* ☐ MISC | | | AGENCY | ☐ CA DMV | ☐ US State Dept | EXPIRES | ❶

CW #2 — #2 WITNESS's NAME | ☐ P/Known | ADDRESS | ☐ Non-Public | ☐ Driver's License # | ☐ Passport | ☐ Other ID | ISSUED | SIGNATURE ☐ (after oath / affirmation)
PHONE C/H/W: / | *or* ☐ MISC | | | AGENCY | ☐ CA DMV | ☐ US State Dept | EXPIRES | ❷

NOTARY NAME (printed): _____ COMMISSION #: _____

153

| SERVICE | DATE __ - __ -20__ | TIME __ : __ am pm | ADDRESS | ☐ Signer's ☐ Office | NOTES | ☐ Stop | MILES | Notary ☐ Adv. Travel ☐ Rush ☐ Copy ☐ Other TOTAL FEES $__ $__ $__ $__ $__ $__ |

Fingerprint — R T I M R P L

| TYPE | ☐ Acknowledgment ☐ Jurat ☐ Copy Certification ☐ Oath/Affirmation ☐ Oath of Office ☐ Proof of Execution ☐ Protest ☐ Other |

DOCUMENT

DOC TYPE ☐ Deed ☐ DOT ☐ Trust ☐ POA ☐ POAH ☐ Agreement ☐ Affidavit ☐ Other
Grant • Trust Transfer • Gift | Mortgage | Certification | General / Limited | AHCD | Compliance-E&O | Borrower • Occupancy • Ownership • Refi • Survey | Vehicle Title
Interspousal • Quitclaim • ToD • Warranty | Rev / Irrev • Am / Rest | Durable / Springing | Living Will | Correction | Debts & Liens • Name-Signature-ID • Marital • Death • Will | Safe Deposit Box

DOC DATE J F M A M J J A S O N D , ____ | DOC TITLE or TYPE | # OF PAGES ☐ Inspect/Copy Request | Entry X-Ref #

☐ **SATISFACTORY EVIDENCE** ☐ Driver's License / Passport / State ID / Military / Government / Tribal / Inmate / Other ID *or* ☐ Credible Witness(es)

SIGNER
SIGNER's NAME ☐ For | ADDRESS | ☐ Non-Public | ☐ Capacity ☐ Voluntary ☐ Proper ID | ISSUED # | SIGNATURE ☐ (oath / affirmation, if any) ☐ (by Mark)
PHONE C / H / W *or* ☐ MISC / | | AGENCY ☐ CA DMV ☐ US State Dept | EXPIRES | ➡

CW #1
#1 WITNESS's NAME ☐ P/Known | ADDRESS | ☐ Non-Public | ☐ Driver's License ☐ Passport ☐ Other ID | ISSUED # | SIGNATURE ☐ (after oath / affirmation)
PHONE C / H / W *or* ☐ MISC / | | AGENCY ☐ CA DMV ☐ US State Dept | EXPIRES | ❶

CW #2
#2 WITNESS's NAME ☐ P/Known | ADDRESS | ☐ Non-Public | ☐ Driver's License ☐ Passport ☐ Other ID | ISSUED # | SIGNATURE ☐ (after oath / affirmation)
PHONE C / H / W *or* ☐ MISC / | | AGENCY ☐ CA DMV ☐ US State Dept | EXPIRES | ❷

154

| SERVICE | DATE __ - __ -20__ | TIME __ : __ am pm | ADDRESS | ☐ Signer's ☐ Office | NOTES | ☐ Stop | MILES | Notary ☐ Adv. Travel ☐ Rush ☐ Copy ☐ Other TOTAL FEES $__ $__ $__ $__ $__ $__ |

Fingerprint — R T I M R P L

| TYPE | ☐ Acknowledgment ☐ Jurat ☐ Copy Certification ☐ Oath/Affirmation ☐ Oath of Office ☐ Proof of Execution ☐ Protest ☐ Other |

DOCUMENT

DOC TYPE ☐ Deed ☐ DOT ☐ Trust ☐ POA ☐ POAH ☐ Agreement ☐ Affidavit ☐ Other
Grant • Trust Transfer • Gift | Mortgage | Certification | General / Limited | AHCD | Compliance-E&O | Borrower • Occupancy • Ownership • Refi • Survey | Vehicle Title
Interspousal • Quitclaim • ToD • Warranty | Rev / Irrev • Am / Rest | Durable / Springing | Living Will | Correction | Debts & Liens • Name-Signature-ID • Marital • Death • Will | Safe Deposit Box

DOC DATE J F M A M J J A S O N D , ____ | DOC TITLE or TYPE | # OF PAGES ☐ Inspect/Copy Request | Entry X-Ref #

☐ **SATISFACTORY EVIDENCE** ☐ Driver's License / Passport / State ID / Military / Government / Tribal / Inmate / Other ID *or* ☐ Credible Witness(es)

SIGNER
SIGNER's NAME ☐ For | ADDRESS | ☐ Non-Public | ☐ Capacity ☐ Voluntary ☐ Proper ID | ISSUED # | SIGNATURE ☐ (oath / affirmation, if any) ☐ (by Mark)
PHONE C / H / W *or* ☐ MISC / | | AGENCY ☐ CA DMV ☐ US State Dept | EXPIRES | ➡

CW #1
#1 WITNESS's NAME ☐ P/Known | ADDRESS | ☐ Non-Public | ☐ Driver's License ☐ Passport ☐ Other ID | ISSUED # | SIGNATURE ☐ (after oath / affirmation)
PHONE C / H / W *or* ☐ MISC / | | AGENCY ☐ CA DMV ☐ US State Dept | EXPIRES | ❶

CW #2
#2 WITNESS's NAME ☐ P/Known | ADDRESS | ☐ Non-Public | ☐ Driver's License ☐ Passport ☐ Other ID | ISSUED # | SIGNATURE ☐ (after oath / affirmation)
PHONE C / H / W *or* ☐ MISC / | | AGENCY ☐ CA DMV ☐ US State Dept | EXPIRES | ❷

NOTARY NAME (printed): COMMISSION #:

Entry 155

SERVICE | DATE - -20 | TIME : am/pm | ADDRESS ☐ Signer's ☐ Office | NOTES | ☐ Stop MILES | Notary $ | ☐ Adv. Travel $ | ☐ Rush $ | ☐ Copy $ | ☐ Other $ | TOTAL FEES $

DOCUMENT
TYPE: ☐ Acknowledgment ☐ Jurat ☐ Copy Certification ☐ Oath/Affirmation ☐ Oath of Office ☐ Proof of Execution ☐ Protest ☐ Other
DOC TYPE: ☐ Deed (Grant • Trust Transfer • Gift • Interspousal • Quitclaim • ToD • Warranty) ☐ DOT (Mortgage) ☐ Trust (Certification • Rev / Irrev • Am / Rest) ☐ POA (General / Limited • Durable / Springing) ☐ POAH (AHCD • Living Will) ☐ Agreement (Compliance-E&O • Correction) ☐ Affidavit (Borrower • Occupancy • Ownership • Refi • Survey • Debts & Liens • Name-Signature-ID • Marital • Death • Will) ☐ Other (Vehicle Title • Safe Deposit Box)
DOC DATE: J F M A M J J A S O N D , | DOC TITLE or TYPE | # OF PAGES | ☐ Inspect/Copy Request | Entry X-Ref #

Fingerprint: R T I M R P L

☐ **SATISFACTORY EVIDENCE** ☐ Driver's License / Passport / State ID / Military / Government / Tribal / Inmate / Other ID *or* ☐ Credible Witness(es)

SIGNER
SIGNER's NAME | ☐ For | ADDRESS | ☐ Non-Public | ☐ Capacity # | ☐ Voluntary | ☐ Proper ID | ISSUED | SIGNATURE | ☐ (oath / affirmation, if any) | ☐ (by Mark)
PHONE C / H / W / | *or* ☐ MISC | | | AGENCY ☐ CA DMV ☐ US State Dept | EXPIRES | ➤

CW #1
#1 WITNESS's NAME | ☐ P/Known | ADDRESS | ☐ Non-Public | ☐ Driver's License # ☐ Passport ☐ Other ID | ISSUED | SIGNATURE | ☐ (after oath / affirmation)
PHONE C / H / W / | *or* ☐ MISC | | | AGENCY ☐ CA DMV ☐ US State Dept | EXPIRES | ❶

CW #2
#2 WITNESS's NAME | ☐ P/Known | ADDRESS | ☐ Non-Public | ☐ Driver's License # ☐ Passport ☐ Other ID | ISSUED | SIGNATURE | ☐ (after oath / affirmation)
PHONE C / H / W / | *or* ☐ MISC | | | AGENCY ☐ CA DMV ☐ US State Dept | EXPIRES | ❷

Entry 156

SERVICE | DATE - -20 | TIME : am/pm | ADDRESS ☐ Signer's ☐ Office | NOTES | ☐ Stop MILES | Notary $ | ☐ Adv. Travel $ | ☐ Rush $ | ☐ Copy $ | ☐ Other $ | TOTAL FEES $

DOCUMENT
TYPE: ☐ Acknowledgment ☐ Jurat ☐ Copy Certification ☐ Oath/Affirmation ☐ Oath of Office ☐ Proof of Execution ☐ Protest ☐ Other
DOC TYPE: ☐ Deed (Grant • Trust Transfer • Gift • Interspousal • Quitclaim • ToD • Warranty) ☐ DOT (Mortgage) ☐ Trust (Certification • Rev / Irrev • Am / Rest) ☐ POA (General / Limited • Durable / Springing) ☐ POAH (AHCD • Living Will) ☐ Agreement (Compliance-E&O • Correction) ☐ Affidavit (Borrower • Occupancy • Ownership • Refi • Survey • Debts & Liens • Name-Signature-ID • Marital • Death • Will) ☐ Other (Vehicle Title • Safe Deposit Box)
DOC DATE: J F M A M J J A S O N D , | DOC TITLE or TYPE | # OF PAGES | ☐ Inspect/Copy Request | Entry X-Ref #

Fingerprint: R T I M R P L

☐ **SATISFACTORY EVIDENCE** ☐ Driver's License / Passport / State ID / Military / Government / Tribal / Inmate / Other ID *or* ☐ Credible Witness(es)

SIGNER
SIGNER's NAME | ☐ For | ADDRESS | ☐ Non-Public | ☐ Capacity # | ☐ Voluntary | ☐ Proper ID | ISSUED | SIGNATURE | ☐ (oath / affirmation, if any) | ☐ (by Mark)
PHONE C / H / W / | *or* ☐ MISC | | | AGENCY ☐ CA DMV ☐ US State Dept | EXPIRES | ➤

CW #1
#1 WITNESS's NAME | ☐ P/Known | ADDRESS | ☐ Non-Public | ☐ Driver's License # ☐ Passport ☐ Other ID | ISSUED | SIGNATURE | ☐ (after oath / affirmation)
PHONE C / H / W / | *or* ☐ MISC | | | AGENCY ☐ CA DMV ☐ US State Dept | EXPIRES | ❶

CW #2
#2 WITNESS's NAME | ☐ P/Known | ADDRESS | ☐ Non-Public | ☐ Driver's License # ☐ Passport ☐ Other ID | ISSUED | SIGNATURE | ☐ (after oath / affirmation)
PHONE C / H / W / | *or* ☐ MISC | | | AGENCY ☐ CA DMV ☐ US State Dept | EXPIRES | ❷

NOTARY NAME (printed): _____ **COMMISSION #:** _____

Entry 157

SERVICE	DATE ___ - ___ -20	TIME ___ : ___ am/pm	ADDRESS	☐ Signer's ☐ Office NOTES	☐ Stop MILES	Notary ☐ Adv. Travel ☐ Rush ☐ Copy ☐ Other TOTAL FEES
					$ ___ $ ___	$ ___ $ ___ $ ___ $ ___

TYPE ☐ Acknowledgment ☐ Jurat ☐ Copy Certification ☐ Oath/Affirmation ☐ Oath of Office ☐ Proof of Execution ☐ Protest ☐ Other

R T I M R P L | **Fingerprint**

DOCUMENT

DOC TYPE ☐ Deed — Grant • Trust Transfer • Gift, Interspousal • Quitclaim • ToD • Warranty   ☐ DOT — Mortgage, Rev / Irrev • Am / Rest   ☐ Trust — Certification   ☐ POA — General / Limited, Durable / Springing   ☐ POAH — AHCD, Living Will   ☐ Agreement — Compliance-E&O, Correction   ☐ Affidavit — Borrower • Occupancy • Ownership • Refi • Survey, Debts & Liens • Name-Signature-ID • Marital • Death • Will   ☐ Other — Vehicle Title, Safe Deposit Box

DOC DATE J F M A M J J A S O N D , ___   **DOC TITLE or TYPE** ___   **# OF PAGES** ___ ☐ Inspect/Copy Request   Entry X-Ref # ___

☐ **SATISFACTORY EVIDENCE** ☐ Driver's License / Passport / State ID / Military / Government / Tribal / Inmate / Other ID *or* ☐ Credible Witness(es)

SIGNER	SIGNER's NAME	☐ For	ADDRESS	☐ Non-Public	☐ Capacity #	☐ Voluntary	☐ Proper ID	ISSUED	SIGNATURE ☐ (oath / affirmation, if any) ☐ (by Mark)
	PHONE C / H / W	*or* ☐ MISC			AGENCY	☐ CA DMV	☐ US State Dept	EXPIRES	➡

CW #1	#1 WITNESS's NAME	☐ P/Known	ADDRESS	☐ Non-Public	☐ Driver's License #	☐ Passport	☐ Other ID	ISSUED	SIGNATURE ☐ (after oath / affirmation)
	PHONE C / H / W	*or* ☐ MISC			AGENCY	☐ CA DMV	☐ US State Dept	EXPIRES	❶

CW #2	#2 WITNESS's NAME	☐ P/Known	ADDRESS	☐ Non-Public	☐ Driver's License #	☐ Passport	☐ Other ID	ISSUED	SIGNATURE ☐ (after oath / affirmation)
	PHONE C / H / W	*or* ☐ MISC			AGENCY	☐ CA DMV	☐ US State Dept	EXPIRES	❷

Entry 158

SERVICE	DATE ___ - ___ -20	TIME ___ : ___ am/pm	ADDRESS	☐ Signer's ☐ Office NOTES	☐ Stop MILES	Notary ☐ Adv. Travel ☐ Rush ☐ Copy ☐ Other TOTAL FEES
					$ ___ $ ___	$ ___ $ ___ $ ___ $ ___

TYPE ☐ Acknowledgment ☐ Jurat ☐ Copy Certification ☐ Oath/Affirmation ☐ Oath of Office ☐ Proof of Execution ☐ Protest ☐ Other

R T I M R P L | **Fingerprint**

DOCUMENT

DOC TYPE ☐ Deed — Grant • Trust Transfer • Gift, Interspousal • Quitclaim • ToD • Warranty   ☐ DOT — Mortgage, Rev / Irrev • Am / Rest   ☐ Trust — Certification   ☐ POA — General / Limited, Durable / Springing   ☐ POAH — AHCD, Living Will   ☐ Agreement — Compliance-E&O, Correction   ☐ Affidavit — Borrower • Occupancy • Ownership • Refi • Survey, Debts & Liens • Name-Signature-ID • Marital • Death • Will   ☐ Other — Vehicle Title, Safe Deposit Box

DOC DATE J F M A M J J A S O N D , ___   **DOC TITLE or TYPE** ___   **# OF PAGES** ___ ☐ Inspect/Copy Request   Entry X-Ref # ___

☐ **SATISFACTORY EVIDENCE** ☐ Driver's License / Passport / State ID / Military / Government / Tribal / Inmate / Other ID *or* ☐ Credible Witness(es)

SIGNER	SIGNER's NAME	☐ For	ADDRESS	☐ Non-Public	☐ Capacity #	☐ Voluntary	☐ Proper ID	ISSUED	SIGNATURE ☐ (oath / affirmation, if any) ☐ (by Mark)
	PHONE C / H / W	*or* ☐ MISC			AGENCY	☐ CA DMV	☐ US State Dept	EXPIRES	➡

CW #1	#1 WITNESS's NAME	☐ P/Known	ADDRESS	☐ Non-Public	☐ Driver's License #	☐ Passport	☐ Other ID	ISSUED	SIGNATURE ☐ (after oath / affirmation)
	PHONE C / H / W	*or* ☐ MISC			AGENCY	☐ CA DMV	☐ US State Dept	EXPIRES	❶

CW #2	#2 WITNESS's NAME	☐ P/Known	ADDRESS	☐ Non-Public	☐ Driver's License #	☐ Passport	☐ Other ID	ISSUED	SIGNATURE ☐ (after oath / affirmation)
	PHONE C / H / W	*or* ☐ MISC			AGENCY	☐ CA DMV	☐ US State Dept	EXPIRES	❷

NOTARY NAME (printed):   COMMISSION #:

Entry 159

SERVICE — DATE - -20 | TIME : am/pm | ADDRESS ☐ Signer's ☐ Office | NOTES | ☐ Stop | MILES | Notary $ | ☐ Adv. Travel $ | ☐ Rush $ | ☐ Copy $ | ☐ Other $ | TOTAL FEES $

TYPE: ☐ Acknowledgment ☐ Jurat ☐ Copy Certification ☐ Oath/Affirmation ☐ Oath of Office ☐ Proof of Execution ☐ Protest ☐ Other   R T I M R P L   **Fingerprint**

DOCUMENT — DOC TYPE: ☐ Deed (Grant • Trust Transfer • Gift • Interspousal • Quitclaim • ToD • Warranty) ☐ DOT (Mortgage • Rev / Irrev • Am / Rest) ☐ Trust (Certification) ☐ POA (General / Limited • Durable / Springing) ☐ POAH (AHCD • Living Will) ☐ Agreement (Compliance-E&O • Correction) ☐ Affidavit (Borrower • Occupancy • Ownership • Refi • Survey • Debts & Liens • Name-Signature-ID • Marital • Death • Will) ☐ Other (Vehicle Title • Safe Deposit Box)

DOC DATE: J F M A M J / J A S O N D ,   DOC TITLE or TYPE   # OF PAGES   ☐ Inspect/Copy Request   Entry X-Ref #

☐ **SATISFACTORY EVIDENCE** ☐ Driver's License / Passport / State ID / Military / Government / Tribal / Inmate / Other ID   *or*   ☐ Credible Witness(es)

SIGNER — SIGNER's NAME | ☐ For | ADDRESS | ☐ Non-Public | ☐ Capacity | ☐ Voluntary | ☐ Proper ID | ISSUED # | SIGNATURE ☐ (oath / affirmation, if any) ☐ (by Mark)
PHONE C / H / W / | *or* ☐ MISC | | | AGENCY | ☐ CA DMV | ☐ US State Dept | EXPIRES | ➡

CW #1 — #1 WITNESS's NAME | ☐ P/Known | ADDRESS | ☐ Non-Public | ☐ Driver's License ☐ Passport ☐ Other ID | ISSUED # | SIGNATURE ☐ (after oath / affirmation)
PHONE C / H / W / | *or* ☐ MISC | | | AGENCY ☐ CA DMV ☐ US State Dept | EXPIRES | ❶

CW #2 — #2 WITNESS's NAME | ☐ P/Known | ADDRESS | ☐ Non-Public | ☐ Driver's License ☐ Passport ☐ Other ID | ISSUED # | SIGNATURE ☐ (after oath / affirmation)
PHONE C / H / W / | *or* ☐ MISC | | | AGENCY ☐ CA DMV ☐ US State Dept | EXPIRES | ❷

Entry 160

SERVICE — DATE - -20 | TIME : am/pm | ADDRESS ☐ Signer's ☐ Office | NOTES | ☐ Stop | MILES | Notary $ | ☐ Adv. Travel $ | ☐ Rush $ | ☐ Copy $ | ☐ Other $ | TOTAL FEES $

TYPE: ☐ Acknowledgment ☐ Jurat ☐ Copy Certification ☐ Oath/Affirmation ☐ Oath of Office ☐ Proof of Execution ☐ Protest ☐ Other   R T I M R P L   **Fingerprint**

DOCUMENT — DOC TYPE: ☐ Deed (Grant • Trust Transfer • Gift • Interspousal • Quitclaim • ToD • Warranty) ☐ DOT (Mortgage • Rev / Irrev • Am / Rest) ☐ Trust (Certification) ☐ POA (General / Limited • Durable / Springing) ☐ POAH (AHCD • Living Will) ☐ Agreement (Compliance-E&O • Correction) ☐ Affidavit (Borrower • Occupancy • Ownership • Refi • Survey • Debts & Liens • Name-Signature-ID • Marital • Death • Will) ☐ Other (Vehicle Title • Safe Deposit Box)

DOC DATE: J F M A M J / J A S O N D ,   DOC TITLE or TYPE   # OF PAGES   ☐ Inspect/Copy Request   Entry X-Ref #

☐ **SATISFACTORY EVIDENCE** ☐ Driver's License / Passport / State ID / Military / Government / Tribal / Inmate / Other ID   *or*   ☐ Credible Witness(es)

SIGNER — SIGNER's NAME | ☐ For | ADDRESS | ☐ Non-Public | ☐ Capacity | ☐ Voluntary | ☐ Proper ID | ISSUED # | SIGNATURE ☐ (oath / affirmation, if any) ☐ (by Mark)
PHONE C / H / W / | *or* ☐ MISC | | | AGENCY ☐ CA DMV ☐ US State Dept | EXPIRES | ➡

CW #1 — #1 WITNESS's NAME | ☐ P/Known | ADDRESS | ☐ Non-Public | ☐ Driver's License ☐ Passport ☐ Other ID | ISSUED # | SIGNATURE ☐ (after oath / affirmation)
PHONE C / H / W / | *or* ☐ MISC | | | AGENCY ☐ CA DMV ☐ US State Dept | EXPIRES | ❶

CW #2 — #2 WITNESS's NAME | ☐ P/Known | ADDRESS | ☐ Non-Public | ☐ Driver's License ☐ Passport ☐ Other ID | ISSUED # | SIGNATURE ☐ (after oath / affirmation)
PHONE C / H / W / | *or* ☐ MISC | | | AGENCY ☐ CA DMV ☐ US State Dept | EXPIRES | ❷

NOTARY NAME (printed): COMMISSION #:

Entry 161

SERVICE	DATE - -20	TIME : am pm	ADDRESS ☐ Signer's ☐ Office	NOTES	☐ Stop	MILES	Notary ☐ Adv. Travel ☐ Rush ☐ Copy ☐ Other TOTAL FEES	**161**

$ $ $ $ $ $

TYPE ☐ Acknowledgment ☐ Jurat ☐ Copy Certification ☐ Oath/Affirmation ☐ Oath of Office ☐ Proof of Execution ☐ Protest ☐ Other

R **Fingerprint**

DOCUMENT

DOC TYPE ☐ Deed ☐ DOT ☐ Trust ☐ POA ☐ POAH ☐ Agreement ☐ Affidavit ☐ Other
Grant • Trust Transfer • Gift | Mortgage | Certification | General / Limited | AHCD | Compliance-E&O | Borrower • Occupancy • Ownership • Refi • Survey | Vehicle Title
Interspousal • Quitclaim • ToD • Warranty | Rev / Irrev • Am / Rest | Durable / Springing | Living Will | Correction | Debts & Liens • Name-Signature-ID • Marital • Death • Will | Safe Deposit Box

T
I
M
R
P

DOC DATE J F M A M J
J A S O N D ,

DOC TITLE or TYPE

OF PAGES ☐ Inspect/Copy Request
Entry X-Ref #

☐ **SATISFACTORY EVIDENCE** ☐ Driver's License / Passport / State ID / Military / Government / Tribal / Inmate / Other ID *or* ☐ Credible Witness(es) | L

| SIGNER | SIGNER's NAME ☐ For | ADDRESS | ☐ Non-Public | ☐ Capacity # | ☐ Voluntary | ☐ Proper ID | ISSUED | SIGNATURE ☐ (oath / affirmation, if any) ☐ (by Mark) |
| | PHONE C / H / W or ☐ MISC / | | | AGENCY | ☐ CA DMV | ☐ US State Dept | EXPIRES | ➡ |

| CW #1 | #1 WITNESS's NAME ☐ P/Known | ADDRESS | ☐ Non-Public | ☐ Driver's License # | ☐ Passport | ☐ Other ID | ISSUED | SIGNATURE ☐ (after oath / affirmation) |
| | PHONE C / H / W or ☐ MISC | | | AGENCY | ☐ CA DMV | ☐ US State Dept | EXPIRES | ❶ |

| CW #2 | #2 WITNESS's NAME ☐ P/Known | ADDRESS | ☐ Non-Public | ☐ Driver's License # | ☐ Passport | ☐ Other ID | ISSUED | SIGNATURE ☐ (after oath / affirmation) |
| | PHONE C / H / W or ☐ MISC | | | AGENCY | ☐ CA DMV | ☐ US State Dept | EXPIRES | ❷ |

Entry 162

SERVICE	DATE - -20	TIME : am pm	ADDRESS ☐ Signer's ☐ Office	NOTES	☐ Stop	MILES	Notary ☐ Adv. Travel ☐ Rush ☐ Copy ☐ Other TOTAL FEES	**162**

$ $ $ $ $ $

TYPE ☐ Acknowledgment ☐ Jurat ☐ Copy Certification ☐ Oath/Affirmation ☐ Oath of Office ☐ Proof of Execution ☐ Protest ☐ Other

R **Fingerprint**

DOCUMENT

DOC TYPE ☐ Deed ☐ DOT ☐ Trust ☐ POA ☐ POAH ☐ Agreement ☐ Affidavit ☐ Other
Grant • Trust Transfer • Gift | Mortgage | Certification | General / Limited | AHCD | Compliance-E&O | Borrower • Occupancy • Ownership • Refi • Survey | Vehicle Title
Interspousal • Quitclaim • ToD • Warranty | Rev / Irrev • Am / Rest | Durable / Springing | Living Will | Correction | Debts & Liens • Name-Signature-ID • Marital • Death • Will | Safe Deposit Box

T
I
M
R
P

DOC DATE J F M A M J
J A S O N D ,

DOC TITLE or TYPE

OF PAGES ☐ Inspect/Copy Request
Entry X-Ref #

☐ **SATISFACTORY EVIDENCE** ☐ Driver's License / Passport / State ID / Military / Government / Tribal / Inmate / Other ID *or* ☐ Credible Witness(es) | L

| SIGNER | SIGNER's NAME ☐ For | ADDRESS | ☐ Non-Public | ☐ Capacity # | ☐ Voluntary | ☐ Proper ID | ISSUED | SIGNATURE ☐ (oath / affirmation, if any) ☐ (by Mark) |
| | PHONE C / H / W or ☐ MISC / | | | AGENCY | ☐ CA DMV | ☐ US State Dept | EXPIRES | ➡ |

| CW #1 | #1 WITNESS's NAME ☐ P/Known | ADDRESS | ☐ Non-Public | ☐ Driver's License # | ☐ Passport | ☐ Other ID | ISSUED | SIGNATURE ☐ (after oath / affirmation) |
| | PHONE C / H / W or ☐ MISC | | | AGENCY | ☐ CA DMV | ☐ US State Dept | EXPIRES | ❶ |

| CW #2 | #2 WITNESS's NAME ☐ P/Known | ADDRESS | ☐ Non-Public | ☐ Driver's License # | ☐ Passport | ☐ Other ID | ISSUED | SIGNATURE ☐ (after oath / affirmation) |
| | PHONE C / H / W or ☐ MISC | | | AGENCY | ☐ CA DMV | ☐ US State Dept | EXPIRES | ❷ |

NOTARY NAME (printed):						COMMISSION #:	

Entry 163

SERVICE — DATE: - -20 | TIME: : am/pm | ADDRESS ☐ Signer's ☐ Office | NOTES | ☐ Stop MILES | Notary $ ☐ Adv. Travel $ ☐ Rush $ ☐ Copy $ ☐ Other $ TOTAL FEES $

TYPE: ☐ Acknowledgment ☐ Jurat ☐ Copy Certification ☐ Oath/Affirmation ☐ Oath of Office ☐ Proof of Execution ☐ Protest ☐ Other

DOCUMENT — DOC TYPE: ☐ Deed (Grant • Trust Transfer • Gift • Interspousal • Quitclaim • ToD • Warranty) ☐ DOT (Mortgage) ☐ Trust (Certification • Rev / Irrev • Am / Rest) ☐ POA (General / Limited • Durable / Springing) ☐ POAH (AHCD • Living Will) ☐ Agreement (Compliance-E&O • Correction) ☐ Affidavit (Borrower • Occupancy • Ownership • Refi • Survey • Debts & Liens • Name-Signature-ID • Marital • Death • Will) ☐ Other (Vehicle Title • Safe Deposit Box)

DOC DATE: J F M A M J J A S O N D , | DOC TITLE or TYPE | # OF PAGES | ☐ Inspect/Copy Request | Entry X-Ref #

R-T-I-M-R-P-L **Fingerprint**

☐ **SATISFACTORY EVIDENCE** ☐ Driver's License / Passport / State ID / Military / Government / Tribal / Inmate / Other ID ***or*** ☐ Credible Witness(es)

SIGNER — SIGNER's NAME | ☐ For | ADDRESS | ☐ Non-Public | ☐ Capacity # | ☐ Voluntary | ☐ Proper ID | ISSUED | SIGNATURE ☐ (oath / affirmation, if any) ☐ (by Mark)
PHONE C / H / W / | *or* ☐ MISC | | | AGENCY | ☐ CA DMV | ☐ US State Dept | EXPIRES | ➡

CW #1 — #1 WITNESS's NAME | ☐ P/Known | ADDRESS | ☐ Non-Public | ☐ Driver's License ☐ Passport ☐ Other ID # | ISSUED | SIGNATURE ☐ (after oath / affirmation)
PHONE C / H / W / | *or* ☐ MISC | | AGENCY ☐ CA DMV ☐ US State Dept | EXPIRES | ❶

CW #2 — #2 WITNESS's NAME | ☐ P/Known | ADDRESS | ☐ Non-Public | ☐ Driver's License ☐ Passport ☐ Other ID # | ISSUED | SIGNATURE ☐ (after oath / affirmation)
PHONE C / H / W / | *or* ☐ MISC | | AGENCY ☐ CA DMV ☐ US State Dept | EXPIRES | ❷

Entry 164

SERVICE — DATE: - -20 | TIME: : am/pm | ADDRESS ☐ Signer's ☐ Office | NOTES | ☐ Stop MILES | Notary $ ☐ Adv. Travel $ ☐ Rush $ ☐ Copy $ ☐ Other $ TOTAL FEES $

TYPE: ☐ Acknowledgment ☐ Jurat ☐ Copy Certification ☐ Oath/Affirmation ☐ Oath of Office ☐ Proof of Execution ☐ Protest ☐ Other

DOCUMENT — DOC TYPE: ☐ Deed (Grant • Trust Transfer • Gift • Interspousal • Quitclaim • ToD • Warranty) ☐ DOT (Mortgage) ☐ Trust (Certification • Rev / Irrev • Am / Rest) ☐ POA (General / Limited • Durable / Springing) ☐ POAH (AHCD • Living Will) ☐ Agreement (Compliance-E&O • Correction) ☐ Affidavit (Borrower • Occupancy • Ownership • Refi • Survey • Debts & Liens • Name-Signature-ID • Marital • Death • Will) ☐ Other (Vehicle Title • Safe Deposit Box)

DOC DATE: J F M A M J J A S O N D , | DOC TITLE or TYPE | # OF PAGES | ☐ Inspect/Copy Request | Entry X-Ref #

R-T-I-M-R-P-L **Fingerprint**

☐ **SATISFACTORY EVIDENCE** ☐ Driver's License / Passport / State ID / Military / Government / Tribal / Inmate / Other ID ***or*** ☐ Credible Witness(es)

SIGNER — SIGNER's NAME | ☐ For | ADDRESS | ☐ Non-Public | ☐ Capacity # | ☐ Voluntary | ☐ Proper ID | ISSUED | SIGNATURE ☐ (oath / affirmation, if any) ☐ (by Mark)
PHONE C / H / W / | *or* ☐ MISC | | AGENCY ☐ CA DMV ☐ US State Dept | EXPIRES | ➡

CW #1 — #1 WITNESS's NAME | ☐ P/Known | ADDRESS | ☐ Non-Public | ☐ Driver's License ☐ Passport ☐ Other ID # | ISSUED | SIGNATURE ☐ (after oath / affirmation)
PHONE C / H / W / | *or* ☐ MISC | | AGENCY ☐ CA DMV ☐ US State Dept | EXPIRES | ❶

CW #2 — #2 WITNESS's NAME | ☐ P/Known | ADDRESS | ☐ Non-Public | ☐ Driver's License ☐ Passport ☐ Other ID # | ISSUED | SIGNATURE ☐ (after oath / affirmation)
PHONE C / H / W / | *or* ☐ MISC | | AGENCY ☐ CA DMV ☐ US State Dept | EXPIRES | ❷

NOTARY NAME (printed):   COMMISSION #:

165

SERVICE

| DATE - -20 | TIME : am/pm | ADDRESS ☐ Signer's ☐ Office | NOTES | ☐ Stop | MILES | Notary $ | ☐ Adv. Travel $ | ☐ Rush $ | ☐ Copy $ | ☐ Other $ | TOTAL FEES $ |

TYPE ☐ Acknowledgment ☐ Jurat ☐ Copy Certification ☐ Oath/Affirmation ☐ Oath of Office ☐ Proof of Execution ☐ Protest ☐ Other

R T I M R P L — Fingerprint

DOCUMENT

DOC TYPE ☐ Deed ☐ DOT ☐ Trust ☐ POA ☐ POAH ☐ Agreement ☐ Affidavit ☐ Other
Grant • Trust Transfer • Gift | Mortgage | Certification | General / Limited | AHCD | Compliance-E&O | Borrower • Occupancy • Ownership • Refi • Survey | Vehicle Title
Interspousal • Quitclaim • ToD • Warranty | Rev / Irrev • Am / Rest | Durable / Springing | Living Will | Correction | Debts & Liens • Name-Signature-ID • Marital • Death • Will | Safe Deposit Box

DOC DATE J F M A M J J A S O N D , | DOC TITLE or TYPE | # OF PAGES | ☐ Inspect/Copy Request | Entry X-Ref #

☐ **SATISFACTORY EVIDENCE** ☐ Driver's License / Passport / State ID / Military / Government / Tribal / Inmate / Other ID *or* ☐ Credible Witness(es)

SIGNER

| SIGNER's NAME ☐ For | ADDRESS | ☐ Non-Public | ☐ Capacity ☐ Voluntary ☐ Proper ID # | ISSUED | SIGNATURE ☐ (oath / affirmation, if any) ☐ (by Mark) |
| PHONE C / H / W / *or* ☐ MISC | | | AGENCY ☐ CA DMV ☐ US State Dept | EXPIRES | ➡ |

CW #1

| #1 WITNESS's NAME ☐ P/Known | ADDRESS | ☐ Non-Public | ☐ Driver's License ☐ Passport ☐ Other ID # | ISSUED | SIGNATURE ☐ (after oath / affirmation) |
| PHONE C / H / W / *or* ☐ MISC | | | AGENCY ☐ CA DMV ☐ US State Dept | EXPIRES | ❶ |

CW #2

| #2 WITNESS's NAME ☐ P/Known | ADDRESS | ☐ Non-Public | ☐ Driver's License ☐ Passport ☐ Other ID # | ISSUED | SIGNATURE ☐ (after oath / affirmation) |
| PHONE C / H / W / *or* ☐ MISC | | | AGENCY ☐ CA DMV ☐ US State Dept | EXPIRES | ❷ |

166

SERVICE

| DATE - -20 | TIME : am/pm | ADDRESS ☐ Signer's ☐ Office | NOTES | ☐ Stop | MILES | Notary $ | ☐ Adv. Travel $ | ☐ Rush $ | ☐ Copy $ | ☐ Other $ | TOTAL FEES $ |

TYPE ☐ Acknowledgment ☐ Jurat ☐ Copy Certification ☐ Oath/Affirmation ☐ Oath of Office ☐ Proof of Execution ☐ Protest ☐ Other

R T I M R P L — Fingerprint

DOCUMENT

DOC TYPE ☐ Deed ☐ DOT ☐ Trust ☐ POA ☐ POAH ☐ Agreement ☐ Affidavit ☐ Other
Grant • Trust Transfer • Gift | Mortgage | Certification | General / Limited | AHCD | Compliance-E&O | Borrower • Occupancy • Ownership • Refi • Survey | Vehicle Title
Interspousal • Quitclaim • ToD • Warranty | Rev / Irrev • Am / Rest | Durable / Springing | Living Will | Correction | Debts & Liens • Name-Signature-ID • Marital • Death • Will | Safe Deposit Box

DOC DATE J F M A M J J A S O N D , | DOC TITLE or TYPE | # OF PAGES | ☐ Inspect/Copy Request | Entry X-Ref #

☐ **SATISFACTORY EVIDENCE** ☐ Driver's License / Passport / State ID / Military / Government / Tribal / Inmate / Other ID *or* ☐ Credible Witness(es)

SIGNER

| SIGNER's NAME ☐ For | ADDRESS | ☐ Non-Public | ☐ Capacity ☐ Voluntary ☐ Proper ID # | ISSUED | SIGNATURE ☐ (oath / affirmation, if any) ☐ (by Mark) |
| PHONE C / H / W / *or* ☐ MISC | | | AGENCY ☐ CA DMV ☐ US State Dept | EXPIRES | ➡ |

CW #1

| #1 WITNESS's NAME ☐ P/Known | ADDRESS | ☐ Non-Public | ☐ Driver's License ☐ Passport ☐ Other ID # | ISSUED | SIGNATURE ☐ (after oath / affirmation) |
| PHONE C / H / W / *or* ☐ MISC | | | AGENCY ☐ CA DMV ☐ US State Dept | EXPIRES | ❶ |

CW #2

| #2 WITNESS's NAME ☐ P/Known | ADDRESS | ☐ Non-Public | ☐ Driver's License ☐ Passport ☐ Other ID # | ISSUED | SIGNATURE ☐ (after oath / affirmation) |
| PHONE C / H / W / *or* ☐ MISC | | | AGENCY ☐ CA DMV ☐ US State Dept | EXPIRES | ❷ |

NOTARY NAME (printed):   COMMISSION #:

Entry 167

SERVICE — DATE - -20 | TIME : am/pm | ADDRESS ☐ Signer's ☐ Office | NOTES | ☐ Stop | MILES | Notary $ | ☐ Adv. Travel $ | ☐ Rush $ | ☐ Copy $ | ☐ Other $ | TOTAL FEES $

TYPE: ☐ Acknowledgment ☐ Jurat ☐ Copy Certification ☐ Oath/Affirmation ☐ Oath of Office ☐ Proof of Execution ☐ Protest ☐ Other   R T I M R P L   **Fingerprint**

DOCUMENT
DOC TYPE: ☐ Deed (Grant • Trust Transfer • Gift • Interspousal • Quitclaim • ToD • Warranty)   ☐ DOT (Mortgage • Rev / Irrev • Am / Rest)   ☐ Trust (Certification)   ☐ POA (General / Limited • Durable / Springing)   ☐ POAH (AHCD • Living Will)   ☐ Agreement (Compliance-E&O • Correction)   ☐ Affidavit (Borrower • Occupancy • Ownership • Refi • Survey • Debts & Liens • Name-Signature-ID • Marital • Death • Will)   ☐ Other (Vehicle Title • Safe Deposit Box)

DOC DATE: J F M A M J J A S O N D ,   DOC TITLE or TYPE   # OF PAGES   ☐ Inspect/Copy Request   Entry X-Ref #

☐ **SATISFACTORY EVIDENCE** ☐ Driver's License / Passport / State ID / Military / Government / Tribal / Inmate / Other ID   *or*   ☐ Credible Witness(es)

SIGNER
SIGNER's NAME | ☐ For | ADDRESS | ☐ Non-Public | ☐ Capacity ☐ Voluntary ☐ Proper ID | ISSUED # | SIGNATURE ☐ (oath / affirmation, if any) ☐ (by Mark)
PHONE C / H / W / | or ☐ MISC | | | AGENCY ☐ CA DMV ☐ US State Dept | EXPIRES | ➤

CW #1
#1 WITNESS's NAME | ☐ P/Known | ADDRESS | ☐ Non-Public | ☐ Driver's License ☐ Passport ☐ Other ID | ISSUED # | SIGNATURE ☐ (after oath / affirmation)
PHONE C / H / W / | or ☐ MISC | | | AGENCY ☐ CA DMV ☐ US State Dept | EXPIRES | ❶

CW #2
#2 WITNESS's NAME | ☐ P/Known | ADDRESS | ☐ Non-Public | ☐ Driver's License ☐ Passport ☐ Other ID | ISSUED # | SIGNATURE ☐ (after oath / affirmation)
PHONE C / H / W / | or ☐ MISC | | | AGENCY ☐ CA DMV ☐ US State Dept | EXPIRES | ❷

Entry 168

SERVICE — DATE - -20 | TIME : am/pm | ADDRESS ☐ Signer's ☐ Office | NOTES | ☐ Stop | MILES | Notary $ | ☐ Adv. Travel $ | ☐ Rush $ | ☐ Copy $ | ☐ Other $ | TOTAL FEES $

TYPE: ☐ Acknowledgment ☐ Jurat ☐ Copy Certification ☐ Oath/Affirmation ☐ Oath of Office ☐ Proof of Execution ☐ Protest ☐ Other   R T I M R P L   **Fingerprint**

DOCUMENT
DOC TYPE: ☐ Deed (Grant • Trust Transfer • Gift • Interspousal • Quitclaim • ToD • Warranty)   ☐ DOT (Mortgage • Rev / Irrev • Am / Rest)   ☐ Trust (Certification)   ☐ POA (General / Limited • Durable / Springing)   ☐ POAH (AHCD • Living Will)   ☐ Agreement (Compliance-E&O • Correction)   ☐ Affidavit (Borrower • Occupancy • Ownership • Refi • Survey • Debts & Liens • Name-Signature-ID • Marital • Death • Will)   ☐ Other (Vehicle Title • Safe Deposit Box)

DOC DATE: J F M A M J J A S O N D ,   DOC TITLE or TYPE   # OF PAGES   ☐ Inspect/Copy Request   Entry X-Ref #

☐ **SATISFACTORY EVIDENCE** ☐ Driver's License / Passport / State ID / Military / Government / Tribal / Inmate / Other ID   *or*   ☐ Credible Witness(es)

SIGNER
SIGNER's NAME | ☐ For | ADDRESS | ☐ Non-Public | ☐ Capacity ☐ Voluntary ☐ Proper ID | ISSUED # | SIGNATURE ☐ (oath / affirmation, if any) ☐ (by Mark)
PHONE C / H / W / | or ☐ MISC | | | AGENCY ☐ CA DMV ☐ US State Dept | EXPIRES | ➤

CW #1
#1 WITNESS's NAME | ☐ P/Known | ADDRESS | ☐ Non-Public | ☐ Driver's License ☐ Passport ☐ Other ID | ISSUED # | SIGNATURE ☐ (after oath / affirmation)
PHONE C / H / W / | or ☐ MISC | | | AGENCY ☐ CA DMV ☐ US State Dept | EXPIRES | ❶

CW #2
#2 WITNESS's NAME | ☐ P/Known | ADDRESS | ☐ Non-Public | ☐ Driver's License ☐ Passport ☐ Other ID | ISSUED # | SIGNATURE ☐ (after oath / affirmation)
PHONE C / H / W / | or ☐ MISC | | | AGENCY ☐ CA DMV ☐ US State Dept | EXPIRES | ❷

NOTARY NAME (printed): COMMISSION #:

Entry 169

SERVICE	DATE - -20	TIME : am / pm	ADDRESS ☐ Signer's ☐ Office	NOTES	☐ Stop	MILES	Notary ☐ Adv. Travel ☐ Rush ☐ Copy ☐ Other TOTAL FEES $ $ $ $ $ $	**169**

| TYPE | ☐ Acknowledgment ☐ Jurat ☐ Copy Certification ☐ Oath/Affirmation ☐ Oath of Office ☐ Proof of Execution ☐ Protest ☐ Other |

Fingerprint (R T I M R P L)

DOCUMENT

DOC TYPE	☐ Deed	☐ DOT	☐ Trust	☐ POA	☐ POAH	☐ Agreement	☐ Affidavit	☐ Other
	Grant • Trust Transfer • Gift	Mortgage	Certification	General / Limited	AHCD	Compliance-E&O	Borrower • Occupancy • Ownership • Refi • Survey	Vehicle Title
	Interspousal • Quitclaim • ToD • Warranty	Rev / Irrev • Am / Rest	Durable / Springing	Living Will		Correction	Debts & Liens • Name-Signature-ID • Marital • Death • Will	Safe Deposit Box

DOC DATE   J F M A M J   J A S O N D ,   DOC TITLE or TYPE   # OF PAGES   ☐ Inspect/Copy Request   Entry X-Ref #

☐ **SATISFACTORY EVIDENCE** ☐ Driver's License / Passport / State ID / Military / Government / Tribal / Inmate / Other ID   *or*   ☐ Credible Witness(es)

SIGNER

SIGNER's NAME	☐ For	ADDRESS	☐ Non-Public	☐ Capacity ☐ Voluntary ☐ Proper ID	ISSUED	SIGNATURE ☐ *(oath / affirmation, if any)* ☐ *(by Mark)*
				#		
PHONE C / H / W	*or* ☐ MISC			AGENCY ☐ CA DMV ☐ US State Dept	EXPIRES	➡

CW #1

#1 WITNESS's NAME	☐ P/Known	ADDRESS	☐ Non-Public	☐ Driver's License ☐ Passport ☐ Other ID	ISSUED	SIGNATURE ☐ *(after oath / affirmation)*
				#		
PHONE C / H / W	*or* ☐ MISC			AGENCY ☐ CA DMV ☐ US State Dept	EXPIRES	❶

CW #2

#2 WITNESS's NAME	☐ P/Known	ADDRESS	☐ Non-Public	☐ Driver's License ☐ Passport ☐ Other ID	ISSUED	SIGNATURE ☐ *(after oath / affirmation)*
				#		
PHONE C / H / W	*or* ☐ MISC			AGENCY ☐ CA DMV ☐ US State Dept	EXPIRES	❷

Entry 170

SERVICE	DATE - -20	TIME : am / pm	ADDRESS ☐ Signer's ☐ Office	NOTES	☐ Stop	MILES	Notary ☐ Adv. Travel ☐ Rush ☐ Copy ☐ Other TOTAL FEES $ $ $ $ $ $	**170**

| TYPE | ☐ Acknowledgment ☐ Jurat ☐ Copy Certification ☐ Oath/Affirmation ☐ Oath of Office ☐ Proof of Execution ☐ Protest ☐ Other |

Fingerprint (R T I M R P L)

DOCUMENT

DOC TYPE	☐ Deed	☐ DOT	☐ Trust	☐ POA	☐ POAH	☐ Agreement	☐ Affidavit	☐ Other
	Grant • Trust Transfer • Gift	Mortgage	Certification	General / Limited	AHCD	Compliance-E&O	Borrower • Occupancy • Ownership • Refi • Survey	Vehicle Title
	Interspousal • Quitclaim • ToD • Warranty	Rev / Irrev • Am / Rest	Durable / Springing	Living Will		Correction	Debts & Liens • Name-Signature-ID • Marital • Death • Will	Safe Deposit Box

DOC DATE   J F M A M J   J A S O N D ,   DOC TITLE or TYPE   # OF PAGES   ☐ Inspect/Copy Request   Entry X-Ref #

☐ **SATISFACTORY EVIDENCE** ☐ Driver's License / Passport / State ID / Military / Government / Tribal / Inmate / Other ID   *or*   ☐ Credible Witness(es)

SIGNER

SIGNER's NAME	☐ For	ADDRESS	☐ Non-Public	☐ Capacity ☐ Voluntary ☐ Proper ID	ISSUED	SIGNATURE ☐ *(oath / affirmation, if any)* ☐ *(by Mark)*
				#		
PHONE C / H / W	*or* ☐ MISC			AGENCY ☐ CA DMV ☐ US State Dept	EXPIRES	➡

CW #1

#1 WITNESS's NAME	☐ P/Known	ADDRESS	☐ Non-Public	☐ Driver's License ☐ Passport ☐ Other ID	ISSUED	SIGNATURE ☐ *(after oath / affirmation)*
				#		
PHONE C / H / W	*or* ☐ MISC			AGENCY ☐ CA DMV ☐ US State Dept	EXPIRES	❶

CW #2

#2 WITNESS's NAME	☐ P/Known	ADDRESS	☐ Non-Public	☐ Driver's License ☐ Passport ☐ Other ID	ISSUED	SIGNATURE ☐ *(after oath / affirmation)*
				#		
PHONE C / H / W	*or* ☐ MISC			AGENCY ☐ CA DMV ☐ US State Dept	EXPIRES	❷

NOTARY NAME (printed):   COMMISSION #:

Entry 171

SERVICE — DATE: - -20 | TIME: : am/pm | ADDRESS ☐ Signer's ☐ Office | NOTES | ☐ Stop MILES | Notary $ | ☐ Adv. Travel $ | ☐ Rush $ | ☐ Copy $ | ☐ Other $ | TOTAL FEES $

TYPE: ☐ Acknowledgment ☐ Jurat ☐ Copy Certification ☐ Oath/Affirmation ☐ Oath of Office ☐ Proof of Execution ☐ Protest ☐ Other

DOCUMENT — DOC TYPE: ☐ Deed (Grant • Trust Transfer • Gift • Interspousal • Quitclaim • ToD • Warranty) ☐ DOT (Mortgage) ☐ Trust (Certification • Rev / Irrev • Am / Rest) ☐ POA (General / Limited • Durable / Springing) ☐ POAH (AHCD • Living Will) ☐ Agreement (Compliance-E&O • Correction) ☐ Affidavit (Borrower • Occupancy • Ownership • Refi • Survey • Debts & Liens • Name-Signature-ID • Marital • Death • Will) ☐ Other (Vehicle Title • Safe Deposit Box)

DOC DATE: J F M A M J J A S O N D , _____ | DOC TITLE or TYPE | # OF PAGES | ☐ Inspect/Copy Request | Entry X-Ref #

R T I M R P L   **Fingerprint**

☐ **SATISFACTORY EVIDENCE** ☐ Driver's License / Passport / State ID / Military / Government / Tribal / Inmate / Other ID *or* ☐ Credible Witness(es)

SIGNER — SIGNER's NAME | ☐ For | ADDRESS | ☐ Non-Public | ☐ Capacity # | ☐ Voluntary | ☐ Proper ID | ISSUED | SIGNATURE ☐ (oath / affirmation, if any) ☐ (by Mark)
PHONE C / H / W / | *or* ☐ MISC | | | AGENCY | ☐ CA DMV | ☐ US State Dept | EXPIRES | ➤

CW #1 — #1 WITNESS's NAME | ☐ P/Known | ADDRESS | ☐ Non-Public | ☐ Driver's License ☐ Passport ☐ Other ID # | ISSUED | SIGNATURE ☐ (after oath / affirmation)
PHONE C / H / W / | *or* ☐ MISC | | | AGENCY | ☐ CA DMV | ☐ US State Dept | EXPIRES | ❶

CW #2 — #2 WITNESS's NAME | ☐ P/Known | ADDRESS | ☐ Non-Public | ☐ Driver's License ☐ Passport ☐ Other ID # | ISSUED | SIGNATURE ☐ (after oath / affirmation)
PHONE C / H / W / | *or* ☐ MISC | | | AGENCY | ☐ CA DMV | ☐ US State Dept | EXPIRES | ❷

Entry 172

SERVICE — DATE: - -20 | TIME: : am/pm | ADDRESS ☐ Signer's ☐ Office | NOTES | ☐ Stop MILES | Notary $ | ☐ Adv. Travel $ | ☐ Rush $ | ☐ Copy $ | ☐ Other $ | TOTAL FEES $

TYPE: ☐ Acknowledgment ☐ Jurat ☐ Copy Certification ☐ Oath/Affirmation ☐ Oath of Office ☐ Proof of Execution ☐ Protest ☐ Other

DOCUMENT — DOC TYPE: ☐ Deed (Grant • Trust Transfer • Gift • Interspousal • Quitclaim • ToD • Warranty) ☐ DOT (Mortgage) ☐ Trust (Certification • Rev / Irrev • Am / Rest) ☐ POA (General / Limited • Durable / Springing) ☐ POAH (AHCD • Living Will) ☐ Agreement (Compliance-E&O • Correction) ☐ Affidavit (Borrower • Occupancy • Ownership • Refi • Survey • Debts & Liens • Name-Signature-ID • Marital • Death • Will) ☐ Other (Vehicle Title • Safe Deposit Box)

DOC DATE: J F M A M J J A S O N D , _____ | DOC TITLE or TYPE | # OF PAGES | ☐ Inspect/Copy Request | Entry X-Ref #

R T I M R P L   **Fingerprint**

☐ **SATISFACTORY EVIDENCE** ☐ Driver's License / Passport / State ID / Military / Government / Tribal / Inmate / Other ID *or* ☐ Credible Witness(es)

SIGNER — SIGNER's NAME | ☐ For | ADDRESS | ☐ Non-Public | ☐ Capacity # | ☐ Voluntary | ☐ Proper ID | ISSUED | SIGNATURE ☐ (oath / affirmation, if any) ☐ (by Mark)
PHONE C / H / W / | *or* ☐ MISC | | | AGENCY | ☐ CA DMV | ☐ US State Dept | EXPIRES | ➤

CW #1 — #1 WITNESS's NAME | ☐ P/Known | ADDRESS | ☐ Non-Public | ☐ Driver's License ☐ Passport ☐ Other ID # | ISSUED | SIGNATURE ☐ (after oath / affirmation)
PHONE C / H / W / | *or* ☐ MISC | | | AGENCY | ☐ CA DMV | ☐ US State Dept | EXPIRES | ❶

CW #2 — #2 WITNESS's NAME | ☐ P/Known | ADDRESS | ☐ Non-Public | ☐ Driver's License ☐ Passport ☐ Other ID # | ISSUED | SIGNATURE ☐ (after oath / affirmation)
PHONE C / H / W / | *or* ☐ MISC | | | AGENCY | ☐ CA DMV | ☐ US State Dept | EXPIRES | ❷

NOTARY NAME (printed):   COMMISSION #:

Entry 173

SERVICE

DATE	TIME	am	ADDRESS	☐ Signer's	☐ Office	NOTES	☐ Stop	MILES	Notary	☐ Adv. Travel	☐ Rush	☐ Copy	☐ Other	TOTAL FEES
- -20	:	pm							$	$		$	$	$ $

TYPE ☐ Acknowledgment ☐ Jurat ☐ Copy Certification ☐ Oath/Affirmation ☐ Oath of Office ☐ Proof of Execution ☐ Protest ☐ Other   **Fingerprint**

DOCUMENT

DOC TYPE ☐ Deed ☐ DOT ☐ Trust ☐ POA ☐ POAH ☐ Agreement ☐ Affidavit ☐ Other
Grant • Trust Transfer • Gift   Mortgage   Certification   General / Limited   AHCD   Compliance-E&O   Borrower • Occupancy • Ownership • Refi • Survey   Vehicle Title
Interspousal • Quitclaim • ToD • Warranty   Rev / Irrev • Am / Rest   Durable / Springing   Living Will   Correction   Debts & Liens • Name-Signature-ID • Marital • Death • Will   Safe Deposit Box

DOC DATE   J F M A M J   J A S O N D   ,   DOC TITLE or TYPE   # OF PAGES   ☐ Inspect/Copy Request   Entry X-Ref #

☐ **SATISFACTORY EVIDENCE** ☐ Driver's License / Passport / State ID / Military / Government / Tribal / Inmate / Other ID *or* ☐ Credible Witness(es)

SIGNER

SIGNER's NAME	☐ For	ADDRESS	☐ Non-Public	☐ Capacity	☐ Voluntary	☐ Proper ID	ISSUED	SIGNATURE ☐ (oath / affirmation, if any) ☐ (by Mark)
				#				
PHONE C / H / W *or* ☐ MISC				AGENCY	☐ CA DMV	☐ US State Dept	EXPIRES	➡

CW #1

#1 WITNESS's NAME	☐ P/Known	ADDRESS	☐ Non-Public	☐ Driver's License	☐ Passport	☐ Other ID	ISSUED	SIGNATURE ☐ (after oath / affirmation)
				#				
PHONE C / H / W *or* ☐ MISC				AGENCY	☐ CA DMV	☐ US State Dept	EXPIRES	❶

CW #2

#2 WITNESS's NAME	☐ P/Known	ADDRESS	☐ Non-Public	☐ Driver's License	☐ Passport	☐ Other ID	ISSUED	SIGNATURE ☐ (after oath / affirmation)
				#				
PHONE C / H / W *or* ☐ MISC				AGENCY	☐ CA DMV	☐ US State Dept	EXPIRES	❷

Entry 174

SERVICE

DATE	TIME	am	ADDRESS	☐ Signer's	☐ Office	NOTES	☐ Stop	MILES	Notary	☐ Adv. Travel	☐ Rush	☐ Copy	☐ Other	TOTAL FEES
- -20	:	pm							$	$		$	$	$ $

TYPE ☐ Acknowledgment ☐ Jurat ☐ Copy Certification ☐ Oath/Affirmation ☐ Oath of Office ☐ Proof of Execution ☐ Protest ☐ Other   **Fingerprint**

DOCUMENT

DOC TYPE ☐ Deed ☐ DOT ☐ Trust ☐ POA ☐ POAH ☐ Agreement ☐ Affidavit ☐ Other
Grant • Trust Transfer • Gift   Mortgage   Certification   General / Limited   AHCD   Compliance-E&O   Borrower • Occupancy • Ownership • Refi • Survey   Vehicle Title
Interspousal • Quitclaim • ToD • Warranty   Rev / Irrev • Am / Rest   Durable / Springing   Living Will   Correction   Debts & Liens • Name-Signature-ID • Marital • Death • Will   Safe Deposit Box

DOC DATE   J F M A M J   J A S O N D   ,   DOC TITLE or TYPE   # OF PAGES   ☐ Inspect/Copy Request   Entry X-Ref #

☐ **SATISFACTORY EVIDENCE** ☐ Driver's License / Passport / State ID / Military / Government / Tribal / Inmate / Other ID *or* ☐ Credible Witness(es)

SIGNER

SIGNER's NAME	☐ For	ADDRESS	☐ Non-Public	☐ Capacity	☐ Voluntary	☐ Proper ID	ISSUED	SIGNATURE ☐ (oath / affirmation, if any) ☐ (by Mark)
				#				
PHONE C / H / W *or* ☐ MISC				AGENCY	☐ CA DMV	☐ US State Dept	EXPIRES	➡

CW #1

#1 WITNESS's NAME	☐ P/Known	ADDRESS	☐ Non-Public	☐ Driver's License	☐ Passport	☐ Other ID	ISSUED	SIGNATURE ☐ (after oath / affirmation)
				#				
PHONE C / H / W *or* ☐ MISC				AGENCY	☐ CA DMV	☐ US State Dept	EXPIRES	❶

CW #2

#2 WITNESS's NAME	☐ P/Known	ADDRESS	☐ Non-Public	☐ Driver's License	☐ Passport	☐ Other ID	ISSUED	SIGNATURE ☐ (after oath / affirmation)
				#				
PHONE C / H / W *or* ☐ MISC				AGENCY	☐ CA DMV	☐ US State Dept	EXPIRES	❷

NOTARY NAME (printed):   COMMISSION #:

Entry 175

SERVICE — DATE: - -20 | TIME: : am/pm | ADDRESS: ☐ Signer's ☐ Office | NOTES | ☐ Stop | MILES $ | Notary $ | ☐ Adv. Travel $ | ☐ Rush $ | ☐ Copy $ | ☐ Other | TOTAL FEES $

TYPE: ☐ Acknowledgment ☐ Jurat ☐ Copy Certification ☐ Oath/Affirmation ☐ Oath of Office ☐ Proof of Execution ☐ Protest ☐ Other

DOCUMENT
- DOC TYPE: ☐ Deed (Grant • Trust Transfer • Gift • Interspousal • Quitclaim • ToD • Warranty) ☐ DOT (Mortgage • Certification • Rev / Irrev • Am / Rest) ☐ Trust ☐ POA (General / Limited • Durable / Springing) ☐ POAH (AHCD • Living Will) ☐ Agreement (Compliance-E&O • Correction) ☐ Affidavit (Borrower • Occupancy • Ownership • Refi • Survey • Debts & Liens • Name-Signature-ID • Marital • Death • Will) ☐ Other (Vehicle Title • Safe Deposit Box)
- DOC DATE: J F M A M J J A S O N D ,
- DOC TITLE or TYPE:
- # OF PAGES:
- ☐ Inspect/Copy Request
- Entry X-Ref #:

Fingerprint — R T I M R P L

☐ **SATISFACTORY EVIDENCE** ☐ Driver's License / Passport / State ID / Military / Government / Tribal / Inmate / Other ID ***or*** ☐ Credible Witness(es)

SIGNER
- SIGNER's NAME | ☐ For | ADDRESS | ☐ Non-Public | ☐ Capacity | ☐ Voluntary | ☐ Proper ID | ISSUED # | SIGNATURE | ☐ (oath / affirmation, if any) | ☐ (by Mark)
- PHONE C / H / W / | *or* ☐ MISC | AGENCY | ☐ CA DMV | ☐ US State Dept | EXPIRES | ➡

CW #1
- #1 WITNESS's NAME | ☐ P/Known | ADDRESS | ☐ Non-Public | ☐ Driver's License ☐ Passport ☐ Other ID | ISSUED # | SIGNATURE | ☐ (after oath / affirmation)
- PHONE C / H / W / | *or* ☐ MISC | AGENCY | ☐ CA DMV | ☐ US State Dept | EXPIRES | ❶

CW #2
- #2 WITNESS's NAME | ☐ P/Known | ADDRESS | ☐ Non-Public | ☐ Driver's License ☐ Passport ☐ Other ID | ISSUED # | SIGNATURE | ☐ (after oath / affirmation)
- PHONE C / H / W / | *or* ☐ MISC | AGENCY | ☐ CA DMV | ☐ US State Dept | EXPIRES | ❷

Entry 176

SERVICE — DATE: - -20 | TIME: : am/pm | ADDRESS: ☐ Signer's ☐ Office | NOTES | ☐ Stop | MILES $ | Notary $ | ☐ Adv. Travel $ | ☐ Rush $ | ☐ Copy $ | ☐ Other | TOTAL FEES $

TYPE: ☐ Acknowledgment ☐ Jurat ☐ Copy Certification ☐ Oath/Affirmation ☐ Oath of Office ☐ Proof of Execution ☐ Protest ☐ Other

DOCUMENT
- DOC TYPE: ☐ Deed (Grant • Trust Transfer • Gift • Interspousal • Quitclaim • ToD • Warranty) ☐ DOT (Mortgage • Certification • Rev / Irrev • Am / Rest) ☐ Trust ☐ POA (General / Limited • Durable / Springing) ☐ POAH (AHCD • Living Will) ☐ Agreement (Compliance-E&O • Correction) ☐ Affidavit (Borrower • Occupancy • Ownership • Refi • Survey • Debts & Liens • Name-Signature-ID • Marital • Death • Will) ☐ Other (Vehicle Title • Safe Deposit Box)
- DOC DATE: J F M A M J J A S O N D ,
- DOC TITLE or TYPE:
- # OF PAGES:
- ☐ Inspect/Copy Request
- Entry X-Ref #:

Fingerprint — R T I M R P L

☐ **SATISFACTORY EVIDENCE** ☐ Driver's License / Passport / State ID / Military / Government / Tribal / Inmate / Other ID ***or*** ☐ Credible Witness(es)

SIGNER
- SIGNER's NAME | ☐ For | ADDRESS | ☐ Non-Public | ☐ Capacity | ☐ Voluntary | ☐ Proper ID | ISSUED # | SIGNATURE | ☐ (oath / affirmation, if any) | ☐ (by Mark)
- PHONE C / H / W / | *or* ☐ MISC | AGENCY | ☐ CA DMV | ☐ US State Dept | EXPIRES | ➡

CW #1
- #1 WITNESS's NAME | ☐ P/Known | ADDRESS | ☐ Non-Public | ☐ Driver's License ☐ Passport ☐ Other ID | ISSUED # | SIGNATURE | ☐ (after oath / affirmation)
- PHONE C / H / W / | *or* ☐ MISC | AGENCY | ☐ CA DMV | ☐ US State Dept | EXPIRES | ❶

CW #2
- #2 WITNESS's NAME | ☐ P/Known | ADDRESS | ☐ Non-Public | ☐ Driver's License ☐ Passport ☐ Other ID | ISSUED # | SIGNATURE | ☐ (after oath / affirmation)
- PHONE C / H / W / | *or* ☐ MISC | AGENCY | ☐ CA DMV | ☐ US State Dept | EXPIRES | ❷

NOTARY NAME (printed):   **COMMISSION #:**

Entry 177

SERVICE — DATE - -20   TIME : am/pm   ADDRESS   ☐ Signer's   ☐ Office   NOTES   ☐ Stop   MILES   Notary ☐ Adv. Travel ☐ Rush ☐ Copy ☐ Other   TOTAL FEES $ $ $ $ $ $

TYPE ☐ Acknowledgment ☐ Jurat ☐ Copy Certification ☐ Oath/Affirmation ☐ Oath of Office ☐ Proof of Execution ☐ Protest ☐ Other

R T I M R P L   **Fingerprint**

DOCUMENT

DOC TYPE ☐ Deed   ☐ DOT   ☐ Trust   ☐ POA   ☐ POAH   ☐ Agreement   ☐ Affidavit   ☐ Other

- Grant • Trust Transfer • Gift   Mortgage   Certification   General / Limited   AHCD   Compliance-E&O   Borrower • Occupancy • Ownership • Refi • Survey   Vehicle Title
- Interspousal • Quitclaim • ToD • Warranty   Rev / Irrev • Am / Rest   Durable / Springing   Living Will   Correction   Debts & Liens • Name-Signature-ID • Marital • Death • Will   Safe Deposit Box

DOC DATE   J F M A M J   J A S O N D   ,   DOC TITLE or TYPE   # OF PAGES ☐ Inspect/Copy Request   Entry X-Ref #

☐ **SATISFACTORY EVIDENCE** ☐ Driver's License / Passport / State ID / Military / Government / Tribal / Inmate / Other ID   *or*   ☐ Credible Witness(es)

SIGNER

SIGNER's NAME   ☐ For   ADDRESS   ☐ Non-Public ☐ Capacity ☐ Voluntary ☐ Proper ID   ISSUED #   SIGNATURE ☐ (oath / affirmation, if any) ☐ (by Mark)

PHONE C / H / W   *or* ☐ MISC   /   AGENCY ☐ CA DMV ☐ US State Dept   EXPIRES   ➡

CW #1

#1 WITNESS's NAME   ☐ P/Known   ADDRESS   ☐ Non-Public ☐ Driver's License ☐ Passport ☐ Other ID   ISSUED #   SIGNATURE ☐ (after oath / affirmation)

PHONE C / H / W   *or* ☐ MISC   /   AGENCY ☐ CA DMV ☐ US State Dept   EXPIRES   ❶

CW #2

#2 WITNESS's NAME   ☐ P/Known   ADDRESS   ☐ Non-Public ☐ Driver's License ☐ Passport ☐ Other ID   ISSUED #   SIGNATURE ☐ (after oath / affirmation)

PHONE C / H / W   *or* ☐ MISC   /   AGENCY ☐ CA DMV ☐ US State Dept   EXPIRES   ❷

Entry 178

SERVICE — DATE - -20   TIME : am/pm   ADDRESS   ☐ Signer's   ☐ Office   NOTES   ☐ Stop   MILES   Notary ☐ Adv. Travel ☐ Rush ☐ Copy ☐ Other   TOTAL FEES $ $ $ $ $ $

TYPE ☐ Acknowledgment ☐ Jurat ☐ Copy Certification ☐ Oath/Affirmation ☐ Oath of Office ☐ Proof of Execution ☐ Protest ☐ Other

R T I M R P L   **Fingerprint**

DOCUMENT

DOC TYPE ☐ Deed   ☐ DOT   ☐ Trust   ☐ POA   ☐ POAH   ☐ Agreement   ☐ Affidavit   ☐ Other

- Grant • Trust Transfer • Gift   Mortgage   Certification   General / Limited   AHCD   Compliance-E&O   Borrower • Occupancy • Ownership • Refi • Survey   Vehicle Title
- Interspousal • Quitclaim • ToD • Warranty   Rev / Irrev • Am / Rest   Durable / Springing   Living Will   Correction   Debts & Liens • Name-Signature-ID • Marital • Death • Will   Safe Deposit Box

DOC DATE   J F M A M J   J A S O N D   ,   DOC TITLE or TYPE   # OF PAGES ☐ Inspect/Copy Request   Entry X-Ref #

☐ **SATISFACTORY EVIDENCE** ☐ Driver's License / Passport / State ID / Military / Government / Tribal / Inmate / Other ID   *or*   ☐ Credible Witness(es)

SIGNER

SIGNER's NAME   ☐ For   ADDRESS   ☐ Non-Public ☐ Capacity ☐ Voluntary ☐ Proper ID   ISSUED #   SIGNATURE ☐ (oath / affirmation, if any) ☐ (by Mark)

PHONE C / H / W   *or* ☐ MISC   /   AGENCY ☐ CA DMV ☐ US State Dept   EXPIRES   ➡

CW #1

#1 WITNESS's NAME   ☐ P/Known   ADDRESS   ☐ Non-Public ☐ Driver's License ☐ Passport ☐ Other ID   ISSUED #   SIGNATURE ☐ (after oath / affirmation)

PHONE C / H / W   *or* ☐ MISC   /   AGENCY ☐ CA DMV ☐ US State Dept   EXPIRES   ❶

CW #2

#2 WITNESS's NAME   ☐ P/Known   ADDRESS   ☐ Non-Public ☐ Driver's License ☐ Passport ☐ Other ID   ISSUED #   SIGNATURE ☐ (after oath / affirmation)

PHONE C / H / W   *or* ☐ MISC   /   AGENCY ☐ CA DMV ☐ US State Dept   EXPIRES   ❷

NOTARY NAME (printed):   **COMMISSION #:**

Entry 179

SERVICE — DATE: - -20   TIME: : am/pm   ADDRESS   ☐ Signer's   ☐ Office   NOTES   ☐ Stop   MILES   Notary $ Adv. Travel $ ☐ Rush $ ☐ Copy $ ☐ Other $ TOTAL FEES $

TYPE: ☐ Acknowledgment   ☐ Jurat   ☐ Copy Certification   ☐ Oath/Affirmation   ☐ Oath of Office   ☐ Proof of Execution   ☐ Protest   ☐ Other

Fingerprint (RTIMRPL)

DOCUMENT — DOC TYPE:
- ☐ **Deed** — Grant • Trust Transfer • Gift • Interspousal • Quitclaim • ToD • Warranty
- ☐ **DOT** — Mortgage
- ☐ **Trust** — Certification • Rev / Irrev • Am / Rest
- ☐ **POA** — General / Limited • Durable / Springing
- ☐ **POAH** — AHCD • Living Will
- ☐ **Agreement** — Compliance-E&O • Correction
- ☐ **Affidavit** — Borrower • Occupancy • Ownership • Refi • Survey • Debts & Liens • Name-Signature-ID • Marital • Death • Will
- ☐ **Other** — Vehicle Title • Safe Deposit Box

DOC DATE: J F M A M J / J A S O N D ,   DOC TITLE or TYPE   # OF PAGES   ☐ Inspect/Copy Request   Entry X-Ref #

☐ **SATISFACTORY EVIDENCE** ☐ Driver's License / Passport / State ID / Military / Government / Tribal / Inmate / Other ID *or* ☐ Credible Witness(es)

SIGNER — SIGNER's NAME   ☐ For   ADDRESS   ☐ Non-Public   ☐ Capacity   ☐ Voluntary   ☐ Proper ID   ISSUED #   SIGNATURE   ☐ (oath / affirmation, if any)   ☐ (by Mark)
PHONE C / H / W   *or* ☐ MISC   AGENCY   ☐ CA DMV   ☐ US State Dept   EXPIRES   ➡

CW #1 — #1 WITNESS's NAME   ☐ P/Known   ADDRESS   ☐ Non-Public   ☐ Driver's License   ☐ Passport   ☐ Other ID   ISSUED #   SIGNATURE   ☐ (after oath / affirmation)
PHONE C / H / W   *or* ☐ MISC   AGENCY   ☐ CA DMV   ☐ US State Dept   EXPIRES   ❶

CW #2 — #2 WITNESS's NAME   ☐ P/Known   ADDRESS   ☐ Non-Public   ☐ Driver's License   ☐ Passport   ☐ Other ID   ISSUED #   SIGNATURE   ☐ (after oath / affirmation)
PHONE C / H / W   *or* ☐ MISC   AGENCY   ☐ CA DMV   ☐ US State Dept   EXPIRES   ❷

Entry 180

SERVICE — DATE: - -20   TIME: : am/pm   ADDRESS   ☐ Signer's   ☐ Office   NOTES   ☐ Stop   MILES   Notary $ Adv. Travel $ ☐ Rush $ ☐ Copy $ ☐ Other $ TOTAL FEES $

TYPE: ☐ Acknowledgment   ☐ Jurat   ☐ Copy Certification   ☐ Oath/Affirmation   ☐ Oath of Office   ☐ Proof of Execution   ☐ Protest   ☐ Other

Fingerprint (RTIMRPL)

DOCUMENT — DOC TYPE:
- ☐ **Deed** — Grant • Trust Transfer • Gift • Interspousal • Quitclaim • ToD • Warranty
- ☐ **DOT** — Mortgage
- ☐ **Trust** — Certification • Rev / Irrev • Am / Rest
- ☐ **POA** — General / Limited • Durable / Springing
- ☐ **POAH** — AHCD • Living Will
- ☐ **Agreement** — Compliance-E&O • Correction
- ☐ **Affidavit** — Borrower • Occupancy • Ownership • Refi • Survey • Debts & Liens • Name-Signature-ID • Marital • Death • Will
- ☐ **Other** — Vehicle Title • Safe Deposit Box

DOC DATE: J F M A M J / J A S O N D ,   DOC TITLE or TYPE   # OF PAGES   ☐ Inspect/Copy Request   Entry X-Ref #

☐ **SATISFACTORY EVIDENCE** ☐ Driver's License / Passport / State ID / Military / Government / Tribal / Inmate / Other ID *or* ☐ Credible Witness(es)

SIGNER — SIGNER's NAME   ☐ For   ADDRESS   ☐ Non-Public   ☐ Capacity   ☐ Voluntary   ☐ Proper ID   ISSUED #   SIGNATURE   ☐ (oath / affirmation, if any)   ☐ (by Mark)
PHONE C / H / W   *or* ☐ MISC   AGENCY   ☐ CA DMV   ☐ US State Dept   EXPIRES   ➡

CW #1 — #1 WITNESS's NAME   ☐ P/Known   ADDRESS   ☐ Non-Public   ☐ Driver's License   ☐ Passport   ☐ Other ID   ISSUED #   SIGNATURE   ☐ (after oath / affirmation)
PHONE C / H / W   *or* ☐ MISC   AGENCY   ☐ CA DMV   ☐ US State Dept   EXPIRES   ❶

CW #2 — #2 WITNESS's NAME   ☐ P/Known   ADDRESS   ☐ Non-Public   ☐ Driver's License   ☐ Passport   ☐ Other ID   ISSUED #   SIGNATURE   ☐ (after oath / affirmation)
PHONE C / H / W   *or* ☐ MISC   AGENCY   ☐ CA DMV   ☐ US State Dept   EXPIRES   ❷

NOTARY NAME (printed):   COMMISSION #:

Entry 181

SERVICE

DATE	TIME	am	ADDRESS	☐ Signer's	☐ Office	NOTES	☐ Stop	MILES	Notary	☐ Adv. Travel	☐ Rush	☐ Copy	☐ Other	TOTAL FEES
- -20	:	pm							$	$	$	$	$	$

TYPE ☐ Acknowledgment ☐ Jurat ☐ Copy Certification ☐ Oath/Affirmation ☐ Oath of Office ☐ Proof of Execution ☐ Protest ☐ Other

R   **Fingerprint**

DOCUMENT

DOC TYPE ☐ **Deed**   ☐ **DOT**   ☐ **Trust**   ☐ **POA**   ☐ **POAH**   ☐ **Agreement**   ☐ **Affidavit**   ☐ **Other**

Grant • Trust Transfer • Gift   Mortgage   Certification   General / Limited   AHCD   Compliance-E&O   Borrower • Occupancy • Ownership • Refi • Survey   Vehicle Title
Interspousal • Quitclaim • ToD • Warranty   Rev / Irrev • Am / Rest   Durable / Springing   Living Will   Correction   Debts & Liens • Name-Signature-ID • Marital • Death • Will   Safe Deposit Box

T
I
M

DOC DATE   J F M A M J   J A S O N D   ,   DOC TITLE or TYPE   # OF PAGES   ☐ Inspect/Copy Request   Entry X-Ref #

R
P

☐ **SATISFACTORY EVIDENCE** ☐ Driver's License / Passport / State ID / Military / Government / Tribal / Inmate / Other ID *or* ☐ Credible Witness(es)

L

SIGNER

SIGNER's NAME	☐ For	ADDRESS	☐ Non-Public	☐ Capacity	☐ Voluntary	☐ Proper ID	ISSUED	SIGNATURE	☐ (oath / affirmation, if any)	☐ (by Mark)
				#						
PHONE C / H / W	*or* ☐ MISC			AGENCY	☐ CA DMV	☐ US State Dept	EXPIRES	➡		

CW #1

#1 WITNESS's NAME	☐ P/Known	ADDRESS	☐ Non-Public	☐ Driver's License	☐ Passport	☐ Other ID	ISSUED	SIGNATURE	☐ (after oath / affirmation)
				#					
PHONE C / H / W	*or* ☐ MISC			AGENCY	☐ CA DMV	☐ US State Dept	EXPIRES	❶	

CW #2

#2 WITNESS's NAME	☐ P/Known	ADDRESS	☐ Non-Public	☐ Driver's License	☐ Passport	☐ Other ID	ISSUED	SIGNATURE	☐ (after oath / affirmation)
				#					
PHONE C / H / W	*or* ☐ MISC			AGENCY	☐ CA DMV	☐ US State Dept	EXPIRES	❷	

Entry 182

SERVICE

DATE	TIME	am	ADDRESS	☐ Signer's	☐ Office	NOTES	☐ Stop	MILES	Notary	☐ Adv. Travel	☐ Rush	☐ Copy	☐ Other	TOTAL FEES
- -20	:	pm							$	$	$	$	$	$

TYPE ☐ Acknowledgment ☐ Jurat ☐ Copy Certification ☐ Oath/Affirmation ☐ Oath of Office ☐ Proof of Execution ☐ Protest ☐ Other

R   **Fingerprint**

DOCUMENT

DOC TYPE ☐ **Deed**   ☐ **DOT**   ☐ **Trust**   ☐ **POA**   ☐ **POAH**   ☐ **Agreement**   ☐ **Affidavit**   ☐ **Other**

Grant • Trust Transfer • Gift   Mortgage   Certification   General / Limited   AHCD   Compliance-E&O   Borrower • Occupancy • Ownership • Refi • Survey   Vehicle Title
Interspousal • Quitclaim • ToD • Warranty   Rev / Irrev • Am / Rest   Durable / Springing   Living Will   Correction   Debts & Liens • Name-Signature-ID • Marital • Death • Will   Safe Deposit Box

T
I
M

DOC DATE   J F M A M J   J A S O N D   ,   DOC TITLE or TYPE   # OF PAGES   ☐ Inspect/Copy Request   Entry X-Ref #

R
P

☐ **SATISFACTORY EVIDENCE** ☐ Driver's License / Passport / State ID / Military / Government / Tribal / Inmate / Other ID *or* ☐ Credible Witness(es)

L

SIGNER

SIGNER's NAME	☐ For	ADDRESS	☐ Non-Public	☐ Capacity	☐ Voluntary	☐ Proper ID	ISSUED	SIGNATURE	☐ (oath / affirmation, if any)	☐ (by Mark)
				#						
PHONE C / H / W	*or* ☐ MISC			AGENCY	☐ CA DMV	☐ US State Dept	EXPIRES	➡		

CW #1

#1 WITNESS's NAME	☐ P/Known	ADDRESS	☐ Non-Public	☐ Driver's License	☐ Passport	☐ Other ID	ISSUED	SIGNATURE	☐ (after oath / affirmation)
				#					
PHONE C / H / W	*or* ☐ MISC			AGENCY	☐ CA DMV	☐ US State Dept	EXPIRES	❶	

CW #2

#2 WITNESS's NAME	☐ P/Known	ADDRESS	☐ Non-Public	☐ Driver's License	☐ Passport	☐ Other ID	ISSUED	SIGNATURE	☐ (after oath / affirmation)
				#					
PHONE C / H / W	*or* ☐ MISC			AGENCY	☐ CA DMV	☐ US State Dept	EXPIRES	❷	

NOTARY NAME (printed): COMMISSION #:

Entry 183

SERVICE — DATE: - -20 TIME: : am/pm ADDRESS: ☐ Signer's ☐ Office NOTES ☐ Stop MILES Notary $ ☐ Adv. Travel $ ☐ Rush $ ☐ Copy $ ☐ Other $ TOTAL FEES $

TYPE: ☐ Acknowledgment ☐ Jurat ☐ Copy Certification ☐ Oath/Affirmation ☐ Oath of Office ☐ Proof of Execution ☐ Protest ☐ Other

R T I M R P L — **Fingerprint**

DOCUMENT

DOC TYPE: ☐ Deed (Grant • Trust Transfer • Gift • Interspousal • Quitclaim • ToD • Warranty) ☐ DOT (Mortgage • Certification • Rev / Irrev • Am / Rest) ☐ Trust ☐ POA (General / Limited • Durable / Springing) ☐ POAH (AHCD • Living Will) ☐ Agreement (Compliance-E&O • Correction) ☐ Affidavit (Borrower • Occupancy • Ownership • Refi • Survey • Debts & Liens • Name-Signature-ID • Marital • Death • Will) ☐ Other (Vehicle Title • Safe Deposit Box)

DOC DATE: J F M A M J J A S O N D ,   DOC TITLE or TYPE   # OF PAGES   ☐ Inspect/Copy Request   Entry X-Ref #

☐ **SATISFACTORY EVIDENCE** ☐ Driver's License / Passport / State ID / Military / Government / Tribal / Inmate / Other ID *or* ☐ Credible Witness(es)

SIGNER

SIGNER's NAME ☐ For ADDRESS ☐ Non-Public ☐ Capacity ☐ Voluntary ☐ Proper ID ISSUED SIGNATURE ☐ (oath / affirmation, if any) ☐ (by Mark)
PHONE C / H / W / *or* ☐ MISC # AGENCY ☐ CA DMV ☐ US State Dept EXPIRES ➡

CW #1

#1 WITNESS's NAME ☐ P/Known ADDRESS ☐ Non-Public ☐ Driver's License ☐ Passport ☐ Other ID ISSUED SIGNATURE ☐ (after oath / affirmation)
PHONE C / H / W / *or* ☐ MISC # AGENCY ☐ CA DMV ☐ US State Dept EXPIRES ❶

CW #2

#2 WITNESS's NAME ☐ P/Known ADDRESS ☐ Non-Public ☐ Driver's License ☐ Passport ☐ Other ID ISSUED SIGNATURE ☐ (after oath / affirmation)
PHONE C / H / W / *or* ☐ MISC # AGENCY ☐ CA DMV ☐ US State Dept EXPIRES ❷

Entry 184

SERVICE — DATE: - -20 TIME: : am/pm ADDRESS: ☐ Signer's ☐ Office NOTES ☐ Stop MILES Notary $ ☐ Adv. Travel $ ☐ Rush $ ☐ Copy $ ☐ Other $ TOTAL FEES $

TYPE: ☐ Acknowledgment ☐ Jurat ☐ Copy Certification ☐ Oath/Affirmation ☐ Oath of Office ☐ Proof of Execution ☐ Protest ☐ Other

R T I M R P L — **Fingerprint**

DOCUMENT

DOC TYPE: ☐ Deed (Grant • Trust Transfer • Gift • Interspousal • Quitclaim • ToD • Warranty) ☐ DOT (Mortgage • Certification • Rev / Irrev • Am / Rest) ☐ Trust ☐ POA (General / Limited • Durable / Springing) ☐ POAH (AHCD • Living Will) ☐ Agreement (Compliance-E&O • Correction) ☐ Affidavit (Borrower • Occupancy • Ownership • Refi • Survey • Debts & Liens • Name-Signature-ID • Marital • Death • Will) ☐ Other (Vehicle Title • Safe Deposit Box)

DOC DATE: J F M A M J J A S O N D ,   DOC TITLE or TYPE   # OF PAGES   ☐ Inspect/Copy Request   Entry X-Ref #

☐ **SATISFACTORY EVIDENCE** ☐ Driver's License / Passport / State ID / Military / Government / Tribal / Inmate / Other ID *or* ☐ Credible Witness(es)

SIGNER

SIGNER's NAME ☐ For ADDRESS ☐ Non-Public ☐ Capacity ☐ Voluntary ☐ Proper ID ISSUED SIGNATURE ☐ (oath / affirmation, if any) ☐ (by Mark)
PHONE C / H / W / *or* ☐ MISC # AGENCY ☐ CA DMV ☐ US State Dept EXPIRES ➡

CW #1

#1 WITNESS's NAME ☐ P/Known ADDRESS ☐ Non-Public ☐ Driver's License ☐ Passport ☐ Other ID ISSUED SIGNATURE ☐ (after oath / affirmation)
PHONE C / H / W / *or* ☐ MISC # AGENCY ☐ CA DMV ☐ US State Dept EXPIRES ❶

CW #2

#2 WITNESS's NAME ☐ P/Known ADDRESS ☐ Non-Public ☐ Driver's License ☐ Passport ☐ Other ID ISSUED SIGNATURE ☐ (after oath / affirmation)
PHONE C / H / W / *or* ☐ MISC # AGENCY ☐ CA DMV ☐ US State Dept EXPIRES ❷

NOTARY NAME (printed):   COMMISSION #:

185

SERVICE

DATE	TIME	am	ADDRESS	☐ Signer's	☐ Office	NOTES		☐ Stop	MILES	Notary	☐ Adv. Travel	☐ Rush	☐ Copy	☐ Other	TOTAL FEES
- -20	:	pm								$	$	$	$	$	$

TYPE ☐ Acknowledgment ☐ Jurat ☐ Copy Certification ☐ Oath/Affirmation ☐ Oath of Office ☐ Proof of Execution ☐ Protest ☐ Other

Fingerprint   R T I M R P L

DOCUMENT

DOC TYPE ☐ Deed ☐ DOT ☐ Trust ☐ POA ☐ POAH ☐ Agreement ☐ Affidavit ☐ Other
Grant • Trust Transfer • Gift | Mortgage | Certification | General / Limited | AHCD | Compliance-E&O | Borrower • Occupancy • Ownership • Refi • Survey | Vehicle Title
Interspousal • Quitclaim • ToD • Warranty | Rev / Irrev • Am / Rest | Durable / Springing | Living Will | Correction | Debts & Liens • Name-Signature-ID • Marital • Death • Will | Safe Deposit Box

DOC DATE J F M A M J   DOC TITLE or TYPE   # OF PAGES ☐ Inspect/Copy Request
J A S O N D ,   Entry X-Ref #

☐ **SATISFACTORY EVIDENCE** ☐ Driver's License / Passport / State ID / Military / Government / Tribal / Inmate / Other ID *or* ☐ Credible Witness(es)

SIGNER

SIGNER's NAME ☐ For | ADDRESS   ☐ Non-Public | ☐ Capacity ☐ Voluntary ☐ Proper ID | ISSUED # | SIGNATURE ☐ (oath / affirmation, if any) ☐ (by Mark)
PHONE C / H / W   *or* ☐ MISC / | | AGENCY ☐ CA DMV ☐ US State Dept | EXPIRES | ➡

CW #1

#1 WITNESS's NAME ☐ P/Known | ADDRESS   ☐ Non-Public | ☐ Driver's License ☐ Passport ☐ Other ID | ISSUED # | SIGNATURE ☐ (after oath / affirmation)
PHONE C / H / W   *or* ☐ MISC / | | AGENCY ☐ CA DMV ☐ US State Dept | EXPIRES | ❶

CW #2

#2 WITNESS's NAME ☐ P/Known | ADDRESS   ☐ Non-Public | ☐ Driver's License ☐ Passport ☐ Other ID | ISSUED # | SIGNATURE ☐ (after oath / affirmation)
PHONE C / H / W   *or* ☐ MISC / | | AGENCY ☐ CA DMV ☐ US State Dept | EXPIRES | ❷

186

SERVICE

DATE	TIME	am	ADDRESS	☐ Signer's	☐ Office	NOTES		☐ Stop	MILES	Notary	☐ Adv. Travel	☐ Rush	☐ Copy	☐ Other	TOTAL FEES
- -20	:	pm								$	$	$	$	$	$

TYPE ☐ Acknowledgment ☐ Jurat ☐ Copy Certification ☐ Oath/Affirmation ☐ Oath of Office ☐ Proof of Execution ☐ Protest ☐ Other

Fingerprint   R T I M R P L

DOCUMENT

DOC TYPE ☐ Deed ☐ DOT ☐ Trust ☐ POA ☐ POAH ☐ Agreement ☐ Affidavit ☐ Other
Grant • Trust Transfer • Gift | Mortgage | Certification | General / Limited | AHCD | Compliance-E&O | Borrower • Occupancy • Ownership • Refi • Survey | Vehicle Title
Interspousal • Quitclaim • ToD • Warranty | Rev / Irrev • Am / Rest | Durable / Springing | Living Will | Correction | Debts & Liens • Name-Signature-ID • Marital • Death • Will | Safe Deposit Box

DOC DATE J F M A M J   DOC TITLE or TYPE   # OF PAGES ☐ Inspect/Copy Request
J A S O N D ,   Entry X-Ref #

☐ **SATISFACTORY EVIDENCE** ☐ Driver's License / Passport / State ID / Military / Government / Tribal / Inmate / Other ID *or* ☐ Credible Witness(es)

SIGNER

SIGNER's NAME ☐ For | ADDRESS   ☐ Non-Public | ☐ Capacity ☐ Voluntary ☐ Proper ID | ISSUED # | SIGNATURE ☐ (oath / affirmation, if any) ☐ (by Mark)
PHONE C / H / W   *or* ☐ MISC / | | AGENCY ☐ CA DMV ☐ US State Dept | EXPIRES | ➡

CW #1

#1 WITNESS's NAME ☐ P/Known | ADDRESS   ☐ Non-Public | ☐ Driver's License ☐ Passport ☐ Other ID | ISSUED # | SIGNATURE ☐ (after oath / affirmation)
PHONE C / H / W   *or* ☐ MISC / | | AGENCY ☐ CA DMV ☐ US State Dept | EXPIRES | ❶

CW #2

#2 WITNESS's NAME ☐ P/Known | ADDRESS   ☐ Non-Public | ☐ Driver's License ☐ Passport ☐ Other ID | ISSUED # | SIGNATURE ☐ (after oath / affirmation)
PHONE C / H / W   *or* ☐ MISC / | | AGENCY ☐ CA DMV ☐ US State Dept | EXPIRES | ❷

NOTARY NAME (printed):								COMMISSION #:	

Entry 187

SERVICE	DATE --20	TIME : am/pm	ADDRESS	☐ Signer's ☐ Office NOTES	☐ Stop MILES	Notary $	☐ Adv. Travel $	☐ Rush $	☐ Copy $	☐ Other $	TOTAL FEES $

TYPE ☐ Acknowledgment ☐ Jurat ☐ Copy Certification ☐ Oath/Affirmation ☐ Oath of Office ☐ Proof of Execution ☐ Protest ☐ Other — **Fingerprint** (R/T/I/M/R/P/L)

DOCUMENT
DOC TYPE: ☐ Deed (Grant • Trust Transfer • Gift / Interspousal • Quitclaim • ToD • Warranty) ☐ DOT (Mortgage) ☐ Trust (Certification / Rev / Irrev • Am / Rest) ☐ POA (General / Limited / Durable / Springing) ☐ POAH (AHCD / Living Will) ☐ Agreement (Compliance-E&O / Correction) ☐ Affidavit (Borrower • Occupancy • Ownership • Refi • Survey / Debts & Liens • Name-Signature-ID • Marital • Death • Will) ☐ Other (Vehicle Title / Safe Deposit Box)

DOC DATE: J F M A M J / J A S O N D , ____ DOC TITLE or TYPE: ____ # OF PAGES: ____ ☐ Inspect/Copy Request Entry X-Ref #: ____

☐ **SATISFACTORY EVIDENCE** ☐ Driver's License / Passport / State ID / Military / Government / Tribal / Inmate / Other ID *or* ☐ Credible Witness(es)

| SIGNER | SIGNER's NAME | ☐ For | ADDRESS | ☐ Non-Public # | ☐ Capacity | ☐ Voluntary | ☐ Proper ID | ISSUED | SIGNATURE ☐ (oath / affirmation, if any) ☐ (by Mark) |
| | PHONE C/H/W / | *or* ☐ MISC | | AGENCY | ☐ CA DMV | ☐ US State Dept | EXPIRES | → |

| CW #1 | #1 WITNESS's NAME | ☐ P/Known | ADDRESS | ☐ Non-Public # | ☐ Driver's License | ☐ Passport | ☐ Other ID | ISSUED | SIGNATURE ☐ (after oath / affirmation) |
| | PHONE C/H/W / | *or* ☐ MISC | | AGENCY | ☐ CA DMV | ☐ US State Dept | EXPIRES | ❶ |

| CW #2 | #2 WITNESS's NAME | ☐ P/Known | ADDRESS | ☐ Non-Public # | ☐ Driver's License | ☐ Passport | ☐ Other ID | ISSUED | SIGNATURE ☐ (after oath / affirmation) |
| | PHONE C/H/W / | *or* ☐ MISC | | AGENCY | ☐ CA DMV | ☐ US State Dept | EXPIRES | ❷ |

Entry 188

SERVICE	DATE --20	TIME : am/pm	ADDRESS	☐ Signer's ☐ Office NOTES	☐ Stop MILES	Notary $	☐ Adv. Travel $	☐ Rush $	☐ Copy $	☐ Other $	TOTAL FEES $

TYPE ☐ Acknowledgment ☐ Jurat ☐ Copy Certification ☐ Oath/Affirmation ☐ Oath of Office ☐ Proof of Execution ☐ Protest ☐ Other — **Fingerprint** (R/T/I/M/R/P/L)

DOCUMENT
DOC TYPE: ☐ Deed (Grant • Trust Transfer • Gift / Interspousal • Quitclaim • ToD • Warranty) ☐ DOT (Mortgage) ☐ Trust (Certification / Rev / Irrev • Am / Rest) ☐ POA (General / Limited / Durable / Springing) ☐ POAH (AHCD / Living Will) ☐ Agreement (Compliance-E&O / Correction) ☐ Affidavit (Borrower • Occupancy • Ownership • Refi • Survey / Debts & Liens • Name-Signature-ID • Marital • Death • Will) ☐ Other (Vehicle Title / Safe Deposit Box)

DOC DATE: J F M A M J / J A S O N D , ____ DOC TITLE or TYPE: ____ # OF PAGES: ____ ☐ Inspect/Copy Request Entry X-Ref #: ____

☐ **SATISFACTORY EVIDENCE** ☐ Driver's License / Passport / State ID / Military / Government / Tribal / Inmate / Other ID *or* ☐ Credible Witness(es)

| SIGNER | SIGNER's NAME | ☐ For | ADDRESS | ☐ Non-Public # | ☐ Capacity | ☐ Voluntary | ☐ Proper ID | ISSUED | SIGNATURE ☐ (oath / affirmation, if any) ☐ (by Mark) |
| | PHONE C/H/W / | *or* ☐ MISC | | AGENCY | ☐ CA DMV | ☐ US State Dept | EXPIRES | → |

| CW #1 | #1 WITNESS's NAME | ☐ P/Known | ADDRESS | ☐ Non-Public # | ☐ Driver's License | ☐ Passport | ☐ Other ID | ISSUED | SIGNATURE ☐ (after oath / affirmation) |
| | PHONE C/H/W / | *or* ☐ MISC | | AGENCY | ☐ CA DMV | ☐ US State Dept | EXPIRES | ❶ |

| CW #2 | #2 WITNESS's NAME | ☐ P/Known | ADDRESS | ☐ Non-Public # | ☐ Driver's License | ☐ Passport | ☐ Other ID | ISSUED | SIGNATURE ☐ (after oath / affirmation) |
| | PHONE C/H/W / | *or* ☐ MISC | | AGENCY | ☐ CA DMV | ☐ US State Dept | EXPIRES | ❷ |

NOTARY NAME (printed):   COMMISSION #:

189

SERVICE

DATE	TIME	am	ADDRESS	☐ Signer's	☐ Office	NOTES	☐ Stop	MILES	Notary	☐ Adv. Travel	☐ Rush	☐ Copy	☐ Other	TOTAL FEES
- -20	:	pm						$	$		$	$	$	$

TYPE ☐ Acknowledgment ☐ Jurat ☐ Copy Certification ☐ Oath/Affirmation ☐ Oath of Office ☐ Proof of Execution ☐ Protest ☐ Other

R T I M R P L **Fingerprint**

DOCUMENT

DOC TYPE ☐ Deed ☐ DOT ☐ Trust ☐ POA ☐ POAH ☐ Agreement ☐ Affidavit ☐ Other
Grant • Trust Transfer • Gift   Mortgage   Certification   General / Limited   AHCD   Compliance-E&O   Borrower • Occupancy • Ownership • Refi • Survey   Vehicle Title
Interspousal • Quitclaim • ToD • Warranty   Rev / Irrev • Am / Rest   Durable / Springing   Living Will   Correction   Debts & Liens • Name-Signature-ID • Marital • Death • Will   Safe Deposit Box

DOC DATE J F M A M J   DOC TITLE or TYPE   # OF PAGES   ☐ Inspect/Copy Request
J A S O N D   ,   Entry X-Ref #

☐ **SATISFACTORY EVIDENCE** ☐ Driver's License / Passport / State ID / Military / Government / Tribal / Inmate / Other ID *or* ☐ Credible Witness(es)

SIGNER

SIGNER's NAME	☐ For	ADDRESS	☐ Non-Public	☐ Capacity	☐ Voluntary	☐ Proper ID	ISSUED	SIGNATURE	☐ (oath / affirmation, if any)	☐ (by Mark)
				#						
PHONE C / H / W	or ☐ MISC			AGENCY	☐ CA DMV	☐ US State Dept	EXPIRES	➡		
/										

CW #1

#1 WITNESS's NAME	☐ P/Known	ADDRESS	☐ Non-Public	☐ Driver's License	☐ Passport	☐ Other ID	ISSUED	SIGNATURE	☐ (after oath / affirmation)
				#					
PHONE C / H / W	or ☐ MISC			AGENCY	☐ CA DMV	☐ US State Dept	EXPIRES	❶	
/									

CW #2

#2 WITNESS's NAME	☐ P/Known	ADDRESS	☐ Non-Public	☐ Driver's License	☐ Passport	☐ Other ID	ISSUED	SIGNATURE	☐ (after oath / affirmation)
				#					
PHONE C / H / W	or ☐ MISC			AGENCY	☐ CA DMV	☐ US State Dept	EXPIRES	❷	
/									

190

SERVICE

DATE	TIME	am	ADDRESS	☐ Signer's	☐ Office	NOTES	☐ Stop	MILES	Notary	☐ Adv. Travel	☐ Rush	☐ Copy	☐ Other	TOTAL FEES
- -20	:	pm						$	$		$	$	$	$

TYPE ☐ Acknowledgment ☐ Jurat ☐ Copy Certification ☐ Oath/Affirmation ☐ Oath of Office ☐ Proof of Execution ☐ Protest ☐ Other

R T I M R P L **Fingerprint**

DOCUMENT

DOC TYPE ☐ Deed ☐ DOT ☐ Trust ☐ POA ☐ POAH ☐ Agreement ☐ Affidavit ☐ Other
Grant • Trust Transfer • Gift   Mortgage   Certification   General / Limited   AHCD   Compliance-E&O   Borrower • Occupancy • Ownership • Refi • Survey   Vehicle Title
Interspousal • Quitclaim • ToD • Warranty   Rev / Irrev • Am / Rest   Durable / Springing   Living Will   Correction   Debts & Liens • Name-Signature-ID • Marital • Death • Will   Safe Deposit Box

DOC DATE J F M A M J   DOC TITLE or TYPE   # OF PAGES   ☐ Inspect/Copy Request
J A S O N D   ,   Entry X-Ref #

☐ **SATISFACTORY EVIDENCE** ☐ Driver's License / Passport / State ID / Military / Government / Tribal / Inmate / Other ID *or* ☐ Credible Witness(es)

SIGNER

SIGNER's NAME	☐ For	ADDRESS	☐ Non-Public	☐ Capacity	☐ Voluntary	☐ Proper ID	ISSUED	SIGNATURE	☐ (oath / affirmation, if any)	☐ (by Mark)
				#						
PHONE C / H / W	or ☐ MISC			AGENCY	☐ CA DMV	☐ US State Dept	EXPIRES	➡		
/										

CW #1

#1 WITNESS's NAME	☐ P/Known	ADDRESS	☐ Non-Public	☐ Driver's License	☐ Passport	☐ Other ID	ISSUED	SIGNATURE	☐ (after oath / affirmation)
				#					
PHONE C / H / W	or ☐ MISC			AGENCY	☐ CA DMV	☐ US State Dept	EXPIRES	❶	
/									

CW #2

#2 WITNESS's NAME	☐ P/Known	ADDRESS	☐ Non-Public	☐ Driver's License	☐ Passport	☐ Other ID	ISSUED	SIGNATURE	☐ (after oath / affirmation)
				#					
PHONE C / H / W	or ☐ MISC			AGENCY	☐ CA DMV	☐ US State Dept	EXPIRES	❷	
/									

NOTARY NAME (printed): _____   COMMISSION #: _____

Entry 191

SERVICE
- DATE: __ - __ -20__   TIME: __:__ am/pm   ADDRESS: _____ ☐ Signer's ☐ Office   NOTES: _____   ☐ Stop   MILES: ____   Notary $____   ☐ Adv. Travel $____   ☐ Rush $____   ☐ Copy $____   ☐ Other $____   TOTAL FEES $____
- TYPE: ☐ Acknowledgment ☐ Jurat ☐ Copy Certification ☐ Oath/Affirmation ☐ Oath of Office ☐ Proof of Execution ☐ Protest ☐ Other

DOCUMENT
- DOC TYPE: ☐ Deed (Grant • Trust Transfer • Gift / Interspousal • Quitclaim • ToD • Warranty)   ☐ DOT (Mortgage / Certification / Rev / Irrev • Am / Rest)   ☐ Trust   ☐ POA (General / Limited / Durable / Springing)   ☐ POAH (AHCD / Living Will)   ☐ Agreement (Compliance-E&O / Correction)   ☐ Affidavit (Borrower • Occupancy • Ownership • Refi • Survey / Debts & Liens • Name-Signature-ID • Marital • Death • Will)   ☐ Other (Vehicle Title / Safe Deposit Box)
- DOC DATE: J F M A M J J A S O N D , ____   DOC TITLE or TYPE: _____   # OF PAGES: ____   ☐ Inspect/Copy Request   Entry X-Ref #: ____

☐ **SATISFACTORY EVIDENCE** ☐ Driver's License / Passport / State ID / Military / Government / Tribal / Inmate / Other ID *or* ☐ Credible Witness(es)

SIGNER
- SIGNER's NAME: _____   ☐ For   ADDRESS: _____   ☐ Non-Public   ☐ Capacity   ☐ Voluntary   ☐ Proper ID   ISSUED #: ____   SIGNATURE   ☐ (oath / affirmation, if any)   ☐ (by Mark)
- PHONE C/H/W: ____ / ____   or ☐ MISC: ____   AGENCY: ____   ☐ CA DMV   ☐ US State Dept   EXPIRES: ____   →

CW #1
- #1 WITNESS's NAME: _____   ☐ P/Known   ADDRESS: _____   ☐ Non-Public   ☐ Driver's License ☐ Passport ☐ Other ID   ISSUED #: ____   SIGNATURE   ☐ (after oath / affirmation)
- PHONE C/H/W: ____ / ____   or ☐ MISC: ____   AGENCY: ____   ☐ CA DMV   ☐ US State Dept   EXPIRES: ____   ❶

CW #2
- #2 WITNESS's NAME: _____   ☐ P/Known   ADDRESS: _____   ☐ Non-Public   ☐ Driver's License ☐ Passport ☐ Other ID   ISSUED #: ____   SIGNATURE   ☐ (after oath / affirmation)
- PHONE C/H/W: ____ / ____   or ☐ MISC: ____   AGENCY: ____   ☐ CA DMV   ☐ US State Dept   EXPIRES: ____   ❷

Fingerprint R T I M R P L

Entry 192

SERVICE
- DATE: __ - __ -20__   TIME: __:__ am/pm   ADDRESS: _____ ☐ Signer's ☐ Office   NOTES: _____   ☐ Stop   MILES: ____   Notary $____   ☐ Adv. Travel $____   ☐ Rush $____   ☐ Copy $____   ☐ Other $____   TOTAL FEES $____
- TYPE: ☐ Acknowledgment ☐ Jurat ☐ Copy Certification ☐ Oath/Affirmation ☐ Oath of Office ☐ Proof of Execution ☐ Protest ☐ Other

DOCUMENT
- DOC TYPE: ☐ Deed (Grant • Trust Transfer • Gift / Interspousal • Quitclaim • ToD • Warranty)   ☐ DOT (Mortgage / Certification / Rev / Irrev • Am / Rest)   ☐ Trust   ☐ POA (General / Limited / Durable / Springing)   ☐ POAH (AHCD / Living Will)   ☐ Agreement (Compliance-E&O / Correction)   ☐ Affidavit (Borrower • Occupancy • Ownership • Refi • Survey / Debts & Liens • Name-Signature-ID • Marital • Death • Will)   ☐ Other (Vehicle Title / Safe Deposit Box)
- DOC DATE: J F M A M J J A S O N D , ____   DOC TITLE or TYPE: _____   # OF PAGES: ____   ☐ Inspect/Copy Request   Entry X-Ref #: ____

☐ **SATISFACTORY EVIDENCE** ☐ Driver's License / Passport / State ID / Military / Government / Tribal / Inmate / Other ID *or* ☐ Credible Witness(es)

SIGNER
- SIGNER's NAME: _____   ☐ For   ADDRESS: _____   ☐ Non-Public   ☐ Capacity   ☐ Voluntary   ☐ Proper ID   ISSUED #: ____   SIGNATURE   ☐ (oath / affirmation, if any)   ☐ (by Mark)
- PHONE C/H/W: ____ / ____   or ☐ MISC: ____   AGENCY: ____   ☐ CA DMV   ☐ US State Dept   EXPIRES: ____   →

CW #1
- #1 WITNESS's NAME: _____   ☐ P/Known   ADDRESS: _____   ☐ Non-Public   ☐ Driver's License ☐ Passport ☐ Other ID   ISSUED #: ____   SIGNATURE   ☐ (after oath / affirmation)
- PHONE C/H/W: ____ / ____   or ☐ MISC: ____   AGENCY: ____   ☐ CA DMV   ☐ US State Dept   EXPIRES: ____   ❶

CW #2
- #2 WITNESS's NAME: _____   ☐ P/Known   ADDRESS: _____   ☐ Non-Public   ☐ Driver's License ☐ Passport ☐ Other ID   ISSUED #: ____   SIGNATURE   ☐ (after oath / affirmation)
- PHONE C/H/W: ____ / ____   or ☐ MISC: ____   AGENCY: ____   ☐ CA DMV   ☐ US State Dept   EXPIRES: ____   ❷

Fingerprint R T I M R P L

NOTARY NAME (printed):   COMMISSION #:

Entry 193

SERVICE

DATE - -20   TIME : am/pm   ADDRESS   ☐ Signer's   ☐ Office   NOTES   ☐ Stop   MILES   Notary ☐ Adv. Travel ☐ Rush ☐ Copy ☐ Other   TOTAL FEES $ $ $ $ $ $

TYPE ☐ Acknowledgment ☐ Jurat ☐ Copy Certification ☐ Oath/Affirmation ☐ Oath of Office ☐ Proof of Execution ☐ Protest ☐ Other

R T I M R P L — Fingerprint

DOCUMENT

DOC TYPE ☐ Deed   ☐ DOT   ☐ Trust   ☐ POA   ☐ POAH   ☐ Agreement   ☐ Affidavit   ☐ Other

Grant • Trust Transfer • Gift   Mortgage   Certification   General / Limited   AHCD   Compliance-E&O   Borrower • Occupancy • Ownership • Refi • Survey   Vehicle Title

Interspousal • Quitclaim • ToD • Warranty   Rev / Irrev • Am / Rest   Durable / Springing   Living Will   Correction   Debts & Liens • Name-Signature-ID • Marital • Death • Will   Safe Deposit Box

DOC DATE J F M A M J J A S O N D ,   DOC TITLE or TYPE   # OF PAGES ☐ Inspect/Copy Request   Entry X-Ref #

☐ **SATISFACTORY EVIDENCE** ☐ Driver's License / Passport / State ID / Military / Government / Tribal / Inmate / Other ID   *or*   ☐ Credible Witness(es)

SIGNER

SIGNER's NAME   ☐ For   ADDRESS   ☐ Non-Public ☐ Capacity ☐ Voluntary ☐ Proper ID   ISSUED #   SIGNATURE ☐ (oath / affirmation, if any) ☐ (by Mark)

PHONE C / H / W   *or* ☐ MISC /   AGENCY ☐ CA DMV ☐ US State Dept   EXPIRES   ➡

CW #1

#1 WITNESS's NAME   ☐ P/Known   ADDRESS   ☐ Non-Public ☐ Driver's License ☐ Passport ☐ Other ID   ISSUED #   SIGNATURE ☐ (after oath / affirmation)

PHONE C / H / W   *or* ☐ MISC /   AGENCY ☐ CA DMV ☐ US State Dept   EXPIRES   ❶

CW #2

#2 WITNESS's NAME   ☐ P/Known   ADDRESS   ☐ Non-Public ☐ Driver's License ☐ Passport ☐ Other ID   ISSUED #   SIGNATURE ☐ (after oath / affirmation)

PHONE C / H / W   *or* ☐ MISC /   AGENCY ☐ CA DMV ☐ US State Dept   EXPIRES   ❷

Entry 194

SERVICE

DATE - -20   TIME : am/pm   ADDRESS   ☐ Signer's   ☐ Office   NOTES   ☐ Stop   MILES   Notary ☐ Adv. Travel ☐ Rush ☐ Copy ☐ Other   TOTAL FEES $ $ $ $ $ $

TYPE ☐ Acknowledgment ☐ Jurat ☐ Copy Certification ☐ Oath/Affirmation ☐ Oath of Office ☐ Proof of Execution ☐ Protest ☐ Other

R T I M R P L — Fingerprint

DOCUMENT

DOC TYPE ☐ Deed   ☐ DOT   ☐ Trust   ☐ POA   ☐ POAH   ☐ Agreement   ☐ Affidavit   ☐ Other

Grant • Trust Transfer • Gift   Mortgage   Certification   General / Limited   AHCD   Compliance-E&O   Borrower • Occupancy • Ownership • Refi • Survey   Vehicle Title

Interspousal • Quitclaim • ToD • Warranty   Rev / Irrev • Am / Rest   Durable / Springing   Living Will   Correction   Debts & Liens • Name-Signature-ID • Marital • Death • Will   Safe Deposit Box

DOC DATE J F M A M J J A S O N D ,   DOC TITLE or TYPE   # OF PAGES ☐ Inspect/Copy Request   Entry X-Ref #

☐ **SATISFACTORY EVIDENCE** ☐ Driver's License / Passport / State ID / Military / Government / Tribal / Inmate / Other ID   *or*   ☐ Credible Witness(es)

SIGNER

SIGNER's NAME   ☐ For   ADDRESS   ☐ Non-Public ☐ Capacity ☐ Voluntary ☐ Proper ID   ISSUED #   SIGNATURE ☐ (oath / affirmation, if any) ☐ (by Mark)

PHONE C / H / W   *or* ☐ MISC /   AGENCY ☐ CA DMV ☐ US State Dept   EXPIRES   ➡

CW #1

#1 WITNESS's NAME   ☐ P/Known   ADDRESS   ☐ Non-Public ☐ Driver's License ☐ Passport ☐ Other ID   ISSUED #   SIGNATURE ☐ (after oath / affirmation)

PHONE C / H / W   *or* ☐ MISC /   AGENCY ☐ CA DMV ☐ US State Dept   EXPIRES   ❶

CW #2

#2 WITNESS's NAME   ☐ P/Known   ADDRESS   ☐ Non-Public ☐ Driver's License ☐ Passport ☐ Other ID   ISSUED #   SIGNATURE ☐ (after oath / affirmation)

PHONE C / H / W   *or* ☐ MISC /   AGENCY ☐ CA DMV ☐ US State Dept   EXPIRES   ❷

NOTARY NAME (printed): COMMISSION #:

Entry 195

SERVICE — DATE - -20 TIME : am/pm ADDRESS ☐ Signer's ☐ Office NOTES ☐ Stop MILES Notary $ ☐ Adv. Travel $ ☐ Rush $ ☐ Copy $ ☐ Other $ TOTAL FEES $

TYPE: ☐ Acknowledgment ☐ Jurat ☐ Copy Certification ☐ Oath/Affirmation ☐ Oath of Office ☐ Proof of Execution ☐ Protest ☐ Other

Fingerprint — R T I M R P L

DOCUMENT
DOC TYPE: ☐ Deed (Grant • Trust Transfer • Gift • Interspousal • Quitclaim • ToD • Warranty) ☐ DOT (Mortgage) ☐ Trust (Certification • Rev / Irrev • Am / Rest) ☐ POA (General / Limited • Durable / Springing) ☐ POAH (AHCD • Living Will) ☐ Agreement (Compliance-E&O • Correction) ☐ Affidavit (Borrower • Occupancy • Ownership • Refi • Survey • Debts & Liens • Name-Signature-ID • Marital • Death • Will) ☐ Other (Vehicle Title • Safe Deposit Box)

DOC DATE: J F M A M J J A S O N D ,   DOC TITLE or TYPE   # OF PAGES   ☐ Inspect/Copy Request   Entry X-Ref #

☐ **SATISFACTORY EVIDENCE** ☐ Driver's License / Passport / State ID / Military / Government / Tribal / Inmate / Other ID *or* ☐ Credible Witness(es)

SIGNER — SIGNER's NAME ☐ For ADDRESS ☐ Non-Public ☐ Capacity ☐ Voluntary ☐ Proper ID ISSUED SIGNATURE ☐ (oath / affirmation, if any) ☐ (by Mark)
PHONE C / H / W /   or ☐ MISC   # AGENCY ☐ CA DMV ☐ US State Dept EXPIRES

CW #1 — #1 WITNESS's NAME ☐ P/Known ADDRESS ☐ Non-Public ☐ Driver's License ☐ Passport ☐ Other ID ISSUED SIGNATURE ☐ (after oath / affirmation)
PHONE C / H / W /   or ☐ MISC   # AGENCY ☐ CA DMV ☐ US State Dept EXPIRES   ❶

CW #2 — #2 WITNESS's NAME ☐ P/Known ADDRESS ☐ Non-Public ☐ Driver's License ☐ Passport ☐ Other ID ISSUED SIGNATURE ☐ (after oath / affirmation)
PHONE C / H / W /   or ☐ MISC   # AGENCY ☐ CA DMV ☐ US State Dept EXPIRES   ❷

Entry 196

SERVICE — DATE - -20 TIME : am/pm ADDRESS ☐ Signer's ☐ Office NOTES ☐ Stop MILES Notary $ ☐ Adv. Travel $ ☐ Rush $ ☐ Copy $ ☐ Other $ TOTAL FEES $

TYPE: ☐ Acknowledgment ☐ Jurat ☐ Copy Certification ☐ Oath/Affirmation ☐ Oath of Office ☐ Proof of Execution ☐ Protest ☐ Other

Fingerprint — R T I M R P L

DOCUMENT
DOC TYPE: ☐ Deed (Grant • Trust Transfer • Gift • Interspousal • Quitclaim • ToD • Warranty) ☐ DOT (Mortgage) ☐ Trust (Certification • Rev / Irrev • Am / Rest) ☐ POA (General / Limited • Durable / Springing) ☐ POAH (AHCD • Living Will) ☐ Agreement (Compliance-E&O • Correction) ☐ Affidavit (Borrower • Occupancy • Ownership • Refi • Survey • Debts & Liens • Name-Signature-ID • Marital • Death • Will) ☐ Other (Vehicle Title • Safe Deposit Box)

DOC DATE: J F M A M J J A S O N D ,   DOC TITLE or TYPE   # OF PAGES   ☐ Inspect/Copy Request   Entry X-Ref #

☐ **SATISFACTORY EVIDENCE** ☐ Driver's License / Passport / State ID / Military / Government / Tribal / Inmate / Other ID *or* ☐ Credible Witness(es)

SIGNER — SIGNER's NAME ☐ For ADDRESS ☐ Non-Public ☐ Capacity ☐ Voluntary ☐ Proper ID ISSUED SIGNATURE ☐ (oath / affirmation, if any) ☐ (by Mark)
PHONE C / H / W /   or ☐ MISC   # AGENCY ☐ CA DMV ☐ US State Dept EXPIRES

CW #1 — #1 WITNESS's NAME ☐ P/Known ADDRESS ☐ Non-Public ☐ Driver's License ☐ Passport ☐ Other ID ISSUED SIGNATURE ☐ (after oath / affirmation)
PHONE C / H / W /   or ☐ MISC   # AGENCY ☐ CA DMV ☐ US State Dept EXPIRES   ❶

CW #2 — #2 WITNESS's NAME ☐ P/Known ADDRESS ☐ Non-Public ☐ Driver's License ☐ Passport ☐ Other ID ISSUED SIGNATURE ☐ (after oath / affirmation)
PHONE C / H / W /   or ☐ MISC   # AGENCY ☐ CA DMV ☐ US State Dept EXPIRES   ❷

NOTARY NAME (printed):   **COMMISSION #:**

Entry 197

SERVICE

DATE ___ - ___ -20___ TIME ___:___ am/pm ADDRESS ___ ☐ Signer's ☐ Office NOTES ___ ☐ Stop MILES ___ Notary $___ ☐ Adv. Travel $___ ☐ Rush $___ ☐ Copy $___ ☐ Other $___ TOTAL FEES $___

TYPE ☐ Acknowledgment ☐ Jurat ☐ Copy Certification ☐ Oath/Affirmation ☐ Oath of Office ☐ Proof of Execution ☐ Protest ☐ Other

DOCUMENT

DOC TYPE ☐ Deed (Grant • Trust Transfer • Gift / Interspousal • Quitclaim • ToD • Warranty) ☐ DOT (Mortgage) ☐ Trust (Certification / Rev / Irrev • Am / Rest) ☐ POA (General / Limited / Durable / Springing) ☐ POAH (AHCD / Living Will) ☐ Agreement (Compliance-E&O / Correction) ☐ Affidavit (Borrower • Occupancy • Ownership • Refi • Survey / Debts & Liens • Name-Signature-ID • Marital • Death • Will) ☐ Other (Vehicle Title / Safe Deposit Box)

DOC DATE J F M A M J J A S O N D , ___ DOC TITLE or TYPE ___ # OF PAGES ___ ☐ Inspect/Copy Request Entry X-Ref # ___

☐ **SATISFACTORY EVIDENCE** ☐ Driver's License / Passport / State ID / Military / Government / Tribal / Inmate / Other ID *or* ☐ Credible Witness(es)

SIGNER

SIGNER's NAME ___ ☐ For ADDRESS ___ ☐ Non-Public ☐ Capacity ☐ Voluntary ☐ Proper ID ISSUED ___ # ___ SIGNATURE ___ ☐ (oath / affirmation, if any) ☐ (by Mark)

PHONE C / H / W ___ *or* ☐ MISC AGENCY ___ ☐ CA DMV ☐ US State Dept EXPIRES ___ ➡

CW #1

#1 WITNESS's NAME ___ ☐ P/Known ADDRESS ___ ☐ Non-Public ☐ Driver's License ☐ Passport ☐ Other ID ISSUED ___ # ___ SIGNATURE ___ ☐ (after oath / affirmation)

PHONE C / H / W ___ *or* ☐ MISC AGENCY ___ ☐ CA DMV ☐ US State Dept EXPIRES ___ ❶

CW #2

#2 WITNESS's NAME ___ ☐ P/Known ADDRESS ___ ☐ Non-Public ☐ Driver's License ☐ Passport ☐ Other ID ISSUED ___ # ___ SIGNATURE ___ ☐ (after oath / affirmation)

PHONE C / H / W ___ *or* ☐ MISC AGENCY ___ ☐ CA DMV ☐ US State Dept EXPIRES ___ ❷

Fingerprint — R T I M R P L

Entry 198

SERVICE

DATE ___ - ___ -20___ TIME ___:___ am/pm ADDRESS ___ ☐ Signer's ☐ Office NOTES ___ ☐ Stop MILES ___ Notary $___ ☐ Adv. Travel $___ ☐ Rush $___ ☐ Copy $___ ☐ Other $___ TOTAL FEES $___

TYPE ☐ Acknowledgment ☐ Jurat ☐ Copy Certification ☐ Oath/Affirmation ☐ Oath of Office ☐ Proof of Execution ☐ Protest ☐ Other

DOCUMENT

DOC TYPE ☐ Deed (Grant • Trust Transfer • Gift / Interspousal • Quitclaim • ToD • Warranty) ☐ DOT (Mortgage) ☐ Trust (Certification / Rev / Irrev • Am / Rest) ☐ POA (General / Limited / Durable / Springing) ☐ POAH (AHCD / Living Will) ☐ Agreement (Compliance-E&O / Correction) ☐ Affidavit (Borrower • Occupancy • Ownership • Refi • Survey / Debts & Liens • Name-Signature-ID • Marital • Death • Will) ☐ Other (Vehicle Title / Safe Deposit Box)

DOC DATE J F M A M J J A S O N D , ___ DOC TITLE or TYPE ___ # OF PAGES ___ ☐ Inspect/Copy Request Entry X-Ref # ___

☐ **SATISFACTORY EVIDENCE** ☐ Driver's License / Passport / State ID / Military / Government / Tribal / Inmate / Other ID *or* ☐ Credible Witness(es)

SIGNER

SIGNER's NAME ___ ☐ For ADDRESS ___ ☐ Non-Public ☐ Capacity ☐ Voluntary ☐ Proper ID ISSUED ___ # ___ SIGNATURE ___ ☐ (oath / affirmation, if any) ☐ (by Mark)

PHONE C / H / W ___ *or* ☐ MISC AGENCY ___ ☐ CA DMV ☐ US State Dept EXPIRES ___ ➡

CW #1

#1 WITNESS's NAME ___ ☐ P/Known ADDRESS ___ ☐ Non-Public ☐ Driver's License ☐ Passport ☐ Other ID ISSUED ___ # ___ SIGNATURE ___ ☐ (after oath / affirmation)

PHONE C / H / W ___ *or* ☐ MISC AGENCY ___ ☐ CA DMV ☐ US State Dept EXPIRES ___ ❶

CW #2

#2 WITNESS's NAME ___ ☐ P/Known ADDRESS ___ ☐ Non-Public ☐ Driver's License ☐ Passport ☐ Other ID ISSUED ___ # ___ SIGNATURE ___ ☐ (after oath / affirmation)

PHONE C / H / W ___ *or* ☐ MISC AGENCY ___ ☐ CA DMV ☐ US State Dept EXPIRES ___ ❷

Fingerprint — R T I M R P L

NOTARY NAME (printed): _____ COMMISSION #: _____

Entry 199

| SERVICE | DATE __-__-20__ | TIME __:__ am/pm | ADDRESS | ☐ Signer's ☐ Office | NOTES | ☐ Stop | MILES $__ | Notary $__ | ☐ Adv. Travel $__ | ☐ Rush $__ | ☐ Copy $__ | ☐ Other $__ | TOTAL FEES $__ |

TYPE: ☐ Acknowledgment ☐ Jurat ☐ Copy Certification ☐ Oath/Affirmation ☐ Oath of Office ☐ Proof of Execution ☐ Protest ☐ Other

DOCUMENT
DOC TYPE: ☐ Deed ☐ DOT ☐ Trust ☐ POA ☐ POAH ☐ Agreement ☐ Affidavit ☐ Other
- Deed: Grant • Trust Transfer • Gift • Interspousal • Quitclaim • ToD • Warranty
- DOT: Mortgage • Rev / Irrev • Am / Rest
- Trust: Certification
- POA: General / Limited • Durable / Springing
- POAH: AHCD • Living Will
- Agreement: Compliance-E&O • Correction
- Affidavit: Borrower • Occupancy • Ownership • Refi • Survey • Debts & Liens • Name-Signature-ID • Marital • Death • Will
- Other: Vehicle Title • Safe Deposit Box

DOC DATE: J F M A M J J A S O N D , ____ DOC TITLE or TYPE: _____ # OF PAGES: __ ☐ Inspect/Copy Request Entry X-Ref #: __

☐ **SATISFACTORY EVIDENCE** ☐ Driver's License / Passport / State ID / Military / Government / Tribal / Inmate / Other ID *or* ☐ Credible Witness(es)

SIGNER
- SIGNER's NAME: ____ ☐ For ADDRESS: ____ ☐ Non-Public ☐ Capacity ☐ Voluntary ☐ Proper ID ISSUED #: ____ SIGNATURE ☐ (oath / affirmation, if any) ☐ (by Mark)
- PHONE C / H / W / ____ *or* ☐ MISC AGENCY ☐ CA DMV ☐ US State Dept EXPIRES ____ ➤

CW #1
- #1 WITNESS's NAME: ____ ☐ P/Known ADDRESS: ____ ☐ Non-Public ☐ Driver's License ☐ Passport ☐ Other ID ISSUED #: ____ SIGNATURE ☐ (after oath / affirmation)
- PHONE C / H / W / ____ *or* ☐ MISC AGENCY ☐ CA DMV ☐ US State Dept EXPIRES ____ ❶

CW #2
- #2 WITNESS's NAME: ____ ☐ P/Known ADDRESS: ____ ☐ Non-Public ☐ Driver's License ☐ Passport ☐ Other ID ISSUED #: ____ SIGNATURE ☐ (after oath / affirmation)
- PHONE C / H / W / ____ *or* ☐ MISC AGENCY ☐ CA DMV ☐ US State Dept EXPIRES ____ ❷

Fingerprint: R T I M R P L

Entry 200

| SERVICE | DATE __-__-20__ | TIME __:__ am/pm | ADDRESS | ☐ Signer's ☐ Office | NOTES | ☐ Stop | MILES $__ | Notary $__ | ☐ Adv. Travel $__ | ☐ Rush $__ | ☐ Copy $__ | ☐ Other $__ | TOTAL FEES $__ |

TYPE: ☐ Acknowledgment ☐ Jurat ☐ Copy Certification ☐ Oath/Affirmation ☐ Oath of Office ☐ Proof of Execution ☐ Protest ☐ Other

DOCUMENT
DOC TYPE: ☐ Deed ☐ DOT ☐ Trust ☐ POA ☐ POAH ☐ Agreement ☐ Affidavit ☐ Other
- Deed: Grant • Trust Transfer • Gift • Interspousal • Quitclaim • ToD • Warranty
- DOT: Mortgage • Rev / Irrev • Am / Rest
- Trust: Certification
- POA: General / Limited • Durable / Springing
- POAH: AHCD • Living Will
- Agreement: Compliance-E&O • Correction
- Affidavit: Borrower • Occupancy • Ownership • Refi • Survey • Debts & Liens • Name-Signature-ID • Marital • Death • Will
- Other: Vehicle Title • Safe Deposit Box

DOC DATE: J F M A M J J A S O N D , ____ DOC TITLE or TYPE: _____ # OF PAGES: __ ☐ Inspect/Copy Request Entry X-Ref #: __

☐ **SATISFACTORY EVIDENCE** ☐ Driver's License / Passport / State ID / Military / Government / Tribal / Inmate / Other ID *or* ☐ Credible Witness(es)

SIGNER
- SIGNER's NAME: ____ ☐ For ADDRESS: ____ ☐ Non-Public ☐ Capacity ☐ Voluntary ☐ Proper ID ISSUED #: ____ SIGNATURE ☐ (oath / affirmation, if any) ☐ (by Mark)
- PHONE C / H / W / ____ *or* ☐ MISC AGENCY ☐ CA DMV ☐ US State Dept EXPIRES ____ ➤

CW #1
- #1 WITNESS's NAME: ____ ☐ P/Known ADDRESS: ____ ☐ Non-Public ☐ Driver's License ☐ Passport ☐ Other ID ISSUED #: ____ SIGNATURE ☐ (after oath / affirmation)
- PHONE C / H / W / ____ *or* ☐ MISC AGENCY ☐ CA DMV ☐ US State Dept EXPIRES ____ ❶

CW #2
- #2 WITNESS's NAME: ____ ☐ P/Known ADDRESS: ____ ☐ Non-Public ☐ Driver's License ☐ Passport ☐ Other ID ISSUED #: ____ SIGNATURE ☐ (after oath / affirmation)
- PHONE C / H / W / ____ *or* ☐ MISC AGENCY ☐ CA DMV ☐ US State Dept EXPIRES ____ ❷

Fingerprint: R T I M R P L

NOTARY NAME (printed): _____ COMMISSION #: _____

Entry 201

SERVICE													

SERVICE

DATE ___ - ___ -20___ TIME ___:___ ☐ am ☐ pm ADDRESS _____ ☐ Signer's ☐ Office NOTES _____ ☐ Stop MILES ___ Notary ☐ Adv. Travel ☐ Rush ☐ Copy ☐ Other TOTAL FEES
$___ $___ $___ $___ $___ $___

201

DOCUMENT

TYPE ☐ Acknowledgment ☐ Jurat ☐ Copy Certification ☐ Oath/Affirmation ☐ Oath of Office ☐ Proof of Execution ☐ Protest ☐ Other

R	Fingerprint
T	
I	
M	
R	
P	
L	

DOC TYPE ☐ Deed ☐ DOT ☐ Trust ☐ POA ☐ POAH ☐ Agreement ☐ Affidavit ☐ Other
Grant • Trust Transfer • Gift / Mortgage / Certification / General / Limited / AHCD / Compliance-E&O / Borrower • Occupancy • Ownership • Refi • Survey / Vehicle Title
Interspousal • Quitclaim • ToD • Warranty / Rev / Irrev • Am / Rest / Durable / Springing / Living Will / Correction / Debts & Liens • Name-Signature-ID • Marital • Death • Will / Safe Deposit Box

DOC DATE J F M A M J J A S O N D , _____ DOC TITLE or TYPE _____ # OF PAGES ___ ☐ Inspect/Copy Request Entry X-Ref # ___

☐ **SATISFACTORY EVIDENCE** ☐ Driver's License / Passport / State ID / Military / Government / Tribal / Inmate / Other ID or ☐ Credible Witness(es)

SIGNER

SIGNER's NAME _____ ☐ For ADDRESS _____ ☐ Non-Public ☐ Capacity ☐ Voluntary ☐ Proper ID ISSUED #___ SIGNATURE ☐ (oath / affirmation, if any) ☐ (by Mark)
PHONE C / H / W _____ or ☐ MISC AGENCY ☐ CA DMV ☐ US State Dept EXPIRES ➡

CW #1

#1 WITNESS's NAME _____ ☐ P/Known ADDRESS _____ ☐ Non-Public ☐ Driver's License ☐ Passport ☐ Other ID ISSUED #___ SIGNATURE ☐ (after oath / affirmation)
PHONE C / H / W _____ or ☐ MISC AGENCY ☐ CA DMV ☐ US State Dept EXPIRES ❶

CW #2

#2 WITNESS's NAME _____ ☐ P/Known ADDRESS _____ ☐ Non-Public ☐ Driver's License ☐ Passport ☐ Other ID ISSUED #___ SIGNATURE ☐ (after oath / affirmation)
PHONE C / H / W _____ or ☐ MISC AGENCY ☐ CA DMV ☐ US State Dept EXPIRES ❷

Entry 202

SERVICE

DATE ___ - ___ -20___ TIME ___:___ ☐ am ☐ pm ADDRESS _____ ☐ Signer's ☐ Office NOTES _____ ☐ Stop MILES ___ Notary ☐ Adv. Travel ☐ Rush ☐ Copy ☐ Other TOTAL FEES
$___ $___ $___ $___ $___ $___

202

DOCUMENT

TYPE ☐ Acknowledgment ☐ Jurat ☐ Copy Certification ☐ Oath/Affirmation ☐ Oath of Office ☐ Proof of Execution ☐ Protest ☐ Other

R	Fingerprint
T	
I	
M	
R	
P	
L	

DOC TYPE ☐ Deed ☐ DOT ☐ Trust ☐ POA ☐ POAH ☐ Agreement ☐ Affidavit ☐ Other
Grant • Trust Transfer • Gift / Mortgage / Certification / General / Limited / AHCD / Compliance-E&O / Borrower • Occupancy • Ownership • Refi • Survey / Vehicle Title
Interspousal • Quitclaim • ToD • Warranty / Rev / Irrev • Am / Rest / Durable / Springing / Living Will / Correction / Debts & Liens • Name-Signature-ID • Marital • Death • Will / Safe Deposit Box

DOC DATE J F M A M J J A S O N D , _____ DOC TITLE or TYPE _____ # OF PAGES ___ ☐ Inspect/Copy Request Entry X-Ref # ___

☐ **SATISFACTORY EVIDENCE** ☐ Driver's License / Passport / State ID / Military / Government / Tribal / Inmate / Other ID or ☐ Credible Witness(es)

SIGNER

SIGNER's NAME _____ ☐ For ADDRESS _____ ☐ Non-Public ☐ Capacity ☐ Voluntary ☐ Proper ID ISSUED #___ SIGNATURE ☐ (oath / affirmation, if any) ☐ (by Mark)
PHONE C / H / W _____ or ☐ MISC AGENCY ☐ CA DMV ☐ US State Dept EXPIRES ➡

CW #1

#1 WITNESS's NAME _____ ☐ P/Known ADDRESS _____ ☐ Non-Public ☐ Driver's License ☐ Passport ☐ Other ID ISSUED #___ SIGNATURE ☐ (after oath / affirmation)
PHONE C / H / W _____ or ☐ MISC AGENCY ☐ CA DMV ☐ US State Dept EXPIRES ❶

CW #2

#2 WITNESS's NAME _____ ☐ P/Known ADDRESS _____ ☐ Non-Public ☐ Driver's License ☐ Passport ☐ Other ID ISSUED #___ SIGNATURE ☐ (after oath / affirmation)
PHONE C / H / W _____ or ☐ MISC AGENCY ☐ CA DMV ☐ US State Dept EXPIRES ❷

NOTARY NAME (printed): COMMISSION #:

Entry 203

SERVICE — DATE: - -20 | TIME: : am/pm | ADDRESS | ☐ Signer's ☐ Office | NOTES | ☐ Stop | MILES | Notary $ | ☐ Adv. Travel $ | ☐ Rush $ | ☐ Copy $ | ☐ Other $ | TOTAL FEES $

TYPE: ☐ Acknowledgment ☐ Jurat ☐ Copy Certification ☐ Oath/Affirmation ☐ Oath of Office ☐ Proof of Execution ☐ Protest ☐ Other

Fingerprint R T I M R P L

DOCUMENT
DOC TYPE: ☐ Deed | ☐ DOT | ☐ Trust | ☐ POA | ☐ POAH | ☐ Agreement | ☐ Affidavit | ☐ Other
Grant • Trust Transfer • Gift | Mortgage | Certification | General / Limited | AHCD | Compliance-E&O | Borrower • Occupancy • Ownership • Refi • Survey | Vehicle Title
Interspousal • Quitclaim • ToD • Warranty | Rev / Irrev • Am / Rest | Durable / Springing | Living Will | Correction | Debts & Liens • Name-Signature-ID • Marital • Death • Will | Safe Deposit Box

DOC DATE: J F M A M J / J A S O N D , | DOC TITLE or TYPE | # OF PAGES | ☐ Inspect/Copy Request | Entry X-Ref #

☐ **SATISFACTORY EVIDENCE** ☐ Driver's License / Passport / State ID / Military / Government / Tribal / Inmate / Other ID *or* ☐ Credible Witness(es)

SIGNER
SIGNER's NAME | ☐ For | ADDRESS | ☐ Non-Public | ☐ Capacity # | ☐ Voluntary | ☐ Proper ID | ISSUED | SIGNATURE | ☐ (oath / affirmation, if any) | ☐ (by Mark)
PHONE C / H / W / | *or* ☐ MISC | | | AGENCY | ☐ CA DMV | ☐ US State Dept | EXPIRES | ➡

CW #1
#1 WITNESS's NAME | ☐ P/Known | ADDRESS | ☐ Non-Public | ☐ Driver's License ☐ Passport ☐ Other ID # | ISSUED | SIGNATURE | ☐ (after oath / affirmation)
PHONE C / H / W / | *or* ☐ MISC | | | AGENCY ☐ CA DMV ☐ US State Dept | EXPIRES | ❶

CW #2
#2 WITNESS's NAME | ☐ P/Known | ADDRESS | ☐ Non-Public | ☐ Driver's License ☐ Passport ☐ Other ID # | ISSUED | SIGNATURE | ☐ (after oath / affirmation)
PHONE C / H / W / | *or* ☐ MISC | | | AGENCY ☐ CA DMV ☐ US State Dept | EXPIRES | ❷

Entry 204

SERVICE — DATE: - -20 | TIME: : am/pm | ADDRESS | ☐ Signer's ☐ Office | NOTES | ☐ Stop | MILES | Notary $ | ☐ Adv. Travel $ | ☐ Rush $ | ☐ Copy $ | ☐ Other $ | TOTAL FEES $

TYPE: ☐ Acknowledgment ☐ Jurat ☐ Copy Certification ☐ Oath/Affirmation ☐ Oath of Office ☐ Proof of Execution ☐ Protest ☐ Other

Fingerprint R T I M R P L

DOCUMENT
DOC TYPE: ☐ Deed | ☐ DOT | ☐ Trust | ☐ POA | ☐ POAH | ☐ Agreement | ☐ Affidavit | ☐ Other
Grant • Trust Transfer • Gift | Mortgage | Certification | General / Limited | AHCD | Compliance-E&O | Borrower • Occupancy • Ownership • Refi • Survey | Vehicle Title
Interspousal • Quitclaim • ToD • Warranty | Rev / Irrev • Am / Rest | Durable / Springing | Living Will | Correction | Debts & Liens • Name-Signature-ID • Marital • Death • Will | Safe Deposit Box

DOC DATE: J F M A M J / J A S O N D , | DOC TITLE or TYPE | # OF PAGES | ☐ Inspect/Copy Request | Entry X-Ref #

☐ **SATISFACTORY EVIDENCE** ☐ Driver's License / Passport / State ID / Military / Government / Tribal / Inmate / Other ID *or* ☐ Credible Witness(es)

SIGNER
SIGNER's NAME | ☐ For | ADDRESS | ☐ Non-Public | ☐ Capacity # | ☐ Voluntary | ☐ Proper ID | ISSUED | SIGNATURE | ☐ (oath / affirmation, if any) | ☐ (by Mark)
PHONE C / H / W / | *or* ☐ MISC | | | AGENCY ☐ CA DMV ☐ US State Dept | EXPIRES | ➡

CW #1
#1 WITNESS's NAME | ☐ P/Known | ADDRESS | ☐ Non-Public | ☐ Driver's License ☐ Passport ☐ Other ID # | ISSUED | SIGNATURE | ☐ (after oath / affirmation)
PHONE C / H / W / | *or* ☐ MISC | | | AGENCY ☐ CA DMV ☐ US State Dept | EXPIRES | ❶

CW #2
#2 WITNESS's NAME | ☐ P/Known | ADDRESS | ☐ Non-Public | ☐ Driver's License ☐ Passport ☐ Other ID # | ISSUED | SIGNATURE | ☐ (after oath / affirmation)
PHONE C / H / W / | *or* ☐ MISC | | | AGENCY ☐ CA DMV ☐ US State Dept | EXPIRES | ❷

NOTARY NAME (printed):   COMMISSION #:

205

SERVICE

DATE	TIME	am	ADDRESS	☐ Signer's	☐ Office	NOTES	☐ Stop	MILES	Notary	☐ Adv. Travel	☐ Rush	☐ Copy	☐ Other	TOTAL FEES
- -20	:	pm						$	$	$		$	$	$ $

TYPE ☐ Acknowledgment ☐ Jurat ☐ Copy Certification ☐ Oath/Affirmation ☐ Oath of Office ☐ Proof of Execution ☐ Protest ☐ Other

R	**Fingerprint**

DOCUMENT

DOC TYPE ☐ Deed ☐ DOT ☐ Trust ☐ POA ☐ POAH ☐ Agreement ☐ Affidavit ☐ Other

Grant • Trust Transfer • Gift   Mortgage   Certification   General / Limited   AHCD   Compliance-E&O   Borrower • Occupancy • Ownership • Refi • Survey   Vehicle Title

Interspousal • Quitclaim • ToD • Warranty   Rev / Irrev • Am / Rest   Durable / Springing   Living Will   Correction   Debts & Liens • Name-Signature-ID • Marital • Death • Will   Safe Deposit Box

DOC DATE	J F M A M J	DOC TITLE or TYPE	# OF PAGES	☐ Inspect/Copy Request	T I M R P
	J A S O N D ,			Entry X-Ref #	

☐ **SATISFACTORY EVIDENCE** ☐ Driver's License / Passport / State ID / Military / Government / Tribal / Inmate / Other ID **or** ☐ Credible Witness(es) | L |

SIGNER

SIGNER's NAME	☐ For	ADDRESS	☐ Non-Public	☐ Capacity	☐ Voluntary	☐ Proper ID	ISSUED	SIGNATURE	☐ (oath / affirmation, if any)	☐ (by Mark)
				#						
PHONE C / H / W	**or** ☐ MISC			AGENCY	☐ CA DMV	☐ US State Dept	EXPIRES	➡		
/										

CW #1

#1 WITNESS's NAME	☐ P/Known	ADDRESS	☐ Non-Public	☐ Driver's License	☐ Passport	☐ Other ID	ISSUED	SIGNATURE	☐ (after oath / affirmation)
				#					
PHONE C / H / W	**or** ☐ MISC			AGENCY	☐ CA DMV	☐ US State Dept	EXPIRES	❶	
/									

CW #2

#2 WITNESS's NAME	☐ P/Known	ADDRESS	☐ Non-Public	☐ Driver's License	☐ Passport	☐ Other ID	ISSUED	SIGNATURE	☐ (after oath / affirmation)
				#					
PHONE C / H / W	**or** ☐ MISC			AGENCY	☐ CA DMV	☐ US State Dept	EXPIRES	❷	
/									

206

SERVICE

DATE	TIME	am	ADDRESS	☐ Signer's	☐ Office	NOTES	☐ Stop	MILES	Notary	☐ Adv. Travel	☐ Rush	☐ Copy	☐ Other	TOTAL FEES
- -20	:	pm						$	$	$		$	$	$ $

TYPE ☐ Acknowledgment ☐ Jurat ☐ Copy Certification ☐ Oath/Affirmation ☐ Oath of Office ☐ Proof of Execution ☐ Protest ☐ Other

R	**Fingerprint**

DOCUMENT

DOC TYPE ☐ Deed ☐ DOT ☐ Trust ☐ POA ☐ POAH ☐ Agreement ☐ Affidavit ☐ Other

Grant • Trust Transfer • Gift   Mortgage   Certification   General / Limited   AHCD   Compliance-E&O   Borrower • Occupancy • Ownership • Refi • Survey   Vehicle Title

Interspousal • Quitclaim • ToD • Warranty   Rev / Irrev • Am / Rest   Durable / Springing   Living Will   Correction   Debts & Liens • Name-Signature-ID • Marital • Death • Will   Safe Deposit Box

DOC DATE	J F M A M J	DOC TITLE or TYPE	# OF PAGES	☐ Inspect/Copy Request	T I M R P
	J A S O N D ,			Entry X-Ref #	

☐ **SATISFACTORY EVIDENCE** ☐ Driver's License / Passport / State ID / Military / Government / Tribal / Inmate / Other ID **or** ☐ Credible Witness(es) | L |

SIGNER

SIGNER's NAME	☐ For	ADDRESS	☐ Non-Public	☐ Capacity	☐ Voluntary	☐ Proper ID	ISSUED	SIGNATURE	☐ (oath / affirmation, if any)	☐ (by Mark)
				#						
PHONE C / H / W	**or** ☐ MISC			AGENCY	☐ CA DMV	☐ US State Dept	EXPIRES	➡		
/										

CW #1

#1 WITNESS's NAME	☐ P/Known	ADDRESS	☐ Non-Public	☐ Driver's License	☐ Passport	☐ Other ID	ISSUED	SIGNATURE	☐ (after oath / affirmation)
				#					
PHONE C / H / W	**or** ☐ MISC			AGENCY	☐ CA DMV	☐ US State Dept	EXPIRES	❶	
/									

CW #2

#2 WITNESS's NAME	☐ P/Known	ADDRESS	☐ Non-Public	☐ Driver's License	☐ Passport	☐ Other ID	ISSUED	SIGNATURE	☐ (after oath / affirmation)
				#					
PHONE C / H / W	**or** ☐ MISC			AGENCY	☐ CA DMV	☐ US State Dept	EXPIRES	❷	
/									

NOTARY NAME (printed):   COMMISSION #:

Entry 207

SERVICE — DATE: - -20 | TIME: : am/pm | ADDRESS | ☐ Signer's ☐ Office | NOTES | ☐ Stop | MILES | Notary $ | ☐ Adv. Travel $ | ☐ Rush $ | ☐ Copy $ | ☐ Other $ | TOTAL FEES $

TYPE: ☐ Acknowledgment ☐ Jurat ☐ Copy Certification ☐ Oath/Affirmation ☐ Oath of Office ☐ Proof of Execution ☐ Protest ☐ Other   R T I M R P L   **Fingerprint**

DOCUMENT — DOC TYPE: ☐ Deed (Grant • Trust Transfer • Gift • Interspousal • Quitclaim • ToD • Warranty) ☐ DOT (Mortgage • Rev / Irrev • Am / Rest) ☐ Trust (Certification) ☐ POA (General / Limited • Durable / Springing) ☐ POAH (AHCD • Living Will) ☐ Agreement (Compliance-E&O • Correction) ☐ Affidavit (Borrower • Occupancy • Ownership • Refi • Survey • Debts & Liens • Name-Signature-ID • Marital • Death • Will) ☐ Other (Vehicle Title • Safe Deposit Box)

DOC DATE: J F M A M J J A S O N D ,   DOC TITLE or TYPE   # OF PAGES   ☐ Inspect/Copy Request   Entry X-Ref #

☐ **SATISFACTORY EVIDENCE** ☐ Driver's License / Passport / State ID / Military / Government / Tribal / Inmate / Other ID **or** ☐ Credible Witness(es)

SIGNER — SIGNER's NAME | ☐ For | ADDRESS | ☐ Non-Public | ☐ Capacity # | ☐ Voluntary | ☐ Proper ID | ISSUED | SIGNATURE ☐ (oath / affirmation, if any) ☐ (by Mark)
PHONE C / H / W / | or ☐ MISC | | | AGENCY | ☐ CA DMV | ☐ US State Dept | EXPIRES | ➡

CW #1 — #1 WITNESS's NAME | ☐ P/Known | ADDRESS | ☐ Non-Public | ☐ Driver's License ☐ Passport ☐ Other ID # | ISSUED | SIGNATURE ☐ (after oath / affirmation)
PHONE C / H / W / | or ☐ MISC | | | AGENCY | ☐ CA DMV | ☐ US State Dept | EXPIRES | ❶

CW #2 — #2 WITNESS's NAME | ☐ P/Known | ADDRESS | ☐ Non-Public | ☐ Driver's License ☐ Passport ☐ Other ID # | ISSUED | SIGNATURE ☐ (after oath / affirmation)
PHONE C / H / W / | or ☐ MISC | | | AGENCY | ☐ CA DMV | ☐ US State Dept | EXPIRES | ❷

Entry 208

SERVICE — DATE: - -20 | TIME: : am/pm | ADDRESS | ☐ Signer's ☐ Office | NOTES | ☐ Stop | MILES | Notary $ | ☐ Adv. Travel $ | ☐ Rush $ | ☐ Copy $ | ☐ Other $ | TOTAL FEES $

TYPE: ☐ Acknowledgment ☐ Jurat ☐ Copy Certification ☐ Oath/Affirmation ☐ Oath of Office ☐ Proof of Execution ☐ Protest ☐ Other   R T I M R P L   **Fingerprint**

DOCUMENT — DOC TYPE: ☐ Deed (Grant • Trust Transfer • Gift • Interspousal • Quitclaim • ToD • Warranty) ☐ DOT (Mortgage • Rev / Irrev • Am / Rest) ☐ Trust (Certification) ☐ POA (General / Limited • Durable / Springing) ☐ POAH (AHCD • Living Will) ☐ Agreement (Compliance-E&O • Correction) ☐ Affidavit (Borrower • Occupancy • Ownership • Refi • Survey • Debts & Liens • Name-Signature-ID • Marital • Death • Will) ☐ Other (Vehicle Title • Safe Deposit Box)

DOC DATE: J F M A M J J A S O N D ,   DOC TITLE or TYPE   # OF PAGES   ☐ Inspect/Copy Request   Entry X-Ref #

☐ **SATISFACTORY EVIDENCE** ☐ Driver's License / Passport / State ID / Military / Government / Tribal / Inmate / Other ID **or** ☐ Credible Witness(es)

SIGNER — SIGNER's NAME | ☐ For | ADDRESS | ☐ Non-Public | ☐ Capacity # | ☐ Voluntary | ☐ Proper ID | ISSUED | SIGNATURE ☐ (oath / affirmation, if any) ☐ (by Mark)
PHONE C / H / W / | or ☐ MISC | | | AGENCY | ☐ CA DMV | ☐ US State Dept | EXPIRES | ➡

CW #1 — #1 WITNESS's NAME | ☐ P/Known | ADDRESS | ☐ Non-Public | ☐ Driver's License ☐ Passport ☐ Other ID # | ISSUED | SIGNATURE ☐ (after oath / affirmation)
PHONE C / H / W / | or ☐ MISC | | | AGENCY | ☐ CA DMV | ☐ US State Dept | EXPIRES | ❶

CW #2 — #2 WITNESS's NAME | ☐ P/Known | ADDRESS | ☐ Non-Public | ☐ Driver's License ☐ Passport ☐ Other ID # | ISSUED | SIGNATURE ☐ (after oath / affirmation)
PHONE C / H / W / | or ☐ MISC | | | AGENCY | ☐ CA DMV | ☐ US State Dept | EXPIRES | ❷

NOTARY NAME (printed): COMMISSION #:

Entry 209

SERVICE												

DATE - -20 **TIME** : am pm **ADDRESS** ☐ Signer's ☐ Office **NOTES** ☐ Stop **MILES** **Notary** ☐ Adv. Travel ☐ Rush ☐ Copy ☐ Other **TOTAL FEES** $ $ $ $ $ $ **209**

TYPE ☐ Acknowledgment ☐ Jurat ☐ Copy Certification ☐ Oath/Affirmation ☐ Oath of Office ☐ Proof of Execution ☐ Protest ☐ Other

R T I M R P L **Fingerprint**

DOCUMENT

DOC TYPE ☐ Deed ☐ DOT ☐ Trust ☐ POA ☐ POAH ☐ Agreement ☐ Affidavit ☐ Other
Grant • Trust Transfer • Gift / Mortgage / Certification / General / Limited / AHCD / Compliance-E&O / Borrower • Occupancy • Ownership • Refi • Survey / Vehicle Title
Interspousal • Quitclaim • ToD • Warranty / Rev / Irrev • Am / Rest / Durable / Springing / Living Will / Correction / Debts & Liens • Name-Signature-ID • Marital • Death • Will / Safe Deposit Box

DOC DATE J F M A M J J A S O N D , **DOC TITLE or TYPE** **# OF PAGES** ☐ Inspect/Copy Request / Entry X-Ref #

☐ **SATISFACTORY EVIDENCE** ☐ Driver's License / Passport / State ID / Military / Government / Tribal / Inmate / Other ID *or* ☐ Credible Witness(es)

SIGNER

SIGNER's NAME ☐ For **ADDRESS** ☐ Non-Public ☐ Capacity ☐ Voluntary ☐ Proper ID **ISSUED** **#** **SIGNATURE** ☐ (oath / affirmation, if any) ☐ (by Mark)

PHONE C / H / W *or* ☐ MISC / **AGENCY** ☐ CA DMV ☐ US State Dept **EXPIRES** ➡

CW #1

#1 WITNESS's NAME ☐ P/Known **ADDRESS** ☐ Non-Public ☐ Driver's License ☐ Passport ☐ Other ID **ISSUED** **#** **SIGNATURE** ☐ (after oath / affirmation)

PHONE C / H / W *or* ☐ MISC / **AGENCY** ☐ CA DMV ☐ US State Dept **EXPIRES** ❶

CW #2

#2 WITNESS's NAME ☐ P/Known **ADDRESS** ☐ Non-Public ☐ Driver's License ☐ Passport ☐ Other ID **ISSUED** **#** **SIGNATURE** ☐ (after oath / affirmation)

PHONE C / H / W *or* ☐ MISC / **AGENCY** ☐ CA DMV ☐ US State Dept **EXPIRES** ❷

Entry 210

DATE - -20 **TIME** : am pm **ADDRESS** ☐ Signer's ☐ Office **NOTES** ☐ Stop **MILES** **Notary** ☐ Adv. Travel ☐ Rush ☐ Copy ☐ Other **TOTAL FEES** $ $ $ $ $ $ **210**

TYPE ☐ Acknowledgment ☐ Jurat ☐ Copy Certification ☐ Oath/Affirmation ☐ Oath of Office ☐ Proof of Execution ☐ Protest ☐ Other

R T I M R P L **Fingerprint**

DOC TYPE ☐ Deed ☐ DOT ☐ Trust ☐ POA ☐ POAH ☐ Agreement ☐ Affidavit ☐ Other
Grant • Trust Transfer • Gift / Mortgage / Certification / General / Limited / AHCD / Compliance-E&O / Borrower • Occupancy • Ownership • Refi • Survey / Vehicle Title
Interspousal • Quitclaim • ToD • Warranty / Rev / Irrev • Am / Rest / Durable / Springing / Living Will / Correction / Debts & Liens • Name-Signature-ID • Marital • Death • Will / Safe Deposit Box

DOC DATE J F M A M J J A S O N D , **DOC TITLE or TYPE** **# OF PAGES** ☐ Inspect/Copy Request / Entry X-Ref #

☐ **SATISFACTORY EVIDENCE** ☐ Driver's License / Passport / State ID / Military / Government / Tribal / Inmate / Other ID *or* ☐ Credible Witness(es)

SIGNER

SIGNER's NAME ☐ For **ADDRESS** ☐ Non-Public ☐ Capacity ☐ Voluntary ☐ Proper ID **ISSUED** **#** **SIGNATURE** ☐ (oath / affirmation, if any) ☐ (by Mark)

PHONE C / H / W *or* ☐ MISC / **AGENCY** ☐ CA DMV ☐ US State Dept **EXPIRES** ➡

CW #1

#1 WITNESS's NAME ☐ P/Known **ADDRESS** ☐ Non-Public ☐ Driver's License ☐ Passport ☐ Other ID **ISSUED** **#** **SIGNATURE** ☐ (after oath / affirmation)

PHONE C / H / W *or* ☐ MISC / **AGENCY** ☐ CA DMV ☐ US State Dept **EXPIRES** ❶

CW #2

#2 WITNESS's NAME ☐ P/Known **ADDRESS** ☐ Non-Public ☐ Driver's License ☐ Passport ☐ Other ID **ISSUED** **#** **SIGNATURE** ☐ (after oath / affirmation)

PHONE C / H / W *or* ☐ MISC / **AGENCY** ☐ CA DMV ☐ US State Dept **EXPIRES** ❷

NOTARY NAME (printed): COMMISSION #:

Entry 211

SERVICE — DATE: - -20   TIME: : am/pm   ADDRESS ☐ Signer's ☐ Office   NOTES ☐ Stop   MILES   Notary $ ☐ Adv. Travel $ ☐ Rush $ ☐ Copy $ ☐ Other $ TOTAL FEES $

TYPE: ☐ Acknowledgment ☐ Jurat ☐ Copy Certification ☐ Oath/Affirmation ☐ Oath of Office ☐ Proof of Execution ☐ Protest ☐ Other

Fingerprint — R T I M R P L

DOCUMENT — DOC TYPE:
- ☐ Deed — Grant • Trust Transfer • Gift • Interspousal • Quitclaim • ToD • Warranty
- ☐ DOT — Mortgage
- ☐ Trust — Certification • Rev / Irrev • Am / Rest
- ☐ POA — General / Limited • Durable / Springing
- ☐ POAH — AHCD • Living Will
- ☐ Agreement — Compliance-E&O • Correction
- ☐ Affidavit — Borrower • Occupancy • Ownership • Refi • Survey • Debts & Liens • Name-Signature-ID • Marital • Death • Will
- ☐ Other — Vehicle Title • Safe Deposit Box

DOC DATE: J F M A M J J A S O N D ,   DOC TITLE or TYPE   # OF PAGES   ☐ Inspect/Copy Request   Entry X-Ref #

☐ **SATISFACTORY EVIDENCE** ☐ Driver's License / Passport / State ID / Military / Government / Tribal / Inmate / Other ID *or* ☐ Credible Witness(es)

SIGNER — SIGNER's NAME ☐ For   ADDRESS ☐ Non-Public   # ☐ Capacity ☐ Voluntary ☐ Proper ID   ISSUED   SIGNATURE ☐ (oath / affirmation, if any) ☐ (by Mark)
PHONE C / H / W   /   or ☐ MISC   AGENCY ☐ CA DMV ☐ US State Dept   EXPIRES   ➡

CW #1 — #1 WITNESS's NAME ☐ P/Known   ADDRESS ☐ Non-Public ☐ Driver's License ☐ Passport ☐ Other ID   ISSUED   SIGNATURE ☐ (after oath / affirmation)
PHONE C / H / W   /   or ☐ MISC   AGENCY ☐ CA DMV ☐ US State Dept   EXPIRES   ❶

CW #2 — #2 WITNESS's NAME ☐ P/Known   ADDRESS ☐ Non-Public ☐ Driver's License ☐ Passport ☐ Other ID   ISSUED   SIGNATURE ☐ (after oath / affirmation)
PHONE C / H / W   /   or ☐ MISC   AGENCY ☐ CA DMV ☐ US State Dept   EXPIRES   ❷

Entry 212

SERVICE — DATE: - -20   TIME: : am/pm   ADDRESS ☐ Signer's ☐ Office   NOTES ☐ Stop   MILES   Notary $ ☐ Adv. Travel $ ☐ Rush $ ☐ Copy $ ☐ Other $ TOTAL FEES $

TYPE: ☐ Acknowledgment ☐ Jurat ☐ Copy Certification ☐ Oath/Affirmation ☐ Oath of Office ☐ Proof of Execution ☐ Protest ☐ Other

Fingerprint — R T I M R P L

DOCUMENT — DOC TYPE:
- ☐ Deed — Grant • Trust Transfer • Gift • Interspousal • Quitclaim • ToD • Warranty
- ☐ DOT — Mortgage
- ☐ Trust — Certification • Rev / Irrev • Am / Rest
- ☐ POA — General / Limited • Durable / Springing
- ☐ POAH — AHCD • Living Will
- ☐ Agreement — Compliance-E&O • Correction
- ☐ Affidavit — Borrower • Occupancy • Ownership • Refi • Survey • Debts & Liens • Name-Signature-ID • Marital • Death • Will
- ☐ Other — Vehicle Title • Safe Deposit Box

DOC DATE: J F M A M J J A S O N D ,   DOC TITLE or TYPE   # OF PAGES   ☐ Inspect/Copy Request   Entry X-Ref #

☐ **SATISFACTORY EVIDENCE** ☐ Driver's License / Passport / State ID / Military / Government / Tribal / Inmate / Other ID *or* ☐ Credible Witness(es)

SIGNER — SIGNER's NAME ☐ For   ADDRESS ☐ Non-Public   # ☐ Capacity ☐ Voluntary ☐ Proper ID   ISSUED   SIGNATURE ☐ (oath / affirmation, if any) ☐ (by Mark)
PHONE C / H / W   /   or ☐ MISC   AGENCY ☐ CA DMV ☐ US State Dept   EXPIRES   ➡

CW #1 — #1 WITNESS's NAME ☐ P/Known   ADDRESS ☐ Non-Public ☐ Driver's License ☐ Passport ☐ Other ID   ISSUED   SIGNATURE ☐ (after oath / affirmation)
PHONE C / H / W   /   or ☐ MISC   AGENCY ☐ CA DMV ☐ US State Dept   EXPIRES   ❶

CW #2 — #2 WITNESS's NAME ☐ P/Known   ADDRESS ☐ Non-Public ☐ Driver's License ☐ Passport ☐ Other ID   ISSUED   SIGNATURE ☐ (after oath / affirmation)
PHONE C / H / W   /   or ☐ MISC   AGENCY ☐ CA DMV ☐ US State Dept   EXPIRES   ❷

NOTARY NAME (printed): _____ COMMISSION #: _____

Entry 213

SERVICE	DATE __ – __ -20__	TIME __ : __ ☐ am ☐ pm	ADDRESS ☐ Signer's ☐ Office	NOTES	☐ Stop	MILES	Notary	☐ Adv. Travel	☐ Rush	☐ Copy	☐ Other	TOTAL FEES	**213**
							$	$	$	$	$	$	

TYPE ☐ Acknowledgment ☐ Jurat ☐ Copy Certification ☐ Oath/Affirmation ☐ Oath of Office ☐ Proof of Execution ☐ Protest ☐ Other

R	**Fingerprint**
T	
I	
M	
R	
P	
L	

DOCUMENT

DOC TYPE ☐ Deed ☐ DOT ☐ Trust ☐ POA ☐ POAH ☐ Agreement ☐ Affidavit ☐ Other
Grant • Trust Transfer • Gift Mortgage Certification General / Limited AHCD Compliance-E&O Borrower • Occupancy • Ownership • Refi • Survey Vehicle Title
Interspousal • Quitclaim • ToD • Warranty Rev / Irrev • Am / Rest Durable / Springing Living Will Correction Debts & Liens • Name-Signature-ID • Marital • Death • Will Safe Deposit Box

DOC DATE J F M A M J J A S O N D , ____ DOC TITLE or TYPE ____ # OF PAGES ____ ☐ Inspect/Copy Request   Entry X-Ref # ____

☐ **SATISFACTORY EVIDENCE** ☐ Driver's License / Passport / State ID / Military / Government / Tribal / Inmate / Other ID *or* ☐ Credible Witness(es)

SIGNER

SIGNER's NAME	☐ For	ADDRESS	☐ Non-Public	☐ Capacity	☐ Voluntary	☐ Proper ID	ISSUED	SIGNATURE	☐ (oath / affirmation, if any)	☐ (by Mark)
				#						
PHONE C / H / W *or* ☐ MISC				AGENCY	☐ CA DMV	☐ US State Dept	EXPIRES	➡		

CW #1

#1 WITNESS's NAME	☐ P/Known	ADDRESS	☐ Non-Public	☐ Driver's License	☐ Passport	☐ Other ID	ISSUED	SIGNATURE	☐ (after oath / affirmation)
				#					
PHONE C / H / W *or* ☐ MISC				AGENCY	☐ CA DMV	☐ US State Dept	EXPIRES	❶	

CW #2

#2 WITNESS's NAME	☐ P/Known	ADDRESS	☐ Non-Public	☐ Driver's License	☐ Passport	☐ Other ID	ISSUED	SIGNATURE	☐ (after oath / affirmation)
				#					
PHONE C / H / W *or* ☐ MISC				AGENCY	☐ CA DMV	☐ US State Dept	EXPIRES	❷	

Entry 214

SERVICE	DATE __ – __ -20__	TIME __ : __ ☐ am ☐ pm	ADDRESS ☐ Signer's ☐ Office	NOTES	☐ Stop	MILES	Notary	☐ Adv. Travel	☐ Rush	☐ Copy	☐ Other	TOTAL FEES	**214**
							$	$	$	$	$	$	

TYPE ☐ Acknowledgment ☐ Jurat ☐ Copy Certification ☐ Oath/Affirmation ☐ Oath of Office ☐ Proof of Execution ☐ Protest ☐ Other

R	**Fingerprint**
T	
I	
M	
R	
P	
L	

DOCUMENT

DOC TYPE ☐ Deed ☐ DOT ☐ Trust ☐ POA ☐ POAH ☐ Agreement ☐ Affidavit ☐ Other
Grant • Trust Transfer • Gift Mortgage Certification General / Limited AHCD Compliance-E&O Borrower • Occupancy • Ownership • Refi • Survey Vehicle Title
Interspousal • Quitclaim • ToD • Warranty Rev / Irrev • Am / Rest Durable / Springing Living Will Correction Debts & Liens • Name-Signature-ID • Marital • Death • Will Safe Deposit Box

DOC DATE J F M A M J J A S O N D , ____ DOC TITLE or TYPE ____ # OF PAGES ____ ☐ Inspect/Copy Request   Entry X-Ref # ____

☐ **SATISFACTORY EVIDENCE** ☐ Driver's License / Passport / State ID / Military / Government / Tribal / Inmate / Other ID *or* ☐ Credible Witness(es)

SIGNER

SIGNER's NAME	☐ For	ADDRESS	☐ Non-Public	☐ Capacity	☐ Voluntary	☐ Proper ID	ISSUED	SIGNATURE	☐ (oath / affirmation, if any)	☐ (by Mark)
				#						
PHONE C / H / W *or* ☐ MISC				AGENCY	☐ CA DMV	☐ US State Dept	EXPIRES	➡		

CW #1

#1 WITNESS's NAME	☐ P/Known	ADDRESS	☐ Non-Public	☐ Driver's License	☐ Passport	☐ Other ID	ISSUED	SIGNATURE	☐ (after oath / affirmation)
				#					
PHONE C / H / W *or* ☐ MISC				AGENCY	☐ CA DMV	☐ US State Dept	EXPIRES	❶	

CW #2

#2 WITNESS's NAME	☐ P/Known	ADDRESS	☐ Non-Public	☐ Driver's License	☐ Passport	☐ Other ID	ISSUED	SIGNATURE	☐ (after oath / affirmation)
				#					
PHONE C / H / W *or* ☐ MISC				AGENCY	☐ CA DMV	☐ US State Dept	EXPIRES	❷	

NOTARY NAME (printed):   COMMISSION #:

Entry 215

SERVICE — DATE: - -20   TIME: : am/pm   ADDRESS ☐ Signer's ☐ Office   NOTES   ☐ Stop   MILES   Notary $ ☐ Adv. Travel $ ☐ Rush $ ☐ Copy $ ☐ Other $ TOTAL FEES $

TYPE: ☐ Acknowledgment ☐ Jurat ☐ Copy Certification ☐ Oath/Affirmation ☐ Oath of Office ☐ Proof of Execution ☐ Protest ☐ Other

DOCUMENT — DOC TYPE: ☐ Deed (Grant • Trust Transfer • Gift, Interspousal • Quitclaim • ToD • Warranty) ☐ DOT (Mortgage) ☐ Trust (Certification, Rev / Irrev • Am / Rest) ☐ POA (General / Limited, Durable / Springing) ☐ POAH (AHCD, Living Will) ☐ Agreement (Compliance-E&O, Correction) ☐ Affidavit (Borrower • Occupancy • Ownership • Refi • Survey, Debts & Liens • Name-Signature-ID • Marital • Death • Will) ☐ Other (Vehicle Title, Safe Deposit Box)

DOC DATE: J F M A M J / J A S O N D ,   DOC TITLE or TYPE   # OF PAGES   ☐ Inspect/Copy Request   Entry X-Ref #

Fingerprint: R T I M R P L

☐ **SATISFACTORY EVIDENCE** ☐ Driver's License / Passport / State ID / Military / Government / Tribal / Inmate / Other ID   *or*   ☐ Credible Witness(es)

SIGNER — SIGNER's NAME   ☐ For   ADDRESS   ☐ Non-Public ☐ Capacity ☐ Voluntary ☐ Proper ID   ISSUED #   SIGNATURE ☐ (oath / affirmation, if any) ☐ (by Mark)   PHONE C / H / W   *or* ☐ MISC   AGENCY ☐ CA DMV ☐ US State Dept   EXPIRES

CW #1 — #1 WITNESS's NAME ☐ P/Known   ADDRESS   ☐ Non-Public ☐ Driver's License ☐ Passport ☐ Other ID   ISSUED #   SIGNATURE ☐ (after oath / affirmation)   PHONE C / H / W   *or* ☐ MISC   AGENCY ☐ CA DMV ☐ US State Dept   EXPIRES ❶

CW #2 — #2 WITNESS's NAME ☐ P/Known   ADDRESS   ☐ Non-Public ☐ Driver's License ☐ Passport ☐ Other ID   ISSUED #   SIGNATURE ☐ (after oath / affirmation)   PHONE C / H / W   *or* ☐ MISC   AGENCY ☐ CA DMV ☐ US State Dept   EXPIRES ❷

Entry 216

SERVICE — DATE: - -20   TIME: : am/pm   ADDRESS ☐ Signer's ☐ Office   NOTES   ☐ Stop   MILES   Notary $ ☐ Adv. Travel $ ☐ Rush $ ☐ Copy $ ☐ Other $ TOTAL FEES $

TYPE: ☐ Acknowledgment ☐ Jurat ☐ Copy Certification ☐ Oath/Affirmation ☐ Oath of Office ☐ Proof of Execution ☐ Protest ☐ Other

DOCUMENT — DOC TYPE: ☐ Deed (Grant • Trust Transfer • Gift, Interspousal • Quitclaim • ToD • Warranty) ☐ DOT (Mortgage) ☐ Trust (Certification, Rev / Irrev • Am / Rest) ☐ POA (General / Limited, Durable / Springing) ☐ POAH (AHCD, Living Will) ☐ Agreement (Compliance-E&O, Correction) ☐ Affidavit (Borrower • Occupancy • Ownership • Refi • Survey, Debts & Liens • Name-Signature-ID • Marital • Death • Will) ☐ Other (Vehicle Title, Safe Deposit Box)

DOC DATE: J F M A M J / J A S O N D ,   DOC TITLE or TYPE   # OF PAGES   ☐ Inspect/Copy Request   Entry X-Ref #

Fingerprint: R T I M R P L

☐ **SATISFACTORY EVIDENCE** ☐ Driver's License / Passport / State ID / Military / Government / Tribal / Inmate / Other ID   *or*   ☐ Credible Witness(es)

SIGNER — SIGNER's NAME   ☐ For   ADDRESS   ☐ Non-Public ☐ Capacity ☐ Voluntary ☐ Proper ID   ISSUED #   SIGNATURE ☐ (oath / affirmation, if any) ☐ (by Mark)   PHONE C / H / W   *or* ☐ MISC   AGENCY ☐ CA DMV ☐ US State Dept   EXPIRES

CW #1 — #1 WITNESS's NAME ☐ P/Known   ADDRESS   ☐ Non-Public ☐ Driver's License ☐ Passport ☐ Other ID   ISSUED #   SIGNATURE ☐ (after oath / affirmation)   PHONE C / H / W   *or* ☐ MISC   AGENCY ☐ CA DMV ☐ US State Dept   EXPIRES ❶

CW #2 — #2 WITNESS's NAME ☐ P/Known   ADDRESS   ☐ Non-Public ☐ Driver's License ☐ Passport ☐ Other ID   ISSUED #   SIGNATURE ☐ (after oath / affirmation)   PHONE C / H / W   *or* ☐ MISC   AGENCY ☐ CA DMV ☐ US State Dept   EXPIRES ❷

NOTARY NAME (printed):   **COMMISSION #:**

Entry 217

| SERVICE | DATE - -20 | TIME : am pm | ADDRESS | ☐ Signer's ☐ Office | NOTES | ☐ Stop | MILES | Notary ☐ Adv. Travel ☐ Rush ☐ Copy ☐ Other TOTAL FEES $ $ $ $ $ $ | 217 |

| | TYPE ☐ Acknowledgment ☐ Jurat ☐ Copy Certification ☐ Oath/Affirmation ☐ Oath of Office ☐ Proof of Execution ☐ Protest ☐ Other | R | **Fingerprint** |

DOCUMENT

DOC TYPE	☐ Deed	☐ DOT	☐ Trust	☐ POA	☐ POAH	☐ Agreement		☐ Affidavit	☐ Other
	Grant • Trust Transfer • Gift	Mortgage	Certification	General / Limited	AHCD	Compliance-E&O	Borrower • Occupancy • Ownership • Refi • Survey		Vehicle Title
	Interspousal • Quitclaim • ToD • Warranty	Rev / Irrev • Am / Rest	Durable / Springing	Living Will		Correction	Debts & Liens • Name-Signature-ID • Marital • Death • Will		Safe Deposit Box

DOC DATE   J F M A M J   J A S O N D   ,   DOC TITLE or TYPE   # OF PAGES   ☐ Inspect/Copy Request   Entry X-Ref #

☐ **SATISFACTORY EVIDENCE** ☐ Driver's License / Passport / State ID / Military / Government / Tribal / Inmate / Other ID   *or*   ☐ Credible Witness(es)

SIGNER

| SIGNER's NAME | ☐ For | ADDRESS | ☐ Non-Public | ☐ Capacity ☐ Voluntary ☐ Proper ID # | ISSUED | SIGNATURE ☐ (oath / affirmation, if any) ☐ (by Mark) |
| PHONE C / H / W   *or* ☐ MISC   / | | | | AGENCY ☐ CA DMV ☐ US State Dept | EXPIRES | ➡ |

CW #1

| #1 WITNESS's NAME | ☐ P/Known | ADDRESS | ☐ Non-Public | ☐ Driver's License ☐ Passport ☐ Other ID # | ISSUED | SIGNATURE ☐ (after oath / affirmation) |
| PHONE C / H / W   *or* ☐ MISC   / | | | | AGENCY ☐ CA DMV ☐ US State Dept | EXPIRES | ❶ |

CW #2

| #2 WITNESS's NAME | ☐ P/Known | ADDRESS | ☐ Non-Public | ☐ Driver's License ☐ Passport ☐ Other ID # | ISSUED | SIGNATURE ☐ (after oath / affirmation) |
| PHONE C / H / W   *or* ☐ MISC   / | | | | AGENCY ☐ CA DMV ☐ US State Dept | EXPIRES | ❷ |

Entry 218

| SERVICE | DATE - -20 | TIME : am pm | ADDRESS | ☐ Signer's ☐ Office | NOTES | ☐ Stop | MILES | Notary ☐ Adv. Travel ☐ Rush ☐ Copy ☐ Other TOTAL FEES $ $ $ $ $ $ | 218 |

| | TYPE ☐ Acknowledgment ☐ Jurat ☐ Copy Certification ☐ Oath/Affirmation ☐ Oath of Office ☐ Proof of Execution ☐ Protest ☐ Other | R | **Fingerprint** |

DOCUMENT

DOC TYPE	☐ Deed	☐ DOT	☐ Trust	☐ POA	☐ POAH	☐ Agreement		☐ Affidavit	☐ Other
	Grant • Trust Transfer • Gift	Mortgage	Certification	General / Limited	AHCD	Compliance-E&O	Borrower • Occupancy • Ownership • Refi • Survey		Vehicle Title
	Interspousal • Quitclaim • ToD • Warranty	Rev / Irrev • Am / Rest	Durable / Springing	Living Will		Correction	Debts & Liens • Name-Signature-ID • Marital • Death • Will		Safe Deposit Box

DOC DATE   J F M A M J   J A S O N D   ,   DOC TITLE or TYPE   # OF PAGES   ☐ Inspect/Copy Request   Entry X-Ref #

☐ **SATISFACTORY EVIDENCE** ☐ Driver's License / Passport / State ID / Military / Government / Tribal / Inmate / Other ID   *or*   ☐ Credible Witness(es)

SIGNER

| SIGNER's NAME | ☐ For | ADDRESS | ☐ Non-Public | ☐ Capacity ☐ Voluntary ☐ Proper ID # | ISSUED | SIGNATURE ☐ (oath / affirmation, if any) ☐ (by Mark) |
| PHONE C / H / W   *or* ☐ MISC   / | | | | AGENCY ☐ CA DMV ☐ US State Dept | EXPIRES | ➡ |

CW #1

| #1 WITNESS's NAME | ☐ P/Known | ADDRESS | ☐ Non-Public | ☐ Driver's License ☐ Passport ☐ Other ID # | ISSUED | SIGNATURE ☐ (after oath / affirmation) |
| PHONE C / H / W   *or* ☐ MISC   / | | | | AGENCY ☐ CA DMV ☐ US State Dept | EXPIRES | ❶ |

CW #2

| #2 WITNESS's NAME | ☐ P/Known | ADDRESS | ☐ Non-Public | ☐ Driver's License ☐ Passport ☐ Other ID # | ISSUED | SIGNATURE ☐ (after oath / affirmation) |
| PHONE C / H / W   *or* ☐ MISC   / | | | | AGENCY ☐ CA DMV ☐ US State Dept | EXPIRES | ❷ |

NOTARY NAME (printed): COMMISSION #:

Entry 219

SERVICE — DATE: - -20 TIME: : am/pm ADDRESS ☐ Signer's ☐ Office NOTES ☐ Stop MILES Notary $ ☐ Adv. Travel $ ☐ Rush $ ☐ Copy $ ☐ Other $ TOTAL FEES $

TYPE: ☐ Acknowledgment ☐ Jurat ☐ Copy Certification ☐ Oath/Affirmation ☐ Oath of Office ☐ Proof of Execution ☐ Protest ☐ Other

Fingerprint — R T I M R P L

DOCUMENT
DOC TYPE: ☐ Deed (Grant • Trust Transfer • Gift • Interspousal • Quitclaim • ToD • Warranty) ☐ DOT (Mortgage) ☐ Trust (Certification • Rev/Irrev • Am/Rest) ☐ POA (General/Limited • Durable/Springing) ☐ POAH (AHCD • Living Will) ☐ Agreement (Compliance-E&O • Correction) ☐ Affidavit (Borrower • Occupancy • Ownership • Refi • Survey • Debts & Liens • Name-Signature-ID • Marital • Death • Will) ☐ Other (Vehicle Title • Safe Deposit Box)

DOC DATE: J F M A M J J A S O N D ,   DOC TITLE or TYPE   # OF PAGES   ☐ Inspect/Copy Request   Entry X-Ref #

☐ **SATISFACTORY EVIDENCE** ☐ Driver's License / Passport / State ID / Military / Government / Tribal / Inmate / Other ID *or* ☐ Credible Witness(es)

SIGNER — SIGNER's NAME ☐ For ADDRESS ☐ Non-Public # ☐ Capacity ☐ Voluntary ☐ Proper ID ISSUED SIGNATURE ☐ (oath/affirmation, if any) ☐ (by Mark)
PHONE C/H/W / *or* ☐ MISC AGENCY ☐ CA DMV ☐ US State Dept EXPIRES ➡

CW #1 — #1 WITNESS's NAME ☐ P/Known ADDRESS ☐ Non-Public # ☐ Driver's License ☐ Passport ☐ Other ID ISSUED SIGNATURE ☐ (after oath/affirmation)
PHONE C/H/W / *or* ☐ MISC AGENCY ☐ CA DMV ☐ US State Dept EXPIRES ❶

CW #2 — #2 WITNESS's NAME ☐ P/Known ADDRESS ☐ Non-Public # ☐ Driver's License ☐ Passport ☐ Other ID ISSUED SIGNATURE ☐ (after oath/affirmation)
PHONE C/H/W / *or* ☐ MISC AGENCY ☐ CA DMV ☐ US State Dept EXPIRES ❷

Entry 220

SERVICE — DATE: - -20 TIME: : am/pm ADDRESS ☐ Signer's ☐ Office NOTES ☐ Stop MILES Notary $ ☐ Adv. Travel $ ☐ Rush $ ☐ Copy $ ☐ Other $ TOTAL FEES $

TYPE: ☐ Acknowledgment ☐ Jurat ☐ Copy Certification ☐ Oath/Affirmation ☐ Oath of Office ☐ Proof of Execution ☐ Protest ☐ Other

Fingerprint — R T I M R P L

DOCUMENT
DOC TYPE: ☐ Deed (Grant • Trust Transfer • Gift • Interspousal • Quitclaim • ToD • Warranty) ☐ DOT (Mortgage) ☐ Trust (Certification • Rev/Irrev • Am/Rest) ☐ POA (General/Limited • Durable/Springing) ☐ POAH (AHCD • Living Will) ☐ Agreement (Compliance-E&O • Correction) ☐ Affidavit (Borrower • Occupancy • Ownership • Refi • Survey • Debts & Liens • Name-Signature-ID • Marital • Death • Will) ☐ Other (Vehicle Title • Safe Deposit Box)

DOC DATE: J F M A M J J A S O N D ,   DOC TITLE or TYPE   # OF PAGES   ☐ Inspect/Copy Request   Entry X-Ref #

☐ **SATISFACTORY EVIDENCE** ☐ Driver's License / Passport / State ID / Military / Government / Tribal / Inmate / Other ID *or* ☐ Credible Witness(es)

SIGNER — SIGNER's NAME ☐ For ADDRESS ☐ Non-Public # ☐ Capacity ☐ Voluntary ☐ Proper ID ISSUED SIGNATURE ☐ (oath/affirmation, if any) ☐ (by Mark)
PHONE C/H/W / *or* ☐ MISC AGENCY ☐ CA DMV ☐ US State Dept EXPIRES ➡

CW #1 — #1 WITNESS's NAME ☐ P/Known ADDRESS ☐ Non-Public # ☐ Driver's License ☐ Passport ☐ Other ID ISSUED SIGNATURE ☐ (after oath/affirmation)
PHONE C/H/W / *or* ☐ MISC AGENCY ☐ CA DMV ☐ US State Dept EXPIRES ❶

CW #2 — #2 WITNESS's NAME ☐ P/Known ADDRESS ☐ Non-Public # ☐ Driver's License ☐ Passport ☐ Other ID ISSUED SIGNATURE ☐ (after oath/affirmation)
PHONE C/H/W / *or* ☐ MISC AGENCY ☐ CA DMV ☐ US State Dept EXPIRES ❷

NOTARY NAME (printed):   **COMMISSION #:**

Record 221

| SERVICE | DATE   -   -20 | TIME   :   am / pm | ADDRESS   ☐ Signer's   ☐ Office   NOTES | ☐ Stop   MILES   Notary ☐ Adv. Travel ☐ Rush ☐ Copy ☐ Other   TOTAL FEES $ $ $ $ $ $ | **221** |

TYPE ☐ Acknowledgment ☐ Jurat ☐ Copy Certification ☐ Oath/Affirmation ☐ Oath of Office ☐ Proof of Execution ☐ Protest ☐ Other

R T I M R P L   **Fingerprint**

DOC TYPE ☐ Deed   ☐ DOT   ☐ Trust   ☐ POA   ☐ POAH   ☐ Agreement   ☐ Affidavit   ☐ Other

Grant • Trust Transfer • Gift | Mortgage | Certification | General / Limited | AHCD | Compliance-E&O | Borrower • Occupancy • Ownership • Refi • Survey | Vehicle Title
Interspousal • Quitclaim • ToD • Warranty | Rev / Irrev • Am / Rest | Durable / Springing | Living Will | Correction | Debts & Liens • Name-Signature-ID • Marital • Death • Will | Safe Deposit Box

DOC DATE J F M A M J J A S O N D ,   **DOC TITLE or TYPE**   **# OF PAGES**   ☐ Inspect/Copy Request   Entry X-Ref #

☐ **SATISFACTORY EVIDENCE** ☐ Driver's License / Passport / State ID / Military / Government / Tribal / Inmate / Other ID   *or*   ☐ Credible Witness(es)

SIGNER
SIGNER's NAME   ☐ For   ADDRESS   ☐ Non-Public   ☐ Capacity   ☐ Voluntary   ☐ Proper ID   ISSUED   SIGNATURE ☐ (oath / affirmation, if any) ☐ (by Mark)

PHONE C / H / W   *or* ☐ MISC   AGENCY   ☐ CA DMV   ☐ US State Dept   EXPIRES   ➡

CW #1
#1 WITNESS's NAME   ☐ P/Known   ADDRESS   ☐ Non-Public   ☐ Driver's License ☐ Passport ☐ Other ID   ISSUED   SIGNATURE ☐ (after oath / affirmation)

PHONE C / H / W   *or* ☐ MISC   AGENCY   ☐ CA DMV   ☐ US State Dept   EXPIRES   ❶

CW #2
#2 WITNESS's NAME   ☐ P/Known   ADDRESS   ☐ Non-Public   ☐ Driver's License ☐ Passport ☐ Other ID   ISSUED   SIGNATURE ☐ (after oath / affirmation)

PHONE C / H / W   *or* ☐ MISC   AGENCY   ☐ CA DMV   ☐ US State Dept   EXPIRES   ❷

Record 222

| SERVICE | DATE   -   -20 | TIME   :   am / pm | ADDRESS   ☐ Signer's   ☐ Office   NOTES | ☐ Stop   MILES   Notary ☐ Adv. Travel ☐ Rush ☐ Copy ☐ Other   TOTAL FEES $ $ $ $ $ $ | **222** |

TYPE ☐ Acknowledgment ☐ Jurat ☐ Copy Certification ☐ Oath/Affirmation ☐ Oath of Office ☐ Proof of Execution ☐ Protest ☐ Other

R T I M R P L   **Fingerprint**

DOC TYPE ☐ Deed   ☐ DOT   ☐ Trust   ☐ POA   ☐ POAH   ☐ Agreement   ☐ Affidavit   ☐ Other

Grant • Trust Transfer • Gift | Mortgage | Certification | General / Limited | AHCD | Compliance-E&O | Borrower • Occupancy • Ownership • Refi • Survey | Vehicle Title
Interspousal • Quitclaim • ToD • Warranty | Rev / Irrev • Am / Rest | Durable / Springing | Living Will | Correction | Debts & Liens • Name-Signature-ID • Marital • Death • Will | Safe Deposit Box

DOC DATE J F M A M J J A S O N D ,   **DOC TITLE or TYPE**   **# OF PAGES**   ☐ Inspect/Copy Request   Entry X-Ref #

☐ **SATISFACTORY EVIDENCE** ☐ Driver's License / Passport / State ID / Military / Government / Tribal / Inmate / Other ID   *or*   ☐ Credible Witness(es)

SIGNER
SIGNER's NAME   ☐ For   ADDRESS   ☐ Non-Public   ☐ Capacity   ☐ Voluntary   ☐ Proper ID   ISSUED   SIGNATURE ☐ (oath / affirmation, if any) ☐ (by Mark)

PHONE C / H / W   *or* ☐ MISC   AGENCY   ☐ CA DMV   ☐ US State Dept   EXPIRES   ➡

CW #1
#1 WITNESS's NAME   ☐ P/Known   ADDRESS   ☐ Non-Public   ☐ Driver's License ☐ Passport ☐ Other ID   ISSUED   SIGNATURE ☐ (after oath / affirmation)

PHONE C / H / W   *or* ☐ MISC   AGENCY   ☐ CA DMV   ☐ US State Dept   EXPIRES   ❶

CW #2
#2 WITNESS's NAME   ☐ P/Known   ADDRESS   ☐ Non-Public   ☐ Driver's License ☐ Passport ☐ Other ID   ISSUED   SIGNATURE ☐ (after oath / affirmation)

PHONE C / H / W   *or* ☐ MISC   AGENCY   ☐ CA DMV   ☐ US State Dept   EXPIRES   ❷

NOTARY NAME (printed): COMMISSION #:

Entry 223

SERVICE: DATE - -20 | TIME : am/pm | ADDRESS ☐ Signer's ☐ Office | NOTES | ☐ Stop | MILES | Notary $ | ☐ Adv. Travel $ | ☐ Rush $ | ☐ Copy $ | ☐ Other $ | TOTAL FEES $

TYPE: ☐ Acknowledgment ☐ Jurat ☐ Copy Certification ☐ Oath/Affirmation ☐ Oath of Office ☐ Proof of Execution ☐ Protest ☐ Other

Fingerprint R T I M R P L

DOCUMENT:
- DOC TYPE: ☐ Deed (Grant • Trust Transfer • Gift • Interspousal • Quitclaim • ToD • Warranty) ☐ DOT (Mortgage • Rev / Irrev • Am / Rest) ☐ Trust (Certification) ☐ POA (General / Limited • Durable / Springing) ☐ POAH (AHCD • Living Will) ☐ Agreement (Compliance-E&O • Correction) ☐ Affidavit (Borrower • Occupancy • Ownership • Refi • Survey • Debts & Liens • Name-Signature-ID • Marital • Death • Will) ☐ Other (Vehicle Title • Safe Deposit Box)
- DOC DATE: J F M A M J J A S O N D , | DOC TITLE or TYPE | # OF PAGES | ☐ Inspect/Copy Request | Entry X-Ref #

☐ **SATISFACTORY EVIDENCE** ☐ Driver's License / Passport / State ID / Military / Government / Tribal / Inmate / Other ID *or* ☐ Credible Witness(es)

SIGNER: SIGNER's NAME | ☐ For | ADDRESS | ☐ Non-Public | ☐ Capacity # | ☐ Voluntary | ☐ Proper ID | ISSUED | SIGNATURE ☐ (oath / affirmation, if any) ☐ (by Mark)
PHONE C / H / W / | or ☐ MISC | | | AGENCY ☐ CA DMV ☐ US State Dept | EXPIRES | ➤

CW #1: #1 WITNESS's NAME | ☐ P/Known | ADDRESS | ☐ Non-Public | ☐ Driver's License # ☐ Passport ☐ Other ID | ISSUED | SIGNATURE ☐ (after oath / affirmation)
PHONE C / H / W / | or ☐ MISC | | | AGENCY ☐ CA DMV ☐ US State Dept | EXPIRES | ❶

CW #2: #2 WITNESS's NAME | ☐ P/Known | ADDRESS | ☐ Non-Public | ☐ Driver's License # ☐ Passport ☐ Other ID | ISSUED | SIGNATURE ☐ (after oath / affirmation)
PHONE C / H / W / | or ☐ MISC | | | AGENCY ☐ CA DMV ☐ US State Dept | EXPIRES | ❷

Entry 224

SERVICE: DATE - -20 | TIME : am/pm | ADDRESS ☐ Signer's ☐ Office | NOTES | ☐ Stop | MILES | Notary $ | ☐ Adv. Travel $ | ☐ Rush $ | ☐ Copy $ | ☐ Other $ | TOTAL FEES $

TYPE: ☐ Acknowledgment ☐ Jurat ☐ Copy Certification ☐ Oath/Affirmation ☐ Oath of Office ☐ Proof of Execution ☐ Protest ☐ Other

Fingerprint R T I M R P L

DOCUMENT:
- DOC TYPE: ☐ Deed (Grant • Trust Transfer • Gift • Interspousal • Quitclaim • ToD • Warranty) ☐ DOT (Mortgage • Rev / Irrev • Am / Rest) ☐ Trust (Certification) ☐ POA (General / Limited • Durable / Springing) ☐ POAH (AHCD • Living Will) ☐ Agreement (Compliance-E&O • Correction) ☐ Affidavit (Borrower • Occupancy • Ownership • Refi • Survey • Debts & Liens • Name-Signature-ID • Marital • Death • Will) ☐ Other (Vehicle Title • Safe Deposit Box)
- DOC DATE: J F M A M J J A S O N D , | DOC TITLE or TYPE | # OF PAGES | ☐ Inspect/Copy Request | Entry X-Ref #

☐ **SATISFACTORY EVIDENCE** ☐ Driver's License / Passport / State ID / Military / Government / Tribal / Inmate / Other ID *or* ☐ Credible Witness(es)

SIGNER: SIGNER's NAME | ☐ For | ADDRESS | ☐ Non-Public | ☐ Capacity # | ☐ Voluntary | ☐ Proper ID | ISSUED | SIGNATURE ☐ (oath / affirmation, if any) ☐ (by Mark)
PHONE C / H / W / | or ☐ MISC | | | AGENCY ☐ CA DMV ☐ US State Dept | EXPIRES | ➤

CW #1: #1 WITNESS's NAME | ☐ P/Known | ADDRESS | ☐ Non-Public | ☐ Driver's License # ☐ Passport ☐ Other ID | ISSUED | SIGNATURE ☐ (after oath / affirmation)
PHONE C / H / W / | or ☐ MISC | | | AGENCY ☐ CA DMV ☐ US State Dept | EXPIRES | ❶

CW #2: #2 WITNESS's NAME | ☐ P/Known | ADDRESS | ☐ Non-Public | ☐ Driver's License # ☐ Passport ☐ Other ID | ISSUED | SIGNATURE ☐ (after oath / affirmation)
PHONE C / H / W / | or ☐ MISC | | | AGENCY ☐ CA DMV ☐ US State Dept | EXPIRES | ❷

NOTARY NAME (printed):   COMMISSION #:

225

SERVICE

DATE   -   -20   TIME   :   am pm   ADDRESS   ☐ Signer's   ☐ Office   NOTES   ☐ Stop   MILES   Notary ☐ Adv. Travel ☐ Rush ☐ Copy ☐ Other   TOTAL FEES $ $ $ $ $ $

TYPE ☐ Acknowledgment ☐ Jurat ☐ Copy Certification ☐ Oath/Affirmation ☐ Oath of Office ☐ Proof of Execution ☐ Protest ☐ Other

DOCUMENT

DOC TYPE ☐ Deed   ☐ DOT   ☐ Trust   ☐ POA   ☐ POAH   ☐ Agreement   ☐ Affidavit   ☐ Other
Grant • Trust Transfer • Gift   Mortgage   Certification   General / Limited   AHCD   Compliance-E&O   Borrower • Occupancy • Ownership • Refi • Survey   Vehicle Title
Interspousal • Quitclaim • ToD • Warranty   Rev / Irrev • Am / Rest   Durable / Springing   Living Will   Correction   Debts & Liens • Name-Signature-ID • Marital • Death • Will   Safe Deposit Box

DOC DATE   J F M A M J   J A S O N D   ,   DOC TITLE or TYPE   # OF PAGES   ☐ Inspect/Copy Request   Entry X-Ref #

R T I M R P L   **Fingerprint**

☐ **SATISFACTORY EVIDENCE** ☐ Driver's License / Passport / State ID / Military / Government / Tribal / Inmate / Other ID   **or**   ☐ Credible Witness(es)

SIGNER

SIGNER's NAME   ☐ For   ADDRESS   ☐ Non-Public   ☐ Capacity   ☐ Voluntary   ☐ Proper ID   ISSUED   SIGNATURE ☐ (oath / affirmation, if any) ☐ (by Mark)
    #
PHONE C / H / W   **or** ☐ MISC   /   AGENCY   ☐ CA DMV   ☐ US State Dept   EXPIRES   ➡

CW #1

#1 WITNESS's NAME   ☐ P/Known   ADDRESS   ☐ Non-Public   ☐ Driver's License ☐ Passport ☐ Other ID   ISSUED   SIGNATURE ☐ (after oath / affirmation)
    #
PHONE C / H / W   **or** ☐ MISC   /   AGENCY   ☐ CA DMV   ☐ US State Dept   EXPIRES   ❶

CW #2

#2 WITNESS's NAME   ☐ P/Known   ADDRESS   ☐ Non-Public   ☐ Driver's License ☐ Passport ☐ Other ID   ISSUED   SIGNATURE ☐ (after oath / affirmation)
    #
PHONE C / H / W   **or** ☐ MISC   /   AGENCY   ☐ CA DMV   ☐ US State Dept   EXPIRES   ❷

226

SERVICE

DATE   -   -20   TIME   :   am pm   ADDRESS   ☐ Signer's   ☐ Office   NOTES   ☐ Stop   MILES   Notary ☐ Adv. Travel ☐ Rush ☐ Copy ☐ Other   TOTAL FEES $ $ $ $ $ $

TYPE ☐ Acknowledgment ☐ Jurat ☐ Copy Certification ☐ Oath/Affirmation ☐ Oath of Office ☐ Proof of Execution ☐ Protest ☐ Other

DOCUMENT

DOC TYPE ☐ Deed   ☐ DOT   ☐ Trust   ☐ POA   ☐ POAH   ☐ Agreement   ☐ Affidavit   ☐ Other
Grant • Trust Transfer • Gift   Mortgage   Certification   General / Limited   AHCD   Compliance-E&O   Borrower • Occupancy • Ownership • Refi • Survey   Vehicle Title
Interspousal • Quitclaim • ToD • Warranty   Rev / Irrev • Am / Rest   Durable / Springing   Living Will   Correction   Debts & Liens • Name-Signature-ID • Marital • Death • Will   Safe Deposit Box

DOC DATE   J F M A M J   J A S O N D   ,   DOC TITLE or TYPE   # OF PAGES   ☐ Inspect/Copy Request   Entry X-Ref #

R T I M R P L   **Fingerprint**

☐ **SATISFACTORY EVIDENCE** ☐ Driver's License / Passport / State ID / Military / Government / Tribal / Inmate / Other ID   **or**   ☐ Credible Witness(es)

SIGNER

SIGNER's NAME   ☐ For   ADDRESS   ☐ Non-Public   ☐ Capacity   ☐ Voluntary   ☐ Proper ID   ISSUED   SIGNATURE ☐ (oath / affirmation, if any) ☐ (by Mark)
    #
PHONE C / H / W   **or** ☐ MISC   /   AGENCY   ☐ CA DMV   ☐ US State Dept   EXPIRES   ➡

CW #1

#1 WITNESS's NAME   ☐ P/Known   ADDRESS   ☐ Non-Public   ☐ Driver's License ☐ Passport ☐ Other ID   ISSUED   SIGNATURE ☐ (after oath / affirmation)
    #
PHONE C / H / W   **or** ☐ MISC   /   AGENCY   ☐ CA DMV   ☐ US State Dept   EXPIRES   ❶

CW #2

#2 WITNESS's NAME   ☐ P/Known   ADDRESS   ☐ Non-Public   ☐ Driver's License ☐ Passport ☐ Other ID   ISSUED   SIGNATURE ☐ (after oath / affirmation)
    #
PHONE C / H / W   **or** ☐ MISC   /   AGENCY   ☐ CA DMV   ☐ US State Dept   EXPIRES   ❷

227		

NOTARY NAME (printed): COMMISSION #:

Entry 227
- SERVICE: DATE - -20 | TIME : am/pm | ADDRESS □ Signer's □ Office | NOTES | □ Stop MILES | Notary $ □ Adv. Travel $ □ Rush $ □ Copy $ □ Other $ TOTAL FEES $
- TYPE: □ Acknowledgment □ Jurat □ Copy Certification □ Oath/Affirmation □ Oath of Office □ Proof of Execution □ Protest □ Other
- DOCUMENT DOC TYPE: □ Deed (Grant • Trust Transfer • Gift • Interspousal • Quitclaim • ToD • Warranty) □ DOT (Mortgage) □ Trust (Certification • Rev/Irrev • Am/Rest) □ POA (General/Limited • Durable/Springing) □ POAH (AHCD • Living Will) □ Agreement (Compliance-E&O • Correction) □ Affidavit (Borrower • Occupancy • Ownership • Refi • Survey • Debts & Liens • Name-Signature-ID • Marital • Death • Will) □ Other (Vehicle Title • Safe Deposit Box)
- DOC DATE: J F M A M J J A S O N D , | DOC TITLE or TYPE | # OF PAGES | □ Inspect/Copy Request | Entry X-Ref #
- Fingerprint: R T I M R P L
- □ SATISFACTORY EVIDENCE □ Driver's License / Passport / State ID / Military / Government / Tribal / Inmate / Other ID *or* □ Credible Witness(es)
- SIGNER: SIGNER's NAME | □ For ADDRESS | □ Non-Public | □ Capacity □ Voluntary □ Proper ID | ISSUED # | SIGNATURE □ (oath/affirmation, if any) □ (by Mark)
- PHONE C/H/W / | or □ MISC | AGENCY □ CA DMV □ US State Dept | EXPIRES →
- CW #1: #1 WITNESS's NAME | □ P/Known ADDRESS | □ Non-Public | □ Driver's License □ Passport □ Other ID | ISSUED # | SIGNATURE □ (after oath/affirmation)
- PHONE C/H/W / | or □ MISC | AGENCY □ CA DMV □ US State Dept | EXPIRES ❶
- CW #2: #2 WITNESS's NAME | □ P/Known ADDRESS | □ Non-Public | □ Driver's License □ Passport □ Other ID | ISSUED # | SIGNATURE □ (after oath/affirmation)
- PHONE C/H/W / | or □ MISC | AGENCY □ CA DMV □ US State Dept | EXPIRES ❷

Entry 228
- SERVICE: DATE - -20 | TIME : am/pm | ADDRESS □ Signer's □ Office | NOTES | □ Stop MILES | Notary $ □ Adv. Travel $ □ Rush $ □ Copy $ □ Other $ TOTAL FEES $
- TYPE: □ Acknowledgment □ Jurat □ Copy Certification □ Oath/Affirmation □ Oath of Office □ Proof of Execution □ Protest □ Other
- DOCUMENT DOC TYPE: □ Deed (Grant • Trust Transfer • Gift • Interspousal • Quitclaim • ToD • Warranty) □ DOT (Mortgage) □ Trust (Certification • Rev/Irrev • Am/Rest) □ POA (General/Limited • Durable/Springing) □ POAH (AHCD • Living Will) □ Agreement (Compliance-E&O • Correction) □ Affidavit (Borrower • Occupancy • Ownership • Refi • Survey • Debts & Liens • Name-Signature-ID • Marital • Death • Will) □ Other (Vehicle Title • Safe Deposit Box)
- DOC DATE: J F M A M J J A S O N D , | DOC TITLE or TYPE | # OF PAGES | □ Inspect/Copy Request | Entry X-Ref #
- Fingerprint: R T I M R P L
- □ SATISFACTORY EVIDENCE □ Driver's License / Passport / State ID / Military / Government / Tribal / Inmate / Other ID *or* □ Credible Witness(es)
- SIGNER: SIGNER's NAME | □ For ADDRESS | □ Non-Public | □ Capacity □ Voluntary □ Proper ID | ISSUED # | SIGNATURE □ (oath/affirmation, if any) □ (by Mark)
- PHONE C/H/W / | or □ MISC | AGENCY □ CA DMV □ US State Dept | EXPIRES →
- CW #1: #1 WITNESS's NAME | □ P/Known ADDRESS | □ Non-Public | □ Driver's License □ Passport □ Other ID | ISSUED # | SIGNATURE □ (after oath/affirmation)
- PHONE C/H/W / | or □ MISC | AGENCY □ CA DMV □ US State Dept | EXPIRES ❶
- CW #2: #2 WITNESS's NAME | □ P/Known ADDRESS | □ Non-Public | □ Driver's License □ Passport □ Other ID | ISSUED # | SIGNATURE □ (after oath/affirmation)
- PHONE C/H/W / | or □ MISC | AGENCY □ CA DMV □ US State Dept | EXPIRES ❷

NOTARY NAME (printed):   COMMISSION #:

229

SERVICE

DATE   -   -20   TIME   :   am / pm   ADDRESS   ☐ Signer's   ☐ Office   NOTES   ☐ Stop   MILES   Notary ☐ Adv. Travel ☐ Rush ☐ Copy ☐ Other   TOTAL FEES $ $ $ $ $ $

TYPE   ☐ Acknowledgment   ☐ Jurat   ☐ Copy Certification   ☐ Oath/Affirmation   ☐ Oath of Office   ☐ Proof of Execution   ☐ Protest   ☐ Other

R T I M R P L   **Fingerprint**

DOCUMENT

DOC TYPE   ☐ Deed   ☐ DOT   ☐ Trust   ☐ POA   ☐ POAH   ☐ Agreement   ☐ Affidavit   ☐ Other

Grant • Trust Transfer • Gift   Mortgage   Certification   General / Limited   AHCD   Compliance-E&O   Borrower • Occupancy • Ownership • Refi • Survey   Vehicle Title

Interspousal • Quitclaim • ToD • Warranty   Rev / Irrev • Am / Rest   Durable / Springing   Living Will   Correction   Debts & Liens • Name-Signature-ID • Marital • Death • Will   Safe Deposit Box

DOC DATE   J F M A M J   J A S O N D   ,   DOC TITLE or TYPE   # OF PAGES   ☐ Inspect/Copy Request   Entry X-Ref #

☐ **SATISFACTORY EVIDENCE** ☐ Driver's License / Passport / State ID / Military / Government / Tribal / Inmate / Other ID   *or*   ☐ Credible Witness(es)

SIGNER

SIGNER's NAME   ☐ For   ADDRESS   ☐ Non-Public   ☐ Capacity   ☐ Voluntary   ☐ Proper ID   ISSUED #   SIGNATURE   ☐ *(oath / affirmation, if any)*   ☐ *(by Mark)*

PHONE C / H / W   /   *or* ☐ MISC   AGENCY   ☐ CA DMV   ☐ US State Dept   EXPIRES   ➡

CW #1

#1 WITNESS's NAME   ☐ P/Known   ADDRESS   ☐ Non-Public   ☐ Driver's License   ☐ Passport   ☐ Other ID   ISSUED #   SIGNATURE   ☐ *(after oath / affirmation)*

PHONE C / H / W   /   *or* ☐ MISC   AGENCY   ☐ CA DMV   ☐ US State Dept   EXPIRES   ❶

CW #2

#2 WITNESS's NAME   ☐ P/Known   ADDRESS   ☐ Non-Public   ☐ Driver's License   ☐ Passport   ☐ Other ID   ISSUED #   SIGNATURE   ☐ *(after oath / affirmation)*

PHONE C / H / W   /   *or* ☐ MISC   AGENCY   ☐ CA DMV   ☐ US State Dept   EXPIRES   ❷

230

SERVICE

DATE   -   -20   TIME   :   am / pm   ADDRESS   ☐ Signer's   ☐ Office   NOTES   ☐ Stop   MILES   Notary ☐ Adv. Travel ☐ Rush ☐ Copy ☐ Other   TOTAL FEES $ $ $ $ $ $

TYPE   ☐ Acknowledgment   ☐ Jurat   ☐ Copy Certification   ☐ Oath/Affirmation   ☐ Oath of Office   ☐ Proof of Execution   ☐ Protest   ☐ Other

R T I M R P L   **Fingerprint**

DOCUMENT

DOC TYPE   ☐ Deed   ☐ DOT   ☐ Trust   ☐ POA   ☐ POAH   ☐ Agreement   ☐ Affidavit   ☐ Other

Grant • Trust Transfer • Gift   Mortgage   Certification   General / Limited   AHCD   Compliance-E&O   Borrower • Occupancy • Ownership • Refi • Survey   Vehicle Title

Interspousal • Quitclaim • ToD • Warranty   Rev / Irrev • Am / Rest   Durable / Springing   Living Will   Correction   Debts & Liens • Name-Signature-ID • Marital • Death • Will   Safe Deposit Box

DOC DATE   J F M A M J   J A S O N D   ,   DOC TITLE or TYPE   # OF PAGES   ☐ Inspect/Copy Request   Entry X-Ref #

☐ **SATISFACTORY EVIDENCE** ☐ Driver's License / Passport / State ID / Military / Government / Tribal / Inmate / Other ID   *or*   ☐ Credible Witness(es)

SIGNER

SIGNER's NAME   ☐ For   ADDRESS   ☐ Non-Public   ☐ Capacity   ☐ Voluntary   ☐ Proper ID   ISSUED #   SIGNATURE   ☐ *(oath / affirmation, if any)*   ☐ *(by Mark)*

PHONE C / H / W   /   *or* ☐ MISC   AGENCY   ☐ CA DMV   ☐ US State Dept   EXPIRES   ➡

CW #1

#1 WITNESS's NAME   ☐ P/Known   ADDRESS   ☐ Non-Public   ☐ Driver's License   ☐ Passport   ☐ Other ID   ISSUED #   SIGNATURE   ☐ *(after oath / affirmation)*

PHONE C / H / W   /   *or* ☐ MISC   AGENCY   ☐ CA DMV   ☐ US State Dept   EXPIRES   ❶

CW #2

#2 WITNESS's NAME   ☐ P/Known   ADDRESS   ☐ Non-Public   ☐ Driver's License   ☐ Passport   ☐ Other ID   ISSUED #   SIGNATURE   ☐ *(after oath / affirmation)*

PHONE C / H / W   /   *or* ☐ MISC   AGENCY   ☐ CA DMV   ☐ US State Dept   EXPIRES   ❷

NOTARY NAME (printed): _____ COMMISSION #: _____

Entry 231

SERVICE
- DATE: __-__-20__ TIME: __:__ am/pm ADDRESS: _____ ☐ Signer's ☐ Office NOTES: _____ ☐ Stop MILES: ____ Notary $____ ☐ Adv. Travel $____ ☐ Rush $____ ☐ Copy $____ ☐ Other $____ TOTAL FEES $____

TYPE: ☐ Acknowledgment ☐ Jurat ☐ Copy Certification ☐ Oath/Affirmation ☐ Oath of Office ☐ Proof of Execution ☐ Protest ☐ Other

Fingerprint — R T I M R P L

DOCUMENT
- DOC TYPE: ☐ Deed (Grant • Trust Transfer • Gift • Interspousal • Quitclaim • ToD • Warranty) ☐ DOT (Mortgage • Certification • Rev / Irrev • Am / Rest) ☐ Trust ☐ POA (General / Limited • Durable / Springing) ☐ POAH (AHCD • Living Will) ☐ Agreement (Compliance-E&O • Correction) ☐ Affidavit (Borrower • Occupancy • Ownership • Refi • Survey • Debts & Liens • Name-Signature-ID • Marital • Death • Will) ☐ Other (Vehicle Title • Safe Deposit Box)
- DOC DATE: J F M A M J J A S O N D , ____ DOC TITLE or TYPE: _____ # OF PAGES: ____ ☐ Inspect/Copy Request Entry X-Ref #: ____

☐ **SATISFACTORY EVIDENCE** ☐ Driver's License / Passport / State ID / Military / Government / Tribal / Inmate / Other ID **or** ☐ Credible Witness(es)

SIGNER
- SIGNER's NAME: _____ ☐ For ADDRESS: _____ ☐ Non-Public ☐ Capacity ☐ Voluntary ☐ Proper ID ISSUED #: ____ SIGNATURE ➤ ☐ (oath / affirmation, if any) ☐ (by Mark)
- PHONE C / H / W: __/__ or ☐ MISC AGENCY: ☐ CA DMV ☐ US State Dept EXPIRES: ____

CW #1
- #1 WITNESS's NAME: _____ ☐ P/Known ADDRESS: _____ ☐ Non-Public ☐ Driver's License ☐ Passport ☐ Other ID ISSUED #: ____ SIGNATURE ☐ (after oath / affirmation)
- PHONE C / H / W: __/__ or ☐ MISC AGENCY: ☐ CA DMV ☐ US State Dept EXPIRES: ____ ❶

CW #2
- #2 WITNESS's NAME: _____ ☐ P/Known ADDRESS: _____ ☐ Non-Public ☐ Driver's License ☐ Passport ☐ Other ID ISSUED #: ____ SIGNATURE ☐ (after oath / affirmation)
- PHONE C / H / W: __/__ or ☐ MISC AGENCY: ☐ CA DMV ☐ US State Dept EXPIRES: ____ ❷

Entry 232

SERVICE
- DATE: __-__-20__ TIME: __:__ am/pm ADDRESS: _____ ☐ Signer's ☐ Office NOTES: _____ ☐ Stop MILES: ____ Notary $____ ☐ Adv. Travel $____ ☐ Rush $____ ☐ Copy $____ ☐ Other $____ TOTAL FEES $____

TYPE: ☐ Acknowledgment ☐ Jurat ☐ Copy Certification ☐ Oath/Affirmation ☐ Oath of Office ☐ Proof of Execution ☐ Protest ☐ Other

Fingerprint — R T I M R P L

DOCUMENT
- DOC TYPE: ☐ Deed (Grant • Trust Transfer • Gift • Interspousal • Quitclaim • ToD • Warranty) ☐ DOT (Mortgage • Certification • Rev / Irrev • Am / Rest) ☐ Trust ☐ POA (General / Limited • Durable / Springing) ☐ POAH (AHCD • Living Will) ☐ Agreement (Compliance-E&O • Correction) ☐ Affidavit (Borrower • Occupancy • Ownership • Refi • Survey • Debts & Liens • Name-Signature-ID • Marital • Death • Will) ☐ Other (Vehicle Title • Safe Deposit Box)
- DOC DATE: J F M A M J J A S O N D , ____ DOC TITLE or TYPE: _____ # OF PAGES: ____ ☐ Inspect/Copy Request Entry X-Ref #: ____

☐ **SATISFACTORY EVIDENCE** ☐ Driver's License / Passport / State ID / Military / Government / Tribal / Inmate / Other ID **or** ☐ Credible Witness(es)

SIGNER
- SIGNER's NAME: _____ ☐ For ADDRESS: _____ ☐ Non-Public ☐ Capacity ☐ Voluntary ☐ Proper ID ISSUED #: ____ SIGNATURE ➤ ☐ (oath / affirmation, if any) ☐ (by Mark)
- PHONE C / H / W: __/__ or ☐ MISC AGENCY: ☐ CA DMV ☐ US State Dept EXPIRES: ____

CW #1
- #1 WITNESS's NAME: _____ ☐ P/Known ADDRESS: _____ ☐ Non-Public ☐ Driver's License ☐ Passport ☐ Other ID ISSUED #: ____ SIGNATURE ☐ (after oath / affirmation)
- PHONE C / H / W: __/__ or ☐ MISC AGENCY: ☐ CA DMV ☐ US State Dept EXPIRES: ____ ❶

CW #2
- #2 WITNESS's NAME: _____ ☐ P/Known ADDRESS: _____ ☐ Non-Public ☐ Driver's License ☐ Passport ☐ Other ID ISSUED #: ____ SIGNATURE ☐ (after oath / affirmation)
- PHONE C / H / W: __/__ or ☐ MISC AGENCY: ☐ CA DMV ☐ US State Dept EXPIRES: ____ ❷

NOTARY NAME (printed): _____   COMMISSION #: _____

Entry 233

SERVICE	DATE - -20	TIME :	am pm	ADDRESS	☐ Signer's	☐ Office	NOTES	☐ Stop	MILES	Notary	☐ Adv. Travel	☐ Rush	☐ Copy	☐ Other	TOTAL FEES
									$	$	$	$	$	$	**233**

TYPE ☐ Acknowledgment ☐ Jurat ☐ Copy Certification ☐ Oath/Affirmation ☐ Oath of Office ☐ Proof of Execution ☐ Protest ☐ Other

R **Fingerprint**

DOCUMENT

DOC TYPE ☐ Deed ☐ DOT ☐ Trust ☐ POA ☐ POAH ☐ Agreement ☐ Affidavit ☐ Other

Grant • Trust Transfer • Gift | Mortgage | Certification | General / Limited | AHCD | Compliance-E&O | Borrower • Occupancy • Ownership • Refi • Survey | Vehicle Title

Interspousal • Quitclaim • ToD • Warranty | Rev / Irrev • Am / Rest | Durable / Springing | Living Will | Correction | Debts & Liens • Name-Signature-ID • Marital • Death • Will | Safe Deposit Box

T I M R P

DOC DATE J F M A M J J A S O N D , | **DOC TITLE or TYPE** | # OF PAGES | ☐ Inspect/Copy Request | Entry X-Ref #

L

☐ **SATISFACTORY EVIDENCE** ☐ Driver's License / Passport / State ID / Military / Government / Tribal / Inmate / Other ID *or* ☐ Credible Witness(es)

SIGNER

SIGNER's NAME | ☐ For | ADDRESS | ☐ Non-Public | ☐ Capacity | ☐ Voluntary | ☐ Proper ID | ISSUED # | SIGNATURE | ☐ (oath / affirmation, if any) | ☐ (by Mark)

PHONE C / H / W or ☐ MISC / | | AGENCY | ☐ CA DMV | ☐ US State Dept | EXPIRES | ➡

CW #1

#1 WITNESS's NAME | ☐ P/Known | ADDRESS | ☐ Non-Public | ☐ Driver's License | ☐ Passport | ☐ Other ID | ISSUED # | SIGNATURE | ☐ (after oath / affirmation)

PHONE C / H / W or ☐ MISC | | AGENCY | ☐ CA DMV | ☐ US State Dept | EXPIRES | ❶

CW #2

#2 WITNESS's NAME | ☐ P/Known | ADDRESS | ☐ Non-Public | ☐ Driver's License | ☐ Passport | ☐ Other ID | ISSUED # | SIGNATURE | ☐ (after oath / affirmation)

PHONE C / H / W or ☐ MISC | | AGENCY | ☐ CA DMV | ☐ US State Dept | EXPIRES | ❷

Entry 234

SERVICE	DATE - -20	TIME :	am pm	ADDRESS	☐ Signer's	☐ Office	NOTES	☐ Stop	MILES	Notary	☐ Adv. Travel	☐ Rush	☐ Copy	☐ Other	TOTAL FEES
									$	$	$	$	$	$	**234**

TYPE ☐ Acknowledgment ☐ Jurat ☐ Copy Certification ☐ Oath/Affirmation ☐ Oath of Office ☐ Proof of Execution ☐ Protest ☐ Other

R **Fingerprint**

DOCUMENT

DOC TYPE ☐ Deed ☐ DOT ☐ Trust ☐ POA ☐ POAH ☐ Agreement ☐ Affidavit ☐ Other

Grant • Trust Transfer • Gift | Mortgage | Certification | General / Limited | AHCD | Compliance-E&O | Borrower • Occupancy • Ownership • Refi • Survey | Vehicle Title

Interspousal • Quitclaim • ToD • Warranty | Rev / Irrev • Am / Rest | Durable / Springing | Living Will | Correction | Debts & Liens • Name-Signature-ID • Marital • Death • Will | Safe Deposit Box

T I M R P

DOC DATE J F M A M J J A S O N D , | **DOC TITLE or TYPE** | # OF PAGES | ☐ Inspect/Copy Request | Entry X-Ref #

L

☐ **SATISFACTORY EVIDENCE** ☐ Driver's License / Passport / State ID / Military / Government / Tribal / Inmate / Other ID *or* ☐ Credible Witness(es)

SIGNER

SIGNER's NAME | ☐ For | ADDRESS | ☐ Non-Public | ☐ Capacity | ☐ Voluntary | ☐ Proper ID | ISSUED # | SIGNATURE | ☐ (oath / affirmation, if any) | ☐ (by Mark)

PHONE C / H / W or ☐ MISC / | | AGENCY | ☐ CA DMV | ☐ US State Dept | EXPIRES | ➡

CW #1

#1 WITNESS's NAME | ☐ P/Known | ADDRESS | ☐ Non-Public | ☐ Driver's License | ☐ Passport | ☐ Other ID | ISSUED # | SIGNATURE | ☐ (after oath / affirmation)

PHONE C / H / W or ☐ MISC | | AGENCY | ☐ CA DMV | ☐ US State Dept | EXPIRES | ❶

CW #2

#2 WITNESS's NAME | ☐ P/Known | ADDRESS | ☐ Non-Public | ☐ Driver's License | ☐ Passport | ☐ Other ID | ISSUED # | SIGNATURE | ☐ (after oath / affirmation)

PHONE C / H / W or ☐ MISC | | AGENCY | ☐ CA DMV | ☐ US State Dept | EXPIRES | ❷

NOTARY NAME (printed):   COMMISSION #:

Entry 235

| SERVICE | DATE - -20 | TIME : am/pm | ADDRESS | ☐ Signer's ☐ Office | NOTES | ☐ Stop MILES | Notary $ | ☐ Adv. Travel $ | ☐ Rush $ | ☐ Copy $ | ☐ Other $ | TOTAL FEES $ |

TYPE: ☐ Acknowledgment ☐ Jurat ☐ Copy Certification ☐ Oath/Affirmation ☐ Oath of Office ☐ Proof of Execution ☐ Protest ☐ Other

Fingerprint — R T I M R P L

DOC TYPE: ☐ Deed (Grant • Trust Transfer • Gift • Interspousal • Quitclaim • ToD • Warranty) ☐ DOT (Mortgage) ☐ Trust (Certification • Rev/Irrev • Am/Rest) ☐ POA (General/Limited • Durable/Springing) ☐ POAH (AHCD • Living Will) ☐ Agreement (Compliance-E&O • Correction) ☐ Affidavit (Borrower • Occupancy • Ownership • Refi • Survey • Debts & Liens • Name-Signature-ID • Marital • Death • Will) ☐ Other (Vehicle Title • Safe Deposit Box)

DOC DATE: J F M A M J J A S O N D ,   **DOC TITLE or TYPE:**   **# OF PAGES:**   ☐ Inspect/Copy Request   **Entry X-Ref #:**

☐ **SATISFACTORY EVIDENCE** ☐ Driver's License / Passport / State ID / Military / Government / Tribal / Inmate / Other ID   *or*   ☐ Credible Witness(es)

| SIGNER | SIGNER's NAME | ☐ For | ADDRESS | ☐ Non-Public | ☐ Capacity # | ☐ Voluntary | ☐ Proper ID | ISSUED | SIGNATURE | ☐ (oath / affirmation, if any) | ☐ (by Mark) |
| | PHONE C/H/W / | or ☐ MISC | | | AGENCY | ☐ CA DMV | ☐ US State Dept | EXPIRES | ➡ | | |

| CW #1 | #1 WITNESS's NAME | ☐ P/Known | ADDRESS | ☐ Non-Public | ☐ Driver's License # | ☐ Passport | ☐ Other ID | ISSUED | SIGNATURE | ☐ (after oath / affirmation) |
| | PHONE C/H/W / | or ☐ MISC | | | AGENCY | ☐ CA DMV | ☐ US State Dept | EXPIRES | ❶ | |

| CW #2 | #2 WITNESS's NAME | ☐ P/Known | ADDRESS | ☐ Non-Public | ☐ Driver's License # | ☐ Passport | ☐ Other ID | ISSUED | SIGNATURE | ☐ (after oath / affirmation) |
| | PHONE C/H/W / | or ☐ MISC | | | AGENCY | ☐ CA DMV | ☐ US State Dept | EXPIRES | ❷ | |

Entry 236

| SERVICE | DATE - -20 | TIME : am/pm | ADDRESS | ☐ Signer's ☐ Office | NOTES | ☐ Stop MILES | Notary $ | ☐ Adv. Travel $ | ☐ Rush $ | ☐ Copy $ | ☐ Other $ | TOTAL FEES $ |

TYPE: ☐ Acknowledgment ☐ Jurat ☐ Copy Certification ☐ Oath/Affirmation ☐ Oath of Office ☐ Proof of Execution ☐ Protest ☐ Other

Fingerprint — R T I M R P L

DOC TYPE: ☐ Deed (Grant • Trust Transfer • Gift • Interspousal • Quitclaim • ToD • Warranty) ☐ DOT (Mortgage) ☐ Trust (Certification • Rev/Irrev • Am/Rest) ☐ POA (General/Limited • Durable/Springing) ☐ POAH (AHCD • Living Will) ☐ Agreement (Compliance-E&O • Correction) ☐ Affidavit (Borrower • Occupancy • Ownership • Refi • Survey • Debts & Liens • Name-Signature-ID • Marital • Death • Will) ☐ Other (Vehicle Title • Safe Deposit Box)

DOC DATE: J F M A M J J A S O N D ,   **DOC TITLE or TYPE:**   **# OF PAGES:**   ☐ Inspect/Copy Request   **Entry X-Ref #:**

☐ **SATISFACTORY EVIDENCE** ☐ Driver's License / Passport / State ID / Military / Government / Tribal / Inmate / Other ID   *or*   ☐ Credible Witness(es)

| SIGNER | SIGNER's NAME | ☐ For | ADDRESS | ☐ Non-Public | ☐ Capacity # | ☐ Voluntary | ☐ Proper ID | ISSUED | SIGNATURE | ☐ (oath / affirmation, if any) | ☐ (by Mark) |
| | PHONE C/H/W / | or ☐ MISC | | | AGENCY | ☐ CA DMV | ☐ US State Dept | EXPIRES | ➡ | | |

| CW #1 | #1 WITNESS's NAME | ☐ P/Known | ADDRESS | ☐ Non-Public | ☐ Driver's License # | ☐ Passport | ☐ Other ID | ISSUED | SIGNATURE | ☐ (after oath / affirmation) |
| | PHONE C/H/W / | or ☐ MISC | | | AGENCY | ☐ CA DMV | ☐ US State Dept | EXPIRES | ❶ | |

| CW #2 | #2 WITNESS's NAME | ☐ P/Known | ADDRESS | ☐ Non-Public | ☐ Driver's License # | ☐ Passport | ☐ Other ID | ISSUED | SIGNATURE | ☐ (after oath / affirmation) |
| | PHONE C/H/W / | or ☐ MISC | | | AGENCY | ☐ CA DMV | ☐ US State Dept | EXPIRES | ❷ | |

NOTARY NAME (printed): _____ **COMMISSION #:** _____

Entry 237

SERVICE	DATE ‑ ‑20	TIME : am pm	ADDRESS ☐ Signer's ☐ Office	NOTES	☐ Stop	MILES	Notary ☐ Adv. Travel ☐ Rush ☐ Copy ☐ Other	TOTAL FEES
						$	$ $ $ $	$

237

TYPE ☐ Acknowledgment ☐ Jurat ☐ Copy Certification ☐ Oath/Affirmation ☐ Oath of Office ☐ Proof of Execution ☐ Protest ☐ Other

R | Fingerprint

DOCUMENT

DOC TYPE ☐ Deed ☐ DOT ☐ Trust ☐ POA ☐ POAH ☐ Agreement ☐ Affidavit ☐ Other

Grant • Trust Transfer • Gift | Mortgage | Certification | General / Limited | AHCD | Compliance-E&O | Borrower • Occupancy • Ownership • Refi • Survey | Vehicle Title
Interspousal • Quitclaim • ToD • Warranty | Rev / Irrev • Am / Rest | Durable / Springing | Living Will | Correction | Debts & Liens • Name-Signature-ID • Marital • Death • Will | Safe Deposit Box

T I M R P

DOC DATE J F M A M J J A S O N D , **DOC TITLE or TYPE** _____ **# OF PAGES** ☐ Inspect/Copy Request — Entry X-Ref #

L

☐ **SATISFACTORY EVIDENCE** ☐ Driver's License / Passport / State ID / Military / Government / Tribal / Inmate / Other ID *or* ☐ Credible Witness(es)

SIGNER	SIGNER's NAME ☐ For	ADDRESS	☐ Non-Public ☐ Capacity # ☐ Voluntary ☐ Proper ID	ISSUED	SIGNATURE ☐ (oath / affirmation, if any) ☐ (by Mark)
	PHONE C / H / W *or* ☐ MISC /		AGENCY ☐ CA DMV ☐ US State Dept	EXPIRES	➡

CW #1	#1 WITNESS's NAME ☐ P/Known	ADDRESS	☐ Non-Public ☐ Driver's License # ☐ Passport ☐ Other ID	ISSUED	SIGNATURE ☐ (after oath / affirmation)
	PHONE C / H / W *or* ☐ MISC /		AGENCY ☐ CA DMV ☐ US State Dept	EXPIRES	❶

CW #2	#2 WITNESS's NAME ☐ P/Known	ADDRESS	☐ Non-Public ☐ Driver's License # ☐ Passport ☐ Other ID	ISSUED	SIGNATURE ☐ (after oath / affirmation)
	PHONE C / H / W *or* ☐ MISC /		AGENCY ☐ CA DMV ☐ US State Dept	EXPIRES	❷

Entry 238

SERVICE	DATE ‑ ‑20	TIME : am pm	ADDRESS ☐ Signer's ☐ Office	NOTES	☐ Stop	MILES	Notary ☐ Adv. Travel ☐ Rush ☐ Copy ☐ Other	TOTAL FEES
						$	$ $ $ $	$

238

TYPE ☐ Acknowledgment ☐ Jurat ☐ Copy Certification ☐ Oath/Affirmation ☐ Oath of Office ☐ Proof of Execution ☐ Protest ☐ Other

R | Fingerprint

DOCUMENT

DOC TYPE ☐ Deed ☐ DOT ☐ Trust ☐ POA ☐ POAH ☐ Agreement ☐ Affidavit ☐ Other

Grant • Trust Transfer • Gift | Mortgage | Certification | General / Limited | AHCD | Compliance-E&O | Borrower • Occupancy • Ownership • Refi • Survey | Vehicle Title
Interspousal • Quitclaim • ToD • Warranty | Rev / Irrev • Am / Rest | Durable / Springing | Living Will | Correction | Debts & Liens • Name-Signature-ID • Marital • Death • Will | Safe Deposit Box

T I M R P

DOC DATE J F M A M J J A S O N D , **DOC TITLE or TYPE** _____ **# OF PAGES** ☐ Inspect/Copy Request — Entry X-Ref #

L

☐ **SATISFACTORY EVIDENCE** ☐ Driver's License / Passport / State ID / Military / Government / Tribal / Inmate / Other ID *or* ☐ Credible Witness(es)

SIGNER	SIGNER's NAME ☐ For	ADDRESS	☐ Non-Public ☐ Capacity # ☐ Voluntary ☐ Proper ID	ISSUED	SIGNATURE ☐ (oath / affirmation, if any) ☐ (by Mark)
	PHONE C / H / W *or* ☐ MISC /		AGENCY ☐ CA DMV ☐ US State Dept	EXPIRES	➡

CW #1	#1 WITNESS's NAME ☐ P/Known	ADDRESS	☐ Non-Public ☐ Driver's License # ☐ Passport ☐ Other ID	ISSUED	SIGNATURE ☐ (after oath / affirmation)
	PHONE C / H / W *or* ☐ MISC /		AGENCY ☐ CA DMV ☐ US State Dept	EXPIRES	❶

CW #2	#2 WITNESS's NAME ☐ P/Known	ADDRESS	☐ Non-Public ☐ Driver's License # ☐ Passport ☐ Other ID	ISSUED	SIGNATURE ☐ (after oath / affirmation)
	PHONE C / H / W *or* ☐ MISC /		AGENCY ☐ CA DMV ☐ US State Dept	EXPIRES	❷

NOTARY NAME (printed):   COMMISSION #:

239

SERVICE | DATE - -20 | TIME : am/pm | ADDRESS ☐ Signer's ☐ Office | NOTES | ☐ Stop | MILES | Notary $ | ☐ Adv. Travel $ | ☐ Rush $ | ☐ Copy $ | ☐ Other $ | TOTAL FEES $

TYPE ☐ Acknowledgment ☐ Jurat ☐ Copy Certification ☐ Oath/Affirmation ☐ Oath of Office ☐ Proof of Execution ☐ Protest ☐ Other   **R T I M R P L**   **Fingerprint**

DOCUMENT
DOC TYPE ☐ Deed   ☐ DOT   ☐ Trust   ☐ POA   ☐ POAH   ☐ Agreement   ☐ Affidavit   ☐ Other
Grant • Trust Transfer • Gift   Mortgage   Certification   General / Limited   AHCD   Compliance-E&O   Borrower • Occupancy • Ownership • Refi • Survey   Vehicle Title
Interspousal • Quitclaim • ToD • Warranty   Rev / Irrev • Am / Rest   Durable / Springing   Living Will   Correction   Debts & Liens • Name-Signature-ID • Marital • Death • Will   Safe Deposit Box

DOC DATE   J F M A M J   DOC TITLE or TYPE   # OF PAGES   ☐ Inspect/Copy Request
         J A S O N D   Entry X-Ref #

☐ **SATISFACTORY EVIDENCE** ☐ Driver's License / Passport / State ID / Military / Government / Tribal / Inmate / Other ID   *or*   ☐ Credible Witness(es)

SIGNER | SIGNER's NAME | ☐ For | ADDRESS | ☐ Non-Public | ☐ Capacity # | ☐ Voluntary | ☐ Proper ID | ISSUED | SIGNATURE ☐ (oath / affirmation, if any) ☐ (by Mark)
PHONE C / H / W   /   *or* ☐ MISC   AGENCY   ☐ CA DMV   ☐ US State Dept   EXPIRES   ➤

CW #1 | #1 WITNESS's NAME | ☐ P/Known | ADDRESS | ☐ Non-Public | ☐ Driver's License ☐ Passport ☐ Other ID # | ISSUED | SIGNATURE ☐ (after oath / affirmation)
PHONE C / H / W   /   *or* ☐ MISC   AGENCY   ☐ CA DMV   ☐ US State Dept   EXPIRES   ❶

CW #2 | #2 WITNESS's NAME | ☐ P/Known | ADDRESS | ☐ Non-Public | ☐ Driver's License ☐ Passport ☐ Other ID # | ISSUED | SIGNATURE ☐ (after oath / affirmation)
PHONE C / H / W   /   *or* ☐ MISC   AGENCY   ☐ CA DMV   ☐ US State Dept   EXPIRES   ❷

240

SERVICE | DATE - -20 | TIME : am/pm | ADDRESS ☐ Signer's ☐ Office | NOTES | ☐ Stop | MILES | Notary $ | ☐ Adv. Travel $ | ☐ Rush $ | ☐ Copy $ | ☐ Other $ | TOTAL FEES $

TYPE ☐ Acknowledgment ☐ Jurat ☐ Copy Certification ☐ Oath/Affirmation ☐ Oath of Office ☐ Proof of Execution ☐ Protest ☐ Other   **R T I M R P L**   **Fingerprint**

DOCUMENT
DOC TYPE ☐ Deed   ☐ DOT   ☐ Trust   ☐ POA   ☐ POAH   ☐ Agreement   ☐ Affidavit   ☐ Other
Grant • Trust Transfer • Gift   Mortgage   Certification   General / Limited   AHCD   Compliance-E&O   Borrower • Occupancy • Ownership • Refi • Survey   Vehicle Title
Interspousal • Quitclaim • ToD • Warranty   Rev / Irrev • Am / Rest   Durable / Springing   Living Will   Correction   Debts & Liens • Name-Signature-ID • Marital • Death • Will   Safe Deposit Box

DOC DATE   J F M A M J   DOC TITLE or TYPE   # OF PAGES   ☐ Inspect/Copy Request
         J A S O N D   Entry X-Ref #

☐ **SATISFACTORY EVIDENCE** ☐ Driver's License / Passport / State ID / Military / Government / Tribal / Inmate / Other ID   *or*   ☐ Credible Witness(es)

SIGNER | SIGNER's NAME | ☐ For | ADDRESS | ☐ Non-Public | ☐ Capacity # | ☐ Voluntary | ☐ Proper ID | ISSUED | SIGNATURE ☐ (oath / affirmation, if any) ☐ (by Mark)
PHONE C / H / W   /   *or* ☐ MISC   AGENCY   ☐ CA DMV   ☐ US State Dept   EXPIRES   ➤

CW #1 | #1 WITNESS's NAME | ☐ P/Known | ADDRESS | ☐ Non-Public | ☐ Driver's License ☐ Passport ☐ Other ID # | ISSUED | SIGNATURE ☐ (after oath / affirmation)
PHONE C / H / W   /   *or* ☐ MISC   AGENCY   ☐ CA DMV   ☐ US State Dept   EXPIRES   ❶

CW #2 | #2 WITNESS's NAME | ☐ P/Known | ADDRESS | ☐ Non-Public | ☐ Driver's License ☐ Passport ☐ Other ID # | ISSUED | SIGNATURE ☐ (after oath / affirmation)
PHONE C / H / W   /   *or* ☐ MISC   AGENCY   ☐ CA DMV   ☐ US State Dept   EXPIRES   ❷

NOTARY NAME (printed): _____   COMMISSION #: _____

241

SERVICE	DATE - -20	TIME :	am pm	ADDRESS	☐ Signer's	☐ Office	NOTES	☐ Stop	MILES	Notary	☐ Adv. Travel	☐ Rush	☐ Copy	☐ Other	TOTAL FEES
									$	$		$	$	$	$

Fingerprint

TYPE ☐ Acknowledgment ☐ Jurat ☐ Copy Certification ☐ Oath/Affirmation ☐ Oath of Office ☐ Proof of Execution ☐ Protest ☐ Other

DOCUMENT

DOC TYPE ☐ Deed ☐ DOT ☐ Trust ☐ POA ☐ POAH ☐ Agreement ☐ Affidavit ☐ Other
Grant • Trust Transfer • Gift | Mortgage | Certification | General / Limited | AHCD | Compliance-E&O | Borrower • Occupancy • Ownership • Refi • Survey | Vehicle Title
Interspousal • Quitclaim • ToD • Warranty | Rev / Irrev • Am / Rest | Durable / Springing | Living Will | Correction | Debts & Liens • Name-Signature-ID • Marital • Death • Will | Safe Deposit Box

DOC DATE J F M A M J / J A S O N D , | DOC TITLE or TYPE | # OF PAGES | ☐ Inspect/Copy Request | Entry X-Ref #

☐ **SATISFACTORY EVIDENCE** ☐ Driver's License / Passport / State ID / Military / Government / Tribal / Inmate / Other ID **or** ☐ Credible Witness(es)

SIGNER

SIGNER's NAME | ☐ For | ADDRESS | ☐ Non-Public | ☐ Capacity | ☐ Voluntary | ☐ Proper ID | ISSUED | SIGNATURE | ☐ (oath / affirmation, if any) | ☐ (by Mark)
#
PHONE C / H / W or ☐ MISC / | AGENCY | ☐ CA DMV | ☐ US State Dept | EXPIRES | ➡

CW #1

#1 WITNESS's NAME | ☐ P/Known | ADDRESS | ☐ Non-Public | ☐ Driver's License | ☐ Passport | ☐ Other ID | ISSUED | SIGNATURE | ☐ (after oath / affirmation)
#
PHONE C / H / W or ☐ MISC / | AGENCY | ☐ CA DMV | ☐ US State Dept | EXPIRES | ❶

CW #2

#2 WITNESS's NAME | ☐ P/Known | ADDRESS | ☐ Non-Public | ☐ Driver's License | ☐ Passport | ☐ Other ID | ISSUED | SIGNATURE | ☐ (after oath / affirmation)
#
PHONE C / H / W or ☐ MISC / | AGENCY | ☐ CA DMV | ☐ US State Dept | EXPIRES | ❷

242

SERVICE	DATE - -20	TIME :	am pm	ADDRESS	☐ Signer's	☐ Office	NOTES	☐ Stop	MILES	Notary	☐ Adv. Travel	☐ Rush	☐ Copy	☐ Other	TOTAL FEES
									$	$		$	$	$	$

Fingerprint

TYPE ☐ Acknowledgment ☐ Jurat ☐ Copy Certification ☐ Oath/Affirmation ☐ Oath of Office ☐ Proof of Execution ☐ Protest ☐ Other

DOCUMENT

DOC TYPE ☐ Deed ☐ DOT ☐ Trust ☐ POA ☐ POAH ☐ Agreement ☐ Affidavit ☐ Other
Grant • Trust Transfer • Gift | Mortgage | Certification | General / Limited | AHCD | Compliance-E&O | Borrower • Occupancy • Ownership • Refi • Survey | Vehicle Title
Interspousal • Quitclaim • ToD • Warranty | Rev / Irrev • Am / Rest | Durable / Springing | Living Will | Correction | Debts & Liens • Name-Signature-ID • Marital • Death • Will | Safe Deposit Box

DOC DATE J F M A M J / J A S O N D , | DOC TITLE or TYPE | # OF PAGES | ☐ Inspect/Copy Request | Entry X-Ref #

☐ **SATISFACTORY EVIDENCE** ☐ Driver's License / Passport / State ID / Military / Government / Tribal / Inmate / Other ID **or** ☐ Credible Witness(es)

SIGNER

SIGNER's NAME | ☐ For | ADDRESS | ☐ Non-Public | ☐ Capacity | ☐ Voluntary | ☐ Proper ID | ISSUED | SIGNATURE | ☐ (oath / affirmation, if any) | ☐ (by Mark)
#
PHONE C / H / W or ☐ MISC / | AGENCY | ☐ CA DMV | ☐ US State Dept | EXPIRES | ➡

CW #1

#1 WITNESS's NAME | ☐ P/Known | ADDRESS | ☐ Non-Public | ☐ Driver's License | ☐ Passport | ☐ Other ID | ISSUED | SIGNATURE | ☐ (after oath / affirmation)
#
PHONE C / H / W or ☐ MISC / | AGENCY | ☐ CA DMV | ☐ US State Dept | EXPIRES | ❶

CW #2

#2 WITNESS's NAME | ☐ P/Known | ADDRESS | ☐ Non-Public | ☐ Driver's License | ☐ Passport | ☐ Other ID | ISSUED | SIGNATURE | ☐ (after oath / affirmation)
#
PHONE C / H / W or ☐ MISC / | AGENCY | ☐ CA DMV | ☐ US State Dept | EXPIRES | ❷

NOTARY NAME (printed):   COMMISSION #:

243

SERVICE
- DATE: - -20
- TIME: : am/pm
- ADDRESS: ☐ Signer's ☐ Office
- NOTES
- ☐ Stop MILES | Notary $ | Adv. Travel $ | Rush $ | Copy $ | Other $ | TOTAL FEES $
- TYPE: ☐ Acknowledgment ☐ Jurat ☐ Copy Certification ☐ Oath/Affirmation ☐ Oath of Office ☐ Proof of Execution ☐ Protest ☐ Other

DOCUMENT
- DOC TYPE: ☐ Deed (Grant • Trust Transfer • Gift • Interspousal • Quitclaim • ToD • Warranty) ☐ DOT (Mortgage Certification Rev / Irrev • Am / Rest) ☐ Trust ☐ POA (General / Limited Durable / Springing) ☐ POAH (AHCD Living Will) ☐ Agreement (Compliance-E&O Correction) ☐ Affidavit (Borrower • Occupancy • Ownership • Refi • Survey Debts & Liens • Name-Signature-ID • Marital • Death • Will) ☐ Other (Vehicle Title Safe Deposit Box)
- DOC DATE: J F M A M J / J A S O N D ,
- DOC TITLE or TYPE
- # OF PAGES | ☐ Inspect/Copy Request
- Entry X-Ref #

☐ **SATISFACTORY EVIDENCE** ☐ Driver's License / Passport / State ID / Military / Government / Tribal / Inmate / Other ID *or* ☐ Credible Witness(es)

Fingerprint R T I M R P L

SIGNER
- SIGNER's NAME | ☐ For | ADDRESS | ☐ Non-Public | ☐ Capacity # | ☐ Voluntary | ☐ Proper ID | ISSUED | SIGNATURE ☐ (oath / affirmation, if any) ☐ (by Mark)
- PHONE C / H / W / | or ☐ MISC | AGENCY | ☐ CA DMV | ☐ US State Dept | EXPIRES | ➡

CW #1
- #1 WITNESS's NAME | ☐ P/Known | ADDRESS | ☐ Non-Public | ☐ Driver's License | ☐ Passport | ☐ Other ID | ISSUED | SIGNATURE ☐ (after oath / affirmation)
- PHONE C / H / W / | or ☐ MISC | AGENCY | ☐ CA DMV | ☐ US State Dept | EXPIRES | ❶

CW #2
- #2 WITNESS's NAME | ☐ P/Known | ADDRESS | ☐ Non-Public | ☐ Driver's License | ☐ Passport | ☐ Other ID | ISSUED | SIGNATURE ☐ (after oath / affirmation)
- PHONE C / H / W / | or ☐ MISC | AGENCY | ☐ CA DMV | ☐ US State Dept | EXPIRES | ❷

244

SERVICE
- DATE: - -20
- TIME: : am/pm
- ADDRESS: ☐ Signer's ☐ Office
- NOTES
- ☐ Stop MILES | Notary $ | Adv. Travel $ | Rush $ | Copy $ | Other $ | TOTAL FEES $
- TYPE: ☐ Acknowledgment ☐ Jurat ☐ Copy Certification ☐ Oath/Affirmation ☐ Oath of Office ☐ Proof of Execution ☐ Protest ☐ Other

DOCUMENT
- DOC TYPE: ☐ Deed (Grant • Trust Transfer • Gift • Interspousal • Quitclaim • ToD • Warranty) ☐ DOT (Mortgage Certification Rev / Irrev • Am / Rest) ☐ Trust ☐ POA (General / Limited Durable / Springing) ☐ POAH (AHCD Living Will) ☐ Agreement (Compliance-E&O Correction) ☐ Affidavit (Borrower • Occupancy • Ownership • Refi • Survey Debts & Liens • Name-Signature-ID • Marital • Death • Will) ☐ Other (Vehicle Title Safe Deposit Box)
- DOC DATE: J F M A M J / J A S O N D ,
- DOC TITLE or TYPE
- # OF PAGES | ☐ Inspect/Copy Request
- Entry X-Ref #

☐ **SATISFACTORY EVIDENCE** ☐ Driver's License / Passport / State ID / Military / Government / Tribal / Inmate / Other ID *or* ☐ Credible Witness(es)

Fingerprint R T I M R P L

SIGNER
- SIGNER's NAME | ☐ For | ADDRESS | ☐ Non-Public | ☐ Capacity # | ☐ Voluntary | ☐ Proper ID | ISSUED | SIGNATURE ☐ (oath / affirmation, if any) ☐ (by Mark)
- PHONE C / H / W / | or ☐ MISC | AGENCY | ☐ CA DMV | ☐ US State Dept | EXPIRES | ➡

CW #1
- #1 WITNESS's NAME | ☐ P/Known | ADDRESS | ☐ Non-Public | ☐ Driver's License | ☐ Passport | ☐ Other ID | ISSUED | SIGNATURE ☐ (after oath / affirmation)
- PHONE C / H / W / | or ☐ MISC | AGENCY | ☐ CA DMV | ☐ US State Dept | EXPIRES | ❶

CW #2
- #2 WITNESS's NAME | ☐ P/Known | ADDRESS | ☐ Non-Public | ☐ Driver's License | ☐ Passport | ☐ Other ID | ISSUED | SIGNATURE ☐ (after oath / affirmation)
- PHONE C / H / W / | or ☐ MISC | AGENCY | ☐ CA DMV | ☐ US State Dept | EXPIRES | ❷

NOTARY NAME (printed):   COMMISSION #:

245

SERVICE

DATE	TIME	am	ADDRESS	☐ Signer's	☐ Office	NOTES	☐ Stop	MILES	Notary	☐ Adv. Travel	☐ Rush	☐ Copy	☐ Other	TOTAL FEES
- -20	:	pm							$	$	$	$	$	$

TYPE ☐ Acknowledgment ☐ Jurat ☐ Copy Certification ☐ Oath/Affirmation ☐ Oath of Office ☐ Proof of Execution ☐ Protest ☐ Other

R   **Fingerprint**

DOCUMENT

DOC TYPE ☐ Deed ☐ DOT ☐ Trust ☐ POA ☐ POAH ☐ Agreement ☐ Affidavit ☐ Other

Grant • Trust Transfer • Gift   Mortgage   Certification   General / Limited   AHCD   Compliance-E&O   Borrower • Occupancy • Ownership • Refi • Survey   Vehicle Title

Interspousal • Quitclaim • ToD • Warranty   Rev / Irrev • Am / Rest   Durable / Springing   Living Will   Correction   Debts & Liens • Name-Signature-ID • Marital • Death • Will   Safe Deposit Box

DOC DATE   J F M A M J   DOC TITLE or TYPE   # OF PAGES ☐ Inspect/Copy Request

J A S O N D   ,   Entry X-Ref #

T I M R P L

☐ **SATISFACTORY EVIDENCE** ☐ Driver's License / Passport / State ID / Military / Government / Tribal / Inmate / Other ID   *or*   ☐ Credible Witness(es)

SIGNER

SIGNER's NAME	☐ For	ADDRESS	☐ Non-Public	☐ Capacity	☐ Voluntary	☐ Proper ID	ISSUED	SIGNATURE ☐ (oath / affirmation, if any) ☐ (by Mark)
				#				
PHONE C / H / W	*or* ☐ MISC			AGENCY	☐ CA DMV	☐ US State Dept	EXPIRES	➡

CW #1

#1 WITNESS's NAME	☐ P/Known	ADDRESS	☐ Non-Public	☐ Driver's License	☐ Passport	☐ Other ID	ISSUED	SIGNATURE ☐ (after oath / affirmation)
				#				
PHONE C / H / W	*or* ☐ MISC			AGENCY	☐ CA DMV	☐ US State Dept	EXPIRES	❶

CW #2

#2 WITNESS's NAME	☐ P/Known	ADDRESS	☐ Non-Public	☐ Driver's License	☐ Passport	☐ Other ID	ISSUED	SIGNATURE ☐ (after oath / affirmation)
				#				
PHONE C / H / W	*or* ☐ MISC			AGENCY	☐ CA DMV	☐ US State Dept	EXPIRES	❷

246

SERVICE

DATE	TIME	am	ADDRESS	☐ Signer's	☐ Office	NOTES	☐ Stop	MILES	Notary	☐ Adv. Travel	☐ Rush	☐ Copy	☐ Other	TOTAL FEES
- -20	:	pm							$	$	$	$	$	$

TYPE ☐ Acknowledgment ☐ Jurat ☐ Copy Certification ☐ Oath/Affirmation ☐ Oath of Office ☐ Proof of Execution ☐ Protest ☐ Other

R   **Fingerprint**

DOCUMENT

DOC TYPE ☐ Deed ☐ DOT ☐ Trust ☐ POA ☐ POAH ☐ Agreement ☐ Affidavit ☐ Other

Grant • Trust Transfer • Gift   Mortgage   Certification   General / Limited   AHCD   Compliance-E&O   Borrower • Occupancy • Ownership • Refi • Survey   Vehicle Title

Interspousal • Quitclaim • ToD • Warranty   Rev / Irrev • Am / Rest   Durable / Springing   Living Will   Correction   Debts & Liens • Name-Signature-ID • Marital • Death • Will   Safe Deposit Box

DOC DATE   J F M A M J   DOC TITLE or TYPE   # OF PAGES ☐ Inspect/Copy Request

J A S O N D   ,   Entry X-Ref #

T I M R P L

☐ **SATISFACTORY EVIDENCE** ☐ Driver's License / Passport / State ID / Military / Government / Tribal / Inmate / Other ID   *or*   ☐ Credible Witness(es)

SIGNER

SIGNER's NAME	☐ For	ADDRESS	☐ Non-Public	☐ Capacity	☐ Voluntary	☐ Proper ID	ISSUED	SIGNATURE ☐ (oath / affirmation, if any) ☐ (by Mark)
				#				
PHONE C / H / W	*or* ☐ MISC			AGENCY	☐ CA DMV	☐ US State Dept	EXPIRES	➡

CW #1

#1 WITNESS's NAME	☐ P/Known	ADDRESS	☐ Non-Public	☐ Driver's License	☐ Passport	☐ Other ID	ISSUED	SIGNATURE ☐ (after oath / affirmation)
				#				
PHONE C / H / W	*or* ☐ MISC			AGENCY	☐ CA DMV	☐ US State Dept	EXPIRES	❶

CW #2

#2 WITNESS's NAME	☐ P/Known	ADDRESS	☐ Non-Public	☐ Driver's License	☐ Passport	☐ Other ID	ISSUED	SIGNATURE ☐ (after oath / affirmation)
				#				
PHONE C / H / W	*or* ☐ MISC			AGENCY	☐ CA DMV	☐ US State Dept	EXPIRES	❷

NOTARY NAME (printed): COMMISSION #:

Entry 247

SERVICE
- DATE: - -20
- TIME: : am/pm
- ADDRESS: ☐ Signer's ☐ Office
- NOTES
- ☐ Stop MILES Notary $ ☐ Adv. Travel $ ☐ Rush $ ☐ Copy $ ☐ Other $ TOTAL FEES $
- TYPE: ☐ Acknowledgment ☐ Jurat ☐ Copy Certification ☐ Oath/Affirmation ☐ Oath of Office ☐ Proof of Execution ☐ Protest ☐ Other

DOCUMENT
- DOC TYPE: ☐ Deed (Grant • Trust Transfer • Gift / Interspousal • Quitclaim • ToD • Warranty) ☐ DOT (Mortgage / Certification / Rev / Irrev • Am / Rest) ☐ Trust ☐ POA (General / Limited / Durable / Springing) ☐ POAH (AHCD / Living Will) ☐ Agreement (Compliance-E&O / Correction) ☐ Affidavit (Borrower • Occupancy • Ownership • Refi • Survey / Debts & Liens • Name-Signature-ID • Marital • Death • Will) ☐ Other (Vehicle Title / Safe Deposit Box)
- DOC DATE: J F M A M J J A S O N D ,
- DOC TITLE or TYPE:
- # OF PAGES:
- ☐ Inspect/Copy Request
- Entry X-Ref #:

Fingerprint: R T I M R P L

☐ **SATISFACTORY EVIDENCE** ☐ Driver's License / Passport / State ID / Military / Government / Tribal / Inmate / Other ID *or* ☐ Credible Witness(es)

SIGNER
- SIGNER's NAME: ☐ For
- ADDRESS: ☐ Non-Public
- ☐ Capacity ☐ Voluntary ☐ Proper ID
- ISSUED #
- SIGNATURE ☐ (oath / affirmation, if any) ☐ (by Mark)
- PHONE C / H / W   /   or ☐ MISC
- AGENCY ☐ CA DMV ☐ US State Dept EXPIRES

CW #1
- #1 WITNESS's NAME ☐ P/Known
- ADDRESS ☐ Non-Public
- ☐ Driver's License ☐ Passport ☐ Other ID ISSUED #
- SIGNATURE ☐ (after oath / affirmation)
- PHONE C / H / W / or ☐ MISC
- AGENCY ☐ CA DMV ☐ US State Dept EXPIRES
- ❶

CW #2
- #2 WITNESS's NAME ☐ P/Known
- ADDRESS ☐ Non-Public
- ☐ Driver's License ☐ Passport ☐ Other ID ISSUED #
- SIGNATURE ☐ (after oath / affirmation)
- PHONE C / H / W / or ☐ MISC
- AGENCY ☐ CA DMV ☐ US State Dept EXPIRES
- ❷

Entry 248

SERVICE
- DATE: - -20
- TIME: : am/pm
- ADDRESS: ☐ Signer's ☐ Office
- NOTES
- ☐ Stop MILES Notary $ ☐ Adv. Travel $ ☐ Rush $ ☐ Copy $ ☐ Other $ TOTAL FEES $
- TYPE: ☐ Acknowledgment ☐ Jurat ☐ Copy Certification ☐ Oath/Affirmation ☐ Oath of Office ☐ Proof of Execution ☐ Protest ☐ Other

DOCUMENT
- DOC TYPE: ☐ Deed (Grant • Trust Transfer • Gift / Interspousal • Quitclaim • ToD • Warranty) ☐ DOT (Mortgage / Certification / Rev / Irrev • Am / Rest) ☐ Trust ☐ POA (General / Limited / Durable / Springing) ☐ POAH (AHCD / Living Will) ☐ Agreement (Compliance-E&O / Correction) ☐ Affidavit (Borrower • Occupancy • Ownership • Refi • Survey / Debts & Liens • Name-Signature-ID • Marital • Death • Will) ☐ Other (Vehicle Title / Safe Deposit Box)
- DOC DATE: J F M A M J J A S O N D ,
- DOC TITLE or TYPE:
- # OF PAGES:
- ☐ Inspect/Copy Request
- Entry X-Ref #:

Fingerprint: R T I M R P L

☐ **SATISFACTORY EVIDENCE** ☐ Driver's License / Passport / State ID / Military / Government / Tribal / Inmate / Other ID *or* ☐ Credible Witness(es)

SIGNER
- SIGNER's NAME: ☐ For
- ADDRESS: ☐ Non-Public
- ☐ Capacity ☐ Voluntary ☐ Proper ID
- ISSUED #
- SIGNATURE ☐ (oath / affirmation, if any) ☐ (by Mark)
- PHONE C / H / W / or ☐ MISC
- AGENCY ☐ CA DMV ☐ US State Dept EXPIRES

CW #1
- #1 WITNESS's NAME ☐ P/Known
- ADDRESS ☐ Non-Public
- ☐ Driver's License ☐ Passport ☐ Other ID ISSUED #
- SIGNATURE ☐ (after oath / affirmation)
- PHONE C / H / W / or ☐ MISC
- AGENCY ☐ CA DMV ☐ US State Dept EXPIRES
- ❶

CW #2
- #2 WITNESS's NAME ☐ P/Known
- ADDRESS ☐ Non-Public
- ☐ Driver's License ☐ Passport ☐ Other ID ISSUED #
- SIGNATURE ☐ (after oath / affirmation)
- PHONE C / H / W / or ☐ MISC
- AGENCY ☐ CA DMV ☐ US State Dept EXPIRES
- ❷

NOTARY NAME (printed):   COMMISSION #:

Entry 249

SERVICE — DATE - -20   TIME : am/pm   ADDRESS   □ Signer's   □ Office   NOTES   □ Stop   MILES   Notary □ Adv. Travel □ Rush □ Copy □ Other   TOTAL FEES $ $ $ $ $ $

TYPE □ Acknowledgment □ Jurat □ Copy Certification □ Oath/Affirmation □ Oath of Office □ Proof of Execution □ Protest □ Other

R   **Fingerprint**

DOCUMENT

DOC TYPE □ Deed   □ DOT   □ Trust   □ POA   □ POAH   □ Agreement   □ Affidavit   □ Other

Grant • Trust Transfer • Gift   Mortgage   Certification   General / Limited   AHCD   Compliance-E&O   Borrower • Occupancy • Ownership • Refi • Survey   Vehicle Title

Interspousal • Quitclaim • ToD • Warranty   Rev / Irrev • Am / Rest   Durable / Springing   Living Will   Correction   Debts & Liens • Name-Signature-ID • Marital • Death • Will   Safe Deposit Box

DOC DATE   J F M A M J   J A S O N D   ,   DOC TITLE or TYPE   # OF PAGES   □ Inspect/Copy Request   Entry X-Ref #

T I M R P L

□ **SATISFACTORY EVIDENCE** □ Driver's License / Passport / State ID / Military / Government / Tribal / Inmate / Other ID   *or*   □ Credible Witness(es)

SIGNER

SIGNER's NAME   □ For   ADDRESS   □ Non-Public   □ Capacity   □ Voluntary   □ Proper ID   ISSUED #   SIGNATURE   □ *(oath / affirmation, if any)*   □ (by Mark)

PHONE C / H / W   *or* □ MISC   /   AGENCY   □ CA DMV   □ US State Dept   EXPIRES   ➡

CW #1

#1 WITNESS's NAME   □ P/Known   ADDRESS   □ Non-Public   □ Driver's License   □ Passport   □ Other ID   ISSUED #   SIGNATURE   □ *(after oath / affirmation)*

PHONE C / H / W   *or* □ MISC   AGENCY   □ CA DMV   □ US State Dept   EXPIRES   ❶

CW #2

#2 WITNESS's NAME   □ P/Known   ADDRESS   □ Non-Public   □ Driver's License   □ Passport   □ Other ID   ISSUED #   SIGNATURE   □ *(after oath / affirmation)*

PHONE C / H / W   *or* □ MISC   AGENCY   □ CA DMV   □ US State Dept   EXPIRES   ❷

Entry 250

SERVICE — DATE - -20   TIME : am/pm   ADDRESS   □ Signer's   □ Office   NOTES   □ Stop   MILES   Notary □ Adv. Travel □ Rush □ Copy □ Other   TOTAL FEES $ $ $ $ $ $

TYPE □ Acknowledgment □ Jurat □ Copy Certification □ Oath/Affirmation □ Oath of Office □ Proof of Execution □ Protest □ Other

R   **Fingerprint**

DOCUMENT

DOC TYPE □ Deed   □ DOT   □ Trust   □ POA   □ POAH   □ Agreement   □ Affidavit   □ Other

Grant • Trust Transfer • Gift   Mortgage   Certification   General / Limited   AHCD   Compliance-E&O   Borrower • Occupancy • Ownership • Refi • Survey   Vehicle Title

Interspousal • Quitclaim • ToD • Warranty   Rev / Irrev • Am / Rest   Durable / Springing   Living Will   Correction   Debts & Liens • Name-Signature-ID • Marital • Death • Will   Safe Deposit Box

DOC DATE   J F M A M J   J A S O N D   ,   DOC TITLE or TYPE   # OF PAGES   □ Inspect/Copy Request   Entry X-Ref #

T I M R P L

□ **SATISFACTORY EVIDENCE** □ Driver's License / Passport / State ID / Military / Government / Tribal / Inmate / Other ID   *or*   □ Credible Witness(es)

SIGNER

SIGNER's NAME   □ For   ADDRESS   □ Non-Public   □ Capacity   □ Voluntary   □ Proper ID   ISSUED #   SIGNATURE   □ *(oath / affirmation, if any)*   □ (by Mark)

PHONE C / H / W   *or* □ MISC   /   AGENCY   □ CA DMV   □ US State Dept   EXPIRES   ➡

CW #1

#1 WITNESS's NAME   □ P/Known   ADDRESS   □ Non-Public   □ Driver's License   □ Passport   □ Other ID   ISSUED #   SIGNATURE   □ *(after oath / affirmation)*

PHONE C / H / W   *or* □ MISC   AGENCY   □ CA DMV   □ US State Dept   EXPIRES   ❶

CW #2

#2 WITNESS's NAME   □ P/Known   ADDRESS   □ Non-Public   □ Driver's License   □ Passport   □ Other ID   ISSUED #   SIGNATURE   □ *(after oath / affirmation)*

PHONE C / H / W   *or* □ MISC   AGENCY   □ CA DMV   □ US State Dept   EXPIRES   ❷

My goal was to create:

- the most **efficient** yet **comprehensive**, **spacious** but **compact** and **methodical** notary journals
- with **truly state-specific** journal entries that
- (most importantly) effectuate the **industry standard** of logging your **notarial protocols** in each journal entry [as instructed by author of *Professor Closen's Notary Best Practices* (2018) / attorney / law professor / notary public / National Notary Association lecturer Michael Closen] to better protect yourself from liability and disciplinary fines. Log all of your notarial protocols (e.g. oath given) . . . in under 3 seconds with any of my 23 quick-fill journals.

Please email questions *or* suggestions to: NotaryRecords@gmail.com. And if you have no suggestions for improvement, **please leave an <u>Amazon star rating</u>** (5 is the best) or better yet, **post a <u>written review</u>** of what you liked the most.

For **free shipping** and a **lower price** (per entry), consider purchasing one of my larger journals next time.

My **website** just launched (July '23) so before your next notarization . . . be sure to read the <u>About</u> tab at:

https://GuardianJournals.WixSite.com/JennaJack

Thank you for choosing a **GUARDIAN NOTARY JOURNAL.**[1]   *Jenna Jack*

---

[1] Ensure you are purchasing an **<u>authentic</u> GUARDIAN NOTARY JOURNAL** by confirming the **<u>author</u> is Jenna Jack**. I cannot vouch for the accuracy or quality of copycat versions [selling for under $9.00] that do not display my author name on Amazon.com and the book title page (page iii). Over time, I will add my (above) trademarked red white & blue **Guardian Notary Journal logo** to the <u>cover</u> and <u>interior pages</u> of my 23 books. Until then, **please help stomp out copyright infringement** by avoiding the counterfeit/fake/fraudulent/knock-off/pirated/bootleg/copycat versions of my notary journals.

Made in the USA
Las Vegas, NV
15 June 2024